Intentional Moves

For Liam and Grace.

I'm so proud to be your mom.

"Imprint your mark upon the world, whatever you shall become."

—Adapted from "Thumbprint" by Eve Merriam

Intentional Moves

How Skillful Team Leaders Impact Learning

Elisa B. MacDonald

A Joint Publication

FOR INFORMATION:

Corwin

A SAGE Company

2455 Teller Road

Thousand Oaks, California 91320

(800) 233-9936

www.corwin.com

SAGE Publications Ltd.

1 Oliver's Yard

55 City Road

London EC1Y 1SP

United Kingdom

SAGE Publications India Pvt. Ltd.

B 1/I 1 Mohan Cooperative Industrial Area

Mathura Road, New Delhi 110 044

India

SAGE Publications Asia-Pacific Pte. Ltd.

18 Cross Street #10-10/11/12

China Square Central

Singapore 048423

President: Mike Soules

Vice President and
  Editorial Director: Monica Eckman

Program Director and
  Publisher: Dan Alpert

Senior Content Development
  Editor: Lucas Schleicher

Content Development
  Editor: Mia Rodriguez

Editorial Assistant: Natalie Delpino

Project Editor: Amy Schroller

Copy Editor: Melinda Masson

Typesetter: C&M Digitals (P) Ltd.

Proofreader: Rae-Ann Goodwin

Cover Designer: Rose Storey

Marketing Manager: Sharon Pendergast

Printed in the United States of America

Library of Congress Cataloging-in-Publication Data

Names: MacDonald, Elisa B., author.

Title: Intentional moves : how skillful team leaders impact learning / Elisa B. MacDonald.

Description: Thousand Oaks, California : Corwin, 2023. | Includes bibliographical references and index.

Identifiers: LCCN 2021056093 | ISBN 9781506392844 (paperback) | ISBN 9781506392851 (epub) | ISBN 9781506392868 (epub) | ISBN 9781506392875 (pdf)

Subjects: LCSH: Teaching teams—United States. | Teachers—Professional relationships—United States. | Educational leadership—United States.

Classification: LCC LB1029.T4 M329 2022 | DDC 371.14/8—dc23/eng/20211222
LC record available at https://lccn.loc.gov/2021056093

This book is printed on acid-free paper.

22 23 24 25 26 10 9 8 7 6 5 4 3 2 1

Contents

List of Figures

Acknowledgments

As someone who had the acting bug as a kid, I made many an Oscar acceptance speech in the mirror. Although I don't get the opportunity to hold a gold statue on stage while wearing an over-the-top gown, I am glad to have the space to thank the many incredible educators, thought partners, friends, and family members who influenced my writing and encouraged me to put forth this book.

I am tremendously grateful to the teachers and school leaders I've worked with over the past 30 years who have greatly influenced my thinking, my practice, and the contents of this book. Each time I led a team, workshop, or course; each time I was invited to the table for a meeting, or to classrooms; each time I coached someone or was coached, I left with new learning. I am especially thankful for my ongoing work with the truly outstanding middle school teacher leaders, principals and assistant principals, and district coordinators of the Newton (MA) Public Schools, and the incredible, visionary teacher leadership work that assistant superintendent of secondary schools Toby N. Romer is spearheading. I'm also extremely thankful for the principals and teachers who opened their schools to me so that I could observe the powerful moves their teams were making and add to the examples in this book. In particular principal Andrew Bott and the teachers at Brighton High (MA); former head of school Steve Wilkins, lower school director Sue Kingman, and the teachers and administrators at the Carroll School (MA); principal Kim Lysaght, assistant principal Ruthe L'Esperance, and the teachers at Charles E. Brown Middle School (MA); founder and head of school Monica Green of Capital Village Public Charter School (Washington, DC); and math co-teacher Emily Sturtevant. And, I am most grateful to the skillful team leaders (STLs) from these schools who I highlight in this book: Osamagbe Osagie, Daryl Campbell, Karen Coyle Aylward, and Michelle Fox—each of you brings a standard of excellence and a deep equity lens to what you do that inspires me each time I see you in action. This book is richer because of your wisdom and lived experiences. (Their bios can be found on page 9.)

I am and will always be grateful to the professionals in the Boston Public Schools, who gave me my first opportunities to teach and lead. I'm thankful to the schools across the nation that opened their doors to me when I led the Turnaround Teacher Team (T³) work at the nonprofit Teach Plus, and to our crackerjack teams of brilliant leadership coaches and teacher leaders who, without question, demonstrated what the power of intentional and skillful collaboration could bring.

Special thanks to my publisher, Dan Alpert, and development editor, Lucas Schleicher, who took this five-year writing journey with me despite the repeated hardships we all faced. Not a pandemic, deaths in the family, serious illness, eye surgery, young children, or the demands of a new puppy stopped us from getting this book out! Many thanks to the professionals at Corwin and Learning Forward: Mia Rodriguez, associate content development editor; Natalie Delpino, editorial assistant; Amy Schroller, project editor; Rose Storey, cover designer; and Sharon Pendergast, marketing manager. I am also appreciative to the reviewers of my manuscript. Your thoughtful and specific feedback greatly influenced my writing.

Thanks to my family who offered encouragement when the sirens of writer's block, perfectionism, insecurity, and discouragement lured me to question my work, and to my dearest friends: Emily Becker, Elizabeth Belkind, Carrie Carman, Sheryl Faye, Sue Forster, Ashot Gheridian, Amanda Good Hennessey, and MaryBeth Ruby. A very special thank-you to Carol Burchard O'Hare: Your actions show so much love, your words fill me with confidence, your mind is brilliant, and your heart is ever-giving.

When I published my first book, I gave thanks to my then 4-year-old twins who used to "pretend to write like Mommy." They will be 13 when this book comes out, and I am so proud of who they are each becoming. "I'm sooo lucky to have a Gracie and a Liam." And lastly, I am most grateful to my husband, Bobby—always believing in me, always helping me not take things too seriously, always making me laugh. I am by your side in sickness and in health—always.

Publisher's Acknowledgments

Corwin gratefully acknowledges the contributions of the following reviewers:

Janet Crews
Coordinator of Professional Learning
Clayton School District
Clayton, MO

Robert Evans
Director of Teaching and Learning
American International School of Johannesburg
South Africa

Matthew Heath
Educational Consultant
State Support Team
Canfield, OH

Jakki S. Jethro
Director of Elementary Education and Federal Programs
New Hanover County Schools
Wilmington, NC

Dr. Bill Macdonald
School Improvement Specialist
Topeka Public Schools USD 501
Topeka, KS

Rachel Manning
Principal
New Hanover County Schools, Snipes Academy of Arts and Design
Wilmington, NC

Dayna Richardson
Executive Director
Learning Forward Kansas
Hutchinson, KS

Quintin Shepherd
School Superintendent
Victoria ISD
Victoria, TX

Kim Tunnell
Educational Consultant
Tunnell Leadership Consultants
Van, TX

About the Author

An educator for 30 years, Elisa B. MacDonald is the author of the best-selling book *The Skillful Team Leader: A Resource for Overcoming Hurdles to Professional Learning for Student Achievement*. Her broad-ranging experience includes roles such as teacher, literacy coach, and assistant principal of instruction in the Boston Public Schools and adjunct professor for teacher action research at Boston College. As national director at Teach Plus, Elisa built up and led a program in six cities in which teams of teachers in chronically underperforming schools achieved rapid gains for students. Currently, Elisa consults with school districts and organizations, training and coaching team leaders and helping to transform teacher, school, and district-level leadership teams.

When Elisa isn't championing students and teachers, she is on stage acting, driving her twins to soccer and theater, or experimenting in the kitchen, pretending she's on the Food Network. Contact Elisa if you want to learn more about skillful intentional team leadership, or if you just want a delicious fudge recipe.

www.elisamacdonald.com

skillfulteamleader@gmail.com

(Twitter) @elisaBmacdonald

(LinkedIn) Elisa B. MacDonald

Part I

Foundations

Skillful Intentional Leadership

Introduction

//

One afternoon I was about to start a meeting with a principal when I noticed another man sidle up to him, scribbling rapidly. The principal smiled and explained, "Don't mind Joe. He is doing a study to see how many minutes a day I spend on instructional tasks." Aside from wanting to make sure that the time I spent with this principal ended up in the right column of Joe's notebook, I got to thinking: *What if Joe recorded the number of minutes that educators spend on instructional talk in team meetings?*

A quick Google search could not point me to a study showing a national average for time spent in school meetings, but basic math can lead us to a good working number. If on average a team meets once a week for 50 minutes, then the minimum amount of time that team is together is almost 2,000 minutes a school year. And more often than not, teams meet more frequently, and educators are on multiple teams, which can put their individual time working in groups at upward of 4,000 minutes a year. That is a lot of time, considering most teachers get 22 minutes a day for lunch. Maybe the better question for Joe is: *What are the outcomes of all that talk?*

When I first work with a school, educators in the room inevitably think of me as "the team lady." *She's here to work with leaders to help our professional learning community teams be more productive. She's going to help our multi-grade-level team align curriculum. She's going to teach us how to manage people who show resistance.* While leadership of teams might be what I do, what I am about is learning. Teaming is the vehicle; student learning is always the outcome. Results such as improved team productivity, better curriculum alignment, and heightened teacher collegiality are each very important, but getting good at these things is not the ultimate outcome we are after. At the end of the day, a team must positively impact students' learning.

With experience over a span of nearly 30 years leading school teams, as well as coaching team leaders and the people who support them, I've learned that not all groups reach this outcome. (If you've picked up this book, you likely know it, too.) I am constantly struck by the fact that two teams, even within the same school, can go through the same motions of setting norms, writing agendas, planning for goals, facilitating protocols, and so on, but only one of those teams makes a positive impact on both teacher and student learning. Of course, different teams are made up of different players, but I am more convinced than before that ultimately it is not individuals who make or break a team's performance; it's the leadership. With skillful, intentional leadership, any team can thrive.

A Skillful Approach

All leaders, regardless of the group they lead or the years of experience they have, encounter hurdles—those things that get in the way of how our teams work together and what they accomplish. "Hurdles . . . come from people we care about, [from] cultures we are proud to work within, and oftentimes from ourselves" (MacDonald, 2013, p. 11). Our approach to these hurdles influences our effectiveness as leaders. A skillful approach, which is explored extensively through reality-based dilemmas in my first book, *The Skillful Team Leader* (MacDonald, 2013), is rooted in four key tenets: values, mindset, emotional intelligence, and responsiveness (formerly called skill). Here is a brief summary of each.

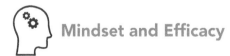 Values

When you reach a fork in the road, when you need to make an unpopular decision or notice your team has lost their way from what's important, your values become your compass. Skillful team leaders (STLs) are guided by their values and principles about such things as equity, inclusion, diversity, social justice, leadership, and teaching and learning. They also draw from personal values that define their character such as hard work, perseverance, honesty, transparency, and humility. They align teamwork to research-based, widely accepted guiding principles about teaching and learning evident in initiatives such as culturally responsive teaching, Universal Design for Learning (UDL), Multi-Tiered System of Supports (MTSS), social-emotional learning (SEL), and so on. Values referenced throughout this book include agency, alignment, asset-based collaboration, clarity, community, competency, critical thinking, cross-collaboration, diversity, efficiency, equity, evidence-based learning, focus, harmony, inclusion, investment, learning outcomes, momentum, morale, ownership, productivity, purpose-driven talk, respect, self-awareness, and student understanding.

Mindset and Efficacy

If you are an effective teacher, then you know children's learning is not fixed. It can be cultivated with effort, deliberate practice, and perseverance. STLs extend this growth mindset to adult learners as well as students. Just as you wouldn't give up on a child learner simply because the child was showing resistance, neither should you write off an adult learner who shows resistance.

STLs hold a growth mindset about themselves, too. They expect to make missteps as leaders. I've been doing this for a long time, and I still make facilitation moves that are the wrong call. STLs give themselves permission to stumble and learn.

A close cousin to mindset is efficacy. In the context of teams, it is the idea that educators' beliefs influence outcomes for students and families. STLs who believe that they and their teams can achieve high expectations for all students are more likely to do so than those who don't believe they can.

Emotional Intelligence

A skillful approach to team leadership is more than facilitating meetings; it's about leading people through continuous improvement—in other words, leading people through change. Different people have different emotional responses to change. In accordance with Daniel Goleman's (2004) nominal work on emotional intelligence, STLs demonstrate the following:

- *Awareness of others.* STLs can "read the room." They recognize when their colleagues exhibit emotions that indicate distress, anxiety, insecurity, sadness, boredom, and other feelings.

- *Sensitivity to the emotions of others.* STLs respond to their colleagues in ways that foster cross-cultural sensitivity and empathy. They have a keen ability to bring levity to stressful circumstances, when appropriate, while simultaneously being supportive of their colleagues.

- *Self-awareness.* Leaders feel the same range of emotions as the people they lead. STLs notice their own feelings and their effect on others.

- *Self-regulation.* STLs don't underestimate the influence of their own emotions and moods on a group. They redirect their impulses and think before acting.

Responsiveness

Your values, mindset, and emotional intelligence shape your approach to leadership, but what people most notice are the ways in which you respond to challenges. STLs notice when hurdles arise and seek to understand why they are happening. They recognize that their own cultural positioning, or the cultural lens from which they see the world, and implicit biases shape their interpretation of events. They actively interrupt their own assumptions to skillfully respond to hurdles.

Self-assess your approach to team leadership with the STL Self-Assessment Tool provided in Primary Intention 10 (see Figure 31).

An Intentional Approach

The idea of leading teams with intention surfaced for me in an unexpected moment. Standing in a long line at the airport security headed to Alabama to work with a few districts, I realized something. That morning, I intentionally chose slip-on shoes so no one would be waiting for me to untie my sneakers. I decided to forgo any metal bangles even though they really made my outfit. I put all my toiletries in a clear bag, and made sure the bag wasn't buried at the bottom of my suitcase so that my unmentionables wouldn't fly out when I went to put it on the conveyor belt, and I chose not to buy my water until I got to the other side. I breezed through the line without a glitch, and I wondered: *What if we led collaborative learning with the same or greater level of intentionality that we put into preparing to move through airport security?* STLs do.

Walk into any team meeting and ask an STL why the seats are set up in the way that they are, why this topic is on the agenda and not that, which pieces of student work a team is analyzing and why, what teachers are looking for when they are observing a colleague teach, and so on. They don't just throw an agenda together and show up to meetings; they make deliberate choices. They think and act with purpose and commitment, always moving the work of teams toward desirable learning outcomes. STLs have a reason behind each thing they do, and it's what makes them effective.

Here are a few examples of how you might act with intention as a team leader:

- "Over the course of two weeks, I intend to set expectations for collaborative inquiry so that people understand the work we are about to do and how it differs from our other meetings."

- "For this upcoming data analysis meeting, I intend to deepen our understanding of the student-learning problem by having us do the question that students got wrong on the assessment."

- "In this difficult conversation, I intend to learn what my colleague's concerns are and convey that they are a valuable member of the team so that going forward they positively contribute to our meetings. I'll do it in a 1:1 check-in rather than in front of the team."

- "In this very moment of our team meeting, I am noticing that we are blaming students. I intend to shift our team talk to take personal responsibility. I want us to feel empowered so that we can positively impact outcomes for our kids."

This book aims to make transparent the intentional moves that STLs make.

10 STL Primary Intentions

Our intentions drive what we do. Like teachers, STLs make hundreds of deliberate moves to facilitate learning. And like teachers, STLs decide which moves to make based on what they intend to accomplish. I call these the 10 STL Primary Intentions and organize this book accordingly. Interestingly, although teachers and STLs might implement the moves differently depending on the age of the learner (child or adult), the intentions behind what they do are most often the same.

Primary Intention 1. Optimize Learning Conditions: Time, Space, and Accommodations

Primary Intention 2. Establish Expectations and Responsibilities: Norms and Roles

Primary Intention 3. Nurture Group Culture: Community and Trust

Primary Intention 4. Design and Plan Learning: Work Plans, Agendas, and Protocols

Primary Intention 5. Engage and Interact: Participation and Conflict Resolution

Primary Intention 6. Lead With Purpose and Direction: Priorities, Inquiry Questions, and Goals

Primary Intention 7. Promote Intentional Data Use: Assessment and Data Analysis

Primary Intention 8. Engage in Analytical Thinking, Creative Problem Solving, and Clear Decision Making: Unbiased Reasoning and Diverse Perspectives

Primary Intention 9. Implement New Learning: Change, Peer Observation, and Accountability

Primary Intention 10. Assess: Feedback, Reflection, and Growth for Teams and Leaders

The Paradox of Intention

The sword of intentionality can be double-edged. Setting intention brings purpose and focus to what leaders do, but it can also cause tunnel vision in which leaders miss opportunities for learning that emerges from the group, or generate a rigidness that makes it difficult to adapt when the unpredictable happens. And herein lies the paradox: As a team leader, how do you set intentions while also being open and flexible to that which you didn't intend?

To understand how STLs manage the paradox, it is helpful to return to what effective teachers do in the classroom. As an effective teacher, you set clear objectives, but are also open to teachable moments, unplanned learning opportunities, and curveballs. Like ballroom dancers, soccer players, stage actors, and surgeons, you are agile. Fully present and mindful, you swiftly and intentionally respond to whatever comes your way without losing sight of your primary intentions.

STLs keep primary intentions front and center at all times, but are fully aware that teams are dynamic. Ideas evolve. People change. Circumstances get uprooted, and plans don't always go as planned. Never was this truer than during the COVID-19 pandemic. Teams and their leaders adapted quickly, learning how to collaborate virtually. Teachers and administrators had to move swiftly to learn new methods for delivering instruction and even learn how to give students the most basic necessities, such as meals. Although I hope we don't ever have to adjust to such a crisis again, as STLs we always have to nimbly adapt, think on our feet, and make in-the-moment moves while simultaneously not losing sight of our primary intentions.

Who Are STLs?

Throughout this book, I abbreviate skillful team leaders who act with intention as STLs. This term refers to anyone who is leading a team, whether they formally hold the role of leader or not. People who will find the material in this book most useful include:

- A teacher leading colleagues.

- An instructional coach/partner leading teachers.

- A principal or assistant principal leading a school leadership or teacher team.

- A district leader leading principals.

- Any person on any team with or without the official title of "team leader." Even a parent leading a parent–teacher organization will likely benefit from the team leadership moves highlighted in this book.

Meet the STLs Highlighted in This Book

I base the examples in this book on a composite of my own experiences and the hundreds of team leaders I have supported; however, I also highlight four standout STLs in particular (see their bios in the following section). All are seasoned educators with varying levels of experience leading different types of teams, illustrating the fact that regardless of where you are in your leadership journey, regardless of who you lead, you can be a skillful intentional team leader.

They and their teams have been so gracious in opening up their meetings to me so that I could observe and write about them. It is worth noting that in many of their team meetings, I not only saw these leaders make moves highlighted in this book, but I also saw other team members do so. This reinforces the point that you don't need to be a formally appointed team leader to move your team toward high function and impact.

Osamagbe Osagie (she, her, hers)

Hailing from a small suburb right outside of Atlanta, Georgia, Osamagbe (Osa) is a lifelong learner who is deeply committed to amplifying the lived experiences of marginalized peoples within her local and global community. Currently, Osamagbe serves as the director of equity and inclusion at the Carroll School, a first- through ninth-grade school for children who have language-based learning differences such as dyslexia and dysgraphia. She leads her colleagues in strategic planning efforts, supporting curriculum design, facilitating group workshops, and engaging in coaching sessions. Osa's love for young people, education, and social justice stems from her work with students, her involvement in state-level politics, and her connections to local grassroots organizations. Osa met Elisa as her son's history teacher and has since been a close thought partner in the work of diversity, equity, and inclusion and team leadership. She loves to spend her free time reading books, learning more about photography, traveling, and spending quality time with her loved ones over good food, spirits, and music.

Daryl Campbell (he, him, his)

Informed by his experience as a Black male growing up in the South and guided by the belief that a quality education is a human right, Daryl has been an educator for over two decades as a classroom math and science teacher, instructional coach, district administrator, and consultant. In 2004, Daryl was the district teacher leader for the Public Schools of Brookline (MA) Educational Equity Project. Daryl worked on Elisa's team at Teach Plus, supporting teacher leaders and coaches in Turnaround schools in Massachusetts and the District of Columbia, and became director of training and development. He moved back to Georgia to be executive director of curriculum and instruction for the City Schools of Decatur. Realizing that his greatest joy is leading from the classroom, Daryl currently serves as the founding lead teacher/instructional coach for Capital Village Public Charter School in Washington, DC. Capital Village PCS opened in 2020 and serves 6% English learners, 42.8% students receiving special education services, and 83.3% economically disadvantaged students. Daryl enjoys reading, hiking, and spending quality time with family and friends.

Karen Coyle Aylward (she, her, hers)

Karen has been a National Board Certified teacher for 16 years and was named a Boston Educator of the Year in 2009. She is a veteran teacher and instructional coach at Brighton High School (MA), a comprehensive urban Turnaround high school with 45.5% English learners, 31.8% students receiving special education services, and 77.1% economically disadvantaged students. She was in the first group of appointed department teacher leaders when Elisa started a teacher leadership program at Brighton High. After 13 years in the classroom teaching English language arts to students from ninth-grade composition through Advanced Placement literature, she transitioned to the role of instructional coach for the past 9 years, helping to lead the work of instructional improvement for the school through mentoring, coaching teachers, and leading professional development. When she is not working to improve educational opportunities at Brighton High, she can be found at home chasing her three young children around.

Michelle Fox (she, her, hers)

Named the Science Educator of the Year for Middlesex County by the Massachusetts Association of Science Teachers (MAST) in 2018, Michelle has been teaching for more than two decades. She is currently an eighth-grade science teacher in a public middle school in the greater Boston metro area with 3.7% English learners and 20% students receiving special education services, in a district with 12.5% economically disadvantaged students. Michelle took part in Elisa's STL course and coaching and has been her school's science department teacher leader for the past three years. Prior to this role, she worked behind the scenes with a small team to rewrite and align the eighth-grade science curriculum to the new science standards and coached a math team. Beyond leading her colleagues, she leads students as the faculty advisor for the student PRIDE club. She lives with her husband, two children, and pet corn snake and loves taking the family out for long, rambling nature walks in their nearby woods. (They leave the snake at home.)

How This Book Is Organized

This book is divided into three parts.

Part I: Foundations

Chapter 1: Skillful Intentional Leadership

This first chapter that you are reading now provides a brief overview of a skillful approach to team leadership and introduces the premise of this book: STLs are doing more than running meetings; they are leading collaborative learning for continuous improvement. Similar to effective teachers in the classroom, they decide what they are aiming to achieve and make small intentional moves to get there.

Chapter 2: Don't Settle for High-Functioning Teams

This chapter emphasizes the critical importance of leading teams from two lenses: *function* (how your team gets along and works together) and *impact* (the learning outcomes, particularly for students, that your team achieves).

I provide an overview of the Team Function, Impact Matrix in Figure 1 (first introduced in my original book, *The Skillful Team Leader* [MacDonald, 2013]), and I define four types of teams:

Q1. High Functioning, High Impact

Q2. High Functioning, Low Impact

Q3. Low Functioning, Low Impact

Q4. Low Functioning, High Impact

Chapter 3: The Real Work of Teams: Collaborative Inquiry

In this chapter, I present my STL Phases of Collaborative Inquiry as a frame for your work with teams, but acknowledge that there are many effective cycles to choose from. The model a team chooses is less important than the leadership of it. I encourage you to choose whatever cycle works for you, whether it be mine or someone else's, so long as you lead each phase with intention, skill, and agility. I also invite you to put the technical process of inquiry aside and reconnect to creating a culture of collaborative inquiry.

Part II: Essential Understandings

This section of the book presents essential understandings about leading teams of adult learners. Having a solid understanding of groups, adult learners, and peer leadership gives you the foundation to effectively implement the moves described in this book. Part II consists of three chapters:

Chapter 4: The Psychology of Groups

Chapter 5: Five Must-Knows About Adult Learners

Chapter 6: The Upside (and Downside) of Being a Peer Leader

Part III: 10 STL Primary Intentions With Moves

I organized my first book, *The Skillful Team Leader* (MacDonald, 2013), around common hurdles team leaders face. "Got a dilemma? Here's what's going on. Try this response." This book comes at the work from a different angle: "Think about what you are trying to accomplish. Try these moves to get there." In Part III I provide close to 150 moves organized into the 10 STL Primary Intentions.

> Primary Intentions 1–5 address collaborative conditions, expectations, culture, planning, and engagement. These moves build what are commonly known as "soft skills."

> Primary Intentions 6–10 build what might be called the "harder" skills. They address goal setting, assessment, data analysis, evidence-based decision making, bias and assumptions, resistance to change, and accountability.

Each primary intention chapter begins with the following:

- An introduction to the primary intention.

- A list of more narrowly defined micro-intentions (what you are aiming to do in a specific moment) with several moves to choose from.

- A list of benefits to using the moves.

- A recommendation for when you might implement the moves.

Where it helps with understanding, each move explored within a primary intention contains the following components:

- Name of the move.

- A brief introduction to the move and why it is needed.

- How to implement the move.

- *In action.* A scripted excerpt from a real or fictional team dialogue.* In some sections, where the moves are intended to build upon one another (e.g., Moves 4.5 and 4.6), the example is provided at the end of the series of moves.

---

*I highlight four outstanding real STLs in this book (see their bios earlier in this chapter). The dialogue from these individuals and their teams is modified but authentic. Permissions were obtained to print and edit. All other scripted examples in the book describe a fictional team leader in a typical scenario intended to illustrate a clear example of each move in action. Although these "in action" examples are not literal dialogue from meetings, they are all based on a composites of real team observations and experiences.

- *STL recommendations.* Tips for how to facilitate the move skillfully.

- *Think like a teacher.*** Connections between using the given move with adult learners and students in the classroom.

- *Find the right words.* Sample language for implementing the move.

- *Related readings.* References to complementary moves in the book.

Where to Begin?

This is a long book. Approach it as you would any field book or practitioner's guide. Rely heavily on the Table of Contents to find what you need when you need it. First, read the front matter in Parts I and II so that you are better equipped to implement the moves in Part III. When you are ready, decide what your primary intention is and turn to the cover page to zero in on which moves might be appropriate to use in your situation.

For example, I am in the *Research & Study* STL phase of collaborative inquiry, and I'm planning to have my team read an article about what we are about to implement. I flip to Primary Intention 4 and look through the suggested moves under "Learn from a text-based discussion." I already know how to select a shared text (Move 4.8), and our team is already in the habit of reading together (Move 4.11), but the last time we had a text-based discussion, people didn't take very much away from it. So, I will try "Design the reading/viewing experience" (Move 4.9) and "Prep the text, the reader, and yourself" (Move 4.10). I will also glance at the moves in the preceding section, "Structure tasks and talk," in case there's a better way for me to facilitate our text-based discussion.

Thanks to Those Who've Written Before Me and to You for What You Bring to This Text

Many texts in the fields of education and organizational psychology influenced the writing of this book, but none influenced the structure more than Jennifer Serravallo's books, *The Reading Strategies Book* (2015) and *The Writing Strategies Book* (2017). In using her texts, I became conscious of the literacy goals we set for our students and the intention with which we reach them. I saw a connection to leading teams. STLs are doing more than running meetings; they are leading collaborative learning for continuous improvement. Similar to effective teachers in the classroom, they decide what they are aiming to achieve and make small intentional moves to get there. I can tell in an instant when I sit to

---

**In a study analyzing classroom discourse dating as far back as the mid-1960s (Bellack et al., 1966), the term *moves* was used to identify effective actions that teachers used when interacting with students. I encourage anyone who has taught students, who is now leading their peers, to draw from their repertoire of effective teacher moves. How you implement a move with adult learners might slightly differ from how you would do so with student learners, but your learning intention behind the move is often the same.

debrief a team meeting with an STL that it's no accident this person is effective. I realized from reading Serravallo's books and from my work with leaders of all types of teams that not everyone is aware of, or knows how to implement, these moves. And why would they be? Many teacher leaders and coaches are skillful at leading *student* learning, but may not have as much knowledge or experience—yet—in leading teams of adult learners. And even team leaders who have been facilitating collaborative learning for years aren't always conscious of what they did in a meeting that made it a "good" one or not. I hope this book changes that. With humility, I hope it can become *the* or at least *one* of your team leadership strategies books.

An important point worth repeating: Two team leaders can implement the same moves in this book and end up with very different outcomes. I encourage you to implement them skillfully and intentionally, considering modifications you might need to make based on the context of your circumstances, the school culture within which you work, and the uniqueness of who you are. I invite you to join me in learning and discussing with others the intentional moves STLs make, while you also discover learning that I did not even intend.

Get in touch: skillfulteamleader@gmail.com

Follow me on Twitter: @elisaBmacdonald

Find out what we offer: www.elisamacdonald.com

Don't Settle for High-Functioning Teams

If there were a pharmaceutical commercial for a struggling team, it would probably sound like this:

> *If you've ever sat in on a team meeting:*
>
> - *Struggling to follow a circuitous conversation*
> - *Wondering what the heck people are talking about*
> - *Feeling as if the meeting could have been shorter*
> - *Fantasizing about joining the awesome team next door that you hear laughing through the wall*
>
> *Then your team is likely suffering from low function.*

No one wants to be a member of the team just described. All teams want to be what is commonly referred to as "high functioning," where members work well together and are productive. But, is getting along and getting things done a high enough bar for our teams when student learning is at stake? Consider the following story.

Say you sat in on two teams, Team A and Team B, and this is what you observed:

TEAM A	TEAM B
• Follows norms.	• Breaks norms.
• Shares team roles.	• All roles fall on the team leader.
• Reaches consensus on goals.	• Fails to reach consensus on goals.
• Adheres to agendas.	• Strays from agendas.
• Follows data protocols.	• Veers off data protocols.

Which team might concern you more? (Put a different way, which team would you *not* want to spend 4,000 minutes with each year?) Chances are you said Team B. This is a team that isn't getting along. They don't share responsibility for team commitments, can't reach agreement, and are off-task in meetings. Conversations wander. Not only do they fail to reach their goals, they struggle just to agree on one. This is a low-functioning team. Team A, on the other hand, seems to be really cooking with gas. Most would describe them as high functioning.

The first chart compares Team A to Team B through what I refer to as a *function lens*. We determine how a team is doing by assessing their collegiality, organization, efficiency, productivity, and so on. Looking through this function lens, it is obvious that we would most likely put our efforts into helping Team B. We have no concerns about Team A, but should we?

Let's look through the same function lens to compare the same Team A against a new team—Team C—and ask the same question: Which team might concern you more?

TEAM A	TEAM C
• Follows norms.	• Follows norms.
• Shares team roles.	• Shares team roles.
• Reaches consensus on goals.	• Reaches consensus on goals.
• Adheres to agendas.	• Adheres to agendas.
• Follows data protocols.	• Follows data protocols.

Through the function lens, Team A and Team C look exactly the same. Both are high functioning; neither is concerning. But, what if we were to switch out our function lens for an *impact* lens? A lens that does not ask: *How is the team working together? Are they getting things done?* But, instead, asks: What *are they getting done? And what student-learning outcomes result from what they are doing together?* In business this lens is often referred to as performance.

When we compare Teams A and C through an *impact* lens, we suddenly see things we didn't see when only looking through the *function* lens. See the examples in the following chart.

TEAM A	TEAM C
• Follows norms (e.g., *We agree to disagree without being disagreeable*).	• Follows norms (e.g., *We agree to actively solicit alternate viewpoints*).
• Shares team roles (e.g., *Mrs. M is the meeting note-taker*).	• Shares team roles (e.g., *Mrs. M is the lesson demonstration teacher*).
• Reaches consensus on goals (e.g., *By the end of our team cycle, teachers will teach a, b, and c*).	• Reaches consensus on goals (e.g., *By the end of our team cycle, students will have learned x, y, and z*).
• Adheres to agendas (e.g., *Item 2: Discussion about . . .*).	• Adheres to agendas (e.g., *Item 2: Discuss . . . so that we leave here with a plan for . . .*).
• Follows data protocols (e.g., *We follow the steps of a data dialogue protocol*).	• Follows data protocols (e.g., *We suspend assumptions during the inference phase of the protocol*).

Through the lens of impact, Team A now becomes a concern. Although Team A stays productive by following norms, distributing roles, setting goals, and using agendas and protocols, they will not impact student learning in the way that Team C can.

For instance, both Teams A and C follow norms. But Team A is only focused on the manner in which the team members talk to one another, not the impact of their talk. Make no mistake; this is important for how the group functions, but Team C goes a step further. They set an agreement to value diversity of thought and flexible thinking, two things known to help groups avoid groupthink and arrive at better decisions.

The word *impact* is ubiquitous thanks to the body of works from leaders in the professional learning field, such as Jim Knight (e.g., 2013), Joellen Killion (e.g., 2018), Nancy Love (e.g., Love et al., 2015), Thomas Guskey (e.g., 2016), Paul Bloomberg and Barb Pitchford (e.g., Bloomberg & Pitchford, 2017), and many others. And thank goodness it is. This makes us pause and evaluate the effects of what we do. John Hattie (2021) in his visible learning meta-analyses makes clear that not all practices have the same effect size on student learning and achievement. "Know thy impact" is a meme I'm sure you've seen. This is as true for our individual work with students as it is for our teams' work.

In fact, through an impact lens, even our pharmaceutical commercial would sound differently:

If you've ever sat in on a team meeting:

- *Unsure if the work your team gets done is the stuff kids need*
- *Wondering why your kids' learning problems keep persisting*
- *Excited to implement change, but not knowing how*
- *Enjoying the collegiality, but wishing you left the meeting with more*
- *Fantasizing about joining the awesome team next door that you see is making a measurable difference for kids*

Then your team is likely suffering from low impact.

There are a number of studies and syntheses over the last two decades in which researchers and thought leaders study what successful schools do in their teams versus what those in low-performing schools do. Most differences fall within the area of impact. (There can be pockets of high-performing teams in low-performing schools and vice versa.) The characteristics of these teams seem to be consistent. Here are a few standouts. Teams in highly successful schools have been reported to:

- View collaboration as a catalyst for improvement (Little, 2012)
- Challenge conventional notions (Horn, 2007)
- Openly express uncertainty and seek help (Timperley, 2008)

- Engage in talk that plunges people into consciousness (MacDonald, 2013)
- Discover insight into teaching and learning (Little, 2012)
- Establish social relationships of equal status, intellectual openness, and possibilities for critique and creative thought (O'Connor & Michaels, 2007)
- Feel a moral responsibility to meet the social and cognitive needs of all children (Lindsey et al., 2009)
- Apply learning to practice (Argyris, 1993)

The moves in this book provide actionable ways to do all of this and more.

Teams in less successful schools have been reported to:

- Get caught up in activity traps with vaguely defined purposes for looking at data (Timperley, 2008)
- Engage in talk that resembles an organizational routine rather than a deliberate means to improve outcomes for students (MacDonald, 2013)
- Participate in protocols that privilege form over substance—in other words, teams value procedures more than insightful, actionable learning (Timperley, 2008)

The Team Function, Impact Matrix

Skillful team leaders (STLs) and their teams intentionally view their teams through dual lenses: function *and* impact. Once you begin to do so, you see that being successful in one does not guarantee success in the other. Put function and impact side by side on a matrix, and four types of teams emerge (see Figure 1).

FIGURE 1   Team Function, Impact Matrix

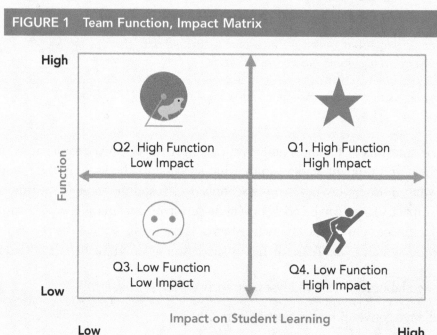

For those unfamiliar with the Team Function, Impact Matrix (first presented in *The Skillful Team Leader* [MacDonald, 2013, p. 31]), I include a primer as follows:

Q1. High Function, High Impact

- *Greatest asset: Progress*
- *Greatest hurdle: Sustainability*

Quadrant 1 (Q1) teams are most desirable. These teams are consistently high functioning and high impact. They most often work well together, enjoy meeting as a group, and move the needle for student learning. Progress is visible.

The biggest challenge for Q1 teams is sustainability of results. Without a plan to sustain success, teams can experience burnout, or adopt a "quit while we are ahead" group mentality, and slip into one of the other quadrants of the matrix.

Q2. High Function, Low Impact

- *Greatest asset: Collegiality and momentum*
- *Greatest hurdle: Collegiality and momentum*

Quadrant 2 (Q2) teams consist of members who get along well, are highly invested in the team's work, and are efficient at doing the work. However, despite functioning like a well-oiled machine, they have little to no collective impact on student learning. Q2 teams end up on a fast-spinning hamster wheel, working really hard but getting nowhere they need to be. The learning challenges students had when the team first met are still there when the team adjourns. For instance, weekly meetings for a Q2 team might be dedicated to writing a thoughtful curriculum unit that is never implemented. Or, team members might implement lessons, but never collectively look at the impact of those lessons on student learning.

The upside of a Q2 team: They are collegial and have momentum. The downside of a Q2 team: They are collegial and have momentum. Yep. Double-edged sword. The team leader won't have any trouble getting this group to meet. There will be little, if any, conflict among group members, and they will accomplish whatever they set out to do. But that collective drive for getting things done makes it hard for leaders of Q2 teams to slow down and change direction to focus on tasks that will have a greater impact on student learning.

Q3. Low Function, Low Impact

- *Greatest asset: Ready for a fresh start*
- *Greatest hurdle: Morale*

No team wants to reside in Quadrant 3 (Q3). Dysfunction and low impact characterize teams that land here on the matrix. It makes sense that a team who can't get along

(Continued)

(Continued)

or be productive would also have little to no impact on learning. Q3 teams typically linger too long in what Bruce Tuckman (1965) calls the forming stage where they can't come to consensus on purpose. Without an agreed-upon direction, they can't collectively have an impact on learning. Some Q3 teams make it past the forming stage but struggle to move past Tuckman's storming stage, which is marked by gossip, bickering, complaining, and overall "fed-up-ness," a clear indicator of low function.

The wheels on Q3 teams don't always squeak from the start. Some groups begin as high-functioning Q2 teams. They start out working well together, but over time the fruits of their labor aren't visible. No matter how collegial the group is, people begin to lose interest if they don't see their collaboration positively impacting their practice or their students' learning. Low interest can take the form of people missing meetings, arriving late, not following through on agreed-upon items, and being compliant. What may once have been a high-functioning team drops to the low-functioning third quadrant in the matrix.

Q3 teams' biggest challenge: People give up on the team. It can be hard for you, as a team leader, to foster ownership and pride in a team that would just prefer not to meet. But the good news is these teams are ready for a fresh start, if you are willing and able to lead them.

Q4. Low Function, High Impact

- *Greatest asset: Competence and potential*

- *Greatest hurdle: Vulnerability-based trust and interdependence*

Quadrant 4 (Q4) teams, low function but high impact, are perhaps the most perplexing in that they don't function well as a group, but they do achieve results for students. People on Q4 teams are often happy to meet with their colleagues socially; however, they don't see much promise in learning with or from one another. When they do want to meet for professional reasons, it's more about collectively fixing something that is getting in the way of their doing what they already do, not examining and changing what they do. There is a strong level of independence that people on Q4 teams are accustomed to, which can make a shift toward interdependence challenging. Because, in isolation, they have an impact on students, members aren't typically convinced that there is a benefit to collaborating as a group. They see no reason, and certainly no urgency, to change what they are doing. (If they really are getting great outcomes for kids, you almost can't blame them for having reservations about changing. "If it ain't broke . . .") While their individual excellence might prove good for the classroom, it can cause dysfunction on a team. A research study showed "the greater the proportion of experts a team had, the more likely it was to disintegrate into nonproductive conflict or stalemate" (Gratton & Erickson, 2007). Despite the outcomes they reach individually, Q4 teams often discover that when they do begin to address their function problems, their collective impact improves as well.

Q4 teams can resemble what the authors of *Team Genius* (Karlgaard & Malone, 2015) describe as "unhealthy, successful teams" (p. 241). Here are the characteristics exactly as they describe them in their book:

- A team that, despite its internal strife, just gets lucky

- A team that features so much talent that, despite itself, still manages to get across the finish line—though much less successfully than it might have otherwise

- A team that is composed of some top-quality members, and others who just played easy riders, but took a share of the credit

- A team that fakes results to look like it succeeded

The problem for Q4 teams is that they never reach their full potential (Karlgaard & Malone, 2015). Problems in student learning *do* exist; they are just not talked about openly and collectively, nor are they brushed off as someone else's responsibility. While a Q4 team might have a few members who are a little more ego than impact, most are composed of people who genuinely care, are continuous learners with high standards, take pride in their accomplishments, and take ownership of the problems they see. They just prefer solving those problems alone. They are used to being solo "superheroes" who consistently make strides with students and find it easier to do what's been working for them thus far. It's not uncommon for one of those superheroes to be the team leader carrying the weight of the team.

The strength of a Q4 team is that students are learning. Their weakness is that educators are not. Q4 team members might exchange resources or recommendations with one another, or even look for solutions to problems outside of their zone of responsibility, but being vulnerable and reflecting publicly on their roles in student failure is not this group's MO. Members are not invested in being a professional learning team. This translates into compliance or disengagement.

Q4 teams have a missed opportunity: The team does not reach their potential learning and wider impact. Members have expertise, but they don't know how to work interdependently. They have not yet figured out how to hold on to their individuality, share their expertise, and continue doing what they do well while also being vulnerable and collectively learning with a group. For a Q4 team leader, it can be tough getting this group to meet and tougher getting this group to publicly expose real struggles in their teaching practice.

Six Key Points When Using the Team Function, Impact Matrix

1. **Don't get hung up on labels.** I've presented the Team Function, Impact Matrix hundreds of times and find that most often principals, administrators, and teacher leaders who have context for it from reading my work, or taking my courses, or attending a workshop, really like the framework, but when they go

(Continued)

(Continued)

to present it to teachers themselves, it gets mixed reactions. Without context, some teachers (not all) see it as another thing they need to do, or new language they now have to use. This is the *last* thing I want for them or you. Decide if showing the matrix or using language from it will help or hinder your team. The important takeaway is not that your colleagues know the difference between Q2 and Q3, but that your teams continuously reflect on two things: how well you work together *and* the impact of what you do together on student learning. (Note: While I make reference in this book to teams as low-functioning, low-impact Q3, etc., it is only to help distinguish characteristics between teams. In real life, I would *never* call or refer to a team by quadrant.)

2. **Teams might not be high or low, but somewhere in between.** View the matrix as a continuum with teams landing anywhere between high and low. It's common to have a moderately functioning team where they get along but are not always productive. Or, you might have a team that is getting results for some student populations but not for others, causing them to identify as moderately impactful.

3. **Your team has hidden strengths.** Teams that are low-functioning and/or low-impact still have many strengths. Drill down to specifics on the STL Meeting Reflection Tool (Figure 29, page 444) to help identify them. For instance, a team might struggle with coming to consensus on decisions (a sign of low function), but they are adept at designing well-run, purposeful meetings (an indicator of high function).

4. **The matrix is a tool for dialogue, not evaluation.** If using the matrix with your team to informally assess in which quadrant people perceive the team to "live," don't aim for consensus. Learning happens when people explain where they perceive their team falls on the matrix. If you so choose, you can even plot points on the matrix to see where people think a team is. But do not turn this process into an evaluation—it should only be used to inform a discussion about the team's strengths and areas for growth.)

5. **Teams can move in and out of any quadrant.** Teams are made up of people, and people can learn how to better function as a group and achieve greater impact. A low-functioning Q3 team, for example, can put organizational systems in place and become a high-functioning Q2 team. On the flip side, teams can also move away from Q1. For instance, a once high-functioning, high-impact Q1 team might gain new members who create friction in the group and cause the team to slip to the low-functioning, high-impact Q4.

6. **Even a Q1 team can have a low-functioning, low-impact meeting.** The matrix is best used to get a sense of how a team is doing over many meetings. *Overall, do we tend to live in Q1 or somewhere else?* But any team, regardless of self-placement on the matrix, can have a meeting that goes either well or poorly. If you lead a struggling team that experiences that

rare high-functioning, high-impact meeting, it can be a good sign that the team is on the verge of shifting quadrants! Debrief what you did so that you can do it again.

On the flip side, a high-functioning, high-impact Q1 team can have one meeting that is full of conflict and hurt feelings, where no intended outcomes are met. This might simply be viewed as one random bad meeting, but the leader and members to reflect on what happened so that the team doesn't slip into an undesirable quadrant with low function for the long term.

The Real Work of Teams: Collaborative Inquiry

3

Teacher team collaboration has merit. Studies show it has the potential to improve teacher practice at a greater rate than when teachers don't collaborate. It brings about better student outcomes and contributes to a cohesive professional school culture (Berry, 2019; Donohoo, 2013; Rennie Center for Education Research and Policy, 2014; Timperley, 2008, 2011, 2014). However, not every group that collaborates experiences such benefits. Those that do often have skillful team leaders (STLs) at the helm who facilitate powerful collaboration in three ways:

1. Engage in cycles of inquiry

2. Lead inquiry with intention and flexibility

3. Foster a culture of collaborative inquiry

1. STLs engage teams in cycles of inquiry.

Collaborative inquiry starts with curiosity or wondering among a group of educators about a challenge or problem. This question launches them into a shared quest for learning and better outcomes. While every team's quest is different, successful journeys follow a predictable cycle.

Robert Shand of the Shanker Institute in a 2017 blog post captures a cycle-based approach with a traditional team example. He writes,

> Teams of teachers, administrators, and other professionals with some shared goal or challenge would assemble—most often, the teams would map on to some existing collaborative structure within a school, such as a team of teachers within the same grade level, teachers of the same subject, or teachers who worked with one specific population of high-needs students. The team would then identify a small target group of students who were struggling with a particular skill and use refined assessment instruments and data analysis protocols to identify a very specific sub-skill to serve as the team's initial area of focus. With a sub-group and sub-skill in hand to give focus and discipline to the team's work, the team would enter into a series of iterative cycles by which they would locate or develop instructional strategies to help improve student performance in the sub-skill, systematically monitor improvement and revise or test new strategies, and then, as they found

strategies that were effective, share them with colleagues and move on to new or more carefully refined sub-skills.

Collaborative inquiry can bring about significant visible changes for students when teams focus on targeting subskills for subgroups of students, as described by Shand (2017). But school teams are also widening their inquiry focus beyond academic achievement and proficiency goals. Today collaborative inquiry can be used to bring about improved social-emotional and wellness outcomes, as well as life skills. Teacher teams also use inquiry to tap into the assets of students' diverse cultures (Hargreaves & O'Connor, 2018a, 2018b) and close opportunity gaps (Jhagroo, 2020).

The STL Phases of Collaborative Inquiry

Regardless of the topic for collaborative inquiry, successful groups typically structure it around a cycle. There are many inquiry cycle models that leaders and their teams can choose to follow. (See the box later in this chapter.) My own experience from training and supporting hundreds of team leaders has led me to put forth the STL Phases of Collaborative Inquiry, as shown in Figure 2.

FIGURE 2   STL Phases of Collaborative Inquiry

STL Phases of Collaborative Inquiry in a Nutshell

Student-centered challenge: At the core of your inquiry cycle is an important student-centered challenge—something that is tugging at you and your colleagues, something that "keeps you up at night." The challenge on which you choose to focus must in some way connect to a school* priority and, most important, should matter to students, families, and your team.

Ask & Aim: Frame the student-centered challenge as a compelling question, one that everyone is eager to pursue. Aim your inquiry work toward gaining answers to your question. Don't fret if your initial question is too broad. As you move through the inquiry cycle, expect that your question will grow more specific and evolve. Exit this phase when you have a strong inquiry question. (Criteria for a strong inquiry question are found in Move 6.6).

Assess & Analyze: Further your understanding about the student-centered problem by examining carefully selected assessment data. Make intentional decisions about which assessments to give (even if you have to create them), who to assess and when, and how to prepare data for analysis. During analysis, suspend bias and assumptions to draw sound and valid conclusions. Exit this phase when you discover evidence-based areas of need.

Target & Plan: Target a bite-sized goal based on student needs, and draw a preliminary road map to reach it. Get specific in naming which students need what goal, by when. Exit this phase with a S-M-A-A-H-R-T goal—one that is specific, measurable, attainable, aligned to priorities, heartfelt, results-driven, and time-bound. Draft an initial work plan to reach your goal.

Research & Study: Expand your team's knowledge base through study. Engage in text-based discussions. Read professional articles and book excerpts, view videos, listen to podcasts, consult with experts, and share best practices. Exit this phase with new educator learning and a collective interest to implement strategies.

Strategize & Design: Decide what idea or strategy to test out, and design a means to implement it. Design and practice with colleagues in a dry-demo (explained in Primary Intention 9) to obtain feedback before doing so with students. Tweak your implementation design. Decide how you will collect evidence. Exit this phase with a specific plan for people to implement.

"School" priorities connote any district, school, department, or grade-level priorities.

Act & Evaluate: This is where the rubber meets the road. Implement what you designed. Get into classrooms and observe each other. Examine data (e.g., student work) collected from implementation. Draw conclusions and adopt new practices. Exit this phase when your team has critically examined the impact of the changes put into practice. Decide what to adopt going forward.

Repeat the Cycle

Ask & Aim: After completion of a cycle of inquiry, new dilemmas, questions, and goals are likely to emerge. If you choose, you can narrow your focus and pursue learning about these questions in a new cycle of inquiry.

Noteworthy Collaborative Inquiry Cycles

The STL Phases of Collaborative Inquiry (Figure 2) is one of many structures from which teams can choose. Despite obvious differences between cycles, such as the number of steps and what those steps are called, or the effective tools and protocols each model offers, all are similar in that they capture the key components of collaborative inquiry.

STL Tip: If your school or team already follows one of these cycles, then you needn't toss it out and replace it with the STL Phases of Collaborative Inquiry. Simply opt for the one that best serves your purpose and best resonates with your colleagues. You really can't go wrong.

Cycles

- STL Phases of Collaborative Inquiry (described in detail in this chapter).

- Harvard's well-respected Data Wise (Boudett et al., 2005) is an eight-step model that recommends teams (1) *organize for collaborative work*, (2) *build assessment literacy*, (3) *create a data overview*, (4) *dig into student data*, (5) *examine instruction*, (6) *develop an action plan*, (7) *plan to assess progress*, and (8) *act and assess*. A key distinction between this model and others is its explicit approach in preparing all educators for collaborative inquiry by organizing structures for collaboration and helping people become data literate.

- Jenni Donohoo (2013) suggests teams move through four stages: (1) *frame the problem*, (2) *collect evidence*, (3) *analyze evidence*, and (4) *celebrate and share*. This cycle emphasizes the importance of evidence-based decision making.

- Learning Forward's (n.d.) teacher learning team cycle presents five stages: (1) *analyze data*, (2) *set goals*, (3) *learn individually and collaboratively*, (4) *implement new learning*, and (5) *monitor, assess, and adjust practice*. What I particularly like about this cycle is its emphasis on setting both student and teacher goals in the second stage. It also places strong focus on learning through implementation of curriculum, instruction, and assessment. A detailed diagram of the cycle of continuous improvement is available from Learning Forward (Roy, 2013).

- The Coalition for Essential Schools (Cushman, 1999), which no longer exists but had a great influence on my work when I first began leading teams, created a model with six steps: (1) *develop a vision for teaching and learning*, (2) *formulate a researchable question*, (3) *design instruction*, (4) *teach and collect data*, (5) *analyze the data*, and (6) *develop implications for changing practice*. This model is a great fit for teacher teams due to its focus on changing teacher practice.

- Love and colleagues' (2015) Formative Assessment for Results (FAR) cycle taught through Research for Better Teaching grounds team planning and analysis in evidence of student understanding. Teacher teams collaborate in ways that grow their expertise and improve student-learning outcomes. Their four-step model guides teams to (1) *clarify the learning journey*, (2) *infuse formative assessments*, (3) *analyze formative assessments*, and (4) *take FIRME action* (feedback, investigation, reteaching/reengaging/regrouping, moving on, and extension). A key distinction of this cycle from others is its powerful and routine use of collectively infusing and analyzing formative assessments.

- The W. Edwards Deming Institute (2021) has a long-standing cycle made popular through DuFour's work with professional learning communities in schools: *plan, do, check, act* (sometimes referenced as *plan, do, study, act*). The simplicity of the cycle allows all types of teams to adopt it. One point of clarity: The word *study* refers to a team measuring the effects of what they implemented in the *do* step. It is not the point in inquiry where teams research and study from internal and external resources, which is how I define *study* in my model.

2. STLs lead inquiry with intention and flexibility.

While high-functioning, high-impact Q1 teams engage in cycles of collaborative inquiry, Q3 teams usually don't. These low-functioning, low-impact teams have such a hard time figuring out how to work together, it's unlikely that they are even focused on teaching or learning. Instead they might spend a whole meeting disagreeing over which type of pie to serve on Pi Day. (I'm not slighting Pi Day, or pie, but we need to collaborate differently if we expect to begin addressing real student-learning challenges.)

It's no surprise that Q3 teams, contending with so many issues, would not engage in collaborative inquiry. But what about the more nuanced partly impactful Q2 and Q4 teams—those teams who show strength in either how they function or the impact they have, but not in both? If high-functioning, high-impact Q1 teams engage in cycles of collaborative inquiry, then what do these other teams do in their meetings? Well, many will tell you they *are* doing collaborative inquiry. They follow a cycle, just like Q1 teams. So, then, why don't these teams impact learning? Short answer: leadership.

As you might expect, any facilitator can efficiently get any moderately high-functioning group to move around a cycle, but leading inquiry is not paint-by-number. It's more than mechanically following steps. STLs lead cycles of collaborative inquiry with intention and flexibility.

Intention

Whether following my cycle or another's, STLs lead inquiry with intent. They know and communicate to their teams the purpose of each phase and make intentional moves to get there. The table in Figure 3 offers some guidance and also references intentional moves that you might make in each phase of the cycle.

Flexibility

Even when leaders are intentional in what they do, teams don't always breeze through the phases of inquiry. Hurdles arise. STLs are flexible and respond effectively. For example, when a team doesn't have data they need during the *Assess & Analyze* STL phase of collaborative inquiry, STLs don't skip that phase; they lead the team in collaboratively designing an assessment.

They are also flexible in their movement through the inquiry cycle. The term *cycle* can be misleading. Think *life cycle of a frog*. It starts with an egg mass, then develops into a tadpole with two legs, then four. Next, it's a froglet, and finally, at the end of the cycle, it is a frog. Now, unless something is radically wrong, that frog isn't going from four legs to two. This is a one-way cycle. But, that's not always the case for teams engaged in a collaborative inquiry cycle. Cycles provide a predictable path for the team to take, but when people engage in collaborative inquiry, following the sequence of steps does not always feel organic. STLs change course in the cycle based on what the group needs.

For example, an English language arts team learns that according to the Common Core State Standards students should be reading "complex works of literature" (National Governors Association Center for Best Practices & Council of Chief State School Officers, 2010). The concept of text complexity is new to team members, so the STL decides to begin their inquiry cycle in the *Research & Study* STL phase of collaborative inquiry. Through discussion of professional readings, an authentic question emerges: "What effect does text complexity have on student engagement, particularly English learners and students with language-based learning differences?" This question launches the team into the *Ask & Aim* STL phase of collaborative inquiry.

3. STLs foster a culture of collaborative inquiry.

Perhaps what most distinguishes high-functioning, high-impact Q1 teams from their counterparts is not which cycle a team follows, or even how a leader

FIGURE 3 Lead the STL Phases of Collaborative Inquiry With Intention

STL PHASE OF COLLABORATIVE INQUIRY	PURPOSE	STL GUIDING QUESTIONS	SAMPLE STL INTENTIONAL MOVES (NOTE: ALL REFERENCES HERE ARE FOUND IN PART III.)
Ask & Aim	Set direction for inquiry with a compelling question.	• What important student-centered challenge "keeps us up at night"?	• Align with a priority (Primary Intention 6). • Focus on a student-centered challenge (Primary Intention 6).
Assess & Analyze	Further understanding through data.	• Which assessment data further our understanding of our student-centered challenge? • What do we learn from analysis?	• Select (or design) assessments (Primary Intention 7). • Prepare data to examine (Primary Intention 7). • Facilitate data analysis (Primary Intention 7). • Interrupt biased or unsound reasoning (Primary Intention 8).
Target & Plan	Narrow focus on a bite-sized goal and draft a preliminary road map to reach it.	• What's the right goal to target? • What's our initial work plan to get there?	• Work toward a S-M-A-A-H-R-T goal (Primary Intention 6). • Plan purposeful meetings (Primary Intention 4).
Research & Study	Expand knowledge base and gain insight into beliefs, assumptions and practice.	• What can we learn from professional texts?	• Learn from a text-based discussion (Primary Intention 4).
Strategize & Design	Decide and plan what to implement and how to collect evidence.	• What's our plan to try this out with students, and how will we know if it is working?	• Cultivate diverse perspectives (Primary Intention 8). • Lead peer observation (Primary Intention 9). • Make clear impactful decisions (Primary Intention 8).
Act & Evaluate	Implement, observe and collect data in real time to evaluate effectiveness.	• Who will implement and how will we collect data? • How effective was this for students? • What new practices will we adopt? • What new questions emerge?	• Strengthen a culture of vulnerability-based trust (Primary Intention 3) • Invite accountability (Primary Intention 9). • Assess team function and impact (Primary Intention 10).

facilitates each phase, but the collaborative culture in which the team operates. Hargreaves and O'Connor (2018) explain that, in high-performing schools, "collaborative inquiry is embedded in the culture and life of the school, where educators actively care for and have solidarity with each other as fellow-professionals as they pursue their challenging work together in response to the cultures of their students, the society and themselves." Educators in schools that have a culture of collaborative inquiry view working together around student-learning challenges as a key driver in their success and a primary reason that they enjoy working in their schools.

You know when this culture is present. People don't leave thinking and doing things in the same ways that they did before they came together. They don't use team time to spread the word on what people already know and do, to get results they already knew how to get. They don't treat the phases of inquiry or any other inquiry cycle as a series of checkpoints to pass through.

"At its heart, inquiry is not a technical process. Rather, its purpose is to create space for critical reflection, questions, dialogue, meaning-making and action . . . being open to what you don't (yet) know, experimenting intentionally and reflecting on what happens" (Cushman, 1999).

Productive Struggle for Teacher Teams

STLs foster a team culture where productive struggle is an expected part of team learning. To better understand what characterizes a professional culture of collaborative inquiry, let's begin with what is most familiar—a culture of collaborative inquiry in the classroom. Whenever I ask teacher team leaders to describe collaborative inquiry with their students, I hear excitement in their voices. They describe it as "fun," "exploratory," and "connected to students' genuine interests." Teachers welcome questions that students come up with—especially those questions that they had not thought of. They act more as "facilitators" and "co-learners" who are "in it with students" and are "willing to let conversations go down unplanned paths" in the name of inquiry. They present just-right challenges and encourage students to "puzzle," "persist," and "speculate." In a classroom culture of collaborative inquiry, students don't initially have all the answers. Teachers allow students to productively struggle.

Struggling productively is the tipping point for learning. In his podcast *Math for Love* (mathforlove.com; see also MathsPathway, 2020), Dan Finkel speaks about the importance of not starting students off with a series of math steps that we expect them to apply to problem after problem, but instead starting with questions and then giving students time to think and time to struggle productively (and, I would add, to collaborate). Doug Fisher and Nancy Frey write extensively about the need for students to productively struggle (see, e.g., Fisher et al., 2018).

Learners of any age need to reach this tipping point. Yet, how often do we ask each other to productively struggle in our team meetings? What percentage of meetings have you attended in which you were invited to "puzzle and persist"?

High-functioning, low-impact Q2 teams who enter and exit a cycle of inquiry without exploring complex questions, who don't deeply inquire into root causes because they don't want to offend anyone, or who just accept all ideas to keep the peace don't ever experience productive struggle. Members of low-functioning, high-impact Q4 teams who won't dare tackle questions that might expose their weak areas, or who avoid solutions that actually require changes to their beliefs and practices, miss out on a culture of collaborative inquiry.

With the trust and courage of their colleagues, STLs facilitate collaborative inquiry that calls upon people to do many of the following:

- Wrestle with what they thought they knew

- Critically examine evidence that reveals that what they have been doing might not be working as well as they think

- Publicly face difficult truths

- Read from and study sources that present perspectives different from their own

- Publicly try new things, even when unsure

- Rely on each other for solutions before defaulting to whatever school leaders prescribe

- Depend on each other to shape each other's thinking, suspend assumptions, and challenge each other's practice

Are We Ready for This?

If you're concerned that discourse involving productive struggle is too demanding and people won't want to meet if they have to do it, think again. Leading collaborative inquiry in this way actually brings more enjoyment to people than if you just have them talk about whatever they want to or share resources they like. Csikszentmihalyi (1990), in his well-known book *Flow*, says, "Enjoyment appears to be at the boundary between boredom and anxiety, when the challenges are just balanced with the person's capacity to act" (p. 32). Educators are ready for this.

A teacher turned principal friend, Karen McCarthy, once told me, "I want teachers to be the thinkers they are." This phrase is one that has stuck with me for years for two reasons: I believe it and think most would agree with the statement. But, I am also perplexed by the ways in which we manage to often take the thinking out of teaching with scripted curriculums, top-down mandates, spoon-fed professional development, and task-oriented team meetings. Engaging teachers in a culture of collaborative inquiry, not just a protocol with steps to follow, gives people opportunities to be thinkers and doers, as well. There have been countless occasions when I and other team members have thought and acted differently *because* of our inquiry work together. Through productive struggle, we grow. I have witnessed high-functioning, high-impact Q1 teams and their leaders transform students academically, socially, and emotionally through targeted inquiry cycles.

I can't help but be influenced by what I have read about the MIT Media Lab, where faculty members, researchers, and students come together from across disciplines to collaborate and innovate in technology. On their website, it says, "Lab researchers are committed to delving into the questions not yet asked, whose answers could radically improve the way people live, learn, express themselves, work, and play." My impression is that these people work in a culture of collaborative inquiry. They are absolutely intentional in what they aim to achieve, and deliberate in what they try, but they are only successful if they approach collaboration grounded in creativity, exploration, interdependence, productive struggle, and discovery.

Essential Understandings

STLs' Essential Understandings

Thank you for your commitment to leading teams of adult learners. This is complex work. It not only takes a skillful intentional approach, but also requires an understanding of, well, teams, adult learning, and peer leadership. Skillful team leaders (STLs) are aware of the social influences that affect group learning. They are attuned to the unique needs of adult learners. And, they capitalize on the advantages and learn to overcome the challenges of being a peer team leader. With the essential understandings in the following chapters, you will be better prepared to implement the moves in this book.

WHAT SKILLFUL TEAM LEADERS UNDERSTAND ABOUT GROUPS

1. All people are subject to social influence.

2. Personalities and work preferences influence how a group works together.

3. Group diversity improves outcomes if you can get past the function troubles.

4. Groups are dynamic, not static.

WHAT SKILLFUL TEAM LEADERS UNDERSTAND ABOUT ADULT LEARNERS

1. Adults are natural problem solvers and self-directed learners.

2. Adults need to know why they are learning something new, how it is relevant to them, and what practical application it has.

3. Adults are motivated by learning that improves either who they are or what they do.

4. Adults know the best ways in which they learn.

5. Adults want to be treated as professionals with their experience and expertise acknowledged.

WHAT SKILLFUL TEAM LEADERS UNDERSTAND ABOUT PEER LEADERSHIP

1. Peer leaders have a change agent edge over those with authority.

2. Peer leaders have a teacher advantage.

3. Peer leaders face a unique set of hurdles because of their dual role.

4. Peer leaders often start with misconceptions of what it means to lead.

5. Peer leaders possess five key attributes.

The Psychology of Groups

4

Most reality TV shows are about groups—*Survivor*, *Big Brother*, *The Amazing Race*. There's a reason for this: drama. When people are part of a group, even a team of two, doing anything becomes more complex. You may be hugely successful on your own, but working with a group is a completely different undertaking. And yet, the outcomes of teamwork almost always far surpass what an individual can accomplish when skillful team leaders (STLs) understand and can navigate the social psychology of groups.

STLs hold the following essential understandings about groups:*

1. All people are subject to social influence.

2. Personalities and work preferences influence how a group works together.

3. Group diversity improves outcomes if you can get past the function troubles.

4. Groups are dynamic, not static.

1. All people are subject to social influence.

Social psychologists have proven that it isn't only children who are swayed by others; adult learners in a group setting are too. STLs are attuned to how a group can impact the choices an individual team member makes and how a single person can affect the group. STLs have a heightened awareness of groupthink, group polarization, and social loafing. (For a summary of these social influences, see Figure 4.)

Groupthink: "What *He* Said"

Have you ever been in a group where everyone favors something that you don't, but when given the chance to speak, you go along with what the group picks? Social psychologists call this conformity. It's a typical human behavior, so don't feel bad if you've done it.

The famous 1950s Asch experiment illustrates the concept of conformity in a most fascinating way. A group of people who don't know one another are brought into a room and given a very simple task: Select which of three

---

Group size, diversity, meeting location, meeting time of day, and meeting frequency can also influence a team. I explore these on my website: www.elisamacdonald.com.

lines drawn on the right side of a card is equal in length to the one line drawn on the left side of the card. One participant is led to believe that this is a visual-perception test and that the other people in the group are also volunteers. In actuality, this participant is the subject of a social psychology experiment, in a room with actors who were instructed in advance to all give the same wrong answer. Within a few rounds of listening to person after person after person incorrectly name the same line on the right that was obviously not equal in length to the line on the left, the non-actor participant conforms, giving the same wrong answer. (A version of this experiment is available on video from Question Everything [2013] and absolutely worth watching, if for nothing else, to see the face of the unknowing non-actor participant wrestle with deciding to state the right answer or to go along with the group . . . And the 1970s hair makes it worth a watch, too.) When individuals conform to the preferences of a group, as the non-actor participant does in this experiment, they are said to have engaged in groupthink (Janis, 1972).

The Asch experiment was conducted many times, and researchers found that one-third of non-actor participants conformed to the group they were with. There are a few theories as to why people do so.

Peer pressure. No matter your age or self-confidence, wanting to be accepted by your peers is a natural phenomenon dating back to primitive times when we needed groups to survive. Sometimes people dismiss their own preferences in favor of the group's so that they fit in. This can happen on any team, particularly large teams where it is hard for one person to oppose a large number of consenting opinions. People are also more likely to conform in public voting or discussion.

Self-doubt. Some people in the Asch experiment reported afterward that they thought they were right until they heard others give a different answer and convinced themselves that they, then, must be wrong. Low-functioning, high-impact Q4 teams are at high risk for conformity because there are often plenty of strong individual performers, which can make people less comfortable expressing opinions contrary to "experts" on the team either because they are intimidated by them or because they simply assume those "experts" know best and defer to them. Multigenerational teams, in particular, are prone to have people conforming to the group. Those new to teaching with less experience question what they know and go along with the preferences of seasoned teachers; those who are older and have been out of graduate school for a longer time may conform to the younger generation, worried that their own methods might be outdated.

Cultural norms. Some people were taught that to conform is good and that being contrarian is disrespectful. Or they learned to avoid confrontation at all costs in order to keep the peace. A principal once told me that he would often opt to agree with everyone else in a group because growing up he was taught to "take one for the team." He promoted the idea that his teachers should be team players in this way. What he didn't realize, until our work together, was that he was unknowingly promoting groupthink, sending a message to his team that getting along should be put above all else, even if it meant suppressing any dissenting opinions that could create conflict.

High-functioning, low-impact Q2 teams, in particular, are often composed of people who favor harmony over confrontation. This makes them ripe for conformity. I've seen teacher leaders go along with a poor instructional team choice because they did not want to disrupt the positive momentum among their colleagues even though they had reservations about the decision.

Group Polarization: Taking a Side

When groupthink occurs, individuals forgo their own opinions to go along with the will of the team even when they disagree with others. When polarization occurs, individuals come to a group with opinions and, when met with acceptance for their ideas, become emboldened, moving themselves and the group toward a more extreme position. Like metal fibers drawn to a magnet, the group clings to their opinions and won't let go.

Think about the left and right sides of the aisle in the U.S. political climate of 2020. Someone posts a political statement on social media, others "like" it, and suddenly all members of that group post more and more extreme views of the same content. Anyone who tries to offer an alternate viewpoint is shut down. The group is polarized.

I've observed group polarization in school teams countless times, typically when people are interpreting data or making decisions together. It happens very quickly and is almost unnoticeable. The team gathers together. People have thought about the problem or decision in advance. They get to the table, and one person, usually someone with a strong opinion, is the first to speak. Others chime in with similar viewpoints, and before you know it the team is fully backing this one idea, without pausing to consider alternate perspectives.

Group polarization is detrimental to school teams because it can prematurely dismiss good ideas before they can be explored. In some cases, it actually advances bad ideas or emboldens people to continue with the status quo. High-functioning, low-impact Q2 teams are especially subject to this social influence because they are often like-minded and get along. Gravitating toward the same idea comes quite naturally to them. Q3 and Q4 teams, who are known for not getting along too well, also get into polarizing discussions because stronger voices in the group bend a team decision toward what they want. Those "louder" voices might belong to one or two people who intimidate others, or to someone with authority, or to someone who is simply very convincing.

Social Loafing

"Baby, you can sleep while I drive." This lyric from a Melissa Etheridge song is meant as a gesture of love, but if we take it as a metaphor for teams, it captures a less endearing phenomenon called social loafing. That is when someone reduces their individual effort because they know others will get the job done with or without them. When there is no individual evaluation component in a group task, some people social loaf (Latané et al., 1979).

Consider a scenario in which a team decides they don't have an assessment that will give them the data they need, so they have to create their own. They start collaborating, but one teacher is on her phone, not participating. When a team member asks what she would like to include as an assessment question, she responds, "I'm good with whatever you all decide." While this teacher's easygoing attitude might be considered a good quality, in reality she is not taking shared responsibility for the team task. She is social loafing.

It's common to have one or more social loafers on a low-functioning, low-impact Q3 team where inevitably someone doesn't fully contribute as others in the group do. Low-functioning, high-impact Q4 teams, who tend to have one or more competent go-getters in the group, will make it easy for some members to social loaf, either because they know the group will carry them or because they don't see themselves as essential to the team and consequently withdraw to let the "superstars" drive the work.

Having one or more social loafers in a group can weigh a team down, but it's not always the fault of the person doing the loafing. Team leaders can unknowingly enable people to reduce their involvement on the team. Some leaders have difficulty sharing the workload and allowing their colleagues to take ownership and responsibility. As a result, people on the team take a passive role so that the team leader can do everything. Team members can't pick up the ball and run down the field, if the team leader won't pass the ball.

2. Personalities and work preferences influence how a group works together.

Personality

When a team thrives, success is often attributed to the makeup of a "good group of people." And when a team struggles, it's common for people to blame particular personalities. But differences in personalities can be an asset to a team. Understanding the social science of personality can help.

Helen Fisher, whose research influenced Match.com, presents evidence indicating that the way our brains are wired plays a role in our personalities. For instance, people with high serotonin activity are more social and outgoing, but also more prone to social-norm conformity, setting aside their own convictions to go along with the group. (Could the behavior of the conforming individuals in the Asch experiment, described earlier, have simply been a result of them having high levels of serotonin?) While there are many family and twin studies pointing to genetics as the primary determiner of our personalities, there are

FIGURE 4   Social Influence Cheat Sheet

SOCIAL INFLUENCE	WHAT IT IS	WHY IT MATTERS	TEAMS MOST AFFECTED
Groupthink	Individuals dismiss their own ideas to be in accord with the group.	• Alternate viewpoints are not heard. • Individuals are silenced. • Leads to compliance instead of ownership. • Individuals can feel oppressed. • Bad ideas and poor decisions go unchallenged.	Q2, Q3, and Q4 teams or teams with new members or new teachers.
Group polarization	Individuals come to a group with opinions and, when met with acceptance for their ideas, become emboldened, moving themselves and the group toward a more extreme position.	• Alternate viewpoints are not explored. • The team comes to consensus too quickly. • Individuals don't develop empathy toward alternate perspectives. • Bad ideas and poor decisions gain momentum.	Q2, Q3, and Q4 teams or homogeneous teams with no diversity.
Social loafing	An individual reduces their effort because they know others will get the job done with or without them.	• Without everyone's contributions, the team is not as strong as it could be. • Tension may occur between team members. • "Social loafers" may feel as if they are not essential to the team, perpetuating their "loafing" behaviors.	Low-functioning Q3 and Q4 teams or large teams.

other studies pointing to the influence of environment. Whatever the reason for your personality and that of your colleagues, most researchers agree that by adulthood, while subtle changes can happen over time, personalities are unlikely to change much. Case in point: I twice took the Myers–Briggs personality test, a lengthy self-reporting inventory that pegs you as one of 16 personality types. Over the span of 10 years, then and now, I'm still an ENTJ—extroverted, intuitive, thinking, and judging. Although you can't change someone's personality, you can teach people to be mindful of how they choose to show up in meetings.

For example, I know my personality type makes me good at thinking analytically and strategically, giving me the ability to quickly see illogical or inefficient options, but I've learned that offering criticism of what's not working can dampen the mood of a group. I am mindful of this and intentionally present problems more as possibilities so as not to turn people off to my recommendations.

Work Preferences

High-functioning, high-impact teams also aim to understand people's different work preferences and what they need to succeed in the group. For instance, I led a Compass Points activity with a district leadership team in which the majority of principals self-identified as results-oriented *Norths*, while their superintendent self-identified as a relationship-focused *South*. *Norths* and *Souths* are on opposite sides of the compass for a reason, and the tension in this group was apparent. But the team had the courage to seek to understand each other's different styles. When the superintendent skillfully explained how she saw being a *South* leader as a positive because she placed great importance on insight from her principals, the principals suddenly appreciated her style and were better able to work with her. When she learned of their *North* tendencies, she adapted her style to make sure that when it was time to make decisions, there was no ambiguity. Once people gain a better understanding of each other's work-style preferences and personalities, they begin to learn how to function better as a team.

3. Group diversity improves outcomes if you can get past the function troubles.

Imagine a fifth-grade team of like-minded general education teachers deciding which math power standards are essential to teach. They come to agreement swiftly and with no conflict. They are considered a high-functioning team. But what happens when they merge with middle and high school teachers, special education teachers, and experts in teaching English learners, each with differing perspectives and opinions? Most likely this diverse group will engage in debate and some conflict. While it might take them longer to reach consensus, in the end this team will actually come to a better-informed conclusion, more so than if they stayed as a homogenous group.

Diverse teams might include people from different cultural and ethnic backgrounds; people of different genders, ages, and/or levels of experience; people with different roles or functions in an organization; people with distinct approaches to collaboration; people with varying ideologies; neurodiversity, defined as people who think and perceive the world differently (Kharbanda, 2020); and developmental diversity. Across the board, social psychologists have concluded that diverse teams have the potential to be more creative, be more innovative, make better decisions, and get better outcomes than homogeneous ones (Güver & Motschnig, 2017).

Diverse groups bring together people with varying degrees of knowledge, experience, and perspective for problem solving and innovation. They even engage in more evidence-based discourse than their counterparts. In fact, differences among people actually drive individuals to stick more to the facts because facts are the only thing people in diverse groups have in common. (David Rock and Heidi Grant [2016] summarize key studies that support this.) The collaboration of a diverse team of educators helps avoid the blind spots that homogeneous groups can have.

Despite all the advantages of a diverse team, the function hurdles can be hard to get past. Diverse teams are more likely to struggle with cohesion and communication. STLs are intentional about helping people think flexibly, cultivate diverse perspectives in ways that respect differences, and create cross-cultural competence for an inclusive environment.

4. Groups are dynamic, not static.

Assemble a team in the fall, then observe them again in the spring, and you'll likely have a different view of how they are doing. In 1965, Bruce Tuckman put forward the notion that teams move through four stages together: forming, storming, norming, and performing (and later he added a fifth stage, adjourning). A brief description of each stage is provided here, followed by how I view these stages as they relate to function and impact.

Forming. In the forming stage, teams learn how to work with one another. Discourse during this stage is often polite and guarded, as people are testing the waters. This stage is revisited each time there are membership changes in the group.

Storming. In the storming stage, conflicts arise when people disagree about the set course and how to get there. By this stage, differences in roles, work styles, and group dynamics come into play, challenging the group's stability.

Norming. If a team makes it to the norming stage, they have worked out conflicts, or at least have an agreed-upon plan for doing so, and begin to build upon one another's strengths. They start to look like a cohesive group.

Performing. Once at the performing stage, there is evidence of the group advancing toward, or meeting, their intended outcomes. This is where team impact is evident.

Adjourning. After the group has met their goals, they adjourn. This can raise different emotions for different people.

Knowing Tuckman's (1965) model helps you understand what to expect when leading your team over a period of time. High-functioning, high-impact Q1 teams move through all of Tuckman's stages over time. (They go through storming, too, but unlike other types of teams, they get past it.) Q3 teams (low everything) can't reach the norming stage, and high-functioning, low-impact Q2 teams can't get beyond it. Low-functioning, high-impact Q4 teams are made up of individuals who are already performing independent of one another, but because they have skipped the norming stage where they would have learned how to work well interdependently, they never reach their potential collective impact on their learning or that of their students.

Five Must-Knows About Adult Learners

As an effective teacher, you have a strong understanding of how children learn, and this influences the intentional decisions you make in the classroom. For instance, because you understand the primary need for a child to feel a sense of belonging in order to learn, you might manage a student's negative behavior in a way that does not alienate the child, make teaching and learning decisions that communicate that this child belongs in your class, and teach in a culturally responsive way. But, why bring up what teachers understand about child learning in a book about leading teams of adult learners? Well, first, it goes without saying that skillful team leaders (STLs) must be effective educators. They have a good grasp on what to teach, how to teach, how students learn, and what to do when they don't. But being an effective teacher does not guarantee being an effective team leader. STLs have a strong understanding of how adults learn.

Not until the 1970s did the notion start to catch on that the learning needs of adults might be different from those of children. Malcolm Knowles (1975) wrote extensively about adult learning, which he called *andragogy* (the opposite of *pedagogy*, which focuses on child learning). His work developed from that of numerous researchers and psychologists dating back to the 1920s.

In the 21st century, Ellie Drago-Severson (2009) published a helpful tool for understanding how adult learners make meaning of the world. Drago-Severson's "Four Ways of Knowing" (based on Harvard psychologist Robert Kegan's [2009] constructive developmental theory) categorizes adult learners in one of four different stages of development: (1) rule-bound, or *instrumental*; (2) other-focused, or *socializing*; (3) reflective, or *self-authoring*; and (4) interconnected, or *self-transforming*. Figure 5 briefly summarizes each way of knowing as it relates to how a person might engage in learning.

Although the stages are hierarchical, Drago-Severson (2009) makes clear that different circumstances call for different ways of knowing. In other words, being "rule-bound" or "other-focused" is not bad (e.g., you want your accountant to be rule-bound). Moreover, her work emphasizes the importance of providing various supports and challenges to adult learners to help advance their developmental trajectories. Based on my understanding of the ways of knowing and my experiences in working with adult learners, it seems to me that if no adults on a team are developmentally ready to be self-authoring (reflective) or self-transforming (interconnected), then group learning will be limited.

FIGURE 5   Adult Ways of Knowing on a Team

WAYS OF KNOWING	RULE-BOUND (INSTRUMENTAL)	OTHER-FOCUSED (SOCIALIZING)	REFLECTIVE (SELF-AUTHORING)	INTERCONNECTED (SELF-TRANSFORMING)
Characteristics	• Views the world in terms of right and wrong. • Engages with others through a transactional lens. • Rule driven.	• Makes meaning of the world through others' opinions. • Engages with others to seek acceptance. • Relationship driven.	• Views the world through their own system of values and beliefs. • Engages with others to learn about self. • Self-improvement driven.	• Views the world as interconnected; is not intimidated by paradox, contradictions, complexity, or uncertainty. • Engages with others to explore and create new meaning. • Systems driven.
What you might hear	• *Do we have permission to do this?* • *But that's not how we've done this before.* • *This is what we were told to do, so we have to do it.*	• *What will people think if I do this?* • *What do you think I should do?* • *I'll go along with whatever the group thinks we should do.*	• *I need to do this to become better.* • *I'll consider what you say, but I'll come to my own conclusion.* • *I set the standards for myself and others.*	• *I need to hear from others to deepen my understanding of the issues.* • *I challenge conventions and accepted theories and practices, even my own.* • *I seek systemic improvement.*
Feels assured when . . .	• *I know the limits and boundaries.*	• *I am liked and appreciated.*	• *I am confident in my values and beliefs.*	• *I have taken time to pursue ideas and how they interconnect.*
Needs to be successful.	• Clear goals and parameters. • Procedures, timelines, and details. • Direct explicit feedback.	• Time to hear multiple viewpoints. • Feedback couched in appreciation.	• Time for analysis and evaluation. • Feedback that emphasizes the person's competence.	• Time for research, exploration, synthesis, and innovation. • Nuanced feedback.
Needs to grow and develop.	• Flexibility and willingness to question authority.	• Self-awareness of one's own values and beliefs and self-motivation.	• Openness to the influence of others, paradox, and uncertainty.	• N/A

Source: Based on Ellie Drago-Severson's work in *Leading Adult Learning* (Corwin, 2009).

In this chapter, I present five essential understandings about adult learners, a synthesis of what Knowles (1975) and Drago-Severson (2009) have said, together with learning from my own experience and the experience of other STLs. If you have led teams of adult learners, or have simply been an adult learner on a team, then the following essential understandings will likely resonate with your experience.

1. Adults are natural problem solvers and self-directed learners.

2. Adults need to know why they are learning something new, how it is relevant to them, and what practical application it has.

3. Adults are motivated by learning that improves either who they are or what they do.

4. Adults know the best ways in which they learn.

5. Adults want to be treated as professionals with their experience and expertise acknowledged.

Key point: I do believe that adult learners are developmentally distinct from child learners, and yet, I also believe that some principles are common to both. For instance, both students and adults have a need to know why they are learning something.

1. Adults are natural problem solvers and self-directed learners.

YouTube carries nearly 14 billion "How To" videos. Amazon carries over 100,000 books with the words *How To* in the title. Our overwhelming interest in seeking out how to do things speaks to adults' problem-solving nature and predilection for self-directed learning.

While there may be disagreements on what is or isn't a problem, or how to solve it, educators want to make things better for students, families, and their teaching. They, too, enjoy having autonomy in decisions about what they learn, when, and how. The need for autonomy does not start at adulthood. It begins in an individual's formative years, gains momentum during adolescence, and only strengthens with age. Over time, a person's self-concept shifts from being dependent on others to learn, to being self-directed. Malcolm Knowles (1975) describes self-directed learning as "a process in which individuals take the initiative without the help of others in diagnosing their learning needs, formulating goals, identifying human and material resources, and evaluating learning outcomes" (p. 18). His choice of words, "without the help of others," is slightly misleading. Self-direction doesn't mean going solo, so don't go abandoning your team just yet. In fact, studies show that self-directed learners engage with an average of 10 people throughout a learning journey by seeking guidance, expertise, resources, and/or encouragement from them. Self-directed also doesn't necessarily mean self-taught. Many self-directed learners identify problems they wish to resolve and seek traditional methods of education and collaborative opportunities to learn how to do it. In other words, self-directed learning in which adults engage in inquiry and problem solving can very much be a team sport.

The need for adults to solve problems and engage in self-directed learning is one reason that collaborative inquiry is a preferred method of learning for educators. Launch a teacher-directed inquiry cycle focused on a student-learning challenge.

2. Adults need to know why they are learning something new, how it is relevant to them, and what practical application it has.

Why is *why* one of the first questions adults need answered when requested to learn something new? Is it because they expect learning to be worthwhile, or because they've spent a lot of time in mandated professional development that was not useful? Or do they need to see a clear reason for learning something new, or how it applies to the "real" work that they do with students? Yes all around.

When adult learning is self-directed, the *why* is very clear: The learner has identified a compelling problem or gap in their own knowledge or skill, and this motivates them to learn and change. But when the reason to learn does not originate with the adult learner, and is instead mandated from someone else without explanation as to why, then the adult has little reason to invest in new learning.

Embedded within the simple three-letter question, *why*, are more questions: *Why this; why not that? Why me; why not someone else? Why now; why not some other time?* Communicate the answers to these questions, and if the reasons are clearly relevant and applicable to your colleagues, they will embrace new learning.

3. Adults are motivated by learning that improves either who they are or what they do.

It troubles me when I hear someone say that a child or an adult is unmotivated to learn. Humans are wired to learn from a very young age. Babies do not need to be externally motivated to walk; they do so because it's instinctual, and because there are natural rewards built in. They can get around. And, they hear the singing praise of their doting caretakers. Once children enter adolescence, they don't suddenly lose their motivation to learn; they just need teachers who can help them access learning by being responsive to their rapidly developing minds and bodies.

All adult learners, too, are motivated learners—yes, even the person who appears to want nothing to do with your team. STLs understand what intrinsically motivates educators. Studies show that so long as adults can see how team learning will improve their performance with students or how it will better who they are as a person and practitioner, they will be motivated. (This is particularly true for those who are self-authoring/reflective knowers [see Figure 5] for whom competence is important.) It's only when the work of teams does not deliver either, or when the team has been collaborating for a while without any visible progress, that adults lose motivation. Connect new learning to ways in which people will grow or practice will improve.

4. Adults know the best ways in which they learn.

Although learning-style research is debated as of late, adults typically know how they learn best. Adults often say things such as "I need a visual." "I need an oral explanation." "I need some time to process this." "I need to act first, process later." "I need to think through this out loud." "I need to learn this in small chunks." With many learning years behind them, adults have found what works best for them and tend to expect time in teams to allow them the freedom to learn in the ways they need. Trust the adults on your team.

5. Adults want to be treated as professionals with their experience and expertise acknowledged.

Perhaps nothing is more off-putting to adult learners than being talked down to. Adults respond best to leaders who recognize their knowledge and expertise in the design and delivery of learning. This does not mean they want public shout-outs or certificates for what they know (though Ellie Drago-Severson's [2009] research does point to one type of adult learner as someone looking for approval). Be mindful of your word choice, meeting design, and ways in which you celebrate individual and team progress.

The Upside (and Downside) of Being a Peer Leader

6

Team leadership is not about running meetings. (Neither is this book.) It is about leading people. Much has been written on leadership. Whether you work in education, business, or the military, whether you lead an Olympic team or a Boy Scout troop, there are fundamental understandings about leadership that apply to all people. Despite articles claiming to reveal the "Top 10 Secrets Every Leader Must Know" or the "5 Mistakes Every Leader Must Avoid," there is no agreement among experts as to what these are. There are many branded leadership approaches that people swear by (e.g., transformational leadership, servant leadership, distributed leadership, indelible leadership), and if you are now, or are looking to become, an administrative leader, then you have likely had exposure to some or all of them. But, if you are a *peer* leading your colleagues, it is most helpful to develop a deep understanding of not just leadership, but more specifically *peer* leadership.

I define a peer as a person who leads colleagues, who does not hold a top authority position (like a principal), does not evaluate teachers (or does, but is also a member of the same union), and who might have social relationships outside of school with those they lead. You are most likely a peer leader if you are a teacher leader, an instructional coach/partner, a department lead, or, perhaps, an assistant principal. Being a peer leader poses unique challenges, but also offers unexpected advantages. In the following pages, I explore five understandings that skillful team leaders (STLs) have about peer leadership.

1. Peer leaders have a change agent edge over those with authority.

2. Peer leaders have a teacher advantage.

3. Peer leaders face a unique set of hurdles because of their dual role.

4. Peer leaders often start with misconceptions of what it means to lead.

5. Peer leaders possess five key attributes.

1. Peer leaders have a change agent edge over those with authority.

When you took the role of team leader, you likely had to consider if you were up for the job. *Can I run our team meetings? Can I be a resource to my colleagues? Do I work well with my peers? Do I have the capacity to devote the hours this role will require?* These are the right questions to ask, but there is another one that gets to the heart of your most important responsibility as a peer leader, and that is: *Am I ready to lead my colleagues through change?*

The real work of leading teams is not facilitating meetings; it is facilitating learning for continuous improvement. And continuous improvement requires change—changes in thinking, changes to practice, changes to structures and policies, and changes in outcomes. Peer leaders are change agents.

To lead anyone in change is a tall task, particularly as different people have different go-to responses when faced with it. Some are quick to jump on board no matter the change. Others have reservations about doing something differently, and express those concerns in ways that can make them seem resistant. When you have embraced change, but someone else has not, it is common to wish for the authority to make the other person see what you see. I have heard from teacher team leaders, "If I could just tell this person what to do . . . but I'm not their boss." Or, "I can only do so much as a colleague." I understand this thinking, but unfortunately it is based on misconceptions about leadership. The truth is that no one, whether a peer or an authority figure, can *make* another person learn or change. They can only create the conditions for learning and act in ways that demonstrate that change is possible. And while you might wish for the authority, you might be more effective without it.

Peer leaders are actually positioned to bring about authentic change in ways that those who are in a role with the power to demand it cannot (Dimock & McGree, 1995; Katzenmeyer & Moller, 2001; Margolis, 2009). To be clear, I am not minimizing the influence of school leaders, as many are effective in bringing about authentic sustainable change, but the authority they have is not likely what does it. Effective school leaders will tell you that *because* they are in an evaluative role they have had to overcome the hurdle of people being guarded and hiding struggle, which thereby inhibits the change process. Others with authority who have tried to foster understanding and the need for change can end up with compliance simply because they are the "boss" and people want to please them or not "rock the boat." In short, having authority over others can actually be a hindrance.

But being a peer responsible for leading change, while it has its own share of hurdles, is actually an advantage. I'll share just a few reasons why teacher leaders have the edge:

- You've earned credibility from your peers as an effective teacher (or you wouldn't have self-selected, or been chosen, to lead).

- You are held to the same expectations as your peers.

- You have regular contact with students.

- You relate and are empathetic to the hurdles facing your peers, as you face the same ones, while also modeling how you overcome them.

- Your peers relate to you knowing you are in a similar role to them. In challenging school cultures where there is high tension between administrators and teachers, your peers will likely view you as one of them and be less guarded around you than around a school leader.

2. Peer leaders have a teacher advantage.

The question I am most asked by peer leaders is, "How do I lead collaborative learning *with adults*?" And my first response is, "How do you lead it *with students*?" Whether you teach now or have prior teaching experience, you were likely tapped for a team leadership position *because* of your effectiveness with kids. You teach with outcomes in mind; you think about how you will engage all students in learning; you decide what to do when a child exhibits pushback; you deliberately facilitate classroom discourse that stretches students' thinking and abilities. Each move you make with a class full of students is done with intention and skill. This is the teacher advantage that you bring to leading adult learners. In short, you already know how to lead collaborative learning.

Adults and children are, of course, not the same, as I emphasize in the prior chapter, but both *are* learners. *How* you lead collaborative learning with children might differ from *how* you lead it with adults, but the intentions behind what you do—the Ten Primary Intentions—are the same.

3. Peer leaders face a unique set of hurdles because of their dual role.

While the role of peer leader provides an excellent opportunity for you to stretch as a professional and lead change, even the oxymoronic name *peer leader* points to the hurdles that come with leading as a colleague. The following are a few common dilemmas that you may have encountered and an explanation of what could be contributing to them. I also make reference to particular sections of this book that provide moves to address the dilemmas highlighted. (Note: Not meant as a shameless plug, but if you want a deeper dive into team leadership hurdles, what's behind them, and how to skillfully respond, you may want to go back and read my first book, *The Skillful Team Leader: A Resource for Overcoming Hurdles to Professional Learning for Student Achievement* [MacDonald, 2013].)

Hurdles From the Peer Side

The friend dilemma: "What do I do when my friend is the one showing resistance?"

This is one of the most jarring challenges a peer leader faces. You expect pushback from the person who is typically the "school naysayer," but when it comes from a friend, you are likely caught off-guard and might be unsure how to respond. To understand this hurdle, you'll need to tap into your emotional intelligence. Notice your emotional response; notice your friend's. Rule out personal motivations such as they wanted the leadership role that you got. Distinguish resistance aimed at you versus that aimed at your ideas, and push for change. The moves in Primary Intention 9 will help you navigate resistance.

The expertise dilemma: "Should I share my expertise or keep quiet? I don't want to come across as a know-it-all to my colleagues."

This is a real concern expressed not only by peer team leaders but by many teachers, and it is called tall poppy syndrome—when people don't want to stand out from their peers for fear of being put down, ridiculed, or even ostracized. The metaphor refers to the phenomenon that all poppies must grow together, and if one gets taller than the rest, it must be cut down. (Sounds like dystopian fiction, but it's a real thing.) If your students got better results than anyone else at the table and you are worried about sharing the data for fear that others will resent you, you have experienced tall poppy syndrome. If the principal invites teachers to present a best practice to the faculty and they decline for fear that others will snicker at them or think they are the principal's "pet," the syndrome is likely present in the school culture. If you ask individual members of your team to showcase their success, and this isn't yet the norm by which your team operates, don't be surprised if the teachers refuse or downplay their success. Sharing expertise and failure is a key component in collaborative learning. Activities and moves in Primary Intention 3 will help you create a culture in which you offer and seek out others' expertise instead of shying away from it.

Hurdles From the Leader Side

The facilitator's dilemma: "How do I facilitate a team when I'm also a member of it?"

Leading and participating at the same time can feel like juggling while riding a unicycle on a tightrope. It's doable but not easy. Because so often peer leaders are teachers alongside their colleagues, the balancing act can feel much more unsteady. As you become more sure of your intentions during facilitation and you practice the moves in this book, you will get a feel for when to full-on participate and when to pull back and manage the conversation. The "five ways to show up" explained in Move 5.5 can help you decide.

The pseudo-administrator dilemma: "My principal seems to be expecting more from me in this peer leadership role than I signed up for. I'm not sure how to talk to them." Or, "Teachers are coming to me for clarification about what the principal says. Some are asking me to advocate on their behalf. I didn't take on this role to be a go-between."

The moment you wear a leadership hat, particularly if it comes with a title like "teacher leader," people make assumptions about your role. Unless your leadership job description specifies that you are to advocate on behalf of teachers or enforce initiatives that come from administration, then be clear that your role is to facilitate collaborative learning. Similarly, clarify with your principal upfront what your job is and isn't so you know what's expected and so they don't overextend your responsibilities. Ask your principal to also message your role to the faculty. Figure 10, *Team Roles and Responsibilities Examples* (Primary Intention 2) defines roles clearly. Once everyone initially understands your role, be careful not to send mixed messages by acting in ways that extend beyond the accepted parameters.

4. Peer leaders often start with a misconception of what it means to lead.

More often than not, peer leaders start with assumptions about how they are "supposed" to lead their colleagues, and it usually involves the misconception that they must be the person who is in control and has all things figured out. For instance, when I am supporting new teacher leaders in particular, some will arrive at our first planning meeting with 10 weeks' worth of agendas already mapped out, as if it were a syllabus. Or, when I observe a meeting that we've planned together, I notice the peer leader facilitates as if they are the only one at the table, plowing through the meeting while their colleagues sit back and let them "lead." And sometimes team leaders do all the problem solving and decision making on their own, then present a polished, finished product and convince others to adopt it. (By the way, these aren't just rookie missteps. With all my years of experience leading teams, I still catch myself sometimes doing these things.)

Why might peer leaders perceive their role in this way? Here are a few reasons that I've heard from many teacher leaders:

- "I receive a stipend or some other perk that my colleagues don't."
- "I think my colleagues expect me to take charge because I have an official leadership role."
- "My colleagues are so busy; I don't want to burden them."
- "I worry that if I don't take charge, the meeting will end up a waste of people's time."
- "If I let go, I will lose control."

To be clear, peer leaders who think these things are often very smart (usually experts in their field) and have people's best interests at heart; they just haven't figured out how to embrace the "peer" side of their role, in which they show up as learners.

The truth is that you are likely a peer leader because you are an effective practitioner, a thoughtful planner, and a talented coordinator, but this doesn't mean that you have to know it all and do it all for your team. In fact, you're more effective if you don't.

Collaborative inquiry, as described in Chapter 3, is about not yet knowing. STLs respond to the ever-evolving twists and turns of the group, and learn *alongside* their colleagues. They don't know on day one what the aim of inquiry will be, or what data will reveal on day two, or what strategies the team will study and implement, or what hurdles will come their way. This "not knowing" where or how you will "land the plane," as STL Daryl Campbell describes it, can feel very unsettling for any leader, especially for a peer who feels pressure to make team time for colleagues worthwhile. It can take a while for you to realize that you can plan and lead without having all the answers. When you accept this truth about peer leadership, you'll feel tremendous relief, and your colleagues will feel more empowered.

5. Peer leaders possess five key attributes.

I don't want to succumb to the "Top 10" type lists that flood the pages of educational journals; however, I would be remiss if I did not share the five teacher team leader attributes that coaches and teacher leaders crafted with me when I was national director of teacher leader development at Teach Plus. Explained in detail in an article we wrote for ASCD, "Leading in Schools on the Edge" (2013), the five attributes of effective team leaders, particularly those doing the challenging work of transforming underperforming high-poverty schools, are being (1) *purpose driven*, (2) *evidence-based decision makers*, (3) *skillful facilitators*, (4) *ongoing learners*, and (5) *change agents*. (In the last 10 years, Teach Plus has replaced *ongoing learners* with *equity-driven*, a critically important attribute to highlight.) Even in the most challenging schools, teacher leaders who possessed these attributes were able to facilitate high-functioning, high-impact Q1 teams.

If you are a teacher team leader, it is also essential that you explore teacher leadership standards. The Teacher Leader Model Standards published by the Teacher Leadership Exploratory Consortium resonate with me (National Education Association, 2020). The standards promote the idea that teacher leaders are charged with positively influencing teaching and professional learning, in order to positively impact student-learning outcomes. (Sound familiar?) The consortium recognized that teacher leaders must develop a unique set of skills, and the standards aim to concretely define what it means to be a teacher leader. Organized into seven domains (as shown in Figure 6), the standards specify performance indicators for teacher leaders.

Although the standards address skills that teacher leaders need in order to take on a wide array of roles such as mentor, coach, or coordinator, many of the recommendations also apply to peers who lead teams. For instance, within

Domain IV: Facilitating improvements in instruction and student learning, the consortium recommends that teacher leaders learn how to "engage in reflective dialog with colleagues based on observation of instruction, student work, and assessment data and help make connections to research-based effective practices." In Primary Intentions 7–9, I highlight moves that help peer leaders intentionally do this, such as specific considerations when selecting student work to analyze collaboratively.

FIGURE 6   Teacher Leadership Standards

The standards consist of seven domains describing the diverse and varied dimensions of teacher leadership:

Domain I: Fostering a collaborative culture to support educator development and student learning

Domain II: Accessing and using research to improve practice and student achievement

Domain III: Promoting professional learning for continuous improvement

Domain IV: Facilitating improvements in instruction and student learning

Domain V: Using assessments and data for school and district improvement

Domain VI: Improving outreach and collaboration with families and community

Domain VII: Advocating for student learning and the profession

---

Source: Von Frank, V. (2011, February). Teacher leader standards: Consortium seeks to strengthen profession with leadership role. *Teachers Leading Teachers, 6*(5). https://learningforward.org/the-leading-teacher/february-2011-vol-6-no-5/

10 STL Primary Intentions With Moves

10 STL Primary Intentions With Moves

I don't like to bake. Yet, one way I unwind from a long day is to watch the PBS *Great British Baking Show* reality series, in which home bakers compete to demonstrate their skills to produce winning pastries, pies, and treats. You might think it odd that someone who doesn't know the difference between baking soda and baking powder would commit to this show, but I enjoy watching the thoughtful design and planning that bakers put into their creations and seeing the different techniques they execute. Most riveting, however, is when the soufflé doesn't rise and the biscuits bomb. It's in these moments that you witness the intentional moves the bakers make to put forth their best creation. Watching them, it becomes clear who has mastered their craft and who is just hoping to get by on a cake pan and a prayer.

Similar to these bakers, skillful team leaders (STLs) intentionally use varied techniques and deliberate moves. I grappled with writing the main part of this book as moves because I was concerned that doing so would reduce the act of team leadership to a series of prescriptive steps. But, what's true for contestants in the technical challenge who line up their finished baked goods on a table for comparison is also true for team leaders: Two people can follow the same recipe and have the same ingredients, but how things turn out depends on the baker. This book makes the moves visible; you are what makes them work.

Important Tips for Reading

Read this part last.

It is tempting to skip Parts I and II of this book and jump ahead to Part III, which delves into practice. But, to most effectively implement the moves, first read Chapters 1–6 so that you build an understanding of a skillful intentional approach to leading groups of adult learners.

Lead with your primary intention, then select the move that will most likely get you there.

There are over 150 moves in this book organized into the 10 STL Primary Intentions. The moves in Primary Intentions 1–5 address collaborative conditions, expectations, culture, planning, and engagement. These moves build what are commonly known as "soft skills."

The moves in Primary Intentions 6–10 build what might be called the "harder" skills. They address goal setting, assessment, data analysis, evidence-based decision making, bias and assumptions, resistance to change, and accountability.

To best navigate this book, begin thinking about what you are trying to accomplish. Ask yourself, "What's my primary intention?" Then flip to a move that you think will work and try it.

Approach the moves as a guide, not a comprehensive manual.

Some moves in this book will be familiar to you; some will be new. If you're a more experienced team leader, you might wonder why a particular strategy or protocol, for example, isn't in this book. Please remember my purpose for writing is not to provide you with a comprehensive A–Z book of what to do in every situation, but rather to highlight key effective moves that help teams get to and stay in the high-functioning, high-impact Quadrant 1.

For example, I do not include every norm-setting technique that exists, but I do highlight three (one that is original to me) that will help you reach your primary intent of establishing expectations for collaborative learning. Implement the moves that make sense, and draw from what you know if it isn't included here.

Beware of hyper-focusing on yourself.

A whole book of small moves can make an already cautious, conscientious leader more so. New team leaders, in particular, might hyper-focus on what *they* are doing and saying rather than on others. As a result, they might misread signals in a group, miss opportunities for learning, overpower voices in a meeting, or misjudge how a meeting went. (We've all been there.) With time and practice, the moves in this book will become more fluid and natural to you, but if you are just starting out or if you tend to lean toward the "I'm worried I'll make the wrong move" type of thinking, then let go a bit and trust your colleagues. Listening to them will help you organically decide which moves to make when.

Read and study together, observe each other in action, but please don't use this book as an evaluation tool.

This book is great to use as the basis for book study with your school or district's teacher team leaders, coaches, and administrators. People can read and discuss excerpts together, share their own strategies, and observe one another's team meetings noticing effective moves leaders make. There is even a reflection tool in Primary Intention 10 that can help people know what to look for when observing a team (see Figure 29). Principals and administrators, if you need to evaluate the effectiveness of team leaders, then look at the outcomes of their team, but please avoid evaluating the moves a team leader makes as if using a checklist. Instead, use this book as a developmental tool (e.g., "Your team does not have purpose and direction. Let's look at the moves in Primary Intention 6 to see what you can do to bring this about.").

Jump around.

Anyone who read my first book, *The Skillful Team Leader* (MacDonald, 2013), knows that I like professional texts that are packed with resources but designed in an accessible, easy-to-reference format for the busy practitioner. Part III of this book can be a doozy if you try to read it cover to cover. Turn to the moves you need, as you need them. My hope is that you'll return again and again to this section as a reference.

Aim for understanding, not precision.

The goal is not to execute the moves in this book to the letter of the law. Let your intuition, insight into your school's culture, and your personal style, wit, and creativity guide you to implement the moves that make sense. The more you practice the moves, the more nimble you will become with them. Cook up your own moves and never forget your intention behind doing what you are doing.

Primary Intention

Optimize Learning Conditions:
Time, Space, and Accommodations

1

//

I have a tendency to kill plants. On a recent occasion, I received several potted arrangements and placed them around in my house. They looked beautiful until about several weeks in. I kept forgetting to water them. One day I moved them to the ledge behind my kitchen sink. Three months later, they are alive and well. Did I suddenly develop a green thumb? No. Simply relocating the plants to a place where I stood every day, where watering was convenient and sunlight was plentiful, was enough to result in a better outcome.

Teams, too, benefit from optimal learning conditions. Skillful team leaders (STLs) are intentional about time, space, and making accommodations for the adult learners on their teams. They protect meeting time from interruptions and cancellations and are mindful of how they use the time they have. Beyond using meetings to design and plan together, STLs ensure that time is spent collaborating about the student learning that *results* from the team's designs and plans. STLs also know that learning does not end when the meeting ends. They create opportunities for collaboration in between meetings to foster a culture of ongoing learning. STLs thoughtfully utilize the learning space—namely, accessibility, visibility, acoustics, and materials—so that no one's participation is inhibited. And STLs get to know their colleagues as learners. They don't just accommodate adults with learning differences, disabilities, and/or preferences; they also encourage them to showcase their strengths.

Contents

Maximize collaborative time.

1.1 Protect meeting time.

1.2 Allocate time to examine learning outcomes.

1.3 Foster collaboration between meetings.

Enhance the learning space.

1.4 Micro-prep.

1.5 Attend to room details.

Promote equitable access to team learning.

1.6 Accommodate adults with learning differences, disabilities, or preferences.

1.7 Leverage strengths in disability.

Note: This chapter focuses on learning conditions within a team that an individual STL can manage. District leaders and school principals seeking to optimize learning conditions school-wide might check out the resources at www.elisamacdonald.com.

MAXIMIZE COLLABORATIVE TIME

Do any of the following resonate with you as an adult learner?

- I am most fresh at the beginning of a learning journey.

- I am least productive after lunch.

- Time-sensitive demands can pull me away from working toward my goal.

- I hit a slump midway through a long period of learning.

- I give my best effort when I see the finish line ahead.

In his book *When: The Scientific Secrets of Perfect Timing* (2018), Daniel H. Pink reminds us that not all minutes in the day are equal. For instance, people do their best work at different times of the day. Some teams are more productive in a short meeting than a long one. Motivation can vary depending on how far a person is into learning something new. Although a teacher leader, in particular, may not have full control over when or for how long a team meets, skillful team leaders (STLs) are thoughtful and intentional about getting the most out of the time they have.

STL moves:

1.1 Protect meeting time.

1.2 Allocate time to examine learning outcomes.

1.3 Foster collaboration between meetings.

What these moves promote:

Momentum. Teams protect meeting time and extend learning between meetings so that collaboration can steadily build and grow.

Morale. Educators feel their time is appreciated.

Productivity. Teams make the best use of their limited time.

When to use these moves:

When designing conditions for teams to meet and throughout the course of collaborative inquiry.

Related reading:

Part I, Chapter 2, "Don't Settle for High-Functioning Teams." Learn the benefits of looking at teams through an impact lens.

Moves 5.7–5.16, "Maximize productivity." To make the most of the time you have, implement these moves during facilitation of a team meeting.

1.1 Protect meeting time.

Things happen: A last-minute, unexpected staff meeting is called. Teachers are pulled to substitute for someone. Teachers are pulled to proctor a test. Team members are absent. Another meeting runs over time. The data to be analyzed is unavailable. The whole school is having an assembly. The fire alarm won't stop going off. A blizzard is coming. A local official is visiting. A wild animal is loose on campus. People are just too busy.

I've had the privilege of observing and leading a lot of team meetings, with all types of teams, in many different schools, from districts that serve different student populations, in urban, suburban, or rural settings, across a handful of states. And more times than I can count, team meetings have been interrupted or canceled for the real reasons I listed earlier and more. (Yes, a fox really did run amok during dismissal, causing us to cut our meeting short.) Whatever the reason, frequent disruptions can negatively affect the momentum and morale of a group. The most important condition for collaborative learning is actually having the time you need to meet. Each time someone or something cancels or steals time from your meeting, the message received is that your team's work is not a priority. There is only so much that a team leader can do to minimize external disruptions, so skillful team leaders (STLs) protect the meeting time they have.

How to protect meeting time:

Take the following two-prong approach:

1. *Work with school leaders to minimize school-wide disruptions.* If school leaders regularly interrupt teacher team meetings, then you need a systemic solution. Make an appointment with school leaders. Perhaps ask to be put on the agenda in an upcoming administrative team meeting. Present the facts, identifying dates of canceled meetings and/or minutes lost over time. Identify patterns if they exist. Voice your understanding of a school leader's need to sometimes take time from teacher team meetings. Be prepared to offer one solution and, if your solution is not viable, problem solve together. If interruptions continue, make it a regular practice to find out on the morning of your scheduled meeting whether a school leader anticipates an upcoming disruption (e.g., absences requiring teachers to be pulled out of your meeting to substitute, a last-minute staff meeting, etc.). Decide whether you should reschedule your meeting so that you have the full amount of time, or revise your agenda so the time you do have is productive.

2. *Preserve time with your colleagues.* Once you have done what you can to ensure that your team has regularly scheduled and protected meeting times, focus on maximizing time within your meeting. Try the following:
   - Ask in advance that none of your colleagues be scheduled for another meeting at the same time as yours. If they are, do what you can to coordinate with the leader of the other team and your colleague.

Perhaps your colleague only needs to miss a portion of your team's meeting, and you can adjust the agenda so that they are present for what's most important.

- Always start on time regardless of who is present. You can still welcome latecomers and give them a 30-second update when they arrive, but starting on time sets a clear norm for collaboration and honors the time of those who are there. Send a reminder for the start time of your team meeting. Connect privately with anyone who is regularly late. Troubleshoot what has to happen in order for them to arrive on time.

- Protect meeting time by maximizing productivity of the group and keeping people focused (see Moves 5.7–5.16). For example, table a conversation that could be resolved outside the meeting. Frame a conversation with clear parameters so that people stay on topic.

- Consistently end your meeting at the same time, or even a few minutes early, so no one is concerned about getting to their next class or commitment and leaves early.

In action:

The principal has consistently scheduled last-minute staff meetings after school that take time from meetings run by teacher leaders. Austin brings this up in a 1:1 meeting with the principal.

Austin: Our teams have committed to worthwhile student-learning goals and are motivated to accomplish them. However, with the unanticipated staff meetings, my team has met for only one hour this month, not the scheduled two hours. Might we be given advance notice about these staff meetings so that we can plan accordingly? Could I, with other team leaders, assist you in problem-solving to assure fewer disruptions?

Think like a teacher:

In my early teaching years, lessons were frequently interrupted at random times throughout the day by loudspeaker announcements. When teachers voiced concerns to the new principal, he established the norm that, after morning announcements, no one would use the PA system to interrupt teaching and learning unless it was absolutely necessary.

Think of all you do as an effective teacher to protect learning time for students. You intentionally work with colleagues and school leaders to schedule activities such as school-wide testing, assemblies, celebrations, and meetings so that they minimize interruptions to essential classroom learning. Within your classroom, you protect the learning time you have by taking actions such as starting on time, managing disruptive behaviors, and avoiding tangents that take students off course. Approach your team meetings with the same commitment to protect collaborative learning time. You and your colleagues deserve it.

Find the right words:

To a school leader:

- *I want to bring your attention to how many meeting interruptions/ cancellations we have had and to problem solve with you.*

To your team:

- *Before we adjourn, does anyone have any conflicts that might interfere with our next meeting?*

- *Can we commit to meeting (X) consecutive times without interruption in order to build momentum?*

1.2 Allocate time to examine learning outcomes.

As I near completion of this book, my twins will soon turn 13. Although I successfully taught middle and high school for years, parenting teens seems to be quite a different skill set (to put it mildly). So, I turned to a local parenting group that met once a week over the course of five weeks. The facilitator was knowledgeable. I could relate to the stories other parents shared about their battles over the most seemingly simple chores like taking out the trash. We talked about parenting strategies to maintain open communication with our kids. The materials and tips were helpful. I even shared the code word my kids and I came up with in order to stay calm and maintain composure when things got stressful in our house—*ginger*. By the end of five meetings, I felt satisfied with my takeaways and the acronyms we jointly created to help us remember what to do in tough situations. That is, until one challenging night.

The kitchen trash was overflowing so much that I couldn't even reach my oven. My twins were loudly bickering with no end in sight. I had only a few hours to prepare for a presentation the next day. I couldn't remember what the darn six-letter acronym stood for that was supposed to help me manage the situation. And I was yelling the words, "Ginger! Ginger! I said, 'Ginger!'" At that moment, I realized that *this* was the stuff our parenting group should have been collaborating about. Discussing ideas and coming up with acronyms was a good use of our time. But, without also collaborating about the difficulty of implementing change as we were going through it, and without also examining the positive and negative outcomes that we were seeing, our group was not optimizing our time together.

Skillful team leaders (STLs) are deliberate and strategic in how they allocate collaborative time. They ensure that there is time for people to collaborate when they are implementing changes to practice, and that there is time to observe and examine student-learning outcomes resulting from what they do as a team.

How to allocate time to examine learning outcomes:

It can be helpful to think about how you use collaborative time across the following three categories:

1. *Housekeeping.* Together, a team might set testing dates, build schedules, modify shared protocols, update a school handbook, clarify common procedures, and establish professional norms for teams (e.g., "We are using meeting time to create a lunch schedule for half-days").

2. *Planning.* Together, a team might envision, design curriculum, plan strategies, practice an instructional strategy on each other, write questions for an assessment, explore professional readings, set professional-practice and student-learning goals, share websites and resources, or write policies (e.g., "We are using meeting time to revise a lesson").

3. *Implementation.* Together, a team might troubleshoot challenges as they implement plans, observe one or more teachers execute plans to see the effect on students, collect and analyze student-learning data, look at student work, progress-monitor specific targeted goals, or analyze the results of surveys (e.g., "We implemented a common lesson. We are using meeting time to analyze data that show which students met specific objectives. We target new goals for specific groups of students").

Calculate the number of meetings your team plans to have over the course of your collaboration. Allocate your time strategically. Unless you are leading an administrative team, spend the least amount of collaborative time on category 1. Tasks in that category are often necessary for teacher teams to discuss but don't directly impact teacher practice or student learning. However, because housekeeping tasks are necessary, be deliberate about when to allocate time for these. Ten minutes at the end of each meeting or one dedicated meeting a week, if you meet daily, may be sufficient.

Dedicate the bulk of your collaborative time to categories 2 and 3, with particular emphasis on the latter. Be careful that your team does not overcommit meeting time to designing and planning without ever using time to collaborate during implementation, which is the time working together is most needed.

In action:

- Tom's second-grade team does not have common formative assessments. They frontload meetings, designing quizzes and homework for an upcoming unit. Then, when the team begins teaching the unit and administering their newly created assessments, they use meetings to observe one another teach, examine student responses on the assessments, and plan next instructional steps.

- Darnell's Grades 6–8 English department team gives students quarterly assessments. They designate a two-hour meeting to sift through data together and determine next instructional steps in grade-level groups.

- Naomi's ninth-grade interdisciplinary team meets three times a month with the goal of improving students' habits of mind. They dedicate one meeting a month to discuss housekeeping business, such as discipline policies across the grade. They designate the first month of inquiry to learning how to teach "habits of mind" and design a unit. They designate the last two months to implementing and studying the effects of the unit they designed.

STL recommendations:

Track time. After each meeting, jot down the approximate number of minutes that were actually spent collaborating in the aforementioned categories. Graph it with a pie chart. If you aren't spending enough time on category 3, then investigate why and set a goal to prioritize collaborating about student learning.

Allocate time for cross-collaboration. Teachers can magnify their impact on student learning when they collaborate with teachers beyond their grade or content area. Toby N. Romer, assistant superintendent for secondary education and special programs at Newton (Massachusetts) Public Schools, prioritized time for teachers in his district's middle schools to meet once a month as multi-grade "vertical" teams. Vertical teaming creates opportunities for collaboration in category 2 (e.g., to align curriculum, construct a continuum of content skills across grade levels, develop assessments for skills that cross grade levels, and foster understanding of content-specific practice standards) and category 3 (e.g., to improve outcomes for at-risk students to successfully transition between grade levels, implement common literacy practices and examine student data that results from teaching, collect and analyze longitudinal data about students, and use it to inform teaching and learning). Interdisciplinary teams are another form of cross-collaboration that provide opportunities for group design, implementation, and assessment of cross-curricular units of study.

Find the right words:

- *Let's sketch out how we would like to use meetings so that housekeeping business does not monopolize our time and we have plenty of time to design instruction and collaborate during implementation.*

- *Let's reflect on how we have been using our collaborative time. How many meetings have we dedicated to planning and design tasks? To peer observations and looking at student work? To housekeeping business?*

- *What time can we allocate to cross-collaboration? Consider multi-grade teams; interdisciplinary teams; and specialty teams such as the diversity, equity, and inclusion, or DEI, team.*

Related readings:

Move 4.2, "Write a three question agenda: Why? What? How?" Design the intended outcomes you expect to reach in your meeting before planning the activities to get there.

Move 5.15, "Pivot from teaching to learning." When facilitating talk becomes too heavily focused on what teachers do, shift focus to what students are learning.

Move 6.12, "(Results-driven) Distinguish learning outcomes from pathways." Learn how to write student-learning goals as desired outcomes and view teacher-learning goals as pathways to reach them.

1.3 Foster collaboration between meetings.

The greatest predictor of team productivity seems to be the energy and engagement between team members *outside* of a meeting, not in it (Pentland, 2012). Helen Timperley found it standard practice for teachers in high-achieving schools to seek assistance and collaborate with their colleagues between team meetings much more so than those in lower-achieving schools (Earl & Timperley, 2009, p. 72). Skillful team leaders (STLs) aren't super-facilitators who get more done in their 46 minutes than those leading low-impact teams. They don't violate teacher contract rules by squeezing in additional meetings. But they do foster a culture that encourages organic collaboration between meetings in order to extend team learning.

How to foster collaboration between meetings:

Do one or more of the following:

- Initiate collaboration during a common time of day (e.g., lunch duty). Casually reach out with questions, ideas, and problems related to your team's inquiry.

- Make your classroom an open classroom. Invite your colleagues to observe you implement what the team is studying and give you constructive feedback.

- Provide professional texts (e.g., articles, podcasts, or videos) as a no-obligation option for people to extend their learning between meetings.

- Organize a shared document where people can put their questions and wonderings down in real time and where others can respond. Padlet is great for this.

- Invite your colleagues to contribute their between-meeting wonderings and concerns to the upcoming agenda.

- Provide time at the start of a subsequent meeting for people to report on the ways in which their thinking or practice has evolved since the last meeting.

STL recommendations:

Expect shifts from meeting to meeting. Where your last meeting ends is not always where the next one begins. Team members learn and process outside of team meetings as much as within them. They connect with people at lunch, think about what was discussed on their commutes home, talk about it with a partner, and test things out when they are back in their classrooms. Beyond thinking differently from meeting to meeting, people can also *feel* differently. If emotions in one meeting are high, they may have simmered down by the next. If a person is confused in Tuesday's meeting, they might come to Thursday's meeting with greater clarity.

Expect ebb and flow. Teams move through different stages over time as a group (see Chapter 4). Even high-functioning, high-impact Q1 teams might experience a midcycle motivation slump, where weeks into a group's collaboration, the novelty of being a team has settled and the team is deep into inquiry but members are not yet implementing changes. Reenergize the group by finding ways to reconnect to the reason behind doing what you are doing together and celebrating the group's small wins you have accomplished.

Find the right words:

- *[At recess duty] I can't stop thinking about the strategy you shared in our last meeting. Do you have a minute to hear how I plan to try that out?*

- *We won't be able to meet next week and I don't want to lose momentum. Is everyone willing and able to [e.g., read this article] before our next meeting to maximize our time when we come back together?* (Note: Check with union guidelines to make certain you can ask people to do tasks outside of meetings.)

- *I invite to my classroom anyone who is free during B and D blocks, which is when I'll test out the strategy we read about.*

Related reading:

Move 9.14, "Give time and space." Encouraging collaboration between meetings allows for your colleagues who are initially resistant to change to come around.

ENHANCE THE LEARNING SPACE

Physical space can affect a team's collaboration, which is why skillful team leaders (STLs) are intentional in how they prepare it. I hesitated to even include these moves because the concept of creating the right space for learning is often intuitive to teachers; however, having observed too many team meetings where leaders have actually not been intentional about the learning space for adults, and having seen the negative implications of those decisions, I decided it is worthwhile to highlight.

Spatial conditions don't dictate if a team will perform well or not, but they can contribute to people's willingness, desire, and stamina to collaborate. STLs don't assume that because adults are adults they don't need the right conditions for collaborative learning. They do a considerable amount of prep work to ensure a positive learning experience (even when the "space" is virtual). Your colleagues might not notice your attention to setting up the learning space, but they'll feel the effects when you don't.

Side note: The COVID-19 pandemic challenged educators to engage in virtual team meetings in many cases for the first time. Since then, teams have learned key moves when facilitating over a screen. It's more challenging to set up a learning space when everyone is literally in a different space, but the moves that follow still apply.

STL moves:

1.4 Micro-prep.

1.5 Attend to room details.

What these moves promote:

Engagement. Space is used to maximize opportunities for people to fully participate.

Productivity. Learning materials are prepared in advance to save time in the meeting.

When to use these moves:

Before every team meeting.

1.4 Micro-prep.

Prepping small details is second nature to teachers. You know how off-track your lesson can get when kids can't find a handout, or when you go to play a link that doesn't work. Adult learners can certainly handle these types of delays, but skillful team leaders (STLs) micro-prep the details to avoid wasting people's time and maximize productivity. Micro-prepping might sound enabling, but when you only have a limited amount of time with your team, every minute counts. Additionally, people appreciate walking into a meeting and having everything they need. You avoid interruptions such as "Wait. I didn't get that." "Where is that?" "I can't open it." For a leader, knowing people have what they need from the start can actually reduce your stress in a meeting and maximize time.

How to micro-prep:

The following checklists can help you prep the small details before your meeting:

☐ Prior to meeting, paste links into your agenda and test that they work.

☐ Enable edit and share settings on e-docs and share all passwords in advance.

☐ Send an email the day before meeting with an agenda, handouts, and reminders of the date, time, location, roles, and what to bring to the meeting.

☐ Cue videos you intend to show and check audio.

☐ Photocopy texts or student work that you plan on having people interact with. A tangible copy helps keep people engaged.

☐ Prepare any chart paper that you expect to use during brainstorming or protocols (e.g., prepopulate charts with prompts for people to respond to during a Chalk Talk protocol).

☐ Prepare slides you might use in a presentation.

☐ Have writing utensils available and outlets accessible (for people who need to charge their laptops).

Meeting virtually?

☐ Create a video invite and include an audio dial-in option.

☐ Paste the link and password to the virtual meeting in the email that includes an agenda so people don't need to hunt through emails to find it.

☐ Decide in advance which documents and/or video you will use for screen sharing, and have those tabs ready at the start of the meeting.

☐ Close any tabs you don't want people accidentally seeing. (STL Michelle Fox once toggled to a screen with her Chris Isaak playlist. It made for a humorous moment as she said, "I'm not ashamed to admit I like him.") But if it's anything too personal, it can throw you off as a facilitator.

☐ Send links to shared documents that you want people to access during the meeting, but also copy and paste the link to your desktop so that you are ready to input into the chat box during the live meeting.

☐ Preset breakout groups, or when your colleagues sign on, ask them to rename themselves with a group number so you can quickly sort people.

☐ Recommend to your colleagues that they print from home particular handouts that you will be using in the meeting so that they don't have to toggle back and forth between viewing colleagues and looking at documents.

☐ Prepare an exit e-survey in advance of the meeting. Have the link ready to post in the chat so that people can give immediate feedback at the end of the meeting.

☐ Activate all sharing permissions in advance.

☐ If you have a very large group, make a list of names of participants since you will not likely be able to see everyone's faces on the screen at once. This way you can call on people and not leave anyone out.

STL recommendations:

Take time to remind. You may be tempted to think adults don't need reminders, but my stance is this: Educators are busy. If a small paper reminder for people who need that visual cue, an email, or use of a reminding app avoids unnecessary hurdles like lateness to your meeting or misunderstandings that can elevate stress levels, than I am all for it. Even your dentist calls to remind you of your appointment, so why can't a team leader remind colleagues of a meeting? Team members will appreciate it.

Designate a role. Just because you are leading the team doesn't mean you have to be the one to micro-prep. Rotate the role if you are concerned that it's too much to take on every meeting.

Tech it out. Technology has made meeting organization simple. Some schools have sharing platforms like Schoology, Canvas, Google Classroom, or Microsoft Teams. If you don't, you can make your own team website using Wix, a simple-to-use and free tool (although you do have to purchase the domain name), or use Padlet. Consider organizing your e-folders in the following categories: Announcements, Agendas (with meeting notes), Readings, Resources, Data, and Celebration/Inspiration.

1.5 Attend to room details.

I once was invited by a team leader to observe a science department meeting because she wanted feedback on why things weren't going well. The first thing I noticed were teachers sitting at tables arranged in immovable rows—ideal for student experiments, but not conducive for collaborative adult discussion. When teachers in the front of the room spoke, they could not comfortably turn around to face the group—so they didn't. Those sitting in the middle didn't seem to know whether to look at people in front of or behind them, and one or two teachers sitting in the back were disconnected from the group. I've seen meetings go south simply because the room was sweltering hot or the adults were crunched into kindergarten chairs for one hour. Of course, some things are beyond your control, but skillful team leaders (STLs) attend to room details as best as they can. They prepare the room for a learning experience, not a meeting.

How to attend to room details:

Do one or more of the following:

- When possible, minimize sound and visual distractions (e.g., avoid meeting next to the music room where students are practicing, and steer clear of high-traffic areas).

- Set up a projector or whiteboard in advance and ensure that people are able to view and hear each other, as well as see any screens that you might be using.

- Choose and arrange seating so that people feel comfortable and collaboration is encouraged. If you have a large team, set up seating into small groups, so more people have a chance to speak.

- Consider placing a sign on your door that says "Meeting in Progress" in case students come by.

- Take a moment to sit in a chair before your meeting and look around the room to see what others will see. Does it seem like a place where adults will be eager to learn together?

Meeting virtually?

- Advise your colleagues to look around their physical setup before turning on video.

- Avoid sitting in front of a direct light source as it can make your image appear dark to those viewing you. Sit in front of an uncluttered wall or bookcase and avoid meeting from your bed (you've seen it). If opting for a backdrop, consider forgoing that virtual scene. Although it is fun, it can be distracting. (My son once chose a California scene as my background, and every time I moved, half my face would disappear into the Golden Gate Bridge). Opt for a blurred background if you have that option and want to keep your home space private.

- Consider standing up at your computer while virtually meeting, or sit down in an upright chair. This may sound peculiar, but virtual meetings can suck the energy out of the virtual room, so do what you can to keep yourself energized.

In action:
Five minutes before the meeting begins, Audrey positions her classroom desks in a cluster. She intentionally places her binder away from the head of the table,

knowing a person in her group prefers to sit at the end. She wants this team member to sit where he is most at ease, and she actually prefers sitting toward the middle anyway, because it allows her to easily connect to people on both sides of the table. She sets out chips and fruit, and softly sets her phone to play jazz music.

STL recommendations:

Avoid seating charts. Let people sit where they choose. If you notice someone intentionally sits outside of the group (e.g., against a back wall), invite them to the table. If they decline (I've seen and experienced this on multiple occasions), there might be something else going on. Privately *check in 1:1* (Move 5.24) with that person after the meeting. The only time you might opt for a seating chart is if you need to be intentional about who is matched up with whom (e.g., you want a multi-grade-level vertical team to sit in grade-level groups for a specific task).

Meet outside of your classroom. If you sense, or anticipate, that anyone on your team perceives you as "the boss" of these meetings, and you want to convey a message of shared leadership, hold meetings in a neutral space such as the library or another teacher's classroom, or rotate classrooms. (Note: Rotating classrooms is advantageous because it sends a message that all are equal partners, but if you do so, clearly communicate the room number in a morning reminder. Otherwise someone is likely to come late or miss the meeting because they don't know where to go.) If no one takes issue with you leading the team, you are probably fine to hold sessions in your classroom.

Personalize the meeting space. Consider small touches that can make people feel comfortable, connected, and ready to learn. Put your stamp on the design of your space and the way in which you run your meetings. If glitz and bling are your style, go ahead and add some flair to your team binders. If people know you love quotes, include a favorite atop your handouts. If you love music, play your favorite hits as people enter the room. Whatever your personality is, aim to bring in some lighthearted warmth to your meetings. If anyone else on your team has a particular talent or interest that may make people feel more connected in meetings, encourage them to share it. Seek opportunities for others to bring in their culture and style.

Build community through food. This recommendation is not a necessity, particularly if you have daily team meetings, but launching a sign-up where team members rotate bringing in snacks can create community. Sharing food is a common way for people to make personal connections to each other. "Coming together and sharing a meal is the most communal and binding thing in almost every place in the world" (Quora, 2017).

I once led a team where a teacher was not eager to meet with the group, but when it was her week to bring in food, she went all-out with a family recipe that everyone raved about. The teacher's whole persona changed in that meeting.

Even if people on your team aren't cooking up signature dishes, when educators are running nonstop and your team's meeting is the first time they can sit down, it helps them to recharge and personally connect over a treat.

Think like a teacher:

Think of a day when maybe you were short on time and didn't intentionally arrange seating or materials in advance and, as a result, your lesson did not go well. Perhaps it only affected a few students, or maybe it made you feel off your game. Whatever impact it had, upon reflection you likely decided, "OK, next time I'm going to prepare the space for this activity."

Teachers not only enhance space to help all students grasp the objectives of a lesson but also look to the principles of trauma-informed design to set up safe spaces for learning, and they are mindful that "the physical environment has an impact on attitude, mood, and behavior, and that there is a strong link between our physiological state, our emotional state, and the physical environment" (Frey et al., 2020).

PROMOTE EQUITABLE ACCESS TO TEAM LEARNING

"The greatest degree of access and usability for the widest range of individuals." This was the mission of Ronald L. Mace at North Carolina State University when he established a framework for designing and delivering products, environments, and services so that individuals with disabilities had access to them. His philosophy of inclusion in architecture inspired the much-adopted Universal Design for Learning (UDL) framework that schools use today (OCALI, n.d.). You may have seen the meme: "UDL has taught us that it is the environment, not the students, that needs to change." The UDL framework is intended to reduce stigma and give every child, regardless of differences or disability, access to learning.

In alignment with UDL is a point worth remembering: Children with learning differences grow up to be adults with learning differences. Although, by adulthood, atypical learners* and those with physical disability have likely learned how to advocate and succeed in a world that might not always be optimally designed for their needs, they thrive on teams that accommodate them and, also, build-off of their strengths . . . and their teams thrive, too. Skillful team leaders (STLs) design the collaborative environment so that all have equitable access to learning.

STL moves:

1.6 Accommodate adults with learning differences, disabilities, or preferences.

1.7 Leverage strengths in disability.

What these moves promote:

Inclusion. Learning is accessible to all, and no one is excluded.

Equity. Team members are given opportunities to fully contribute to the team.

Asset-based collaboration. Teams capitalize on the strengths of all team members, particularly those with differences and/or disabilities.

When to use these moves:

In preparation for meeting and throughout a team's course of collaboration.

---

*Atypical learners, specifically those who are neuroatypical, might be diagnosed with any of the following: attention deficit disorder (ADD), attention deficit hyperactivity disorder (ADHD), dyslexia, dysgraphia, dyscalculia, speech disorders, autism spectrum disorder (ASD), Asperger syndrome, Down syndrome, or giftedness.

Related reading:

Part II, Chapter 5, "Five Must-Knows About Adult Learners." Before implementing the moves in this section, ground your thinking in two key concepts explored in this chapter about adult learners: Adults know the best ways in which they learn. And, adults want to be treated as professionals with their experience and expertise acknowledged.

1.6 Accommodate adults with learning differences, disabilities, or preferences.

I led professional learning for an individual who was legally blind and could not see small print. The educator had an aide who would read documents to him. Wanting the team member to have access to team handouts, I brought a preloaded iPad to meetings so that he could independently view them by simply enlarging the screen to his needs. Not only was the team member appreciative of the gesture, but he was also better able to actively engage in meetings. Another time, a colleague voiced her preference to get hard copies of electronic documents because it was easier for her to process content when she could mark up a paper copy. Skillful team leaders (STLs) remove barriers to learning by accommodating adults who identify as people with disabilities, learning differences, or particular learning preferences.

How to accommodate adults with learning differences, disabilities, or preferences:

Check in with individuals who identify as having disabilities and/or learning differences. Learn what each person needs to fully engage in the team meeting. Although not a comprehensive list, here are some common challenges that neuroatypical* learners might face when working on a team, even through adulthood:

- Slower processing speed than others

- Need for movement and breaks

- "Motor mouth" where a person talks quickly, almost without pause, and makes it difficult for others to interject

- Struggle with organization and other executive functioning skills

---

Neuroatypical is a term assigned to people who have one or more of the following: attention deficit disorder (ADD), attention deficit hyperactivity disorder (ADHD), dyslexia, dysgraphia, dyscalculia, speech disorders, autism spectrum disorder (ASD), Asperger syndrome, Down syndrome, and giftedness.

- Struggle to access written texts through reading at the same pace as others

- Difficulty interacting with colleagues or challenges picking up social cues

Adult-learner accommodations, like those for students, fall into four categories: presentation, response, setting, and timing.

MODE	SAMPLE ACCOMMODATIONS
Presentation	Closed captions, large print, spacing between print (particularly helpful to people who have dyslexia), color of text on background (black letters on a white background for people who are color blind), color-coded handouts, video, or sign language
Response	Speech-to-text, writing with a scribe, movement opportunities, paired or small-group discussions
Setting	Close or far seating from visuals, noise level, handicap access, or lighting
Timing	Frequent breaks or wait time within or between meetings, time to think or write before speaking

Source: Iris Center (2021).

Meeting virtually? Remove barriers to team learning. In many ways, virtual meetings are ideal for those with visual or auditory impairments. Technology makes it easy for people to enlarge text, see images up close, turn up the volume or tune out extemporaneous sounds with headphones, and record meetings for replay. Review key features with someone in advance of the meeting to make sure they know how to access accommodations.

STL recommendations:

Seek out resources. Many websites offer ideas for accommodating specific disabilities and learning differences. Here are a few examples:

- *ADDitude (www.addituemag.com).* Supports for people with ADHD.

- *Understood (www.understood.org).* Supports for people with a range of learning disabilities.

- *Web Accessibility Initiative (www.w3.org/WAI).* Accommodations for people with dyslexia and visual impairments. (See also Rello & Baeza-Yates, 2012.)

Nurture a culture of self-advocacy. You can't anticipate every need. Sonsoles Alonso of the Gifted Foundation (Kharbanda, 2020) encourages those who are neuroatypical to express what they need to collaborate and learn. This is really good practice for all adult learners on a team.

Related readings:

Moves 3.1–3.2, "Foster inclusivity." Actively seek to include your colleagues who have learning differences or disabilities or are members of traditionally marginalized groups.

1.7 Leverage strengths in disability.

Since my son was diagnosed with a language-based learning disability (LBLD), I discovered and fell in love with the term *dyslexic advantage*. This is the notion that people with dyslexia perceive the world differently and excel at spatial reasoning, interconnected thinking, and creativity (Eide & Eide, 2011). (Cool fact: Steve Jobs, Muhammad Ali, Albert Einstein, and Galileo were dyslexic.) Besides possessing incredible talents, many adults with an LBLD have acquired resilience and perseverance from having to overcome obstacles growing up. (Unfortunately, before FAPE—the right to a free appropriate public education—schools didn't understand or respond to learning differences in the same way they do now, and many older adults with learning disabilities had negative school experiences.) Individuals who learn differently likely have a perspective that can help the team better serve students who have differences similar to their own. Skillful team leaders (STLs) leverage the strengths of their colleagues who have learning differences or disabilities.

How to leverage strengths in disability:

Do one or more of the following:

- Share personal stories to the level of comfort people are willing for the purpose of better understanding learning differences and disabilities in children.

- Invite people to name the assets and challenges of their personal learning differences and/or disabilities for the purpose of better understanding each other and how to work together as a team.

- Invite colleagues who have shared their differences with you or the team to take on roles that cater to their strengths. Examples: A person with ADHD has the gift of hyper-focus and is likely very good at sticking with a high-interest task until completion. A neuroatypical learner who is gifted can be good at systems thinking, capable of solving complex problems. Someone who experiences anxiety might help the team better understand practices that can raise or reduce anxiety in students.

- View your peers who exhibit behaviors different from your own (e.g., someone who misses the social cues of the group) as an opportunity for understanding and learning about others and the assets they hold.

In action:

An interdisciplinary team is doing an inquiry cycle about literacy.

Shannon: In order to better understand how to reach students who regularly struggle with reading and writing, think of someone you know (and it might be you) who faced reading or writing challenges, but also possessed great strengths. Who is comfortable sharing a story?

Teacher 1: My spouse is severely dyslexic. He told me that the hardest thing for him growing up in the '70s was not his struggle with reading, but his school's lack of belief in his abilities. He was put in remedial classes all day where he basically did coloring and was not challenged. He thought he was stupid. It was not until high school, when his mother insisted he be included with students in general education so he could be put into honors math classes, that he saw his affinity for science and math. Today he is a professor with a postdoctorate degree in chemistry. He tells me it is still excruciatingly hard for him to write and he is a slow reader, but he has published many papers, and he is an avid reader. He reads more than me. [*Laughs.*]

[*Shannon captures what she hears on chart paper: "Challenges—school's lack of belief in his abilities; school's low expectations; poor inaccurate self-image. Strengths—exceptional science and math ability; persistence; someone who not only believed in him but advocated for him." Some other teachers share their stories.*]

Shannon: Looking at our list of challenges and strengths, how does this influence the ways in which we might approach a child who has a language-based learning disability?

Think like a teacher.

One of the reasons I most loved doing plays and musicals with middle and high schoolers is because it showed a spotlight on children who were atypical learners and misunderstood. Students who could not sit still in class, had incredible focus and presence on stage. Those who struggled to read even directions on a test could recite a Shakespearean sonnet from memory with incredible expression. Those who held back from speaking in class because of a speech impediment seemed to have no problem speaking in front of an auditorium crowded with people. Students who could not remember steps to solving math problems could remember an entire complex dance routine.

As an effective teacher, you know that disability does not define how smart a child is or put limits on their potential. You focus on students' strengths and resiliency. Bring the same mindset to adult learners with disabilities.

Find the right words:

- *How is a challenge/disability also a gift?*

- *What assets do you have that can benefit our team?*

- *How can our personal experiences with learning differences or physical disabilities help us better understand our students?*

Related reading:

Move 8.10, "Address deficit thinking." Shift a data analysis conversation from a focus on student deficits—what they can't do—to what they can do.

Primary Intention

Establish Expectations and Responsibilities: Norms and Roles

2

What to Expect When You're Expecting (Murkoff et al., 1984) is one of the most influential, best-selling books of all time ("25 Books That Leave a Legacy," 2007). And that's not because it's easy to read. (In fact, many agree it reads like an out-of-touch, scary medical journal.) It's popular because it—along with other less alarmist books of similar content—lays out everything new parents can expect throughout pregnancy and childbirth. When entering any experience for the first time, adults want to know what to expect and, in the case of professional learning teams, what is expected of them. Skillful team leaders (STLs) establish group expectations and responsibilities.

Norm setting is more than a list-generating activity. It's culture building. STLs work to disrupt unhealthy patterns of interaction—those behaviors that are not written down but have become acceptable in a school culture for years. With group agreements, people develop mindfulness and take personal responsibility for their own ways of engaging with others. Team members agree to new expectations for working together.

STLs also set expectations for roles and responsibilities. This is particularly important in schools that are new to collaborative inquiry, where there are likely misconceptions about what it means to lead and follow on a team. Everyone shares responsibility for advancing team learning (e.g., modeling a lesson for colleagues) and meeting tasks (e.g., timekeeping). Beyond team jobs, an individual's role on a team also refers to the ways in which one engages with the group. STLs are mindful of stereotypical roles that limit how people engage.

Contents

Facilitate a group norm-setting process.

2.1 Co-construct norms through consensus.

2.2 Save time with starter norms.

2.3 Promote mindfulness with personal norms.

Institute social norms that maximize team impact.

2.4 Foster sensitivity for cultural norms.

2.5 Surface unspoken norms.

2.6 Set ground rules for potentially difficult conversations.

2.7 Restore a norm after it has been broken.

Share responsibility through roles.

2.8 Clarify the team leader role.

2.9 Commission others to lead learning.

2.10 Break from fixed or imposed roles.

Tools and templates:

Figure 7: Norm-Setting Process Comparison Chart

Figure 8: STL Personal Norming Tool

Figure 9: Two Lenses for Norm Setting

Figure 10: Team Roles and Responsibilities Example

Figure 11: The Benefits of Note-Taking

Related reading:

Part I, Chapter 3, "The Real Work of Teams: Collaborative Inquiry." If your team is new to collaborative inquiry, then set expectations for what a cycle of inquiry can look like and why you do it.

Part II, Chapter 4, "The Psychology of Groups." Revisit this chapter to see how social influences can affect how people interact in your group and the roles they take on.

FACILITATE A GROUP NORM-SETTING PROCESS

Norms. (Audible groan acknowledged.) For some team leaders, collaboratively crafting a list of norms is a must-do, and for others, doing a dramatic group reading of the Pledge of Allegiance would seem like a better use of time. Understandably, norm setting can feel fruitless if you talk for 30 minutes, bicker over adjectives, and end up with a list of obvious agreements such as "Start and end on time." Yes, a punctuality agreement is important, but this isn't what skillful team leaders (STLs) are after when they engage groups in norming.

When facilitated well, a group norming process will engage people in honest discourse about behaviors that help and hinder the team. Discussion results in a short list of agreements that everyone can commit to. When the process is facilitated poorly, people spend a significant chunk of team time brainstorming about how they *should* interact, as if they're in an alternate universe where nothing goes wrong. They fall into a black hole of wordsmithing a norm where they debate prepositions for 10 minutes until someone gives in. By the end of the meeting, the team comes away with either a succinct list that isn't a true representation of the voices in the room or a much-too-long set of agreements that no one will remember, let alone follow. Either way, the time-consuming process results in a meaningless list that has no influence over how people really work together in meetings. STLs intentionally choose and facilitate a norm-setting method that establishes expectations for how people will *actually* work together on a team.

There are many ways to facilitate an authentic group norm-setting process. In the next few pages, I offer three specific methods, outlined in Figure 7. Choose to use what best fits your team.

STL moves:

2.1 Co-construct norms through consensus.

2.2 Save time with starter norms.

2.3 Promote mindfulness with personal norms.

Tools and templates:

Figure 7: Norm-Setting Process Comparison Chart

Figure 8: STL Personal Norming Tool

What these moves promote:

Clarity. All team members know from the start what behaviors are expected of them during collaboration.

Self-awareness. People are called upon to notice the ways in which their behaviors help and hinder the team.

What to call norms:

If you have a team that has had a negative experience with setting norms, change the term. More favorable options include *group agreements, working agreements, rules of engagement, team expectations, social contracts,* and *team pacts.*

When to introduce norms:

When people come together, particularly for the first time, they want to launch into the important work they came together to do, not wordsmith a list of rules they must agree to. Create a need for norms after you have set an initial direction for your team. It might even be in the second or third meeting after you have had time to work together. Once group members figure out what they are trying to accomplish and why, they will be ready to set agreements for working to accomplish these goals.

Whom to create norms for:

You might think teams that know each other well and have worked together before can skip norming, but actually the opposite is more often true. When a group is forming, people are more careful and conscientious of how their words and actions affect others. But once people get comfortable and familiar with each other, the line of what's acceptable can get blurry. (An extreme example: I was in a group where a colleague cut his fingernails at the meeting. Really.) Although you may not encounter that type of "anything goes" behavior, collegiality can hold a team back. Agreeing to ways in which people collaborate can help a team of friends maintain a level of professionalism needed to work well together and engage in impactful discourse.

STL recommendations for any norm-setting process:

Write with action verbs. English teachers know to steer clear of passive verbs. I know you are not writing a paper, but norms are much easier to uphold when they are written as directives that you can keep one another accountable for. Frame your agreements using action verbs. Replace passive verbs such as *be* with small specific actions that people can do. For instance, "Don't be defensive" becomes "Hear what's hard." "Be solutions-oriented" becomes "Offer at least one solution." "Be prepared" could become a more specific actionable norm such as "Prep your data." Changing from passive to active verbs might seem nitpicky, but people actually appreciate having actionable agreements as they provide clarity for what is expected.

Extend your list with school-wide norms. Work with school leaders to establish school-wide norms that educators on all teams are expected to uphold. This cuts back on the agreements you need to make as a team, leaving room on your list for what's most important to your group. (For instance, starting and ending meetings on time should be a school-wide norm.)

FIGURE 7   Norm-Setting Process Comparison Chart

PROCESS	BENEFITS	CHALLENGES
Co-construct norms through consensus.	• Everyone in the group is given an opportunity to speak. • The team feels ownership for norms. • Everyone has a shared understanding of the agreed-upon norms.	• The process is time-consuming. Depending on the size of the group, it may take up to 45 minutes. • Social influences (explored in Part II, Chapter 4) can affect how people participate. This can result in a watered-down list of agreements that holds little meaning for the group, presenting challenges once collaboration is underway.
Save time with starter norms.	• The process is efficient. • The process establishes group agreements without disrupting momentum for the work the team is doing. • People who have had negative experiences with group norm setting appreciate the approach. • Essential, customized norms are selected.	• There's little to no input from team members, which can cause some people to feel a lack of ownership over the list of agreements.
Promote mindfulness with personal norms.	• People are deeply invested in their personal norm. • The process is efficient because the team does not need to spend time reaching consensus. All norms are accepted. • People become mindful of their own behaviors in a team.	• The process is short but requires homework in between meetings. • The process demands self-awareness and vulnerability.

2.1 Co-construct norms through consensus.

If you want norms to stick, involve the people who are expected to follow them in the process of writing them. Build ownership by co-constructing norms. The goal of this approach is to generate many ideas for group agreements, narrow down the choices, and, through consensus, arrive at a few to adopt. Consensus (explored in detail in Move 8.16) does not mean coming to a unanimous decision, and it doesn't mean majority rule wins. It's about collecting information, formulating ideas, listening to and discussing options, and ultimately coming to decisions everyone on the team can live with, even if only temporarily (Massachusetts Institute of Technology, n.d.). Skillful team leaders (STLs) co-construct norms through consensus.

How to co-construct norms through consensus:

Follow this four-step protocol:

1. *Brainstorm challenging behaviors.* Invite colleagues to generate behaviors that they don't want to see on their team—things that really irk them, pet peeves, and behaviors that hinder the function and impact of a team. Write one per sticky note.

2. *Do a quick sort.* Brainstorming leaves you with an endless list of possibilities. To derive meaning from the list and focus the group on the task at hand, quickly sort ideas into categories. Ask your team or small groups to silently cluster the "pet peeve" sticky notes into five piles by common theme. Put any note that doesn't seem to have a place to the side. Discuss the piles made and title each pile.

3. *Reframe with positive language.* You are more likely to get people to keep norms if you write them as things they should do, as opposed to things they shouldn't do. Turn your categories into positively worded agreements.

4. *Reach consensus.* Read through your list of positively worded norms and confirm that everyone in the group can "live" by these agreements.

In action:

Kyle: Let's begin by thinking about the behaviors that might get in the way of our collaboration. What peeves you? Pick something important, but don't write about any specific person. [*Kyle passes out sticky notes.*] . . . Looks like everyone has independently written at least three pet peeve sticky notes by now. Let's put them all out on the table, read through them silently, and begin to move them around to make piles according to common themes. Let's group the following sticky notes together—"people off-task," "side conversations," "grading papers," and "answering email"—and name the category *Distractions*. . . . Let's set an actionable positive norm to address distracting behaviors:

"Fully engage throughout the meeting." . . . Is there anyone who can't live with this agreement? Okay. Let's set the other agreements.

STL recommendations:

Break up. Large teams may need to split into small groups for brainstorming and quick sort. Bring them back together when narrowing down to five piles and reframing in positive language.

Set parameters. Brainstorming the negative can turn into a blame game unless there are guardrails in place for the conversation. Explain from the start that no one should describe specific people or incidents.

Be careful of compromise. Consensus is not compromise. Bargaining in ways such as "I'll give up the confidentiality norm if you let us keep the evidence-based decision-making norm" leads to people advocating or disagreeing until someone who doesn't want to debate any longer gives in. If you are stuck reaching agreement, keep both norms.

Start with the ideal. Often when teams set norms through consensus, they brainstorm a list of desirable behaviors. Although this positive slant helps people envision how they aspire to collaborate, it doesn't always get real in the way that a norm-setting process needs to. This is why I recommend starting with the challenges. However, if you fear this approach will spiral your group into a negative tailspin, then brainstorm the ideal and move to categorizing and choosing up to five norms that you aspire to keep.

Find the right words:

Brainstorm challenging behaviors.

- *What irks you in a team meeting?*

- *What hinders your engagement in a meeting?*

- *What hinders your ability to learn?*

Quick sort.

- *Arrange sticky notes into five or fewer categories.*

- If you have more than five categories: *Let's set aside the challenges that should be addressed with school-wide norms, as well as any challenges that may be obvious things we want to avoid. Let's keep the piles that address the behaviors that could really hinder our team and come up with norms for those.*

Reframe with positive language.

- *If we were to reframe that as a positive agreement, it might sound like . . .*

Reach consensus.

- *Is there anyone who cannot live with these group agreements?*

Related reading:

Move 5.16, "Synthesize ideas." When you have too long a list of norms, turn to this move to lift up and put together ideas.

Move 8.16, "Reach agreement on group decisions." Find consensus-building moves here.

2.2 Save time with starter norms.

When time is limited but you still want to set behavioral expectations for your meetings, starter norms are the way to go. They are a quick method to establish initial ways of working together. It's not a move for leaders who want to facilitate thoughtful discussion around behaviors that hinder a team, but it is an efficient means to set some ground rules upfront. Skillful team leaders (STLs) propose norms for people to follow.

How to save time with starter norms:

Follow this three-step protocol:

1. *Curate.* You likely have a sense of where the wheels could fall off with the team that you are about to lead. Before your team meets, decide on three to five agreements you want to adopt at the start. Think about agreements in such categories as productivity, confidentiality, decision making, participation and engagement, technology, conflict resolution, and implementation.

2. *Check for understanding.* Have you ever been in a circumstance in which you thought you agreed to one thing until someone else said, "I thought we agreed to something different"? Check that everyone has the same understanding of what they are agreeing to. Read aloud your starter norms, give a brief context as to what they mean if any need defining, and explain why you are proposing each one. Give people an opportunity to discuss what the norm will look like in practice.

3. *Gain commitment through consensus.* As with any norming method, you'll want commitment from everyone on your team to uphold the agreements you set. Get people to agree to "live with" the list for now, and inform them that they will have multiple opportunities to revisit and change norms going forward.

In action:

Maya convenes a district-wide content team that will meet only a few times throughout the year.

Maya: We are lucky to come from different schools and hold different perspectives. Because of this I'd like to propose that we make it the norm to *invite multiple perspectives*. Putting this norm into practice means being mindful of when to advocate and when to actively seek others' opinions. Can we commit to upholding this for now?

STL recommendations:

Talk less, listen more. Keep explanations short and dedicate more time to discussing understanding.

Go hybrid. For people who want to contribute to group agreements, propose three starter norms that you feel are essential for the team, and invite anyone who's interested to propose up to two more if they feel the list is insufficient.

Find the right words:

- *I'm proposing this first set of group agreements. After we've worked together for a little longer, we can revisit and revise. Which of these norms need clarification? Is there anyone here who can't commit to this list for now?*

2.3 Promote mindfulness with personal norms.

In my theater days, a director once told me that actors must avoid bringing their own mannerisms—or *-isms*, as he liked to call them—to the stage. These are the default patterns of behavior that we do without even being aware of them. For instance, an actress might play with her hair out of habit, even when the character she is playing wouldn't do that. (Evidently, my acting "Elisa-ism" was touching my neck in scenes.) You don't have to be an actor to have an *-ism*. We have been working in teams since a very young age, and these early experiences, together with ones from adulthood, have cemented some less-than-great habits. While others may learn to tolerate our quirks, some of our behaviors may be debilitating to a team and need to be normed. It's not until we become aware of our *-isms* that we can consciously work to rid ourselves of them.

Traditional consensus-building models for writing team norms do not always produce agreements that break us of our habitualized patterns of behavior that hinder collaboration. Some skillful team leaders (STLs) lead a more reflective approach—personal norm setting.

How to promote mindfulness with personal norms:

Follow this three-step protocol:

1. *Notice how you show up in meetings.* Invite your colleagues to observe and reflect on their own helping and hindering behaviors when they participate

in team meetings. (If self-reflection is challenging, they can ask a trusted friend to give them feedback.)

2. *Name assets.* To keep the tone positive, capitalize on the good. Recognize the strengths that people bring. Invite colleagues to write one positive attribute about every member of the team, or to name their own superpower when working in groups (e.g., "I'm good at synthesizing ideas"). Either of these exercises might initially make people self-conscious, but once people begin sharing, the group will see how strong they can be if they take advantage of these assets.

3. *Set personal goals.* Instruct your colleagues to choose one behavior that they wish to change about themselves—something that they see hinders the function and/or impact of their team. (Figure 8 can be useful.) If needed, reframe the problematic behavior as a positive, actionable norm. Key point: This is not a consensus approach; all personal norms are accepted.

In action:

The following are three examples of individuals coming to their own personal norms.

Neil:

(Helpful behavior) I capture written notes in a meeting with appropriate detail.

(Hindering behavior) I have noticed that I tend to "wing it" in other team meetings, attending them unprepared.

(Personal norm) I commit to carving out a consistent time to review materials before these meetings.

Callie:

(Helpful behavior) I am evidence-based when analyzing data.

(Hindering behavior) I process out loud and tend to voice my ideas in meetings as soon as I have one. I've noticed this doesn't leave much space for others to talk. I think I may need to hold back a bit.

(Personal norm) I commit to inviting others to talk.

Paul:

(Helpful behavior) I always follow through with tasks after a meeting.

(Hindering behavior) A colleague told me that he noticed I tend to get swept away by discussion ideas, which can distract our team from what we are trying to accomplish.

(Personal norm) I commit to contributing in ways that bring the team closer to the meeting's intended outcomes.

FIGURE 8   STL Personal Norming Tool

Directions: Use the left-hand column to identify any behaviors you exhibit when collaborating on other teams. Then look to the right-hand column for ideas you might consider adopting as your personal norm for your work with this team.

BEHAVIORS THAT HINDER FUNCTION AND IMPACT:	NORMS THAT IMPROVE FUNCTION AND IMPACT:
I voice my thinking more than others on the team. I process externally, speaking up often. I express my ideas more than others.	Invite others to speak. Pause and listen. Participate intentionally—know when to step up and step down.
I voice my thinking less than others on the team. I process internally, taking time to speak up. I rely more on others for ideas.	Participate intentionally—know when to step up and step down. Privately jot down my thinking and then share out one idea.
I lean toward my own perspective and ideas. I have trouble listening to perspectives different from my own. I tend to advocate for my ideas before hearing others.	Solicit alternative viewpoints. Encourage pushback on my ideas. Seek first to understand and then to be understood. Hear what's hard. Listen to learn.
I take things personally.	Respond more than react. Pause and ask, "What is another way to interpret this?"
I voice objections and struggle to move past them. I question people's motives.	Strike positive. Find the good and praise it. Assume positive intentions.
I rarely voice objections. I hold back to steer away from conflict.	Solicit alternative viewpoints. Encourage pushback on my ideas.
I get distracted or tune out.	Be present and focused. Only use technology to support my learning and participation.
I inconsistently follow through.	Anticipate obstacles and plan with others how to overcome them. Commit to action.
I do not consistently come prepared to meetings.	Be reliable.
I offer observations based on opinion more often than on evidence.	Annotate data documents with observations before participating.
I permit my bias to influence my inferences about data and/or view of what is possible.	Make evidence-based observations. Use the words *not yet* when speaking about students' deficits.
I frequently get the team off-track from the agenda.	Contribute in ways that move the team toward intended outcomes.

In action:

Anna:	The next time you are in any meeting, take note of the ways in which your participation helps the group, and the ways in which it doesn't. Jot down your observations and bring them to our next meeting. You could also ask a trusted colleague to give you feedback on how they see you as an asset to a team and behaviors that you might consider working on. . . . [*Next meeting.*] As we decide the ways in which we want to work together, let's share one superpower—a special quality that each of us brings to a team. I'll start. It feels weird to tell you all that I'm really good at keeping people on task, but I am. If our conversation starts to wander off the agenda to nowhere land, I'll bring us back.
Teacher 1:	I'll go. I'm awesome at thinking like a kid. [*The team laughs.*] Whenever I'm with a group and we are looking at student work and no one can figure out what the student was thinking, somehow I can.
Teacher 2:	I might have trouble naming my own, but I can say that [Teacher 3] is incredible at bringing a sense of calm to any crisis.
Teacher 3:	Thanks. And I think you are great at envisioning what could be, and telling it in a way that others can see, too.
Anna:	These strengths are important. Let's all commit to using our "superpowers" at each meeting. . . . Now, what about the things we do that hinder collaboration? What do you want to change? For instance, I've been told that I talk . . . a lot. I think I'm just one of those people who processes aloud, but I realize that doesn't leave a lot of space for others to talk. I am setting the personal norm to invite others to speak. To put that norm in action right now . . . Mara, I invite you to share your personal norm. [*People laugh.*]
Mara:	Well, I might have been a bit hard on myself and came up with a bunch of things to work on, but then I talked to my supervisor and realized this personal norm could fit in with what we identified in my teacher evaluation goal. Essentially, I need to be more evidence-based. My personal norm is to stop making assumptions.
Anna:	That is such an important area to work on. To make that positive and actionable, you could agree to *Draw conclusions from evidence.* Does that capture it?

STL recommendations:

Do field research. One New Year, a friend convinced me to take on a cleaning organization challenge, and the first assignment was to tackle my fridge. I thought to myself, "I know I'm not the cleanest person, but my fridge is fine." Once I started cleaning it out, however, I was shocked at what I actually had in there (and, if I'm being honest, how gross my shelves really were). I bring this up because if I had been asked to simply sit and self-reflect on what areas needed work in my kitchen, I would not have named my refrigerator. It took the act of intentionally addressing it for me to see that this was a trouble spot.

The behaviors we exhibit in meetings can resemble that grime in the veggie drawer that we've stopped noticing. Successful norm building requires bringing awareness to our behavior. Rather than asking people to sit quietly and think about how they act in meetings, invite your colleagues to actually do some field research in which they notice and keep records of their behaviors when collaborating on teams.

Partner up. Invite team members to partner with one person at the table during the share-out. This can lower anxiety for people who are nervous about publicly naming their personal norms to the whole team.

Let it be. It might happen that someone on your team will set a personal norm that you and your colleagues feel isn't *the* thing that person needs to work on. There are some people who are either less aware of their own hindering behaviors or aware but not yet ready to tackle those behaviors publicly. (It's not easy to admit "I gossip about my colleagues and want to stop.") Trust that the person selected a norm that is meaningful to them, and at a later date, you can invite people to revisit and revise their personal norms.

Add on personal norms. Ask people to adopt one personal norm in addition to a short list of essential norms that every team needs. For example, "We will start and end all meetings on time, agree to disagree without being disagreeable, and uphold our own personal norms."

Think like a teacher:

Mindfulness has become regular practice in schools. When students become mindful of their behavior, they can actually begin to choose how they want to show up as learners. I remember working with a middle school student to help him curb his blurting out in class. Although this behavior was obvious to me and the other students because it was disruptive to their learning, the child was often not aware that he was doing it. He and I came up with a secret hand signal that I could use to help bring awareness to his blurting-out behavior without embarrassing him in front of the class. We set the intention for him to actively participate in ways that did not involve his voice, such as writing responses on a small whiteboard at his desk, and I agreed to walk by him frequently to see what he wrote and give him acknowledgement. None of these techniques eliminated his disruptive behavior, but they did improve his self-awareness enough to reduce it, which helped him and others participate better in the learning. In essence, what this student and I did was set a personal norm for him and give him the means to successfully uphold it.

You do not need to support educators on your teams as much as I did with my student, but the act of setting personal norms can empower people to show up to meetings as their best selves.

Find the right words:

- *Between now and the next time we meet, be mindful of how you show up in other team meetings or collaborative settings. Make note of what you do that helps the team and what behaviors might hinder the team's collaboration. If helpful, ask a friend who will tell it to you straight what they see as the strengths you bring to team discourse and where they see you need to improve.*

- *What behavior do you exhibit that helps your team get along [function] or achieve its goals [impact]? Put another way, if someone came up to you at the end of a team meeting and said, "Wow, you are really good at X in our meetings," what would X be?*

- *If you have ever left a meeting disappointed in yourself and thought, "I really wish I didn't Y in that meeting," what would Y be?*

INSTITUTE SOCIAL NORMS THAT MAXIMIZE TEAM IMPACT

It's not just about how you play with others in the sandbox; what you build matters, too. Most teams can commit to a set of norms that guide them to get along and be productive. These ways of interacting help the group function like a well-oiled machine. But groups that want better outcomes for their teams look at them through an impact lens. Skillful team leaders (STLs) institute social norms that maximize team members' impact on their own learning and that of their students.

Figure 9 shows a distinction between norms that help your team function and norms that help your team impact learning. Please do not waste time debating if a norm is intended to help the team function better or reach the desired impact on learning. People can argue in circles, and there is often overlap. Instead, use the moves in this section to have rich dialogue about what might get in the way of your team reaching its goals, and agree to a way of behaving that gets past it.

FIGURE 9 Two Lenses for Norm Setting	
NORMS TO HELP YOUR TEAM FUNCTION WELL:	**NORMS TO HELP YOUR TEAM IMPACT LEARNING:**
We agree to make decisions by consensus.	We agree to base decisions on evidence.
We agree to structure conversation with a protocol when analyzing data.	We agree to recognize and interrupt any bias when analyzing data.
We agree to disagree without being disagreeable.	We agree to disagree with practices that compromise our school values.
We agree to speak respectfully of any stakeholders who are not in our meeting.	We agree to seek diverse perspectives from any key stakeholders who are not in our meeting.

STL moves:

2.4 Foster sensitivity for cultural norms.

2.5 Surface unspoken norms.

2.6 Set ground rules for potentially difficult conversations.

2.7 Restore a norm after it has been broken.

What these moves promote:

Empathy. People develop an understanding and appreciation of others as they learn about their colleagues' cultural norms and life experiences that have shaped who they are and how they collaborate.

Healthy school cultures. People engage in courageous conversations about the norms of their school culture that hinder learning, and reflect on how they came about.

Trust. People behave in ways that build relational and vulnerability-based trust.

Accountability. People on the team maintain high expectations of one another and address broken norms, if need be.

When to use these moves:

Throughout the course of collaborative inquiry.

2.4 Foster sensitivity for cultural norms.

"You cannot serve those you don't understand," said Tiffany Anderson, super-intendent of Topeka (Kansas) Public Schools, at an ASCD virtual conference in July 2020 (Motter, 2020). Learn who your colleagues are and where they came from. It is unrealistic to be an expert on every culture,* but you can facilitate a dialogue about the different ways in which adults collaborate so that they can learn how best to work together. When leading adults in a dialogue about expectations, skillful team leaders (STLs) are mindful of diverse cultures and foster sensitivity for cultural norms.

How to foster sensitivity for cultural norms:

Model and lead others in sharing personal stories about your own cultural norms, how you were raised, or the ways in which people behaved in other work settings. Reflect on similarities and differences between norms. Seek to understand differences. Identify points of misunderstanding or conflict that could come into play on your team, and set agreements for working together.

In action:

Claudia: If you're comfortable, please share a story that will help us understand how your cultural upbringing or life experiences shaped the way you collaborate with others now. I'll kick it off: I grew up in a large somewhat Italian family from the south of

---

Culture includes, but is not limited to, race, nationality, region, gender, generation, religious affiliation, and sexual orientation.

Italy, and we'd get together every Sunday as a large extended family with lots of food—my mother makes the best meatballs with gravy—and everyone would talk . . . at the same time. Conversation and debate would get lively. I learned that to be heard you had to jump in and speak up.

Teacher 1:   That's interesting because it's so different than what I've experienced. I lived and worked in Japan for eight years, and groups function differently there, in that it's most important to be polite, maintain harmony, and come to decisions by consensus. When I got back here, I notice I wait to speak and, when I do, I tend to avoid conflict.

Teacher 2:   I don't really have a family or personal story like those.

Claudia: I know you just came here from a different school. What was your experience with collaboration there?

Teacher 2:   I felt like I was really on my own. People kept to themselves. No one really even knew what was going on in your classroom. Even the teachers' break room always had this uncomfortable vibe where some people didn't even say hello to you. When the school day was over, the building felt like a ghost town because everyone booked it out of there. I felt very isolated there and learned to keep to myself. It's one of the reasons I left to come here.

Think like a teacher:

Larry Ferlazzo (2020) highlights a key recommendation for creating a culturally responsive classroom from educational equity specialist Barbara Leilani Brazil Keys. She calls on teachers to ask the question (paraphrased here), "Are my rules and the norms of my classroom culturally empowering to students and inclusive, or do they create a cultural divide?"

As a teacher, you understand that children from different cultures and upbringings are raised with different norms. One teacher shared with me how she learned that in Haiti children are taught not to make direct eye contact with adults, so she had to manage her own expectations of a student who'd recently emigrated from there.

When working with adults, use discussion about cultural norms to foster understanding and establish an inclusive environment.

Find the right words:

- *How do people interact in your home culture? How did people collaborate in your prior work experience?*

- *What have these experiences taught you to expect when collaborating with others?*

- *Where do we have conflicting beliefs about how we are supposed to collaborate? What do we need to understand about each other in order to collaborate effectively?*

Related reading:

Move 3.9, "Share a story-moment." Share cultural norms through personal storytelling to foster empathy.

Move 3.11, "Practice compassion." Practice compassion when you or others hear cultural norms that are very different from your own.

2.5 Surface unspoken norms.

Whether you and your team make a list or not, norms are present even before you get to the table. Anyone new to a team can usually pick up on them. If you come a few minutes late to a meeting and notice people have started without you, you quickly learn that the norm here is to be on time. If a colleague voices an idea that gets shut down, you learn that dissenting viewpoints are not welcome. If gossip prevails throughout your school, then you can bet it will have its place among members of your team. Tacit norms are not typically found on any publicized list. They are long-established behaviors typically not talked about, and they represent the good, the bad, and the ugly ways people *really* collaborate within a team and/or school culture. And it's the bad and the ugly—those things we have gotten accustomed to, don't talk about, and let slide—that we need to start understanding and replacing with new behaviors. Skillful team leaders (STLs) surface unspoken norms. Some examples of unhealthy accepted behaviors that STLs might surface include working in silos instead of working interdependently, keeping teaching practices private instead of publicly opening classroom doors, and allowing gossip and cliques to fester instead of engaging in honest upfront communication.

How to surface unspoken norms:

Whatever the ways of being that people in your school building have come to see as an acceptable part of the organizational culture, these become the norms of behavior on your team—unless you set different expectations. Norm setting is the opportunity for new expectation setting. Begin with the positive. Next, shift to discussing those hindering behaviors that have somehow become acceptable in your school. Aim to understand how these behaviors came to be. Envision the way in which you would like everyone to interact regularly on your team. Finally, commit to norms that you are ready to adopt.

In action:

Justine: When I first came to work at this school, I instantly noticed a caring and genuine interest in one another among the staff. I remember suffering through a cold early in the year, and Joanna bringing me soup for lunch. It's not written anywhere that we take care of one another, but we just do. I think there is an unspoken norm that we treat each other as family here, not just as people we work along-side. What positive ways do you see people interacting that aren't necessarily in the "rule book"?

[Teachers share positive experiences.]

And, if I were to name an unspoken norm that I see in our building that I wish I could change—and this is hard to share—I guess it would be that although we are very collegial here and I feel like I could ask a favor of anyone, I don't know that we push each other's practice enough. Is there anyone else who sees this, too?

[Teachers nod and comment in agreement.]

I would welcome working in a place where asking critical questions of each other were the norm. Can we do this for each other?

STL recommendations:

Remind people of the intent behind this move. This move calls on people to engage in courageous conversations about the norms of their school culture that they want to change. People are encouraged to be honest and vulnerable, two building blocks to fostering trust. But, things can quickly go sour if surfacing unspoken norms turns into a blame game. Make clear that the purpose of this conversation is to call attention to behaviors that get in the way of reaching goals, and agree to collaborate differently.

Dig down to the roots. Beyond naming hindering behaviors that have become acceptable ways of being, get to the why. According to psychologist Edgar Schein (quoted in Kuppler, 2015), organizational culture is like a lily pond: "On the surface, you've got leaves and flowers and things that are very visible. That's the 'how we do things around here' but the explanation of why we do things in that way forces you to look at the root system, what's feeding it and the history of the pond, who planted what. If you don't dig down into the reasons for why we do things this way you've only looked at the culture at a very superficial level and you haven't really understood it." Here are a few reasons unhealthy norms might persist in a school:

* *School leadership.* "The old principal used to . . . We don't know why, but we just keep doing it that way."

- *Weak incentive or accountability systems.* "We've always done it this way because there were no incentives for doing it differently." "No one came down on us if we did it this way, so we assumed it was fine."

- *Lack of exposure to other ways of doing things.* "We never learned a different way to do this, so we figured we were doing it right."

Do this move in real time. Talking about challenging behaviors in your school culture can be a heavy conversation. You don't have to surface unspoken norms on day one of meeting; instead, do it when you notice unhealthy behaviors that have become acceptable.

Defer to the school leadership team. If there are school-wide hindering behaviors to address, it's probably most effective to surface tacit norms at a school leadership team meeting with the principal present.

Find the right words:

- Pose the following sentence frames to surface tacit norms with your team:
    - *There's no explicit rule about . . . but make sure you . . .*
    - *They say everyone must . . . but no one ever does.*
    - *Make sure you . . . I don't know why, but we've always done it this way.*
    - *Be careful not to . . . It's just not done here.*
    - *You can . . . but people are going to look at you weird.*

- *What are some unspoken norms that a new person will recognize within a week of being in our school? Which ones might be hindering our collaboration or promoting exclusion? How can we address unspoken norms and promote norms of inclusion?*

- *What are some unspoken ways of interacting that help our school function well? What are some of the hindering or even toxic behaviors that we have, perhaps inadvertently, come to see as acceptable in our school culture? What beliefs, values, and assumptions drive these behaviors? Where did they come from? How can we create conditions for better collaboration on this team?*

- In the moment: *I know we've always done it this way, but let's pause to think about why and whether we can get better outcomes if we do it differently this time.*

2.6 Set ground rules for potentially difficult conversations.

Difficult conversations are a regular occurrence in the most high-functioning, high-impact Q1 teams. They involve talk about teacher and student data, race and equity, student trauma, student-learning differences, tragic school events such as suicide, change in school leadership, and even how the team is performing. Lower-functioning teams engage in difficult conversations as well; however, conversation isn't always productive, particularly when emotions run high. Talk can devolve into blame and personal attacks. Assumptions and bias might overrule evidence. Fixed mindsets, if present, can hold the group back from taking responsibility for problems and implementing solutions. Skillful team leaders (STLs) set ground rules for potentially difficult conversations. The following are some examples of norms to prepare for difficult conversations.

Norms for Difficult Conversations

Courageous Conversation norms. These four agreements were put forth by Singleton and Linton (2006) specifically for conversations about race but are also helpful for difficult conversations about unhealthy school cultures and practices.

- Stay engaged. (Notice when you are shutting down.)

- Speak your truth. (Take risks and be honest. Do so in a way others can hear. Don't second-guess someone else's truth.)

- Experience discomfort. (Expect to feel unsettled, uncertain, or disturbed.)

- Expect and accept non-closure. (All's well that doesn't end well or doesn't end at all. Difficult conversations may not wrap up neatly by the time your meeting is over.)

Confidentiality norms. Some teams call this the Vegas norm: "What happens in Vegas stays in Vegas." The spirit of any confidentiality agreement is not to create a secret community or a place to vent without others finding out, but rather to encourage honesty and vulnerability within the team. No one wants to "put themselves out there" to their colleagues, only to find out that what they have said has been parroted to someone outside of the meeting without context. Discuss with your team when and how you will share out from a meeting. Consider agreeing to the following:

- It's your story to tell. (Direct those who want to know what happened to the source.)

- Ask permission before you share outside of the meeting.

- Act to maintain trust.

Decision-making norms. Primary Intention 8 offers moves to make while decision making with a group, but establishing an agreement upfront can reduce tension and gridlock. Here are some examples:

- Speak candidly, but also be sensitive to the impact of your tone and word choice.

- Respond to others with empathy.

- Distinguish the problem from the people.

- Talk about the issues, not who is or isn't responsible for them.

- Focus conversation on causes within your control.

- Maintain a tolerance for ambiguity.

- Agree to disagree and revisit this conversation at a different time.

Data analysis norm. Discussed further in Move 7.9, the following norm that I wrote helps foster empathy for the challenging work of continuous improvement and the genuine belief in everyone's good intentions:

> Behind every number is a student who is trying. Behind every student is a teacher who is trying.

How to set ground rules for potentially difficult conversations:

Anticipate when a conversation might require group agreements beyond what you normally use. Select norms that address the following aspects of facilitating a difficult conversation: speaking and listening, confidentiality, and decision making. Invite people to jot down a norm that they rely on when conversations get challenging. This is also a great place to revisit personal norms. You don't need a long list, but you will want to anticipate one to three things that could spin the conversation into a downward spiral.

STL recommendation:

Normalize discomfort. The Learning Zone Model, based on Lev Vygotsky's (1978) zone of proximal development, suggests that a person learning something falls into three states: comfort, learning, and panic. The panic zone is usually charged with emotion. The amygdala does its fright, flight, or freeze job and no learning can happen. STL Osamagbe (Osa) Osagie recommends that, when talking about equity and race, teams normalize discomfort so people expect feelings they might not be used to. She suggests that, before people enter the panic zone, they pause and decipher the reason for their discomfort—for example, by asking, "I'm sensing myself entering panic mode, but am I really unsafe or is this a healthy learning zone where I need to be pushed?"

Think like a teacher:

As you build social contracts with your students to establish group agreements, so should you, as a leader, build social contracts with your team. Osa reminded teachers in a Carroll School team meeting that norms are a great way to protect the safety of the people who are both in the classroom and not in the classroom. They provide structure and help students make informed decisions about the way they want to engage. They empower the learner.

In order for difficult conversations to succeed, teams must have psychological safety. Setting ground rules in advance helps establish this.

Find the right words:

- *In light of learning this difficult news, let's talk about its effect on our community and ourselves. Because this might be a challenging conversation, I'm going to ask us to agree to . . .*

- *Examining student data together can be fodder for difficult conversation. Let's agree to . . .*

- *It's not often that we need to talk about what's not working on our team, but it's apparent that we do need to address some things that are hindering our collaboration. For this conversation, let's agree to . . .*

2.7 Restore a norm after it has been broken.

Crafting norms is not nearly as hard as following them. And confronting someone who breaks a norm is probably harder than both; yet, it's something we have to do. STL Osamagbe (Osa) Osagie reminds us that when we do not address undesirable behaviors and low expectations on our teams, we send the message that those behaviors are acceptable. Skillful team leaders (STLs) restore norms after they have been broken.

How to restore a norm after it has been broken:

Notice when an individual or group is struggling to maintain a norm that is intended to help the group collaborate. Be aware of any hesitancy you may feel in bringing it forward. Summon the courage to call attention to it. Raise the broken agreement in a way that preserves the dignity of all members of the group. Together, reflect on what makes it hard to keep the agreement. Suspend judgment. Plan actionable ways to live the norm.

In action:

Janet:	Recently we had an email thread that caused a lot of misunderstanding and tension within our group. I appreciate everyone's participation in helping us resolve that specific challenge. To avoid a similar circumstance in the future, I'd like us to restore the norm of assuming positive intentions. It's not always easy to do. What makes this norm hard to keep?
Teacher 1:	I think sometimes we get caught in the moment and rush to judgment before hearing someone out.
Janet:	I certainly do that and not just on our team—sometimes with parents or even students. It's a natural response, and it happens in an instant. So, going forward, what will help our group assume positive intentions?

Teacher 2:	I think literally just pausing and asking, "What else, besides what I'm thinking, might be behind my colleague's words?"
Janet:	That's good, but it can be hard to do when you are in an emotional state.
Teacher 1:	So let's get concrete. How about we all agree not to email a response when we are upset? Instead, we connect with the person directly.
Teacher 2:	And also we should agree to avoid raising issues by email that we have not yet discussed. Instead, add them to the agenda.

Think like a teacher:

You are likely comfortable addressing undesirable behaviors with students and, if you are like me, more reluctant to do so with your colleagues. While we could explore the multitude of reasons you might be hesitant with your peers ("It's not my role," "He is my friend," "What's the point?," etc.), it's more helpful to think about what gives you the courage to discuss such behaviors with children.

First, you are motivated by the desire to maintain a safe optimal learning environment for all children. The moment a child puts that in jeopardy by exhibiting unacceptable behaviors, you are ready to guide them back. Second, you are clear about what the behavioral expectations in your classroom are, so any deviation from them leaves no doubt in your mind that the behavior must be addressed. Third, you have established relational and vulnerability-based trust with your students—they know you care; they take risks with you; they'll call you or another classmate out if you break a class agreement, confident that the relationship will not be affected. And lastly, you are experienced. You've likely had to address broken social contracts with students since day one of your teaching, and you've developed moves that do it in a way that does not embarrass or humiliate the students or jeopardize your relationship with them.

So, take this approach with your colleagues and share the responsibility with other members of your team so that you are holding one another accountable. It will take time and practice, but your team will be better for it.

STL recommendations:

Establish a signal. You might be too young to remember Carol Burnett, a great comedic actress who had her own variety show on TV in the 1970s, but she would pull on her ear every time she wanted to let her daughter know that she loved her. We use nonverbal signals in the classroom with students all the time to redirect unwanted behaviors, indicate transitions, or show agreement with one another. Decide with your colleagues what signal you can use to help keep one another accountable to norms.

Prevent a broken norm. Here are a few ways to keep norms alive:

- Invite a colleague to read aloud norms at the start of each meeting as a reminder.

- Ask people to select one norm that they believe is important for others to uphold, and one norm that they will make an effort to especially uphold. (Gene Thompson-Grove, one of the original developers of Critical Friends Groups, recommended this move in a June 2013 or 2014 training session for teacher leaders I arranged when I was national director of Teach Plus.)

- Deep-dive into a brief discussion about one norm from the list before getting into the day's agenda. For example, say, "Let's talk about what norm two means today and what it might look like in action."

- As the leader, call attention to one norm that you anticipate being particularly important given what's on your agenda for the day.

- Discuss the impact of a broken norm before someone breaks it, and recommit to upholding it.

Find the right words and actions:

Respond during a meeting.

- Pause and reread a norm when you notice your conversation needs it.

- Model. Uphold group agreements, and others will likely follow your lead.

- Call attention to hindering behaviors and identify where they are coming from. Commit to better:

  - *We are not keeping with our norm. Why not? If it's truly the way we aspire to interact, then let's recommit to it.*

Revisit norms at the end of or after a meeting.

- Use norms as a checklist at the end of a meeting to mentally mark off those that you upheld, and share what you plan to do better next time.

- After a meeting, privately approach anyone who broke a norm and reset the expectation. Avoid shaming them. Communicate that you are not seeking explanations, just looking to move forward:

  - *Ms. S, I've noticed you have come late to the last three meetings. This isn't easy for me to bring up, and there's no need to for you explain why. I just wanted to check in and make sure you'll be able to come on time going forward. Thanks.*

SHARE RESPONSIBILITY THROUGH ROLES

As widely accepted as the concept of collaboration is, what it looks like among teams differs greatly, not only between districts or schools but sometimes also within the same school. Nothing illuminated these differences more than the COVID-19 pandemic. Some teacher teams co-planned and distributed the workload. They studied which students were responsive to different technologies. Together, they problem solved and improved their own practice to heights they didn't ever anticipate needing to reach. Teachers on these teams anecdotally reported to me that they felt like, after a few months of team meetings, things were "organized" and "manageable." They felt that they were "supported" and that they were "getting into a good groove." (Interestingly, one school leader shared with me that teachers who were reluctant to collaborate before suddenly felt a strong shared purpose for doing so, and were eager to work with their teams.)

On the flip side, some teacher teams did not take on a collective approach during the pandemic. Individuals were left to figure out plans and implementation on their own. The bizarre thing is, these teams still met regularly, even if not in person. Time was not their challenge; a lack of shared responsibility was. They were, as I name in my first book, "alone together" (MacDonald, 2013, p. 29). These teachers described their work to me during this difficult period as "joyless," "overwhelming," "exhausting," and "lonely."

Skillful team leaders (STLs) share responsibility for roles that both keep the team running well and share responsibility for student (and adult) learning.

STL moves:

2.8 Clarify the team leader role.

2.9 Commission others to lead learning.

2.10 Break from fixed or imposed roles.

Tools and templates:

Figure 10: Team Roles and Responsibilities Example

Figure 11: The Benefits of Note-Taking

What these moves promote:

Clarity. People clarify misconceptions about roles and responsibilities of team leaders.

Shared responsibility. People take on roles that help the team both function well and impact adult learning.

Agency. Teachers are not passive participants on a team. They have a say in how the team collaborates.

When to use these moves:

At the start of collaboration; when roles need clarification; when people seem stuck in one way of working in a group.

2.8 Clarify the team leader role.

"Isn't that the team leader's job?"

If your school is new to, or changing up the way you do, teacher-led teams, the faculty will need to learn what to expect from the team leader and what is expected of them. Skillful team leaders (STLs) and their principal or school leaders clarify leadership roles and how they interface with other roles (see Figure 10).

How to clarify the team leader role.

Take the following three-prong approach:

1. Work with school leaders to write role descriptions (see Figure 10) and message them to staff.

2. Get ahead of misconceptions by defining in your first team meeting what your roles and responsibilities are and are not. For instance, a team leader is not a meeting manager, the only expert at the table, a boss, an assistant or team secretary, or a go-between for teachers and principal.

3. Follow through. Live the roles you defined. For example, if you tell your colleagues that your role is to facilitate meetings, and their role is to help shape the agenda for each meeting, then create opportunities for them to do so.

In action:

Oscar assembles his grade-level math team for the first time.

Oscar: I have been fortunate to participate in training to help lead our team, but in no way does this mean I'm running the show. Our work is collaborative, and we will need to rely on each other and share responsibility for the tasks and learning ahead. My hope is that each of us can lead and contribute in ways that make everyone feel valued and advance our team's student-learning goals.

I'll move us through the phases of inquiry, but there will be many opportunities for anyone ready to co-design meetings, co-facilitate portions of our agenda, bring in readings you find, demonstrate lessons, and bring in student work for us to examine.

FIGURE 10   Team Roles and Responsibilities Example

TEAM LEADERS
Trained facilitators of
collaborative learning

Primary responsibilities:
Attend ongoing leadership training
and coaching; connect with principal,
school, and team leaders across the
school/district; design and plan
collaborative inquiry;
facilitate or co-facilitate agenda items;
actively support colleagues; guide the
team toward high-impact outcomes.

TEAM MEMBERS
Educators engaged in
collaborative inquiry

Primary responsibilities:
Actively contribute; take on shared
meeting tasks and learning
opportunities such as co-plan
and prepare, co-facilitate,
record keep, bring in
data/student work, or
demonstrate instruction.

All hold expertise. All are co-learners.

Shared responsibilities: Advocate for
students and families; suspend and
address assumptions and bias; engage
in evidence-based discourse; implement
new learning; lead and support one
another throughout implementation.

TEAM LEADER "COACHES"
Supportive counsel for the
growth and development of
the team leader and team

Primary responsibilities:
Co-plan with team leader; attend most
meetings and provide feedback;
maintain focus on high-impact
outcomes; troubleshoot problems;
facilitate network opportunities
for team leaders to
collaborate with each other.

**PRINCIPAL and HEADS OF
SCHOOL/DEPARTMENTS**
Visionary leaders who establish
school-wide systems, structures, and
supports for team function and impact

Primary responsibilities:
Identify school priorities; acquire
leadership training for team leaders;
protect team time; establish a short list
of school-wide collaboration norms;
make accountability measures consistent
and explicit; foster collaboration with and
across team leaders and coaches;
observe teams across schools; decide
changes to school-wide collaborative
systems, structures, and policies.

Oscar: I also wanted to let you know that you'll see the math coach sit in on most of our meetings. She is primarily here to support my growth and development as a leader, and also to guide us as we advance our department priorities. The principal, too, might pop in as she circulates among team meetings. Neither's presence should negatively affect how we collaborate. These meetings are meant to give us time to work together and help our kids.

We'll need to share some logistical roles for tasks such as note-taker, timekeeper, and data organizer. I sent you a link to SignUpGenius where I'm asking everyone to sign up three times over the course of our meetings. Choose the roles that feel like the best fit for you.

And finally, we are all peers, and I ask that we keep each other accountable to our school-wide and our own team norms. In other words, if someone breaks an agreement, please don't come to me. Go directly to that person, and let's support one another.

As we engage in the work, additional responsibilities might come up, but for now, what else can I clarify regarding roles?

STL recommendations:

Sign up for tasks in advance. Once you know your meeting dates, ask people to volunteer to sign up for a logistical role from the start so that you aren't taking time each meeting asking for a note-taker, timekeeper, data organizer, or snack supplier.

Highlight other forms of teacher leadership. If your school has newly designated teacher team leaders, there is a risk that a divide can begin to form between staff, particularly if the team leader role comes with "perks" such as a stipend, time off from teaching responsibilities, or exclusive meetings with school leaders. Ask your principal to send the message that teacher team leader is one of many types of teacher leadership roles in the building. Team leaders are learners and members of the team just as much as they are leaders of the team.

Find the right words:

- *Let me clarify what the teacher team leader role is and what it isn't.*

- *Here's what's different between the roles of your team leader, team members, and administrator . . . Here's what's the same . . .*

- *Here's what you can expect from me as the team leader . . . Here's what we should expect from one another . . .*

Related reading:

- Part II, Chapter 6, "The Upside (and Downside) of Being a Peer Leader." Become aware of misconceptions that you, as a peer leader, might have.

2.9 Commission others to lead learning.

Part I, Chapter 2 puts forward the idea that skillful team leaders (STLs) don't only attend to how well team members get along and get things done, but they also look at the impact of what they do together. They intentionally share responsibilities for learning together and support their colleagues as needed.

How to commission others to lead learning:

The following are six responsibilities that any team member can take on to help advance the learning goals of their team.

1. Co-facilitate.

Leading does not need to mean that you are the only person facilitating meetings. Some of your colleagues may want the opportunity. While I do believe in the motto of the Disney-Pixar film *Ratatouille*—"Anyone can cook"—in truth, not everyone is ready to facilitate a whole meeting solo. *Facilitate* means "to make easy," but some people who are not skillfully trained can sometimes "*difficile*–itate." For this reason I'm not a fan of rotating the role in which every person takes a turn. But, you can rotate the role of co-facilitator, someone who plans meetings and facilitates alongside you or facilitates portions of the meeting. As the primary facilitator, you can provide stability in leadership from meeting to meeting while also bringing in multiple voices and leadership styles.

Find the right words:

- *Is there someone who feels ready to facilitate this portion of the meeting?*

- *This work is not in my wheelhouse, and I'd welcome someone else to facilitate.*

- *Given my appointed role as teacher leader, I will remain facilitator but would like to bring in others' talents and voices to rotate co-facilitation with me each week.*

2. Document.

Most people view note-taking as a laborious meeting task, but it is actually a means to impact team learning. When I led teams as a literacy coach, for example, note-taking gave me time to process everything that was discussed, highlight key learning that I wanted us to hold onto, and plan next steps for the group. Note-taking also required me to listen more and talk less, something I wanted to work on. I shared these notes with my teams and made them available to any teacher in our school who was interested in looking at what we were learning. I still have binders of notes from most of my meetings and sometimes read through them, amazed at the learning and insight my teacher teams and I experienced together. See Figure 11 for a list of benefits to the team and the note-taker.

FIGURE 11 The Benefits of Note-Taking	
BENEFITS OF MEETING NOTES TO A TEAM	**BENEFITS OF BEING THE NOTE-TAKER**
• Records a shared understanding of what was discussed in the meeting • Captures essential ideas and important details • Commits a team to decisions • Commits a team to action • Serves as a reference document • Serves as a tool for transparency in which notes can be shared with others not present at the meeting • Engenders an appreciation for your team—the work you've accomplished and the incredible learning you engaged in together	• Allows time for you to process what's being said • Helps you verbally hold back, if you are a person who tends to monopolize airtime in a meeting • Helps you attend to all comments and summarize or synthesize them • Instills a feeling of worth that you are doing a much-needed service for the team

STL recommendations:

Go first. Although the benefits of it are clear, note-taking can still be a burdensome job that no one wants. Sign up for the role yourself several times throughout the course of your team's inquiry work. Also, by going first, you set the expectation for what documenting a meeting should look like.

Skip minutes. Some business or school board meetings require minutes in which almost line-by-line transcripts are recorded. This level of detail is not typically needed in a teacher team or school leadership meeting and can actually cause people to be guarded if they know their name will be attached to every comment they make and then those notes are going public. Notes can simply consist of big ideas, important details, remaining questions, and next steps.

Tag team. Although you did it in your college classes, taking notes and participating at the same time can be challenging for some people. A good rule of thumb to adopt is this: When one person is participating, someone else is jotting down notes. Using a shared electronic document makes this doable. It's helpful to still name one person as the primary note-taker who is responsible at the end of the meeting for making sure things were captured as accurately as possible, and who can also share out to others who were not at the meeting should the team choose to do so.

3. Recap.

This move falls more with decision-making moves in Primary Intention 8, but I include it here because some teams have benefitted from turning summarizing into someone's role. Too often great discussion is had and ideas are generated, but people leave a meeting unclear about what was decided or the next steps to take.

Recap decisions already made, including what or who is responsible, by when, and make clear, any decisions not yet made.

4. Access texts.

During the *Research & Study* STL phase of collaborative inquiry, teams look to research, articles, videos, and other texts to further their learning about how to bring about the outcomes they desire for students. Empower your team members to be on the hunt for worthy texts (see Moves 4.8–4.11).

5. Present student work/data or teacher work.

Bring the classroom to your team meeting. One of the most important responsibilities individual team members can take is sharing their students' work/data. Teachers learn so much from looking at student work (LASW) or looking at teacher work (LATW), such as lesson plans, together. More detail on how to support people taking on this role can be found in Primary Intentions 7 and 9.

6. Demonstrate a lesson.

Bring your team to the classroom. Peer observation, whether live, prerecorded, or dry demo (without students present), is a powerful responsibility for any teacher to undertake and can bring about tremendous learning for educators, about their students and themselves as practitioners. Moves to support teachers in this role are found in Primary Intention 9.

2.10 Break from fixed or imposed roles.

Margaret Hamilton played the Wicked Witch of the West in *The Wizard of Oz* so well that she could never get cast as anything other than a scary witch or villain. While team members are not typecast to this extreme, they can get pigeonholed into playing the same role on a team, and never get to exhibit the complexity of who they really are (Lewis & Woodhull, 2018).

I remember being a teacher on a team in which a well-meaning leader attempted to share how valuable we each were to her. She highlighted something about each of us: "Adrianne, you are good at ensuring we follow through on what we plan. Elisa, you are good at seeing the big picture. And Tammy, you are a good timekeeper." Understandably, Tammy (not her real name) was frustrated by the box in which the leader had placed her, and she was never given opportunities to show how much more she could contribute.

In some cases, people bring these narrowly defined roles onto themselves by going so far as to tell the group, "I'm the naysayer" or "the eternal optimist" or "the instigator." In other cases, a role is assigned *to* a person without permission. This can occur in our own families where parents and siblings fall into roles they can't escape from (e.g., "You are the responsible one, but your sister will always be the impulsive one"). But it's most commonly experienced by people who identify as BIPOC (Black, Indigenous, or a person of color) (Sue et al., 2007). When at the table they are in the minority, others might put them (often unconsciously) in the position of speaking for their entire race or culture. For example, a group of white teachers asks the one Latino male teacher on the team, "What do Hispanic boys like to do?" This is true for any person who identifies with a different social or cultural group (religion, generation, sexuality, etc.) than the others at the table.

Whether you assume a role in a group or someone unconsciously assigns a role to you, you are pressured with the expectation to always act the part. It can be tough to show up to the group differently even if you want to. Skillful team leaders (STLs) offer opportunities for people to take on different roles in a group, and break from fixed roles and stereotypical roles imposed on them.

How to break from fixed or imposed roles:

Heighten awareness of the roles people assign to themselves and those that they unconsciously assign to others. Ask people how they would like to be perceived and how they would not. If you believe someone is imposing a role on you because of your social cultural identity, STL Osamagbe (Osa) Osagie recommends that you first assume positive intentions of the other person, relying on what you know of their character. Then, manage your emotions and respond. Tell the person that you are not comfortable with them asking you to speak for, explain, or defend the words and actions of an entire race, religion, generation, or other group with which you identify.

In action:

Tyrone:	What role, if any, do you tend to take on when in a group, or what role is often assigned to you that you wish to step away from when we are collaborating? I'll start. I have a tendency to assume the role of "fixer." Any time someone presents a problem, it's my nature to jump and offer a solution. Some people get turned off to me when I do this, and others rely too much on me, expecting me to solve their problems. On this team, I'm going to try to take on more of a listening role that empowers others to find their own solutions.

Teacher 1:   I teach art, and sometimes I feel that my contributions are not always given the same weight as that of comments made from my colleagues who teach core classes. I hope people see my role on this team as someone who holds a different, but equally important, perspective about students.

Administrator: I'm the only administrator on this team, and while I know I'm technically an evaluator, I would like to have a partnership role with you. I hope you see me as working things out alongside you.

STL recommendations:

Sense the readiness of the room. This move can feel similar to personal norm setting (Move 2.3), and although you can never be mindful enough, it can feel like overkill if you do this move on the same day that you lead team agreement and expectation setting. Better to implement this move when you notice people are falling into set roles or making assumptions about others.

Discourage debate. If the art teacher says she wants a role on the team where her opinions are given equal weight to those of her colleagues, don't let the conversation turn into people trying to psychoanalyze why she thinks people see her in this way. Simply recognize that this is the role the art teacher wants to play on this team going forward.

Expect a reaction. Chances are, if you explain that you are not comfortable being assigned a role that is based on your social or cultural identity, the person who put you in that position is going to have a reaction. They might feel ashamed, defensive, misunderstood, angry, or something else. That's OK. Provide them a graceful exit (see Move 5.25). And if, indeed, you misconstrued what they said, then own that (see Move 10.9).

Find the right words:

- *What role, if any, do you tend to take on when in a group?*

- *What role is often assigned to you that you wish to step away from when we are collaborating?*

Primary Intention

Nurture Group Culture: Community and Trust

3

Think of a team that you lead or are a member of. Mark off all of the following statements with which you can honestly say you strongly agree:

☐ I get along with all members of this team.

☐ I don't fear judgment, gossip, or shame from any member of this team.

☐ I never feel excluded and never exclude anyone on this team.

☐ I share with this team my missteps, blunders, confusions, and struggles.

☐ I proactively invite others on this team to examine with me my assumptions, biases, and fixed mindsets.

☐ I enjoy working with this team.

Regardless of what you checked off, these statements are some indicators of the health of your team culture. Even if you strongly agreed with every statement for one team, it would not be surprising if you had a different set of responses for another. Teams have their own intangible culture—something that is hard to describe but invokes a feeling when members are together. While outsiders might say they can see the culture of a school when they walk through the doors of the building, or that of a team as soon as they sit at the table, culture is less about what we see and more about what we don't. Psychologist Edgar Schein (quoted in Kuppler, 2015) defines culture as the reasons *why* we do what we do around here. He suggests, as described in Move 2.5, that organizations are like ponds: The health on the surface of the pond depends on what's happening in the roots.

Dig beneath the surface of a high-functioning, high-impact Q1 team, and you see a foundation of trust. Look at the roots of low-functioning Q3 and Q4 teams, and it's obvious there is little to no trust. Members of high-functioning, low-impact Q2 teams (where people get along but their efforts don't yield better outcomes) will likely say that they trust one another. However, upon close examination, it's clear what they actually have is relational trust, not vulnerability-based trust. The first and last statements in the opening checklist are indicators of relational trust; the other statements are examples of what someone might say on a team that has vulnerability-based trust. A brief distinction between the two types of trust follows.

Relational Trust

Relational trust is an authentic partnership between you as team leader and those whom you lead. There is mutual respect. People are compassionate toward one another, assuming positive intentions when things go wrong more so than if a trusting relationship did not exist. Steven Covey (2006) said it best: "In a high-trust relationship, you can say the wrong thing, and people will still get your meaning. In a low-trust relationship, you can be very measured, even precise, and they'll still misinterpret you." You know you have relational trust, for instance, when you ask your colleagues to try for the first time a protocol that you've never led, and they are willing because it's *you* who asked them to do it. They trust that you will never steer them wrong.

When relational trust is present, there is also a strong sense of community and a personal commitment wherein people feel like they have each other's backs. A teacher once told me she knew for a fact that her team trusted one another because, if someone confidentially confessed to the group, "I killed a man," the team would say, "Let's go get the shovels." I'm not condoning crime (nor was she, obviously), but it is that "familyhood" bond that is present on a team that has earned relational trust.

Examples of relational trust on a team include the following:

- I trust you to watch my class for five minutes while I go to the restroom.

- I can't attend the meeting, but I trust you will bring up my concerns.

- We're ordering lunch, and you forgot money. I lend you some because I trust you will pay me back.

Vulnerability-Based Trust

Every December we receive Christmas letters. My all-time favorite comes from a dear friend who doesn't just tell of the awards her kids received, the promotions they got, or the trips they took, but also shares the hardships they overcame that year. It takes courage to share that your children did not have a good year in school and you are still trying to figure out how to best help them, or to say that you lost your job and welcome any leads. My friend's letter stands out each year because it is "real" and shows her vulnerability.

Vulnerability-based trust is often dependent on having relational trust. This is one reason why low-functioning Q3 and Q4 teams typically don't have it. (You're not going to open up to someone about the teaching challenges you face if you fear they'll gossip behind your back.) But, Q4 teams have another reason for having a hard time being vulnerable with their colleagues. Most often, people on these teams are individually competent. This can lead to an unconscious need to protect their social status within the group. They keep their challenges to themselves in order to sustain the way others see them in the group.

People on high-functioning, high-impact Q1 teams are forthcoming to their team about their own missteps, confusions, misunderstandings, struggles, and failures. They may not share their deep personal secrets (although some do), but they are vulnerable about their teaching practice. They risk the possibility of judgment, gossip, or ridicule from others. They are willing to be viewed as amateur or not as amazing as everyone thinks they are, all for the sake of becoming better at what they do. When colleagues are vulnerable with one another and the response from the group is positive and no one shames or shuts them down, then deep learning takes place.

Examples of vulnerability-based trust on a team include the following:

- I don't understand how to use our new portal system. I trust you won't mock me, so I ask you for help.

- I have never taught this lesson before. I trust that you will support me, so I invite you into my classroom to observe the first time I'm doing it and give me feedback.

- My students scored lower than everyone else's students on the same test. I don't know how to help my students. I invite my colleagues to analyze my student work samples because I trust that they will help me without thinking less of me.

Contents

Foster inclusivity.

3.1 Welcome underrepresented voices.

3.2 Instill a sense of belonging.

Build community and relational trust through play.

3.3 Plan play strategically.

3.4 Frame the game.

3.5 Level up language.

3.6 Give simple directions.

3.7 Do a demo.

3.8 Lead community- and trust-building games.

Strengthen a culture of vulnerability-based trust.

3.9 Share a story-moment.

3.10 Make struggle visible.

3.11 Practice compassion.

FOSTER INCLUSIVITY

It's becoming more and more common across schools and workplaces to have a diversity, equity, and inclusion (DEI) director or team. Each word in this title is intentional. Yet, sometimes people refer to them in one breath as if they are one word, and the distinct meanings get lost. I like these simple definitions from Heinz (2021):

- *Diversity:* The presence of differences within a given setting. In the workplace,[*] that can mean differences in [ability, learning,] race, ethnicity, gender, gender identity, sexual orientation, age and socioeconomic class.

- *Equity:* The act of ensuring that processes and programs are impartial, fair and provide equal possible outcomes for every individual.

- *Inclusion:* The practice of ensuring that people feel a sense of belonging in the workplace.

Skillful team leaders (STLs) create inclusive team cultures where all members—particularly those who identify differently from the majority—feel a sense of belonging to the group.

STL moves:

3.1 Welcome underrepresented voices.

3.2 Instill a sense of belonging.

What these moves promote:

Community. People of all diverse backgrounds feel welcome on the team.

Empathy. People develop an appreciation for different cultures and perspectives.

Morale. People are enthusiastic about belonging to this team.

3.1 Welcome underrepresented voices.

"There is wisdom in the minority." Myrna Lewis, a psychologist and founder of Deep Democracy (see Lewis, 2016; Lewis & Woodhull, 2018), speaks of the risk in overlooking the voices of the few who are not with the majority. Most commonly, these are individuals who are underrepresented because of social and cultural identifiers (race, gender, age, sexuality, etc.) or learning or linguistic differences or disabilities. Diversity, explored further in

---

[*]*Workplace* may represent an organization, district, school, team, or classroom.

Primary Intention 9, is a critical component to team creativity and solution finding, but only if people feel that their unique perspectives are welcome. Skillful team leaders (STLs) actively seek ways to involve individuals who might not otherwise feel included.

How to welcome underrepresented voices:

Throughout this book, I offer the following facilitation moves that should help foster inclusivity on your team.

- *Accommodate adults with learning differences, disabilities, or preferences* (Move 1.6). Create conditions where everyone has access to learning.

- *Leverage strengths in disability* (Move 1.7). Create conditions where you celebrate and leverage the gifts of your colleagues.

- *Foster sensitivity for cultural norms* (Move 2.4). Invite your colleagues to share norms present in their cultural upbringing so as to develop empathy for the different ways people collaborate.

- *Break from fixed or imposed roles* (Move 2.10). Recognize how people box themselves and others into roles.

- *Share a story-moment* (Move 3.9). Build vulnerability-based trust and community when people of diverse backgrounds share personal histories.

- *Write a three-question agenda: Why? What? How?* (Move 4.2). Invite people from underrepresented groups or those with roles that offer a different lens than yours to help design and plan team meetings.

- *Prep the text, the reader, and yourself* (Move 4.10). Select texts that represent diverse perspectives to read with your team.

- *Foster equitable airtime* (Move 5.2). Discover ways to bolster the underrepresented voices at the table.

- *Call attention to an assumption* (Move 8.2). Point out thinking and behaviors grounded in bias.

- *Spotlight the minority viewpoint* (Move 8.12). Prevent groupthink (explained in Part II, Chapter 4) by emboldening people to speak who have views that differ from the majority.

Think like a teacher:

Zaretta Hammond (2015a), in her book *Culturally Responsive Teaching and the Brain*, makes us think more deeply about what we mean by inclusivity. Teachers in culturally responsive classrooms don't mold culturally or linguistically diverse students to fit into the mainstream culture, as others have historically done. Instead, they act as allies, acknowledging the reality of inequities in and out of school that make it challenging for students to feel as if they belong. They

PRIMARY INTENTION 3

empower these students to view their differences as assets, not something to be ashamed of or downplay in order to be accepted.

Be an ally to your colleagues, particularly those who identify in an underrepresented population. Even if you share things in common with them, be sensitive to the reality that their experiences in schools might differ from yours or those of others. Listen to them and encourage them to speak out.

Find the right words:

- *I appreciate that you hold a different perspective than others on the team. I welcome your voice in planning our conversation next week about . . .*

- *You have openly shared that you identify as . . . Would you be willing to share your experience with the team?*

- *Thank you for sharing with me that you don't feel included in our meetings because, as you say, you are "the only one at the table who is . . ." What would make you feel more supported and comfortable? Is there something I or others can do or stop doing?*

Related reading:

Move 8.12, "Spotlight the minority viewpoint." Make space in conversation to explore the viewpoints from people who are often underrepresented.

3.2 Instill a sense of belonging.

We know from the social psychology of groups (explored in Part II, Chapter 4) that adults, like children, need to feel accepted by their peers. People on high-functioning Q1 and Q2 teams have this foundation, which is built on community and trust. This is not to say that people on these teams accept all ideas all the time, but they are able to listen and debate ideas without judging or excluding the people who say them.

On the contrary, low-functioning Q3 and Q4 teams, known to have cliques on the team, link belonging to agreement. "You belong if you agree with what we think and say and how we do things." This dynamic especially occurs when one person is distinctly different from others in the group (e.g., one new teacher among veterans; one special educator among a group of general education teachers; one Black male educator among a group of white female educators; one independent schoolteacher among a group of public school teachers; one Generation X teacher among a team of Millennial teachers; etc.). Skillful team leaders (STLs) instill a sense of belonging, especially for those who don't feel accepted by the team.

How to instill a sense of belonging:

Do one or all of the following:

- Welcome new members into the group. Listen to and accept ways in which they might collaborate even if different from how your team typically functions.

- Empower any individuals who seem withdrawn. Explicitly express that you are glad they are on the team. If their behavior is not negatively impacting the group, then accept that they are adults who can set their own pace for group reentry and decide for themselves what participation looks like.

- Practice compassion (see Move 3.11). People cannot feel accepted when they are being judged. Model and encourage others to show compassion instead of judgment. No one should leave a meeting feeling "less than."

Think like a teacher:

You are likely familiar with Maslow's (1943) hierarchy of needs, which identifies a sense of belonging as one of the most basic necessities for children to reach their potential. As an effective teacher, you are intentional in how you interact with each child. You are particularly sensitive to students who are at risk of being ridiculed or marginalized. You create a climate where all children learn from and accept one another.

The fundamentals for nurturing an inclusive culture in your classroom also apply to the learning culture you lead with your colleagues. If you notice that someone withdraws from the group or is being excluded by others, think about how you help students feel a sense of belonging. Use what you know, but also give adults autonomy to fit in with others in ways that make sense for them.

Find the right words:

- *We are fortunate to welcome a new member to our group.*

- *Glad you are here.*

- *We are better because you are a member of our team.*

Related reading:

Move 1.6, "Accommodate adults with learning differences, disabilities, or preferences." Ensure your colleagues with learning differences or disabilities have access to what they need in a meeting to learn and belong.

BUILD COMMUNITY AND RELATIONAL TRUST THROUGH PLAY

Two Truths and a Lie, Would You Rather?, Human Knot, Build a Tower. I am not surprised if you have led one of these or a similar team-building game with your students. You don't need to be a drama teacher to know the value of team building. But do games like these have a place in team meetings?

Adult learners need bonding experiences and opportunities to build relationships just as much as younger learners, and play is a great way to achieve this. Tracy Brower (2019), a sociologist, cites a study by Brigham Young University that discovered adults who played together (granted, it was video games) boost their productivity by 20%. She names four benefits of teams engaging in play: (1) fostering innovation, (2) uniting a team, (3) allowing people to bring other parts of themselves to the group, and (4) helping reduce stress. I'm not advocating that you and your team play *Fortnite*, but games can foster community and trust in ways that discussion cannot. Skillful team leaders (STLs) are extremely intentional in which games they choose, for what purpose, and when and how they lead them.

STL moves:

3.3 Plan play strategically.

3.4 Frame the game.

3.5 Level up language.

3.6 Give simple directions.

3.7 Do a demo.

3.8 Lead community- and trust-building games.

What these moves promote:

Community. People bond over common experiences and group accomplishments.

Relational trust. People get to know one another beyond their professional roles and form connections.

Diversity. People are encouraged to share their diverse opinions, beliefs, perspectives, and experiences.

Empathy. People develop new understandings about colleagues who are different from them.

When to use these moves:

At the beginning of a team's course of collaboration; to launch a meeting; to break up a lengthy meeting.

3.3 Plan play strategically.

If you have ever participated in a community trust-building game in which you were confused about what to do or uncomfortable beyond a healthy stretch point, if you felt unsafe or misunderstood during a "trust" game, or if you just felt like the game was an utter waste of time, then you know that facilitation matters. Games are a great tool to build trust and relations, but only if you are thoughtful about why you are playing the game and how. Skillful team leaders (STLs) plan play strategically.

How to plan play strategically:

Consider the purpose for playing the game, timing and duration, how the game connects to the rest of your meeting, how you will structure the game, and what you'll need to prepare in advance of leading the game with your colleagues. (Note: All games referenced in this section are described in Move 3.8.)

- *Purpose.* Match your game to your intended purpose. Different games are intended to bring about different outcomes. For instance, Two Truths and a Lie is intended to build relationships and break down assumptions that we have of one another by sharing personal information with each other. Human Knot is a team-building game in which people must work together to accomplish something. Don't play something just because it's fun.

- *Timing.* Decide the best time to lead a game so that it does not interrupt the "meat" of the meeting.

- *Duration.* With so little time in the day, some of your colleagues might understandably bristle at the idea of using 45 minutes to collaboratively build a dry noodle bridge. Plan how long you will run the game, ensuring it does not eat up too much time. Many sharing-out games, such as Shamelessly Brag and You Might Know, can be modified to reduce playtime so that only one person shares at the beginning of each meeting over several meetings.

- *Content connection.* Connect the game to the content of your work whenever possible so that the game is not perceived as unrelated to the work of the meeting.

- *Structure.* Consider how much people need to participate, and decide what structure will best allow for that—whole team or smaller groups, heterogeneous or homogeneous groupings, and so on.

- *Preparation.* Have all materials at the ready including a demo if you are going to do one.

3.4 Frame the game.

Adult learners want to know why they are doing something (see Part II, Chapter 5). Whether they're doing one of the community- and trust-building games in this chapter or leading one of the exercises in Primary Intention 8 aimed at engaging people in analytical thinking, skillful team leaders (STLs) avoid jumping straight into playing a game. They frame it so that people's questions are answered and they know what to expect.

How to frame the game:

Communicate your intended purpose upfront. Manage expectations particularly when a game requires people to be vulnerable. Give people a heads-up when an exercise might surface disagreement or a difficult conversation so your colleagues are mentally prepared. Review norms such as suspending judgment of others, agreeing to disagree without being disagreeable, and responding with cultural sensitivity. Set the expectation that no one will be asked to share something they don't want to, and if someone does share something deeply personal, get people to agree to keep confidentiality and be supportive. Also, preview any speed bumps people might experience when playing the game.

In action:

Walter: We are going to do an exercise called For vs. Against.* In this game, you and your partner must decide who will argue for the mystery statement and who will argue against it. Some of you might be tempted to break the rules of the exercise and switch sides. Please encourage each other to fight this urge and stick to the rules of the game. This exercise is intended to encourage flexible thinking.

STL recommendation:

Replace "touchy-feely" with authenticity. Not going to lie. When I'm on a new team and asked to divulge personal information, I tend to tense up, particularly if I'm not certain of the team leader's skill in leading this type of discussion. I worry it's going to get overly emotional where I feel like I'm in therapy, or I'll be told to hug it out with a colleague. You will likely have members on your team who feel like I do. Games that call on people to be vulnerable can get touchy-feely, but you don't have to lead them that way. Be aware of people's body language. Notice their level of comfort. You want people to reveal information and be vulnerable without feeling naked. If there is any unwillingness to share, reframe the game simply as a means of "truth telling."

*For vs. Against is a game described in Move 8.11.

Find the right words:

- *Here's what we are going to play, and here's what you can expect.*

- *I chose activity X. It requires people to Y. Is anyone not comfortable with that?*

Related reading:

Part II, Chapter 5, "Five Must-Knows About Adult Learners." Framing the game fits in with one of the adult-learning principles explored in this chapter— that adults need to know *why* they are doing something.

3.5 Level up language.

Many community-building games that you play with students can be played by adults, but know your audience and lead the game in a professional manner so that no one feels as if they are being treated like a child. Gen Xers and Boomers can be particularly sensitive to this. Often it's not the activity that they take issue with, but instead it's the name you called it. (I knew a team leader who got a very negative response when she asked high school teachers to make "name tents," a practice used with elementary school students.) Skillful team leaders (STLs) level up language so that what they present has a better chance of being well received.

How to level up language:

Before speaking, think about words that could trigger a negative response from your colleagues. Adults do not want to be treated as students. When you can, use simple but different phrasing and signals to your colleagues. Even the right words can be off-putting with the wrong tone. Watch that your voice is not condescending. Avoid sounding condescending by speaking with respect and humility. Sometimes you can begin with "You might already do this . . ." If you must use the same wording that you use with students, couch it with a disclaimer if you are concerned people will be sensitive to it. For example, "I know we are adults, but because we are a large group I'm going to use this signal that I use with students to get your attention."

In action:

Dominique is a principal team leader who wants teachers to rely on one another. When she was a teacher, she would tell her students, "Ask three before you ask me," but she does not want to use that language with teachers because some might view that as her treating them like students.

Dominique:	Please work this out with your colleagues, first, before checking in with me.

STL recommendations:

Trust matters. I shared the following quote in the introduction to Primary Intention 3: "In a high-trust relationship, you can say the wrong thing, and people will still get your meaning. In a low-trust relationship, you can be very measured, even precise, and they'll still misinterpret you" (Covey, 2006). This especially holds true in picking your words when working with adult learners. If you work in a high-trust Q1 or Q2 team where relational trust is present, you likely don't need to be as sensitive to the language you use because there is less of a chance of someone taking offense to it. You have the advantage of people trusting your intentions. However, if you lead a Q3 or Q4 team, you need to build relational trust as well as carefully choose your words.

Practice cultural sensitivity. There are a number of commonly used American expressions that are now being challenged because of their racist or sexist origins. Many articles have recently been written on the subject. Educate yourself on the history of particular expressions and commit to not using them as a team. If you or someone else does say one, just clarify the intent behind the words, and find a way to say it differently. You might opt to respectfully call attention to a phrase if someone uses it regularly (see Move 8.2).

Find the right words:

- *Turn to the person next to you.* (Instead of *Turn and talk.*)

- *Partner up.* (Instead of *Find a buddy.*)

- *Let's get started.* (Instead of *Settle down.*)

- *Am I making sense?* (Instead of *Do you follow me?*)

- *Please pause your conversation and come back to the group.* (Instead of *If you can hear me, clap once.*)

- *I recently learned that that phrase has racist connotations. The history behind it is . . . I've said it and certainly meant nothing negative by it; however, let's choose to say something else.* (In response to an expression with racist overtones.)

3.6 Give simple directions.

Sometimes team games don't go wrong because people aren't willing to play; they go wrong because people simply don't understand what they are supposed to be doing. It's not just students in the classroom who need explicit directions. Skillful team leaders (STLs) recognize that adult learners, too, need simple understandable directions to avoid confusion.

How to give simple directions:

Be clear and succinct in verbal directions and check for understanding. If directions are complicated, write them out so people can refer to them throughout the game. (Teachers like this, too, because then they can modify the game to play with their students.)

STL recommendations:

Practice in advance. Practice saying directions alone out loud before you lead the game with your colleagues.

Play with your students. Many community- and trust-building games can be played with people of any age. Before you lead a game with your colleagues for the first time, try it out with your students. It will strengthen the bonds in your classroom and help you work out any glitches in the game before leading it with your peers who might be less forgiving of unclear directions.

Google it. There are so many community- and trust-building activities online. Search for what you want and borrow language that is recommended, or watch a video of someone explaining the game. The clearer you are in how to play, the clearer your communication will be.

Don't assume. Teachers are often familiar with many of the icebreaker-type activities because they do them with students, but it's still worth a quick review of directions as there are many iterations of these games and you want to avoid confusion. For instance, I've seen Would You Rather? played sometimes where people move across the room, other times where people partner up, and still other times where people drop pom-poms in the bucket of their choice.

3.7 Do a demo.

Depending on the complexity of the game, people can benefit from a quick demonstration or a practice run just to make sure they understand what to do. For example, Count to 20 (see Move 3.8) is a game that has particular rules about not having people call out a number at the same time or in a repetitive sequence, and this rule is often easier to grasp when you see it modeled. Skillful team leaders (STLs) take a moment to demo a game before a group plays it.

How to do a demo:

If you are about to play a game that requires two or more people, or model a strategy that others will practice, demonstrate with a willing colleague. Be explicit in pointing out any specific moves you made during the demo. Check for understanding or invite people to ask clarifying questions before they go off to play or practice on their own.

STL recommendation:

Prep a partner. If a game is complex, select one colleague in advance with whom you can do the demo. Review what you will do together so that your partner is not caught off-guard when modeling in front of your colleagues.

Show a video. You can find anything on the internet these days including tons of groups playing community- and team-building games. You might opt to show a clip to your colleagues before they play, particularly if the game is complex. Show just enough of people playing for your colleagues to get the gist.

3.8 Lead community- and trust-building games.

Over the following pages, I share some popular games that build community and relational trust. They are presented in alphabetical order.

Count to 20

A community-building game that fosters group cohesiveness and builds relational trust.

Prep: None.

Group size: One or many groups of 5–7 people. Groups of fewer than 5 people do not work.

Playtime: 10 minutes.

How to play: The object of the game is to count aloud sequentially to 20 as a group. All members of a group stand in a line or circle. Without planning or signaling, someone starts the game by calling out the number 1. Play continues with people spontaneously calling out the next sequential number—2, 3, 4, and so on. If two or more players call out a number at the same time, then the team must reset and start back at 1. A new person must begin the count each time. No one is allowed to plan the order in which they will call out or signal someone to speak, and it is best to avoid eye contact. People must sense when it is a good time to speak and when they should hold back. Team members will feel a great sense of accomplishment and a bond after they have completed the challenge.

Variations: If counting to 20 seems like an impossible task, ask team members to count as high as they can and try to beat their own score each time they play. If counting up to 20 is too easy for your group, challenge them by counting backward. If you have a large group, break into small groups with no more than 8 and no fewer than 5 people per group.

Group Problem-Solving Tasks

There are so many engaging tasks that call on people to problem solve as a group for the purpose of surfacing diverse approaches. Popular choices include Build a Tower, Construct a Bridge, and Human Knot.

Group size: One or many groups with a minimum of 5 people, and a maximum of 12, in each group. Human Knot is better with many people.

Prep: Most of these activities require prep of materials. For example, in Construct a Bridge you need dry pasta and sticky tape.

Playtime: Most of these activities take up a significant chunk of your meeting time because most tasks take at least 20 minutes plus time to debrief the game.

How to play: You can find directions to any of these games with a quick online search for "team-building activities," "problem-solving group games," or "cooperative games." Because all the games require a group to work together, you can anticipate conflict occurring. This is good. You want people to work through it, but first make sure you frame the game (Move 3.4) so they know what to expect.

Identity Circle

A community builder that strengthens relational trust by revealing points in common.

Prep: None.

Group size: Any.

Playtime: 10 seconds per round.

How to play: Form a circle with one person at the center and ask that person to reveal a personal statement—for example, "I'm afraid of heights." Anyone who is also, in this case, afraid of heights joins that person at the center of the circle. Then the game resets by having all players do a mad dash to any marked spot in the outer circle. (There should be enough spots for all but one of the players.) The player who is without a spot in the outer circle ends up in the middle, where they reveal a personal statement, and play continues. Play several rounds until everyone has had a chance to participate.

Variations:

Eliminate movement. If you lack space or want team members to remain seated, then have team members move pawns, such as monopoly tokens, on a makeshift game board with a dot inside a circle. Rules are the same except instead of people getting up to move, they move their pawns.

Up the stakes. When giving directions, announce that you will play three rounds with prompts. Each prompt will ask people to share something more revealing.

Round 1: Name something you like (e.g., "I like chocolate").

Round 2: Share a personal fact (e.g., "I am ambidextrous").

Round 3: Share a personal struggle, challenge, or failing experience (e.g., "I struggle with multitasking").

Keep each round to about 2 minutes, and be careful that no one begins storytelling, or people will be standing for too long. When the team meeting is over, people will likely want to connect with one another about some things that were said. This is great because people are building connections beyond the minutes of a meeting.

Penny Memory

A community builder that strengthens relational and vulnerability-based trust through personal stories and memorable events.

Prep: Pennies dated no later than the birth of the oldest person on the team.

Group size: One or many groups of 2–7 people.

Playtime: Up to 1 minute per person.

How to play: Each player selects a coin from a pile, reads the date, and shares a memory from that year if they can. If they can't, they pick another penny.

Variation: One coin is chosen, and all players share a memory from that year.

Personal Object

A community builder that strengthens relational and vulnerability-based trust through personal stories and memorable events.

Prep: People can bring an object from home or from their classroom, or spontaneously choose something on their person (optional).

Group size: One or many groups of 2–7 people.

Playtime: 1 minute per person.

How to play: People pull an item from their bag, on their person, or from their classroom or home, and tell a story about why that piece is meaningful to them. Think show-and-tell, but for adults.

Variation: Play with partners or in trios to cut back on time.

Shamelessly Brag

A community-building game in which members of a team who know each other learn surprising things about one another.

Prep: None.

Group size: Any.

Playtime: Up to 1 minute per person.

How to play: Each person takes up to 1 minute to shamelessly brag about an event, demonstrating something they are good at. It can be as significant a story as the person wants to reveal. I've heard one person share that they climbed Mount Everest, while another "bragged" about eating a whole pint of ice cream in one sitting. All answers are worthy.

Variation: Play with partners or in trios to cut back on time.

Two Truths and a Lie

A community-building game in which members learn things about each other that they may not otherwise have known.

Prep: None.

Group size: Best played in groups of 3–5 people.

Playtime: Approximately 1–2 minutes per person.

How to play: Ask people to silently write down three facts about themselves; two must be true, and one must be false. Have people read the facts off in random order. Other members of the group then guess which "fact" is a lie. Play continues until each person in the group has shared.

Would You Rather? (aka This or That?)

A community-building game in which members of a team learn what they have in common with other people.

Prep: Choose prompts that lend themselves to a binary choice. Create slides so people can read the choices.

Group size: Any.

Playtime: Any; however, playing up to 8 rounds, each at about 30 seconds, is good so people don't fatigue of the game.

How to play: Display a "Would you rather . . . ?" choice statement. Ask people to walk to opposite sides of the room based on their preference. Without discussion, have people do the same for the next statement until all are complete.

Variations: Cafés often have a version of this game as a tip jar. It poses two options, one over each jar, and people place their tip on the side that indicates their preference. Instead of money, you can have people use paper clips or craft pom-poms. For example, "Place your pom-pom in the left jar if you are a morning person, or in the right jar if you are a night owl."

You Might Know

A community-building game in which members of a team who know each other learn surprising things about one another.

Prep: Approach team members outside of the meeting and write down their responses.

Group size: Any.

Playtime: Up to 5 minutes per round.

How to play: It's easiest to understand how this game is played with an example. The facilitator reads from a prompt:

You might know that [Amanda is a teachers' union representative].

You might not know that [Amanda grows orchids].

[Amanda] might not know that someone said this about her: ["Amanda is a true problem solver. She listens carefully, highlights perspectives I don't always see, and gives spot-on advice."]

Before your team meets, approach one team member privately. Ask them to share one fact that people would know about them, and one fact that people would likely not know about them. Then approach a different person from the team (in private before your team meets) and ask them to say a kind specific statement about the first person. Write all responses on a card using the following three prompts:

1. *You might know that [person's name] . . .*

2. *You might not know that [person's name] . . .*

3. *[Person's name] might not know that someone said this about them: . . .*

When you are ready to play this game with your team, read off the responses you gathered. (Note: Because you will be speaking about a colleague in the third person while that person is present, just check that you are using their preferred personal pronoun—*he, she, they,* etc.).

Variations:

Keep names anonymous and see if team members can guess who the person is. (Note: Because guessing adds time to the game, be sure it's the move you want to make.)

Invite vulnerability. When you ask a person to share something others might not know about them, invite them to offer up a struggle. Double-check with them to be sure they understand that what they tell you will be shared publicly with the team.

Example:

You might know that this person has been teaching for 12 years.

You might not know that this person is dyslexic.

This person might not know that someone said this about them: "This person is able to bring out the best in students. They connect with students in a way that motivates them to learn about science. I want to learn better from this person how to spark that excitement in my students."

STRENGTHEN A CULTURE OF VULNERABILITY-BASED TRUST

"Get naked." This was popular advice (not literal, of course) given to people on teams in business, encouraging them to be vulnerable with one another. The framing never resonated with me, though. It makes sense to strip away the protective layers that keep you from learning together, but it seems "getting naked" with peers would only make people uncomfortable and self-conscious to the point where they couldn't learn.

I prefer Brené Brown's (2021a) "take off the armor" analogy, as shared in an episode of her podcast *Dare to Lead*. The armor we wear protects us from what we gravely fear or mistrust—an internal or external threat. She names three types of armor people most commonly put on:

- *Perfectionism:* Do everything right, and no one can judge or blame you.

- *Numbing:* Avoid feeling pain by engaging in things like overworking, isolating, overeating, excessive drinking, or drugs.

- *Foreboding joy:* Do not allow yourself to be too happy for fear of being let down (SXSWedu, 2017).

Teams that have a culture of vulnerability-based trust remove their armor. They have what is known as psychological safety, a group phenomenon in which each member of the group is able to "show and employ one's self without fear of negative consequences of self-image, status or career" (Kahn, 1990, p. 708). They know they can share their struggles and their colleagues will not judge or humiliate them. Vulnerability-based trust is essential for teams to tackle challenges together (TEDxTalks, 2014).

Skillful team leaders (STLs) strengthen a culture of vulnerability-based trust in a group.

STL moves:

3.9 Share a story-moment.

3.10 Make struggle visible.

3.11 Practice compassion.

What these moves promote:

Community. People bond over common experiences.

Vulnerability-based trust. People take risks sharing their struggles and challenges.

Diversity. People are encouraged to share their diverse opinions, beliefs, perspectives, and experiences.

Empathy. People develop new understandings about colleagues who are different from them.

When to use these moves:

Throughout a team's course of inquiry and learning.

Related readings:

Move 9.6, "Strengthen vulnerability-based trust for peer observation." Explore specific strategies to help you and your colleagues embrace peer observations.

Move 10.9, "Admit missteps." A key way to foster vulnerability-based trust among your colleagues is by modeling your own vulnerability. Admitting your own missteps is a great way to do this.

3.9 Share a story-moment.

Teachers had a different view of me as a literacy coach when they learned that reading and writing were hard for me as a child. When a teacher on my team revealed that he had experienced post-traumatic stress disorder in the Vietnam War, I had a little better understanding as to why he was extremely passionate about being a history teacher. When a second-career teacher shared that she left her high-paying profession to teach but now felt completely out of her element because teaching is not what she expected, her colleagues suddenly saw her as a learner, not just someone who couldn't control her class. When a Black teacher shared at a table of white colleagues that she had attended a school in a high-poverty neighborhood where staff turnover was high and opportunities for students were limited, teachers on the team felt a wealth of emotions, and connected with her commitment to equity.

It is surprisingly difficult for many adults to talk about their upbringing or their early learning experiences publicly, particularly when those experiences were challenging, but when they do, they tend to feel more connected to one another. Patrick Lencioni (2002) suggests that the act of sharing personal histories builds psychological safety within a group. Skillful team leaders (STLs) facilitate an activity in which people share story-moments that are hard to reveal—those stories that risk judgment from others—but, when shared, build vulnerability-based trust.

How to share a story-moment:

Prep: You may want to give people a heads-up so they can think in advance of a story to share.

Group size: Any (although smaller groups are more intimate, which can help people feel more comfortable sharing personal histories).

Playtime: 2–5 minutes per story.

How to play: Establish ground rules. Review norms for potentially difficult conversations (Move 2.6). Emphasize the rule of listening without interruption and keeping confidence after people share. (Nothing will break trust on your team faster than if someone blabs to others the story one member just told your team.) Then simply invite people who are ready to tell their story. You might opt to go first to break the ice. Finally, honor the storyteller by thanking them for trusting the group with their story.

Variation: Apply to your inquiry work. Powerful connections can be made when people share histories of themselves as students. WestEd's Reading Apprenticeship recommends that teachers looking to see their students improve as readers reflect upon and share their own personal reading histories with one another and with their students (see WestEd, 2016). If your team aims to lower students' math anxiety, you might invite people to share stories about their own growing-up and school experiences with math.

Think like a teacher:

In the classroom, personal storytelling is a powerful method for developing understanding between teacher and students and students and students. Hearing someone's story, or learning about a person in a different way from what you might expect, fosters empathy and builds community and trust. Students see English learners differently when they learn they had to endure a difficult immigration to this country. If, as a teacher, you have ever shared your struggles from your own school days with your students, I'm sure you noticed they were captivated by your every word as they began to see you in a different light than before. The moment you or your students share a personal story, you show vulnerability, and when people respond with empathy, trust is built.

Similarly, when adults on your team share stories about challenge, hardship, resilience, and so on, people connect and bond.

STL recommendation:

Be prepared. Sometimes people share stories that are difficult to hear. I was once at a company retreat with a very large group of people who did not all know one another, with a facilitator we did not know, when someone revealed through many tears that her dad was an alcoholic. The facilitator was thrown off-guard and did not know how to respond, and it made everyone in the room feel very uncomfortable. It takes a highly skilled team leader to manage this level of disclosure, and I am not convinced that personal sharing on a team needs to get to such depth in order for people to develop empathy for one another. Prepare yourself for whatever is shared, and skillfully bring closure to a highly emotionally charged conversation with a simple acknowledgement of the person's vulnerability and a reminder to the group that they are in charge of how much or how little they wish to share.

Find the right words:

- **Establish ground rules:**
  - *Let's listen with compassion. Let's agree to maintain confidentiality. Each person's story is theirs to share outside of our team, if they so choose, not ours. Can we agree to these things?*

- **Honor the storyteller:**
  - *Thank you for sharing your personal story. It might not have been easy to tell, but we appreciate your trusting us with it.*

3.10 Make struggle visible.

Can you imagine the story of *The Old Man and the Sea* if Hemingway (1952) hadn't written about the multitude of struggles Santiago faced? Or if, instead of making a movie about *Apollo* 13 in which NASA had to figure out how to get the astronauts back safely to Earth after an oxygen tank failed, they made a movie about my last uneventful flight to North Carolina? Hearing about real dilemmas doesn't just make a story interesting; it engages us in thought and problem solving. It fosters empathy and helps us reflect on our own challenges. It builds vulnerability-based trust on a team. Skillful team leaders (STLs) make their own struggles visible and call upon others to do so as well.

How to make struggle visible:

Invite your colleagues to show struggles they and their students have by telling stories, inviting peers to observe them teach, and examining student data together. Validate the hardships and show appreciation. Dive deeper into understanding the challenge or begin to problem solve together.

In action:

Alika: What's a struggle you face right now?

Teacher 1: I just can't get my ninth graders to do homework. I came into this job with such high expectations of kids. I read all about how teachers in high-poverty, underperforming schools have low expectations for kids, and I swore I'd never be that teacher. And yet, day after day, more and more students—capable students—just don't do homework. Maybe they didn't get homework in middle school and aren't used to it, or maybe their families aren't able to support them in doing it. I'm just so tired of them not doing it, and me nagging them or penalizing them, that I'm tempted to stop assigning it. If they aren't going to do it anyway, I feel like I'm just creating a stressful culture.

Alika: You've hit upon the complexity of this work. This is also a struggle for me.

Teacher 2:	For me, too. This conversation is making me realize that I give less homework now than I did in previous years because it's just not worth the fight.
Teacher 3:	My students do the homework, but I guess it's because I've lowered my expectations of them. I think I'm settling for being happy if they just do something, so I don't assign anything too challenging or time-consuming.
Alika:	Thanks for opening up. I'm hearing a few questions emerge from these real struggles: *What things do we have control over that might be contributing to students not doing homework? How do repeated experiences where students don't meet our expectations influence our expectations of them?* Next meeting, let's bring in a recent homework assignment that students didn't complete or did poorly on, with a lesson plan or video clip of students learning how to do it.

Think like a teacher:

One of the best pieces of advice I read that helped me grow as a writing teacher was from Kelly Gallagher (2011), who essentially said, *Don't spend hours sweating out a model essay at home and then only show students your perfect piece the next day. Write live in front of them. They learn more from seeing how you wrestle through the struggles of writing than seeing a perfect piece of writing presented to them.*

As a teacher, you might lead a think-aloud that shows how hard it is for you to organize what you want to say, or read a challenging text aloud to students to demonstrate how you work through passages that are difficult to comprehend. You might wrestle with a complex math story problem live, or show your students your first iteration of an engineering project you undertook gone wrong. Or, you might share stories with your students of the learning hardships you had to overcome when you were in school.

Just as you make your struggles visible to your students so that they can relate to you and learn how to overcome their own, so can you do with your colleagues. Live peer observation (Moves 9.1–9.6) is a great way to make struggle visible.

Find the right words:

- *Is anyone willing to share an example of a situation that didn't go well?*

- *What dilemma are you struggling with now? What can you show that would make that struggle visible?*

- *I'll go first. My mini-lesson "flopped." Here's what's challenging . . . I am interested in hearing your perspective.*

3.11 Practice compassion.

A number of programs that help individuals go through a significant change (e.g., WW [formerly known as Weight Watchers] and Alcoholics Anonymous) offer support group meetings. Now imagine if you went to one of these meetings, you shared something challenging, and everyone judged you for it. You probably wouldn't speak up again. Passing judgment is a normal human response, almost instinctual, but no one on your team will be vulnerable in their practice if they feel judged. Skillful team leaders (STLs) and their teams practice compassion to encourage vulnerability.

A compassionate response isn't holding a "pity party" for someone or enabling them. It doesn't replace being a critical thought partner, and it definitely doesn't give anyone a pass to speak or act in ways that are harmful to students. The Dalai Lama (2019) describes compassion as "concern for others' well-being." It is similar to empathy in that you aim to stand in another person's shoes, but different in that you may not ever come to fully understand what the person is experiencing. Yet, it's worthwhile to do because simply expressing compassion for another person tells them you care, and this can be enough to let someone begin to trust you.

How to practice compassion:

Anstiss and colleagues (2020) believe you can build compassion. They offer three suggestions to teams:

1. Notice your feelings of compassion toward people you love, close friends, family members, and loved pets. "Then extend this 'circle of compassion' towards mere acquaintances and strangers. And then, perhaps, to people you actively dislike."

2. Shift from your own silo perspective to seeing how you and others need to work together for the greater good.

3. Practice self-compassion. Be kind and forgiving to yourself, without compromising high self-expectations.

Notice signs that someone might feel judged by you. This could look like withdrawal, guardedness, or avoidance of failure. Then reflect on any judgment you might be projecting. Where is it coming from? (Your own insecurity or jealousy?) Lead an inner monologue in which you challenge yourself to remain compassionate in your response. Communicate that you care while simultaneously maintaining the high expectations you and your colleague share.

In action:

Teacher: How am I supposed to keep pace with my curriculum if I now need to teach about colonial times from Indigenous peoples' perspective? There's just too much to cover.

Paul: [Silently recognizes his visceral response is judgment: *This teacher is more concerned about fitting things into her lesson plans than presenting an inclusive curriculum?! How can I view this question through a compassionate lens? Where is this teacher coming from? Am I able to express concern for their well-being while simultaneously staying true to the values behind this change?*] I hear your concern about pacing. It's hard to change curriculum. I also recognize the real pressure to "fit everything in." I don't think you are alone. We need to support one another through this change to figure out questions like this that require us to manage our classrooms differently so that we can present an inclusive curriculum.

Think like a teacher:

Why do we say to our students, "There's no such thing as a stupid question"? We want to create a safe space where they can learn. When students feel judged by you or their peers, or when they feel they don't belong in the conversation, they typically withdraw or push back. Even if you are not judging students, so long as they perceive that you are, their engagement changes. But when you show compassion to students, you preserve your relationship and build trust so they will be open to learning.

Regardless of learners' age (child, teen, or adult), they will have questions, ideas, and wonderings that are not yet fully formed. They may even say things that are culturally insensitive or offend someone. If you can offer a compassionate response instead of a judgmental one, your colleagues will more likely be open to learning.

STL recommendations:

Approach with a "beginner's mind." The Zen Buddhist concept known as *shoshin*, or "the beginner's mind," teaches you to approach what you already know as if you're learning it for the first time (Suzuki, 1970). Let go of preconceived notions and remain curious. This approach also helps you practice compassion with people who are actual beginners at something that you already have expertise in. Recognize that everyone is on their own learning continuum. A person needs permission to be a beginner, just like you were at one point. This can be tough to remember when you have lived and breathed for years what this person is now just learning.

Reflect back to when you were learning something for the first time. Think back to the questions, confusions, and needs you had then, as well as the misguided thinking and errors you were permitted to make and learn from. Key point: Being a beginner is not carte blanche to express harmful words and actions. The only way for beginners to learn is by having compassionate people around them to guide their new way of learning and doing.

Accept overly sensitive people. "That person is too sensitive." Maybe some people are hypersensitive by nature, but it is also long recognized that "the more people expose their thoughts and feelings the more vulnerable they become to the reactions of others" (Anderson, 1997). Expect people to be sensitive when you are engaged in conversations that require vulnerability-based trust. It's not uncommon to hear someone say something like "I'm sorry. Was that OK to share?" or to learn that people had a meeting after the meeting because they were worried about how they came across. Convey compassion and stay confident that these conversations are an indication that you are on track to becoming a high-functioning, high-impact team because it means people are being vulnerable—and that's when learning happens.

Find common ground through mission. If you are honestly not judging people yet they think you are, show compassion for their feelings and reconnect to the focus of your shared, joint mission.

Find the right thoughts:

With this move, it's actually less about what you say and more about what you think as you listen to people. Consider asking yourself these questions when you notice yourself judging what someone has said or done:

- *What would happen if I showed this person compassion right now? Am I able to do that at this time? If not, what makes it hard for me to show compassion right now?*

- *Am I able to express concern for this person's well-being while simultaneously staying true to my values? If not, what can I say, and how can I say it in a way that won't shut this person out of the conversation?*

Amy Gallo (2020) offers two additional powerful thinking frames for practicing compassion in her article "What Your Co-Workers Need Right Now Is Compassion":

- *We have different ways of coping with uncertainty, grief, and stress.*

- *Others are under pressures that I don't always see and can't fully understand (and probably aren't entirely my business).*

Related reading:

Move 2.4, "Foster sensitivity to cultural norms." A great time to practice compassion is when listening to others share cultural norms that are different from your own.

Primary Intention

Design and Plan Learning: Work Plans, Agendas, and Protocols

4

Design requires intention. Landscape designers lay out backyards, engineers design prototypes, set designers stage the look of a production, and teachers design engaging and challenging learning for children. So why wouldn't team leaders intentionally design meetings?

Skillful team leaders (STLs) don't just plan meetings; they design collaborative learning experiences. From the team's overarching work plan to the details of what the team does during a meeting, STLs craft purposeful agendas with clear intended outcomes. Thought is given to the readings and protocols that the team will engage with. Tasks are appropriately challenging and explained clearly. Materials are thoughtfully prepared and organized so that the meeting runs smoothly. Attention given to design and planning sets the team up for learning.

Contents

---

*Text *refers to the written word, such as books, articles, excerpts, and studies, and to audio/visual texts, such as podcasts, videos, graphs, charts, slide shows, and pictures.*

4.10 Prep the text, the reader, and yourself.

4.11 Build a collaborative reading habit.

Tools and templates:

Figure 12: STL Team Inquiry Work Plan Guiding Questions

Figure 13: STL Team Inquiry Work Plan Template

Figure 14: STL Team Inquiry Work Plan Example

Figure 15: STL Three-Question Agenda Template

Figure 16: STL Three-Question Agenda Examples

Figure 17: Team Meeting Intended Outcome Language Stems

Figure 18: Multi-Grade Team Meeting Intended Outcome Language Stems

Figure 19: Protocols by Purpose

Related reading:

Part II, Chapter 5, "Five Must-Knows About Adult Learners." Revisit this chapter when designing learning experiences for adults so that your colleagues get the most out of team meetings.

PLAN PURPOSEFUL MEETINGS

Look, I get it. Agendas are likely not something you care to think deeply about. But when you do—when you intentionally *craft* your agenda—you have a better meeting. It's not uncommon to find a low-functioning, low-impact Q3 team without an agenda, or with a thrown-together list of bulleted topics on a page posing as an agenda, such as this:

Agenda:

☑ *Welcome*

☑ *Concerns*

☑ *Upcoming assembly*

Does that look a little too familiar? It's understandable. When people are planning anything, even a day of errands, they often think in terms of categories, such as these:

☑ *Dry cleaners*

☑ *Post office*

☑ *Gas*

But a meeting agenda is more than a to-do list. It serves as a tool to organize time, keep people on task, and act as a record-keeping document to capture notes—essentials for teams to function well. It's also a tool for impact. It calls on leaders to be clear about what people will meet about, why, and how. Skillful team leaders (STLs) design and plan a meeting with specific outcomes in mind. Your colleagues might not notice a well-designed agenda, but they'll notice when there isn't one.

STL moves:

4.1 Draft a team inquiry work plan.

4.2 Write a three-question agenda: Why? What? How?

4.3 Open a meeting to activate learning.

4.4 Close a meeting to establish next steps for learning.

Tools and templates:

Figure 12: STL Team Inquiry Work Plan Guiding Questions

Figure 13: STL Team Inquiry Work Plan Template

Figure 14: STL Team Inquiry Work Plan Example

Figure 15: STL Three-Question Agenda Template

Figure 16: STL Three-Question Agenda Examples

Figure 17: Team Meeting Intended Outcome Language Stems

Figure 18: Multi-Grade Team Meeting Intended Outcome Language Stems

What these moves promote:

Focus. Meetings are designed around intended outcomes.

Clarity. Everyone, whether they have helped write the agenda or not, is clear about why they are meeting and what they must accomplish in the given time.

Productivity. STLs structure meetings in a way that doesn't squander time.

Engagement. STLs design engaging learning experiences.

Assessment. The agenda serves as a tool to check that outcomes were reached.

When to use these moves:

During planning.

4.1 Draft a team inquiry work plan.

Some people want a plan and like to know where a team is headed—reasonable. Skillful team leaders (STLs) draft a work plan for the group shortly after a team formulates an inquiry question or student-learning goal. (See the moves in Primary Intention 6.) Similar to a curriculum map for a teaching unit, a work plan offers the team a preliminary road map for their course of collaboration. This plan is a living document that evolves as the team moves through collaborative inquiry.

How to draft a team inquiry work plan:

If you choose to draft a team inquiry work plan, you can use the questions listed in Figure 12 as a guide or use the template in Figure 13. (An example is also available in Figure 14.)

FIGURE 12   STL Team Inquiry Work Plan Guiding Questions

NOTE: Some questions, particularly those listed later in the inquiry cycle, cannot be planned too far in advance, but you can record your decisions as you go.

Team:

- Who is on our team?

Meeting logistics, roles, and projected timeline:

- How many meetings do we plan to hold, and on what dates?
- Where do we intend for meetings to take place? (Include room numbers, if applicable.)
- Who plans on taking responsibility for meeting tasks and learning roles, and on which dates?
- What is our projected focus for each meeting? Where do we hope to be in the inquiry cycle on that day?

Norms for collaboration:

- What group agreements/norms does our school have in place?
- What group agreements/norms do we intend to adopt?
- What personal norms, if any, do we intend to keep?

Ask & Aim

- What district/school/department/grade-level priority do we intend to align our work to?
- What student-centered challenge do we plan to tackle, and what does it look like now?
- What inquiry question do we intend to pursue?

Assess & Analyze

- What assessments do we plan to give students to further our understanding of their challenge? Do we plan on using an existing assessment, or will we need to create one? If the latter, who will create it, what tasks will students be given, and in what format? What do we intend to do to optimize assessment conditions for students so that we get an authentic read on where they are at?
- (Once inquiry is underway) What findings result from our data analysis? What specific challenges or new questions emerge?

Target & Plan

- What bite-sized student-centered goal do we plan to target?
- What student-performance goals do we expect to reach, and how do we plan to monitor progress?
- What teaching-practice goals do we plan to reach, and how will we monitor progress?

Research & Study

- What texts do we plan to read/view together?
- What strategies do we intend to learn about and practice?

Strategize & Design

- What strategies do we intend to try, and when?
- Who plans on demonstrating strategies for others to observe?
- Who plans to bring in student data, and when?
- How do we plan on measuring effectiveness of what we implement?

Act & Evaluate

The following questions can't be planned in advance, but are useful for recording decisions made.

- What did we implement, and when did we do it?
- What were the effects of what we implemented (a) on student learning and (b) on teacher practice?
- What key findings did we conclude?
- What new questions emerged that we may want to further pursue?

FIGURE 13   STL Team Inquiry Work Plan Template

	OUR TEAM

LOGISTICS, ROLES & PROJECTED TIMELINE

Date	Time	Location	Note-taker	Timekeeper	Food	Learning lead*	Projected focus for this meeting

*The "learning lead" can be responsible for bringing in a reading, bringing in student work, modeling a lesson, asking probing questions, calling out bias or assumptions, facilitating data talk, trying a strategy with students, cross-collaborating with others, and so on.

NORMS FOR COLLABORATION

Expectations and agreements for working together as a high-functioning, high-impact team.

School-wide norms:	Team norms:	Personal norms (optional):

ASK & AIM

Set direction for inquiry with a compelling question about a student-centered challenge that matters.

Priorities:	Student-centered problem/teacher dilemma:	Inquiry question:

ASSESS & ANALYZE		
Further understanding (about a student-centered challenge) through data.		
Assessments to analyze (with dates, if available):	Initial key findings:	Narrowed questions based on data analysis:

TARGET & PLAN
Narrow focus on a bite-sized goal and draft a preliminary road map to reach it.

Based on data analysis we plan to target:	
Student-centered goals with desired outcomes:	Measures to monitor student progress:
Teaching (pathway goals) with desired outcomes:	Measures to monitor teacher learning:

RESEARCH & STUDY
Expand knowledge base and gain insight into beliefs, assumptions, and practice.
Resources:
Questions to explore further:

STRATEGIZE & DESIGN
Decide and plan what to implement and how to collect evidence.
Strategic implementation plan:

ACT & EVALUATE
Implement the strategic plan, observe, and collect data in real time to evaluate effectiveness.
Actions taken:
Post-assessments and learning outcomes:
Emerging questions for further inquiry:

FIGURE 14   STL Team Inquiry Work Plan Example

Team: Middle School Interdisciplinary Team

JT, Math teacher

MM, Science teacher

WL, History teacher

RD, Computer science teacher

LG, English teacher (team leader)

NK, Assistant principal

SG, Music

LOGISTICS, ROLES, & PROJECTED TIMELINE

Date	Time	Location	Note-taker	Timekeeper	Food	Learning lead*	Projected focus for this meeting
9/28	2:15–3:30	Library	—	—	—	—	Whole school launch
10/13	2:15–3:30	201	LG	SG	SG	LG	*Ask & Aim*
11/10	2:15–3:30	202	LG	JT	JT	NK	*Ask & Aim*
12/8	2:15–3:30	203	MM	WL	WL	MM	*Assess & Analyze*
1/12	2:15–3:30	204	MM	WL	WL	RD	*Assess & Analyze*
1/26	2:15–3:30	205	MM	NK	NK	WL	*Target & Plan*
2/16	2:15–3:30	201	LG	RD	RD	LG	*Research & Study*
3/16	2:15–3:30	202	LG	WL	JT	JT	*Strategize & Design*
4/13	2:15–3:30	203	MM	RD	SG	SG	*Act & Evaluate*
5/18	2:15–3:30	204	MM	NK	NK	LG	*Act & Evaluate*
6/12	2:15–3:30	Library	—	—	—	All present	Whole school celebrate

*The "learning lead" can be responsible for bringing in a reading, bringing in student work, modeling a lesson, asking probing questions, calling out bias or assumptions, facilitating data talk, trying a strategy with students, cross-collaborating with others, and so on.

NORMS FOR COLLABORATION

Expectations and agreements for working together as a high-functioning, high-impact team.

School-wide norms:

- Start and end on time.
- Be professional.
- Seek diverse perspectives

Team norms:

- Ground what we say in evidence.
- Hold each other accountable.
- Show vulnerability.

Personal norms (optional):

RD - Invite others to talk.

SG - Try new things.

MM - Listen first, then speak.

JT - Follow through.

WL - Take notes to keep engaged.

NK - Invite pushback.

LG - Respond without reacting.

ASK & AIM

Set direction for inquiry with a compelling question about a student-centered challenge that matters.

Priorities:	Student-Centered Challenge/ Teacher Dilemma	Inquiry Question:
District: Equity School: Literacy Grade level: Vocabulary	• Students across all grade levels perform poorly on reading comprehension of complex texts with challenging vocabulary. • Learning math, science, computers, music, etc., is "like learning another language." • Teachers want to learn strategies for helping students attack vocabulary. • High-needs students "hit a wall" when text is loaded with vocab they don't know. • Students get confused when words have multiple meanings or mean one thing in science class and something different in English class (e.g., *eclipse*). English learners (ELs) in particular struggle with this. • Some teachers have had success with some students when teaching explicit vocab strategies for high-frequency Tier 2 and low-frequency domain-specific Tier 3 words.	We aim to ensure *all* students have access to understanding text in all subjects. How do we improve students' academic vocabulary so that they can make meaning of texts across all classes?

ASSESS & ANALYZE

Further understanding (about the student-centered challenge) through data.

Assessments to analyze (with dates, if available):	Initial key findings:
• i-Ready reading vocab. • (12/8) Based on learning, create quiz with Tier 2 high-frequency words found across most domains. • Student responses to short-answer prompts containing Tier 2 vocab. *Note:* (11/10) Team realizes they need to create an assessment so they jump to *Study & Strategize* phase. Team reads and discusses Common Core academic vocab definition and Reading Rockets "Choosing Words to Teach" (Beck et al., n.d.). Then creates assessment on 12/8 to administer as a baseline.	(1/12) Students seem to demonstrate minimal attack strategies for unknown Tier 2 words. High-needs students skipped prompts containing Tier 2 words more than students who are not identified as high-needs. *Student performance on quiz: EL level 3 and below scored 20% or below accuracy on quiz. Students with language-based learning disabilities scored 40% or below. Students not identified as high-needs scored 75% or below. A few outliers with higher scores were also noted.

Narrowed questions based on data analysis:

• How do we teach students, particularly high-needs students, strategies to attack Tier 2 vocabulary so that they make meaning of text across all domains? (This is our more focused inquiry question going forward.)

• Are written assessments showing what students can do? What effect might oral assessments have, specifically on ELs?

Source: Beck, I., McKeown, M., & Kucan, L. (n.d.). Choosing words to teach. Reading Rockets. https://www.readingrockets.org/article/choosing-words-teach

(Continued)

(Continued)

TARGET & PLAN

Narrow focus on a bite-sized goal and draft a preliminary road map to reach it.

Based on data analysis, we plan to target:

Tier 2 words for all students, particularly high-needs students.

Student-centered goals with desired outcomes:

- SWBAT demonstrate understanding of teacher-identified Tier 2 words in texts. EL level 2s 40% accuracy by Feb. (20% points growth) to 60% (20% points growth) by June. Students w/specific learning disability 60% by Feb. (20% growth) to 80% by June (20% growth). Students not identified as high-needs 95% accuracy (20%–35% growth) by June.

Teaching (pathway goals):

- Grade-level teachers will generate a list of cross-content Tier 2 vocabulary students are expected to master by the end of sixth grade.

- Teachers will learn strategies for teaching Tier 2 vocabulary.

Measures to monitor student progress:

- Vocab quiz.

- Short-answer response.

- Oral conferences w/teacher.

Measures to monitor teacher learning:

- Peer observations w/team debriefs.

RESEARCH & STUDY

Expand knowledge base and gain insight into beliefs, assumptions, and practice.

Resources:

- Common Core defines academic vocabulary.

- Reading Rockets online resource: "Teaching Vocabulary" by Linda Diamond and Linda Gutlohn (www.readingrockets.org/article/teaching-vocabulary).

- Chapter 11 of *The Reading Strategies Book: Your Everything Guide to Developing Skilled Readers* by Jennifer Serravallo (2015).

- WIDA English Language Development Standards (wida.wisc.edu/teach/standards/eld) and Can Do Descriptors (wida.wisc.edu/teach/can-do/descriptors).

Question(s) to explore further:

- How can we help students use cognates to make meaning of unknown words when we do not know students' native languages?

STRATEGIZE & DESIGN

Decide and plan what to implement and how to collect evidence.

Strategic implementation plan:

(2/16) meeting. Read Serravallo 11.8 "Word Part Clues—Prefixes and Suffixes," 11.18 "Help From Cognates," and 11.5 "Multiple Meaning Words."

What we intend to do:

1. Peer observation lessons to teach strategies and decide data to collect.

2. Conduct conferences w/explicit vocab teaching; for example: "How can the Spanish word that you know, *mayoria*, help you make meaning of the word *majority*?" "If *chrono* means time, then *chronological* order means . . ." "*Expression* in math means . . . , in ELA it means . . . , and in music it means . . ."

(3/16) meeting. Do dry-demo lesson to experiment with Serravallo's strategies before doing in classroom with students. Anticipate challenges some students might have and design ways to tap into our ELs' native language advantage.

ACT & EVALUATE
Implement the strategic plan, observe, and collect data in real time to evaluate effectiveness.

Actions taken:

(1/26) Team members extended study to their own vertical content teams where content teachers will explicitly teach domain-specific Tier 3 vocabulary since the focus of this inquiry cycle is on Tier 2 vocabulary across domains.

Ongoing in between meetings: Teacher-led student conferences with explicit teaching. Collected anecdotal notes. Due to time constraints some teachers opted to only lead 1:1 and small-group conferences with high-needs students.

Prior to 4/13. Recorded one teacher modeling peer observation lesson for team to view and collected student work.

(4/13) Viewed recording, debriefed peer observation, and looked at student work. All committed to implementing strategies with a group of students.

(5/18) All implemented model lesson and brought in student work for collaborative analysis.

Post-assessments and learning outcomes:

- Post-cycle quiz and short-answer response to prompts: Of the groups of students who were taught explicit vocab strategies, 100% of students without high needs met targets; 80% of students with specific learning disabilities met targets; 60% English learners met targets. Need new approach for students who didn't meet targets.

- Anecdotal notes from conferences: When unknown vocab had a prefix or cognate, students could typically deduce meaning. Some students shared that they "never heard that word before," or for words with multiple meanings they said they "never heard the word used that way."

- Key finding: Students with language-based learning disabilities and English learners who struggle with reading English don't encounter many texts with these words. Need to increase exposure.

Emerging questions for further inquiry:

- How do we help students attack unknown academic vocab when words don't have prefixes, suffixes, roots, or known cognates?

- How do we increase exposure to Tier 2 (and Tier 3) academic vocab in and beyond our own classrooms, specifically for high-needs students? Would more oral exposure to words help some high-needs students with reading challenges?

STL recommendations:

Use your own cycle of inquiry. I organize the work plan around the STL Phases of Collaborative Inquiry (Figure 2), but you can substitute in whatever inquiry cycle you are following.

Build your plan as you go. Once the work begins and inquiry questions narrow and goals get more targeted, STLs adjust plans and fill in details. Essentially, the plan is more like GPS updating and rerouting as you intentionally (and unintentionally) take turns throughout the course. This can feel a little unsettling to those who like to have a plan and stick to it, but remember that STLs lead with flexibility and responsiveness to the needs of the group.

Make public. Promote cross-collaboration by updating your plan in a shared folder that all school teams can access.

Related readings:

Part I, Chapter 3, "The Real Work of Teams: Collaborative Inquiry." Access the STL Phases of Collaborative Inquiry (Figure 2) and how to approach a cycle of inquiry.

Move 10.6, "Publicly celebrate impact." Figure 30, the "STL Team Inquiry Summary," in this move could be used as an alternate work plan for a team that finds Figure 13, the "Team Inquiry Work Plan Template," overwhelming.

4.2 Write a three-question agenda: Why? What? How?

There are many agenda formats out there. I am particularly fond of the *fabulous* POP model by Leslie Sholl Jaffe and Randy Alford (see Gass, 2013). (Yes, they actually named it fabulous.) I like its emphasis on purpose and outcomes, and thus have adapted their model to create my version: the *amazing* (just kidding) three-question agenda. (See the template in Figure 15 and examples in Figure 16.) If you've been using an agenda format and you don't want to switch to the one I provide in this book, then keep your format, but use the questions in this chapter to inform the planning and design decisions you make. Skillful team leaders (STLs) write agendas that answer the following *why, what,* and *how* questions:

1. Why are we meeting about this?

2. What outcome(s) do we intend to leave with?

3. How will we collaborate about this?

How to write a three-question agenda:

Ask the three questions of each topic you put on your agenda. You do not need to answer the questions in sequence, but it is often best to ask question 3 last. The following describes the thought process behind each question:

1. Why are we meeting about this?

"We are gathered here today . . ." You might hear these words at a wedding, religious service, or community event. They make clear to all in attendance the purpose of coming together at a given time. In contrast, join a team meeting from the start, and as you leave, you are still wondering what the meeting was for. People need to know why they are meeting and why something is on the agenda. First, don't plan a meeting as an isolated event. Instead, determine how it fits into the big-picture work of your team. Connect to your school priorities, inquiry question, or team goal. Your visionary colleagues whose compass points East (see the section of Part II, Chapter 4 on work preferences and personalities) will especially appreciate this bird's-eye view of how this meeting connects to the others. Second, decide the reason for each agenda item. If you don't know why something is on your agenda, it probably shouldn't be there.

2. What outcome(s) do we intend to leave with?

You would advise a new teacher to plan a lesson around an objective, not activities. Yet we often design team meetings around what we will *do* together rather than about what we will *learn and accomplish* together. When crafting your agenda, decide what outcome(s) you hope and intend to achieve as a result of your collaboration. Although it's not always the case, most people collaborate because they are looking for one of the following three outcomes:

- Information or learning (e.g., *We'll leave this meeting with understanding about a policy decision made by the principal*).

- Input or feedback (e.g., *I'll leave this meeting with recommendations from my colleagues for an upcoming lesson*).

- Decision or product (e.g., *We'll leave this meeting with a decision about which assessment to give on Friday*).

Think in terms of what you need to "carry out" of the meeting. In other words, when planning your agenda, ask, "What are we leaving this meeting or conversation with?" An outcome is a noun. Avoid using verbs like *discuss* as that can result in a weak outcome or none at all. Instead, write intended outcomes as you would write a shopping list in a grocery store. You would not write, "Browse the fruit aisle." You would write what needs to be in your bag when you leave the store: *apples, bananas, oranges*, and so on. When possible, name tangible deliverables such as lesson plans, parent letters, test questions, and lists of student names, as well as "soft" outcomes such as *a shared understanding of . . . , consensus about . . . , shared ownership of . . . , positive feelings toward . . . , harmony among . . . ,* and *trust between . . .* (Sentence stems in Figure 17 can help you write intended outcomes for your meeting.)

If you are used to writing objectives (which are written with verbs) instead of outcomes, then do so, but embed outcome language. Add the words *so that we leave with.* To use the shopping example: *We will browse the fruit aisle so that we leave with apples.* Applied to a school setting, it might sound like this: *Discuss surveys so that we leave with a decision about which policy to revise.*

3. How will we collaborate about this?

"Watching paint dry." Sometimes when I tell people that much of my job is observing school team meetings, it's as if I've told them this instead. While I find group collaboration about teaching and learning fascinating, I'm not going to lie—some meetings are a little rough to sit through. Don't plan a meeting. Instead, design an engaging, collaborative learning experience. When you design the structure and activities of your meeting, consider the following:

- *Outcome. What activities will ensure a positive learning experience and lead us to our intended outcomes?* Design every activity in service of aiming for your intended meeting outcomes. Jigsaws, icebreakers, and movement activities are fun, but if they don't support why you are meeting in the first place, or if they don't bring your team closer to what they need to accomplish, then they are just engaging, not impactful.

- *Structure. How will we engage everyone in learning? What protocols will best structure our conversation? How will we group people to facilitate equitable participation?* To create a positive, engaging learning experience, draw from your vast knowledge of and experience with designing lessons for your students. Your box of pedagogical tools (e.g., Chalk Talk, Jigsaw, Think/ Pair/Share) can be very effective with adult learners (again, so long as there is a clear worthwhile purpose for doing them).

- *Sequence. How will we sequence topics so that our meeting has a good flow and things that are important don't get shortchanged? Should we move anything around?* Order agenda items so that the meeting has a good pace and so that important topics are prioritized. Starting with easily attainable outcomes can give your meeting momentum and help people feel productive so that they are more ready to tackle harder-to-achieve goals or controversial discussions.

- *Logistics. Who will lead each process, and for how long? How will we design around the size of our group, the space we have, the duration of our meeting, and the frequency with which we meet?* Make design decisions based on the number of people, the meeting space, the amount of time you have, and what opportunity, if any, you will have to meet again as a group.

- *Grouping.* Plan how you will group people in advance with consideration for the size and makeup of your team.

- *Ownership. In what ways can my colleagues feel ownership over this meeting?* Design a collaborative learning experience that brings in your colleagues' voice and choice. Specify facilitators, keeping in mind that you can have different people leading different parts of your agenda. Consider roles in which people can share responsibility for learning (see Move 2.9).

- *Feelings and experience. How do we want people to feel when the meeting is over?* Elena Aguilar (2013) recommends that coaches name the emotional response they hope teachers will feel after collaboration.

- *Prep. How will the facilitator or I prepare for this meeting? Who will share details in advance of the meeting? Is there anything my colleagues need to do to prepare for this meeting?* You are not done planning for your meeting until you identify the preparation needed to ensure the meeting runs as smoothly as possible. Determine what your colleagues need to do before the meeting (e.g., read, take a survey, or bring in student work), and decide how you will communicate this to them. Additionally, decide what you (or another facilitator) need to prepare before the meeting (e.g., prepare slides, photocopy, or create virtual breakout groups).

In action:

Jay is helping his colleague plan her agenda for an upcoming team meeting.

Colleague: I'm not really sure what we should do in this meeting. We could all bring in the graphic organizers we use. Or, I found this short video that explains logical patterns to writing. But someone last week mentioned peer editing, so maybe we should do that instead.

Jay: There are a lot of ways you could go. Instead of thinking about what you are going to *do* in your next meeting, think about what you want everyone to leave this meeting with. Your focus for inquiry is writing. Have you narrowed that down further?

Colleague: Yes. How to help kids organize their writing, particularly informational text.

Jay: And given that that's your focus, what do you hope to leave *this* meeting with?

Colleague: I know people want mini-lessons, but I don't think we are ready to do that in this meeting.

Jay: Why not?

Colleague: Because, to be honest, I don't really know if we even have agreement on what we all expect for writing at this grade level.

Jay: Sounds like you want to leave the meeting with shared expectations for writing informational text. [*Colleague nods.*] Why?

Colleague: Because students need to know what's expected of them and those expectations can't be different from one teacher to the next. And the same with grading. We need consistency.

[*Jay writes in the* why *column, "For consistent grading practices and clear expectations for students across classrooms."*]

Jay: And is there a deliverable, something people could produce in the meeting that would be helpful?

Colleague: Yes. What we really need to walk out of there with is one common writing rubric for this type of writing. Once we agree to what we are looking for, it's so much easier to communicate expectations to students, teach, give them feedback, and grade. But, I don't think we'll have time to craft a whole rubric in one meeting.

Jay: How about we leave with agreement on the criteria and begin to develop the "meets expectations" column?

Colleague: That's manageable.

Jay: Lastly, what activities or tasks will get you to that outcome? And think about details that will make the meeting both enjoyable and fruitful.

Colleague: I went to a training where they had us think about ourselves as writers, and that helped me think about expectations for my students. I'd like to open with that because I think it will get people's interest and also give us insight into the next task, which will be writing the "Meets Expectations" column. When we work on the rubric, we won't need to start from scratch. I'll have people examine any existing rubrics that they have been using. Then we'll all review standards and student work samples, so that we can make informed decisions when tweaking the existing rubric language.

(*Note:* The agenda they produced is shown in the second example of Figure 16.)

Think like a teacher:

Throughout this book, I emphasize the point that you are doing more than facilitating a meeting; you are facilitating adult learning for continuous improvement. Think about designing learning experiences for your colleagues, in a similar way as you would design lessons for students. When designing a lesson, you see that it fits within your unit. You are clear about learning outcomes you intend to reach and design the sequence, pace, types of activities, and transitions to bring about the learning outcomes students need. Beyond being goal-driven, you think about the experience your students will have.

All this is true for designing a meeting for adult learners as well. When possible, aim for small, specific, attainable learning targets within your outcome as you would with younger learners. In the classroom, this might look like any of the following:

- Students will be able to compare and contrast word choice in two texts.

- By the end of today's lesson, eighth-grade students will be able to apply Pascal's law about pressure and fluid to an everyday example.

- I can distinguish between acute, right, and obtuse angles.

In a team meeting, this might look like any of the following:

- We'll leave this meeting able to implement the think-aloud strategy with students.

- By the end of this meeting, we will know which students have grasped the concept of skip counting and leave with a plan for those who have not.

- We'll leave this meeting with heightened awareness of our own bias (e.g., "I can recognize my implicit bias when grading student essays").

STL recommendations:

Don't get caught up in wordsmithing. Don't spend time perfectly wording a *why* statement or intended outcome. Whether you use the three-question agenda format or something else, just make sure that you and everyone on your team knows the reason they are meeting and what they intend to accomplish in the meeting, and that you have thoughtfully designed an engaging learning experience that will bring about the outcomes you expect.

Bookend. Bookend each meeting with Moves 4.3 and 4.4.

Build in floating minutes. When creating an agenda, include 5 to 10 unplanned floating minutes that can be allocated as needed during the meeting.

Keep two agendas. The three-question agenda format can feel very comfortable to our "Compass Points West" people who love detail (see the section of Part II, Chapter 4 on work preferences and personalities), but a little overwhelming to others. If you are looking to provide a cleaner, less detailed agenda to your team, write two versions: a facilitator's agenda and a meeting agenda for your colleagues that leaves off or simplifies the *how* column.

Plan for your plan with a friend. When possible, plan with someone who can prompt your thinking. Allot 20–30 minutes to write a three-question agenda for every meeting. After you have done it a few times, you'll likely be able to design your meeting in less time. Note: Planning with the entire team is not always the most efficient use of time. Instead, bring in other people through a co-facilitator rotation (see Move 2.9). Or invite people to send suggestions for the agenda prior to planning.

Avoid outcome overload. Be careful not to overload your meeting agenda with a long list of deliverables. (I'm guilty of this.) Simplify. For example, write on your facilitator's agenda: "We will leave this meeting with a list of ideas to reduce test anxiety, names of teachers who will implement the activities, descriptions of activities, and a calendar for when we will do the activities" but on the team agenda write: "We will leave this meeting with a detailed plan for reducing test anxiety."

Plan to assess your outcomes. Make note of which outcomes you meet by the end of your meeting. List outcomes with bullet circles that you can fill in. For example:

- met

- partially met

- not yet met

Make your agenda available in advance. Adults prefer to know what they are doing and why before they get to a meeting. If they didn't have a role in writing a three-question agenda, be sure to share it with them *before* the meeting. This is especially important if there is any prework that needs to be done.

Be adaptive, not goal-obsessed. Just like your grocery store run, what you intend to leave with might not necessarily be what you actually leave with. Don't hold so tightly to your intended outcomes if your team isn't ready for them, and be open to unintended positive outcomes. Great learning that you didn't plan for can emerge, so be prepared to welcome it. (To stick with the grocery analogy, if the apples don't look fresh, you might choose oranges instead.)

Take notes on the agenda. Put the notes from your meeting directly into a digital three-question agenda (e.g., Google Doc). Keep all agendas in one digital file with the most recent ones at the top. This way you have a record of past conversations and can easily reference back.

Take note of what doesn't make the agenda. We constantly make choices when planning and facilitating meetings about what to include, what to spend time on, and what to leave off our agendas. Notice when important things are not given time and attention, and determine why this is happening.

Find the right words:

- Why are we meeting about this?
  - *What is our purpose for coming together?*
  - *Why is collaborating about X important?*
  - *Is every agenda item listed necessary for this meeting? Is there something we can eliminate? If not, why not?*
- What outcome(s) do we intend to leave with?
  - Do we need to leave with information? Input and feedback? Or a decision?
  - Instead of thinking about what we will do in this meeting, let's name what we expect to leave with.
- How will we collaborate? *(See the questions bulleted under "3. How will we collaborate about this?" on pages 165–166.)*

Related readings:

Move 5.1, "Set parameters for breakout groups"; Move 5.2, "Foster equitable airtime"; and Move 5.7, "Form subcommittees." These moves provide strategies for grouping during activities so that all voices are heard.

FIGURE 15   STL Three-Question Agenda Template

DATE: TIME: ROOM/VIRTUAL LINK:	MEMBERS PRESENT & MEETING ROLES:	OUR GROUP AGREEMENTS:

Big-picture connection:

What is our team working toward? (*Name school priorities, the team inquiry question, or the team goal here.*)

Preparation:

How should the facilitator and the team prepare for this meeting?

TIME	TOPIC	WHY Why are we meeting about this?	WHAT? What outcome(s) do we intend to leave with?	HOW How will we collaborate about this?
	1.			
	2.			

Next steps (Who/What/By When): (Completed during the meeting)

Figure 16 presents two examples of the three-question agenda, one belonging to a diversity, equity, and inclusion teacher–parent committee and the other to an English language arts teacher team.

FIGURE 16   STL Three-Question Agenda Examples

Example 1: Diversity, Equity, and Inclusion Committee

MEETING: 1 DATE: 10/5 ROOM: 201 TIME: 4–5 p.m.	MEMBERS PRESENT & ROLES: Parents: CM, BT, DD Educators: KD, DS, MM, GL Food: DS Note-taker: BT	STARTER AGREEMENTS: Respect time agreements. Think, question, and wonder. Invite other voices to speak.

Big-picture connection:

School priority: Diversity, equity, and inclusion (DEI).

Inquiry question: How can a group of parents and educators best work together to serve the DEI mission?

WHAT?

We intend to leave this meeting with . . .

Clarity about our mission, vision, and work as a newly formed DEI committee.

Preparation:

All read school DEI mission statement; bring laptop.

TIME	TOPIC	WHY?	WHAT?	HOW?
10 min.	Welcome/ introduction	To build community.	N/A	(GL) Share name, role, and reason for joining this committee. (Round robin)
10 min.	DEI then and now	To inform new members of, and reconnect existing members to, the mission.	A shared understanding of the DEI mission and how it has evolved.	(KD) Director presents.
15 min.	Shared vision	To hear diverse perspectives for what could be.	Vision phrases.	(GL) Brainstorm prompt: If a documentary film was made about DEI at our school three years from now, what would we see/hear? (Whole group)
20 min.	Projects and communication	To make initial planning decisions.	A list of potential committee projects; a plan for communication to parents.	(GL) Sticky note sort—what's our work, and what isn't? Brainstorm.
5 min.	Debrief	To assess our collaboration as a team.	N/A	(CM) How well did we meet our intended outcome? What intended outcomes resulted? How well did we stick to our norms? What do we need to do differently? (N/A)

Example 2: English Language Arts Team

DATE: TIME: ROOM/VIRTUAL LINK:	MEMBERS PRESENT & MEETING ROLES: OM (facilitator)	OUR GROUP AGREEMENTS:

Big-picture connection:

School priority: Literacy across content areas.

Team aims: Improve student writing and student beliefs about themselves as writers. (See goal for metrics.)

WHAT?

We will leave this meeting with . . .

1. Awareness of ourselves as writers.

2. A revised rubric.

Preparation:

- Review writing standards (www.corestandards.org/ELA-Literacy).
- Bring in 3 student work samples with a "meets" rating on our existing rubric.

TIME	TOPIC	WHY?	HOW?
5 min.	1. **Awareness as writers**	To better understand our students as writers.	Give prompt: Write 1 paragraph introducing yourself to a new principal. Reflect: What was challenging about writing this paragraph? Discuss: What might students find challenging when writing?
45 min.	2. **A revised rubric**	For consistent grading practices and clear expectations for students across classrooms.	OM: • (5 min.) Present original rubric. • (10 min.) Revisit standards as a team. • (15 min.) Examine student work samples in pairs. • (15 min.) Edit criteria for "meets expectations" in pairs and then as a whole group.
5 min.	3. **Meeting feedback**	To solicit feedback so that we can briefly assess our collaboration as a team.	Google feedback form. (Link emailed)

Next steps: Who? What? By when? (Completed during the meeting.)

FIGURE 17   Team Meeting Intended Outcome Language Stems

What outcomes do we intend to leave this meeting with?

We intend for people to inform others or gain new information/learning.

We want to leave this meeting with . . .

- a shared understanding of . . .
- knowledge of [schedule conflicts, new calendar items, etc.]
- awareness of [celebrations, hardships, etc.]
- an update about . . .
- clarification about . . .
- new skills or methods to . . .
- research-based strategies for . . .
- training on . . .

We intend for people to give or receive feedback/input.

We want to leave this meeting with . . .

- a list of [ideas, suggestions, etc.]
- warm and cool feedback on . . .
- opinions about . . .
- recommendations for . . .
- a new perspective into the problem of . . .
- multiple perspectives about . . .
- probing questions to think differently about . . .
- suggestions for [wording, strategies, etc.]
- editing suggestions [keep, toss, revise, add, etc.]

We intend for people to co-construct, decide, or implement something with others.

We want to leave this meeting with . . .

- an initial list of [priority standards, student names, questions to ask, resources, etc.]
- a finalized list
- a decision regarding . . .
- consensus for . . .
- a plan for . . .
- a visual representation of . . .
- a survey
- a summary
- a timeline
- a learning progression

- a working draft of . . .
- a chart or template
- a climate/culture of . . .
- an assessment of . . .
- analysis of data
- a goal for . . .
- a process to . . .
- a graph representing . . .

FIGURE 18   Multi-Grade Team Meeting Intended Outcome Language Stems

Curriculum Outcomes

We will leave our vertical team meeting with . . .

- a shared understanding of the standard(s)
- identified curriculum strengths and gaps across our content
- learning progressions from grade to grade
- a list of specific skills within our priority standard
- a list of language mismatches taught across our content
- consensus on common language across our content
- consensus on which concepts, skills, knowledge, habits, and mindsets are to be taught at each grade level
- a list of social-emotional learning (SEL) skills, habits, and mindsets to be taught across the curriculum
- methods for teaching SEL across the curriculum

Instructional Outcomes

We will leave our vertical team meeting with . . .

- an exchange of teaching ideas and strategies
- methods to implement teaching strategies
- specific improvements to a lesson
- common questions to ask students during instruction
- an SEL mini-lesson
- consensus on homework expectations at different grade levels

(Continued)

(Continued)

Assessment Outcomes

We will leave our vertical team meeting with . . .

- development and analysis of aligned benchmark assessments to inform curriculum decisions
- a common standards-based performance task to assess student mastery
- identified skills and knowledge students have mastered at each grade level
- a strengthened understanding of the relationship between learning goals, instructional practice, and assessment

Professional Learning Outcomes

We will leave our vertical team meeting with . . .

- a shared understanding of students' whole-school experience in our content
- recommendations for grade-level department team goals
- feelings of community, collegiality, and connectedness
- teaching resources for implementation
- probing questions that stretch our thinking as professionals
- new knowledge about pedagogy or content
- a schedule for lesson observations
- goals for peer lesson observation
- consensus on an observation and debrief protocol for peer lesson observation

4.3 Open a meeting to activate learning.

Ever play doubles in tennis with people who are new to the game and you just can't get a good rally going? The first person serves the ball into the net. The next person hits the ball out of bounds. The next person swings their racket and misses. And so on. Like a slow start to a tennis match, meetings can take a while to build momentum. Skillful team leaders (STLs) open their meetings with an engaging learning task or activity.

How to open a meeting to activate learning:

Consider the type of activator, purpose, and method for leading.

Type. Select from community- and trust-building games (see examples in Move 3.8) or launch your meeting with a relevant reading, powerful anecdote, data set, humorous cartoon, computer game such as Kahoot!, or thought-provoking question.

Purpose. Decide the tone you are looking to create in your meeting and what you want from an activator. If you want to build community, you might choose a team-building game; if you want to get people comfortable with talking about data, you might open with an intriguing data point.

Method. How you open the meeting is as important as what you choose to lead at the beginning of your meeting. For example, to engage people in discussion of a complex text, draw attention to a specific standout line and invite people to react. (Articles often have lines in a sidebar that the author or publisher deem important.)

In action:

Example 1: Activate learning through images.

Reina:　　In today's meeting we are going to brainstorm effective strategies for responding to resistance from students. Let's get the conversation going with this quick activator. [*She shows four images on the screen.*] Select the image that best represents your emotional response to a student who shows resistance. Then talk with the person next to you about why you chose that image.

Example 2: Activate learning through text.

With an aim to minimize bias in scoring, Jen leads her team in a discussion about "Minimizing Bias When Assessing Student Work" by Pamela Steinke and Peggy Fitch (2017). The text requires a bit of heavy lifting as it comes from a research journal.

Jen:　　Let's launch our conversation about this research by talking about the quote in the sidebar on page 88 and why we think it was significant enough for the publisher to highlight it: "We argue that the potential for bias is a concern when assessing student work and that when it does occur scorers are often not aware that the bias is operating." Let's start with what the line means and then weigh in on the argument the authors put forth.

Think like a teacher:

How do you start your class lesson? Do you present a thought-provoking question in a "Do Now" exercise? A puzzle students need to solve? A writing prompt that students are eager to speak about? A partner conversation about a photo on the screen? A song with lyrics that relate to the theme of your lesson for the day? A student explaining to their peers how they solved a problem? However you choose to launch learning for the day, you are intentional about finding a way to activate students' thinking, hook them into the lesson, and get them talking. And when you don't start in this way—for example, when you open with a low-engagement task like "Copy this definition off the board" (admittedly, I did this for a while until I saw the positive impact of a high-engagement activator)—you see the sobering effects on your learners.

Adults benefit from an engaging task, just as children do. What you do with your team might be different from what you do to engage students in a lesson, but the intention behind doing it is the same: activate learning.

STL recommendations:

Delay housekeeping tasks. A common energy trap is to begin a meeting by previewing the day's agenda or reading off norms. These are important tasks but can drain people before you even get going. Instead, begin with something that will activate thinking and talk for a few minutes, then shift into housekeeping.

Connect to content. While you certainly could opt for a fun activator that is unrelated to the meeting (and certainly your students wouldn't mind), it's not the best approach to use with your colleagues. Adult learners need to know why they are doing something and how it connects to their work (see Part II, Chapter 5). They don't want to waste time—and neither do you. Engage your colleagues in an opening task that leads into or reinforces the content of this or a previous meeting.

Insert fun. In 2020, at the beginning of the COVID-19 pandemic, teachers were thrown into learning how to teach virtually. I saw a department head teach the features of an online platform by opening with an activity in which people changed their screen names. People chose names of superheroes, names of family pets, and personal descriptors such as Queen Gardener. Instantly, participants were laughing and put at ease with the new technology.

Choose activators that can be used with students. A bonus to doing an activator in a team meeting with your colleagues is that it gives everyone a chance to pick up a strategy to take back to the classroom. I remember being a teacher on a team where my colleague activated our learning with a folded paper organizer (much like a horizontal flip-book) that helped us visually categorize types of questions we could ask students in the classroom. I loved it so much that I adapted it for my student writers.

Skip the game. Some people worry activators take up too much time. You don't need to carve out 10 minutes on your agenda to engage people in learning. A powerful on-topic prompt or controversial data point can work.

Find the right words:

- *The goal of this activator is to . . .*

- *Who wants to lead an opening activity about X for next week? Remember the goal of the activator is to get us thinking, talking, and engaging.*

- *Let's kick off our data analysis with this surprising finding . . . What do you make of this?*

Primary Intention 3, "Nurture Group Culture." Open your meeting with one of many community- and trust-building games explored in this section. See especially Move 3.8.

4.4 Close a meeting to establish next steps for learning.

Seinfeld. Lost. How I Met Your Mother. The Sopranos. Nothing like a disappointing ending to ruin a good run. A team meeting doesn't need to end in an exciting twist like you would expect of a popular TV series, but skillful team leaders (STLs) are intentional about getting closure in a way that helps team members reflect on learning, leave with clarity on the direction for moving forward, and feel connected and confident in the team.

How to close a meeting to establish next steps for learning:

As you close each team meeting, consider posing the following guiding questions either to the group or in an exit ticket:

- *Learning.* What have we learned from our collaboration today? What further learning or support do we need?

- *Decisions.* What decisions, if any, did we make? Is everyone satisfied with our decision-making process?

- *Next steps.* What next steps have we agreed to? Who will do what by when?

- *Collaboration.* What worked today? What could have been better? How well did we uphold our group agreements for collaboration? How do people feel as this meeting ends?

Think like a teacher:

I'm sure this scenario has happened to you: *The bell rings, indicating class is over, but you are still calling out instruction over the bustle of kids packing their bags and running out your classroom door.* Running out of time and ending class without the space for a wrap-up once in a while isn't the end of the world; however, it doesn't provide the grounded time for students to reflect on the lesson and gain clarity for what they need to do that night. And for students who have learning differences, the chaos of nonclosure can actually feel unsettling and make the transition to their next class challenging.

Many adult learners, too, need time to process and get clear on next steps. Our days move at such a rapid pace that taking five minutes at the end of the meeting to button up what's been discussed helps new learning sink in and helps the group avoid misunderstandings around decisions made.

STL recommendations:

Don't shortchange time. It makes sense: You only have so many minutes, and there's so much ground to cover. Wouldn't it be better to work up to the last minute of a team meeting rather than taking time to close the meeting? Usually not. People crave some type of wrap-up even if it's just three minutes. And typically, if you feel you need to finish up what you are talking about by extending to the last second of your meeting, you probably need more time than what's left of your meeting. Table the discussion (see Move 5.9) and put it on the next meeting agenda.

Do a quick learning check. To avoid a lengthy discussion during a closing, you can try some quick prompts and exercises to help people reflect on learning. The ideas listed as follows are similar to the summarizers and synthesizers a teacher might use with students:

- *I used to think . . . but now I know . . .*

- *3, 2, 1: Three things I learned are . . . Two things I wonder are . . . One thing I'll try is . . .*

- *Above the line drawn on the board, write what you have learned. Below the line, write the questions you still have.*

Related readings:

Move 8.15, "Clarify the decision-making process." Be clear about how your team will make a decision before making it.

Move 8.17, "Commit to action." Get clear on next steps and learn key considerations to help people commit to decisions made within a meeting.

PRIMARY
INTENTION 4

STRUCTURE TASKS AND TALK

"We are all adults. We don't need protocols." This is a common misunderstanding often made by peer team leaders who worry that structured talk can be too confining for adults. Yes, adults *can* work together without parameters for discussion, but meeting after meeting of unstructured group talk is not the most effective means for learning and reaching your goals.

I understand why some team leaders opt out. Protocols can feel awkward. But, as a former colleague of mine, Britta Hiester, would say, "Like a pair of jeans out of the dryer, protocols are uncomfortable at first, but after you try them on a few times, you don't even notice them." If you can get past some people's dislike of them, you'll find that protocols give much-needed structure to conversations, which is especially important when those conversations are highly charged about issues such as race, equity, and social justice. Similar to practicing safety protocols in school, regular use of team protocols prepares everyone for difficult situations. People can focus on the substance of the conversation and not the process.

There are many protocols from which to choose, and preparation can make all the difference in facilitation. In addition to selecting tasks that are appropriately challenging for adults and being clear about what is expected of people in the task, skillful team leaders (STLs) structure tasks and conversation so that collaboration brings about new insight and learning.

STL moves:

4.5 Choose a protocol.*

4.6 Preview a task or protocol.

4.7 Facilitate a protocol.

Tools and templates:

Figure 19: Protocols by Purpose

What these moves promote:

Productivity. Teams intentionally choose structures that facilitate productive conversation.

Focus. Protocols lend focus to conversation that might otherwise be aimless.

Evidence-based discourse. Many protocols for analyzing data and looking at student work require people to examine evidence before jumping to conclusions.

---

*STLs often make Moves 4.5 and 4.6 in sequence. Because of this, I include one "in action" example of an STL implementing these moves at the end of this section (see pp. 187–188).

Communication. Protocols suggest time limits and language stems that help people share airtime and listen to one another.

When to use these moves:

For any potentially challenging conversation or data talk.

4.5 Choose a protocol.

When I first learned how to use the Consultancy protocol, I liked it. I mean I *really* liked it. I used it for everything: With my colleagues we would discuss problems of practice, analyze best practices, look at student work, give feedback on lessons. With my students we would collaborate about each other's writing. I even used it with some non-educator friends to support one another in thinking through career decisions. It didn't take long, however, for me to see that the protocol didn't really fit my needs for every conversation, and I would end up tweaking or abandoning it. Later, I learned that there are, of course, a ton of protocols from which facilitators can choose. So how do you know which one to pick?

Different protocols are intended to produce different outcomes. For instance, if you want to further your team's professional learning with a text-based discussion, you can choose from protocols such as Final Word, Jigsaw, and Three Levels of Text. If you are looking to gain insight into a specific child's student learning strengths and areas for need, you can turn to Child Study or another protocol for looking at student work. Skillful team leaders (STLs) decide how to structure a conversation by deciding the purpose for the conversation and then picking a protocol to match.

How to choose a protocol:

Discuss with your colleagues what they want to get out of a conversation. Choose a task that best meets your purpose for collaborating (e.g., read a text together, look at student work together, or debrief a peer observation). If a protocol is helpful in structuring the conversation, then decide what you want the protocol to do. Four common reasons your team might use a protocol include the following:

- To examine what we teach (e.g., standards, curriculum, policy)
- To examine how we teach (e.g., instructional methods and strategies)
- To examine student learning (e.g., assessment and feedback analysis)
- To further professional learning (e.g., text-based discussions)

Figure 19 organizes protocols into these four categories. (Note: This list identifies the *primary* purpose for which you would turn to a particular protocol.) In some cases, a protocol might serve multiple purposes. In other cases, although I only mark one primary purpose, other outcomes might result. For example, the Calibration protocol is most commonly used to examine what people teach, but when people go through the process of norming student work, they will, no doubt, reflect on their mindset about student expectations. Furthering professional learning isn't the main purpose for choosing this protocol, but it's a likely outcome if the protocol is facilitated skillfully.

FIGURE 19 Protocols by Purpose

This figure presents commonly used protocols organized by what you want from your conversation. First decide for what primary purpose you are collaborating, and then explore the protocols in that category to find the best match.

PURPOSE FOR COLLABORATION	EXAMINE WHAT WE TEACH	EXAMINE HOW WE TEACH	EXAMINE STUDENT LEARNING	FURTHER PROFESSIONAL LEARNING
Things a team might do during the protocol	• Unpack standards. • Select curriculum. • Norm success criteria. • Design or tweak lessons and assessments. • Evaluate policies. • Plan for change. • Identify problems of practice.	• Practice a teaching strategy with colleagues. • Observe and analyze live or recorded demonstration lessons. • Share teaching strategies.	• Analyze assessment data. • Look at student work. • Analyze feedback. • Plan instructional steps based on data findings.	• Learn from a text-based discussion. • Reflect on educator habits, mindsets, and practices.
PROTOCOLS THAT MATCH				
Calibration	X			
Chalk Talk				X
Child Study			X	
Consultancy (or Problem of Practice)	X	X	X	
Data Driven Dialogue			X	
Evidence Analysis Action (EAA)			X	
Final Word				X
Fishbone	X			
Five *Whys*	X		X	
Four A's	X			X
Four Corners	X	X	X	X
Gallery Walk	X	X	X	X
Issaquah	X	X	X	

(Continued)

(Continued)

PURPOSE FOR COLLABORATION	EXAMINE WHAT WE TEACH	EXAMINE HOW WE TEACH	EXAMINE STUDENT LEARNING	FURTHER PROFESSIONAL LEARNING
PROTOCOLS THAT MATCH				
Jigsaw	X	X	X	X
Looking at Three Levels of Student Work			X	
Mirrors and Windows	X			X
Peeling the Onion	X		X	
Success Analysis	X	X	X	
Text Rendering				X
Three Levels of Text				X
Tuning	X	X	X	
Unpacking for Success in Action	X			

Note: These protocols can be found at schoolreforminitiative.org and nsrfharmony.org with the exception of EAA and Unpacking for Success in Action, which are described in the book *Leading Impact Teams* (Bloomberg & Pitchford, 2017). This is not a comprehensive list of all protocols from which a facilitator may select, but instead includes those that are commonly used.

Think like a teacher:

When you lead a class discussion, you likely have an outcome in mind and structure talk so that you can reach it. For instance, if you want students to have a dialogue with one another without interruption, you might lead a Chalk Talk in which they silently circulate the room writing their thoughts and questions and responding to others on chart paper.

Many of the same protocols that you use with your students can be implemented with adults so long as you convey to your colleagues that you see them as capable of having adult learning conversations.

For an example, see "Moves 4.5 and 4.6 in action" on page 187.

STL recommendations:

Meet outside of the meeting. If you have arranged for one or two team members to present a challenge or success to the group, uncover their need in advance of meeting with the team. The presenting team member(s) should be able to communicate clearly and succinctly, in the meeting, their dilemma or success and what they are looking for from the group. This will save your team time and focus your conversation at the start.

Distinguish between problem finding and problem solving. Not every protocol is intended to find and solve problems. For instance, Consultancy, Five *Whys*, and Peeling the Onion deep-dive into identifying the core problem but don't get to solutions, whereas Success Analysis and Tuning do the opposite. They do not deeply explore the cause and effect of problems, but instead focus team talk on improvement solutions. Some protocols are designed to do both (e.g., Child Study, Data Driven Dialogue, EAA, Issaquah, and most protocols for looking at student work).

To know which structure to use, consider the amount of time you have in your meeting and the depth with which you might need to explore problems or generate solutions. If you have a complex problem, take time to get to the heart of the issue so that you aren't throwing solutions at the wrong problem. If people already have a good grasp of the issue, choose a protocol that gets to solutions so people don't get frustrated with conversation that only talks about the problem.

Find the right words:

- *What do you need from our group discussion in the next meeting? Which protocol is the best fit?*

- *What question are you wrestling with? Or what success could our team unpack? Which protocol best suits this conversation?*

- *Is your purpose for this upcoming conversation to examine what we teach, examine how we teach, examine student learning, or engage in a text-based discussion to further our own professional learning?*

Related reading:

Move 7.5, "Select student work samples (student data) to examine." If you choose to lead a protocol for looking at student work, first be intentional about the student samples you plan to analyze.

Additional resources:

Schoolreforminitiative.org and *nsrfharmony.org* provide an alphabetized list of protocols that detail the purpose for the protocol and steps for facilitation.

4.6 Preview a task or protocol.

I once made a grave mistake facilitating a problems of practice protocol in which I did not give the presenting teacher a heads-up that she would be silent for about 10 minutes while others talked about her and her challenge. Understandably, she got upset to the point where we had to stop the protocol. She later told me the experience of not being allowed to talk while others talked about her work made her feel disempowered. I felt terrible as, of course, this was not my intention. I took away the lesson that regardless of how familiar *I* am with a protocol, I need to preview and prepare others for it.

Protocols put forth guidelines that can feel unnatural compared to the way in which groups of people normally speak. Skillful team leaders (STLs) preview the protocol or task they plan to use with colleagues so everyone knows what to expect.

How to preview a task or protocol:

Reflect on what you needed to know and understand the first time you engaged in this task or protocol. Anticipate challenges you might encounter, such as not having enough time to move through a protocol in its entirety, and make decisions based on the outcomes you want from the conversation. Preview the format of a new protocol or task with your colleagues. Review roles for participation and what people can expect. Leave time for questions.

For an example, see "Moves 4.5 and 4.6 in action" on page 187.

STL recommendations:

Make the protocol visible. Have the protocol available for viewing during your meeting on chart paper, in a handout, or projected on a screen so that people know what to expect. That way, if you break into small groups, they can facilitate the text-based discussion without you.

Practice facilitation with your students. When I first engaged in a protocol for looking at student work with my colleagues in a team meeting, I was so struck by the insight I gained—not just about the student work we were analyzing but also about my own teaching—that I immediately brought it back to my classroom to do with students. I taught students the protocol to help them give feedback to one another in a group about their writing. It was transformative. Students became better at recognizing strong and weak elements in each other's and their own writing. But, I also discovered an added benefit—I was able to practice the protocol in a comfortable, forgiving setting with my students. Gene Thompson-Grove, co-founder of Critical Friends Groups, would say that the first time you lead a protocol it's likely going to turn out "like the first waffle"—passable but not quite the way you want it. But, the next few waffles you make get better and better. So try it out on your students; they won't mind getting the first waffle.

Abridge with caution. Some protocols, particularly those for data analysis, can be time-consuming. I understand the desire to make a *Reader's Digest* version, but be careful that your changes don't reduce what you are doing to the point where you can't reach the purpose for your conversation. I observed a teacher leader who distilled a 45-minute protocol for looking at student work to 15 minutes. She asked great probing questions as the protocol suggested, but the team didn't have time to thoughtfully explore her questions. For people to engage in robust analysis of any data, they need time to review the work presented to them (and sometimes do the assessment task); make their observations and inferences; thoughtfully discuss, question, and wonder; and commit to next steps.

Find the right words:

(When previewing a protocol with a presenting teacher)

- *Let's look over the task/protocol before we do it with the team to make sure you know what to expect.*

- *What do people need to know about the protocol before we use it?*

- *You'll notice this protocol requires the presenter to be silent for a period of time and for everyone else to talk as if the presenter is not in the room. Expect that this can feel awkward or even uncomfortable.*

- *The protocol indicates time for you to share context/background knowledge. What do you plan to share with the group?*

Moves 4.5 and 4.6 in action:

STLs Michelle Fox and Elisa MacDonald choose a protocol to structure an upcoming problem of practice conversation.

MOVES	CONVERSATION	
4.5 Choose a protocol.	Elisa:	Thanks for agreeing to share a problem of practice. In thinking about our team goal, what are you wrestling with?
	Michelle:	Kids have to write out their experimental design and write a claim, evidence, and reasoning. I'm not sure how I should teach and assess students so that they are able to demonstrate both understanding of the open-endedness of the inquiry process and understanding of the content without misconceptions, specifically right now with what I'm teaching—the force–mass–acceleration relationship.
	Elisa:	Why is this important?
	Michelle:	With inquiry lessons, there is a constant struggle in teaching science—you want students to experience the open-endedness of the process, but you have understandings that you want them to walk away with. Last year kids got the inquiry part, but then they walked away with misconceptions, and I had to spend a ton of time doing damage control afterward. It was partly because I was teaching physical science for the first time, but regardless, I want to do it better this year.
	Elisa:	I think the other team members will be able to relate to this dilemma. Next, let's select a protocol for this conversation. What feels best for us to do as a group? Examine student work you have? Support you with lesson design? Provide feedback on your instruction? Or just broaden our knowledge about something with a text-based discussion?
	Michelle:	I'd love suggestions on how I can improve my lesson and the assessment kids will need to do. We are about to study balance and forces, so I would do it with that. As I mentioned, I did the lesson last year, but it didn't go well because kids walked away with a lot of misconceptions.
	Elisa:	Sounds like you want us to examine your lesson and assessment for the purpose of tweaking it. A good protocol for that purpose is Tuning.

(Continued)

(Continued)

MOVES	CONVERSATION	
4.6 Preview a task or protocol.	Elisa:	In this protocol the team will give you warm and cool feedback on your lesson and the assessment that you intend on giving to your students. Here's what it looks like. [*Elisa goes to schoolreforminitiative.org and shows Michelle the protocol.*] You'll notice there is a short amount of time where you are not permitted to talk. You can take notes, but you won't be able to ask or answer questions (even if people look at you for answers), nor will you be able to provide any more details or context other than what you shared at the beginning of the conversation. Pulling you out of the conversation for a few minutes, although it might feel awkward the first time we do it, allows team members to engage in uninterrupted discourse and lets you be a "fly on the wall" listening. You'll be amazed at what you take away from their talk. It's a good time to take notes. Since I'm facilitating, I'll make sure that I give the team a heads-up about this part of the protocol, because it can be uncomfortable and even frustrating to them if they are doing it for the first time.
		[*Michelle and Elisa decide what to prepare. They want teachers to see the content reading kids received; the lesson the teacher had drafted; the experiment students were tasked to design; the claim, evidence, and reasoning (CER) students were expected to write; and the rubric that went with it.*]

4.7 Facilitate a protocol.

Protocols have been around for a long time, yet not every team embraces them. This can be due to the misconception that protocols stifle organic conversation. They do not, when facilitated skillfully and intentionally. The following pages present skillful team leader (STL) recommendations for facilitating commonly used protocols for data analysis (e.g., looking at student work [LASW] and looking at teacher work [LATW]), defining problems, and leading text-based discussions. I do not include detailed procedures for facilitation because you can easily find directions at schoolreforminitiative.org/protocols or on other sites.

1. Data Analysis Protocols

Calibration

Purpose: To increase consistency in scoring work in alignment to common criteria. To deepen understanding of scoring criteria and student expectations for proficiency.

Materials: Prompt or task, student work samples, criteria for scoring (i.e., rubric), and place to record scores.

Group size: Any size. Break up a large group into 4–7 participants to allow opportunities for everyone to speak.

Summary: Teachers read or do the student prompt or task to gain a better understanding of the demand on students. They also review the scoring criteria so that they have an initial understanding of expectations. Independently, they score papers and report out scores (round-robin style). If there is disagreement about a score, an evidence-based discussion follows in which people pull evidence from the student work sample and from the scoring criteria language to make their case.

Upside:

- Teams build a habit of examining student work for strengths and areas for growth based on a rubric. Teachers take this practice to their classroom when scoring their own students' work.

- The process sometimes results in improved tweaks to a rubric or student task.

- Once consensus is reached on scores, have the team pull anchor documents for each score. These can serve as models for students so they know what to expect (just be sure to use a different prompt with students when it's their turn to produce the work).

Downside:

- Focus is on scoring. If you want instructional next steps for students, you have to prompt people to do so or choose a different protocol for looking at student work.

- The process is time-consuming, particularly if the student work samples are lengthy (e.g., five-paragraph essays).

STL Recommendations:

- Provide sticky notes so that people can jot and place their observations on the actual student work. This makes it easier to reference evidence during discussion.

- Save team time and raise ownership by examining a common prompt or task that teachers helped create and a common rubric that they helped write or know.

- If you have a cumbersome lengthy rubric, focus on one criterion at a time.

- Alternative process: Divvy up the documents. Make three piles (or have three literal buckets)—high, medium, and low—and do a quick sort where people assign a first-impression score to each paper. Pass the papers around so all participants can make an evidence-based determination. Then discuss whether or not you agree that each one was placed in the best score "bucket."

Virtual facilitation tip: Preload documents in a shared drive with different saved names (e.g., Student A, Student B, Student C) so people can flip through easily.

Additional resource: Rhode Island Department of Education & National Center for the Improvement of Educational Assessment, *Calibration Protocol*

for Scoring Student Work (www.ride.ri.gov/Portals/0/Uploads/Documents/
Teachers-and-Administrators-Excellent-Educators/Educator-Evaluation/
Online-Modules/Calibration_Protocol_for_Scoring_Student_Work.pdf).

Child Study

Purpose: To foster shared responsibility across educators for a child.

Materials: Student data.

Group size: Any size. Break up a large group into 4–7 participants to allow opportunities for everyone to speak.

Summary: Presenting teacher(s) share context for a particular student and concerns or a dilemma that they have. Then they share student data, which includes observations, parent/caretaker data, and student work samples. Work samples are typically collected over time so team members can observe characteristics, patterns, and changes. After observation and time for inference, the team makes recommendations (for next instructional steps, curriculum resources, intervention or enrichment, etc.).

Upside:

- The team gains powerful insight into a child learner. Team members who share the same student see aspects of a child they may not otherwise have seen. Similarly, the presenting teacher sees aspects of a child they may not otherwise have noticed.

Downside:

- The process is time-consuming. Teams cannot do this with every student and must be selective.

- The name of the student at the center of the child study is revealed. Teacher bias can shape interpretation of the child's data.

STL Recommendations:

- For a vertical team or multi-subject grade-level team, a single presenting teacher shares context and presents student data to the team. For a grade-level team of teachers who share students, all team members can bring in student work from the same learner.

- Select at-risk students who need a team approach to helping them.

- Select students who fit a particular profile so that recommendations can be applied to more than one student.

Virtual facilitation tip: Screen share student work samples and view them at the same time using the comment box for observations.

Additional resource: School Reform Initiative, *The Descriptive Review of a Child* (schoolreforminitiative.org/doc/descriptive_review_child.pdf).

Data Driven Dialogue

Purpose: Originated by Nancy Love (2008), this protocol intends to engage teams in grade-level, school, or district-level data analysis.

Materials: Data; different-colored highlighters, chart paper, and markers.

Group size: Any size. Break up a large group into 4–7 participants to allow opportunities for everyone to speak.

Summary: Four phases define this data analysis protocol: Predict, Go Visual, Observe, and Infer. Before seeing any results, team members predict what they expect to see in the data. They anticipate findings. Then they create a visual representation of the data using charts, graphs, color-coding—whatever will help them make sense of data. Next, they make evidence-based observations from their visual representation. They withhold all explanations for what they observe, conjectures about what data mean, conclusions that they make, and potential solutions until the last phase (Infer), at which point they also decide how to proceed with what they have discovered from data analysis, and identify additional data needed to learn more.

Upside:

- This protocol requires team members to engage with the data at hand.

- The prediction phase surfaces assumptions and biases that are often challenged when people see the data.

- The protocol is designed to draw data-informed conclusions and propose solutions.

- When generating a visual, team members better understand the data. Patterns and trends jump out, thereby making the observation phase more robust.

Downside:

- The protocol is time consuming, particularly if you have a lot of data available.

- You need a strong facilitator who can keep the phases distinct. People can be tempted to see the data and jump to conclusions and offer solutions before discussing observations.

- Team members have different levels of data literacy. Some may not know how to interpret charts and graphs, let alone make them.

- It is possible to superficially move through each phase without talking about data points that reveal inequities, or to generate solutions that have not worked in the past for all students.

STL Recommendations:

- Save time and make copious amounts of data manageable by divvying up sections of data, by standard, for example. Have pairs or trios create a visual for one section instead of all the data. (Although not as powerful as going visual as a group, you could also have it be one person's role to create visuals for people to observe.)

- Make data analysis a routine part of your team's collaboration. Look at student work regularly and incorporate the phases of Observe and Infer. Examine grade-level or school data when relevant. With practice, people will become more data literate.

- Use the moves in Primary Intention 8 of this book to suspend and interrupt assumptions, bias, and unsound reasoning.

Virtual facilitation tip: Reading spreadsheets that someone screen shares can be challenging for people to see and work with. Highlight key areas for people to look at. Electronically send printable copies of data for people to print and mark up.

Additional resource: School Reform Initiative presents a protocol with fantastic prompts for each phase of the Data Driven Dialogue (schoolreforminitiative.org/download/data-driven-dialogue).

Evidence Analysis Action (EAA)

Purpose: Originated by Paul Bloomberg and Barbara Pitchford (2017), this protocol intends to help teams collectively make evidence-based decisions that impact student learning.

Materials: Success criteria aligned to a focus standard; student data.

Group size: Any size.

Summary: Contains all the elements for analyzing student work based on success criteria in three easy-to-grasp steps. A teacher team presents evidence of success criteria for the prompt or task in the student work samples, which are sorted into performance levels (high–exemplary, medium–mastery/proficiency, and low–approaching proficiency). Next, the team analyzes all available student data (work samples, self- and peer assessment, classroom observation, etc.), to decide student strengths and areas for growth for every group of students, and prioritizes a focus area for each. Lastly, the team creates a goal and high-leverage action plan for each group of students, as well as a means to assess progress and reflect on team impact.

Upside:

- Students are encouraged to participate in the analysis of their own work.

- The protocol emphasizes criteria-based evidence.

- The protocol yields actionable next steps.

- Many teachers find the simple three-step process accessible.

Downside:

- With poor facilitation, this protocol can be oversimplified, causing people to mechanically go through the motions. To focus talk on evidence, to engage in robust data analysis that suspends assumptions and bias, and to generate action plans that actually achieve better outcomes for students, STLs and their colleagues must make intentional moves throughout the protocol.

Additional resource: Leading Impact Teams: Building a Culture of Efficacy by Paul Bloomberg and Barbara Pitchford (2017). This book is an excellent resource for protocols, including Unpacking for Success in Action (see pages 81–85).

Looking at Three Levels of Student Work

Purpose: To observe evidence of student learning and plan instructional strategies to target areas for growth.

Materials: Prompt or task, student work samples, and criteria for success.

Group size: Any size. Break up a large group into 4–7 participants to allow opportunities for everyone to speak.

Summary: One person brings in three samples of student work (high–exemplary, medium–mastery/proficiency, and low–approaching proficiency) in response to the same prompt or task. (Alternatively, many teachers can bring in student work samples, such as responses to the same prompt or task, and look for patterns and trends across students.) The presenting teacher gives context for the prompt/task. Teachers silently observe student work and then share out what they notice. Dialogue moves toward inferring strengths and areas for growth and closes with instructional strategies/interventions and a commitment to implementation.

Upside:

- Teams build a habit of examining student work for strengths and areas for growth based on success criteria. Teachers take this practice to their classroom when determining next instructional steps for their own students.

- Teachers take away new learning about students and agree to strategies for implementation.

- This process occurs during the *Assess & Analyze* STL phase of collaborative inquiry to determine a focus for targeted inquiry and again during the *Act & Evaluate* STL phase of collaborative inquiry when teachers want to see the impact of what they are implementing with students.

Downside: I write this with reservation because looking at student work together is so powerful that it's well worth any downsides that exist.

- If team members are not used to making inferences about student work, you might get responses like "Well, how do I know what the student was thinking?"

- Protocols in general can feel stiff, but protocols for looking at student work can feel particularly so because you need to hold people to making evidence-based observations from the work in front of them before jumping into a conversation about instructional practice.

- The process is time-consuming, particularly if the student work samples are lengthy (e.g., five-paragraph essays).

STL Recommendations: See Moves 7.5–7.8. (Note: Data can include student work samples.)

Additional resources:

Resource 4.1, "Adapted Consultancy Protocol," in *The Skillful Team Leader* (MacDonald, 2013).

Rhode Island Department of Education & National Center for the Improvement of Educational Assessment, *Student Work Analysis Protocol* (www.ride .ri.gov/Portals/0/Uploads/Documents/Teachers-and-Administrators-Excellent -Educators/Educator-Evaluation/Online-Modules/Student_Work_Analysis_ Protocol.pdf).

Tuning

Purpose: To design or refine teaching, learning, or assessment materials based on a focus question.

Materials: Student work samples or learning materials that someone wants feedback on (lesson plans, prompts, or tasks; assessments; policies; surveys; parent/caretaker letters, etc.).

Group size: Any.

Summary: A teacher or group presents student work samples or learning materials with appropriate context and poses a question for feedback while the team listens. The team then asks clarifying questions. Teachers silently examine the document in front of them. Team members offer warm supportive feedback before moving on to giving cool feedback with questions or recommendations while the presenter is silent and listens. Then the presenter rejoins the discussion to share out any takeaways they got out of listening to colleagues.

Upside:

- The protocol provides insight into a student-centered challenge or dilemma.

- Students gain ownership of a lesson before doing peer observation of that lesson.

Downside:

- The protocol is time-consuming. The focus is on one learning material (e.g., one lesson plan) and/or one presenting teacher. It's important to ensure that what is being collectively examined has some relevancy to those who are analyzing the teacher's work.

STL Recommendation:

- End with an application where everyone on the team reports out on how the takeaways from analysis might give insight into their own similar challenges.

Additional resource: School Reform Initiative, *Tuning Protocol* (schoolre forminitiative.org/doc/tuning.pdf).

2. Protocols for Defining a Problem

Cause and Effect Protocols: Fishbone, Five Whys, and Peeling the Onion

Purpose: To narrow down focus and get at the root of a problem for inquiry.

Materials: Any tool for recording (chart paper, whiteboard, shared electronic document, etc.).

Group size: Any.

Summary: Three protocols in particular—Fishbone, Five *Whys*, and Peeling the Onion—demand teams to think deeply about specific root causes of a problem. A fishbone diagram uses a graphic organizer (shaped like a fishbone) in which the group first names the problem and then fills in the "bones" with overarching causes and specific contributing factors leading you to a root cause. Five *Whys* engages the group in asking "Why?" repeatedly until a root cause surfaces. Peeling the Onion "peels" the layers off of the problem to understand the dilemma by investigating assumptions and smaller more specific questions.

Upside: Teams get good at focusing their work on a specific, bite-sized cause of the problem instead of tackling something broad, generic, and overwhelming.

Downside: Each of these protocols takes time and patience, as many educators don't want to spend time pinpointing the problem—they want to jump to strategies. It can be frustrating for "Compass Points North" people who just want to get to solving the problem.

STL Recommendations:

- If your team is having difficulty narrowing questions down to a specific inquiry or goal for the team's work, any of these protocols can help the team articulate a compelling problem/dilemma that they are really concerned about.

- Create categories for the "bones" in the fishbone organizer and then list specific causes within each. Examples of causal categories include policies, people (training and staffing), systems and procedures, curriculum, pedagogy and instruction, and assessment.

Virtual tip: Five *Whys* and Peeling the Onion are very easy to facilitate over a virtual meeting because they are discussion based. Fishbone requires people to see the visual and add to it, so the facilitator can go "old school" by pointing their camera toward a whiteboard and drawing the organizer as people brainstorm.

Additional resources:

- Eye on Tech, *What Is a Fishbone Diagram?* (Video), (www.youtube.com/watch?v=4eteSMuum6k).

- School Reform Initiative, *The 5 Whys for Inquiry* (schoolreforminitiative .org/download/the-5-whys-for-inquiry/).

- School Reform Initiative, *Peeling the Onion: Defining a Dilemma Protocol* (schoolreforminitiative.org/doc/peeling_onion.pdf).

Consultancy (or Problem of Practice)

Purpose: To deep-dive into a problem of practice so that it can be better understood.

Materials: Evidence illustrating a problem.

Group size: Any. Groups of 4–7 are ideal.

Minimum time needed for discussion: 45 minutes.

Summary: An individual presents a dilemma. The group asks clarifying questions followed by probing questions. Then the group discusses what they have heard of the dilemma from the presenter while the presenter listens and takes notes silently. At the end the presenter shares what they have learned, and the group debriefs.

Upside:

- Listening to others talk about a dilemma can be very thought-provoking and bring about new insight for the presenter.

- If you can get through the whole protocol, group members leave with meaningful takeaways, even though the dilemma was not theirs.

Downside:

- It can be hard for some presenters to silently listen without feeling the need to explain or defend something they hear the group discussing.

- People might ask leading questions during the clarification portion of the protocol.

- A Consultancy protocol is meant to deeply unpack a problem, not solve it. This can feel frustrating to people who want to leave with solutions and action steps.

STL Recommendations:

- Keep the topic of the dilemma being explored related to the inquiry work of the team so that the problem of practice is relevant to everyone.

- Close the protocol with connections and takeaways for all participants.

- Review the distinction between clarifying questions and probing questions, and be vigilant in holding off on asking probing questions or offering solutions until people have a deep understanding of the dilemma.
    - Examples of clarifying questions: *What do you mean by . . . ? When did this happen? How much time did you spend on . . . ? I heard you say . . . Did I hear this correctly?*
    - Examples of probing questions: *Why did you . . . ? What would have happened if you didn't . . . ? What impact would X have on Y?*

- Preview the protocol so the presenter, in particular, understands why they are not permitted to talk for a portion of the protocol (see Move 4.6).

Virtual facilitation tip:

- Ask people to mute during different portions of the protocol as this can help them listen.

- Post sample questions in the chat so people can distinguish between clarifying and probing.

Additional resources:

- *The Skillful Team Leader* (MacDonald, 2013, pp. 167–168).

- Digital Promise, *Framing a Problem of Practice* (microcredentials .digitalpromise.org/explore/framing-a-problem-of-practice).

Adaptation: The Consultancy protocol can be used as a Success Analysis protocol to better understand an effective practice and aim to sustain success or replicate it. Instead of presenting a dilemma, the presenter would present a practice that is working. See National School Reform Faculty, *Success Analysis Protocol With Reflective Questions* (www.nsrfharmony.org/wp-content/uploads/2017/10/ success_analysis_reflective_0.pdf).

Related protocol: Issaquah. This is one of my favorite protocols because it not only delves into understanding of a dilemma, but also presses the presenter to actually attempt to answer one of the probing questions asked and then allows the group to make suggestions to help resolve the problem. It's a satisfying protocol for groups who like to leave with potential solutions and action steps, versus just a deeper understanding of a problem. See School Reform Initiative, *The Issaquah Protocol* (schoolreforminitiative.org/doc/issaquah.pdf).

3. Text-Based Protocols

Chalk Talk

Purpose: To brainstorm ideas, or surface people's responses to various quotes or excerpts.

Materials: Multiple quotations from the same or different texts, or questions about a topic.

Group size: Ideal for large groups.

Minimum time needed for discussion: Varies depending on number of quotes or questions.

Summary: Similar to a Gallery Walk (page 201), Chalk Talk has people circulating the room reading and responding to quotes or questions, except in Chalk Talk there is no verbal talking. Instead, people jot down their comments/ideas/ connection/questions, essentially "talking" to each other about the quote/ excerpt through writing.

Upside:

- This activity allows people to express their ideas without interruption.

- People can visually see where there is agreement or disagreement.

Downside: The protocol is time-consuming.

STL Recommendations:

- Write thought-provoking quotes or questions to which people feel compelled to respond.

- Participate. This will allow you to model the type of written "dialogue" you expect.

Virtual tip: Padlet makes it easy for people to jot down notes that everyone can view and comment on at once.

Additional resource: National School Reform Faculty, *Chalk Talk* (www .nsrfharmony.org/wp-content/uploads/2017/10/chalk_talk_0.pdf).

Final Word

Purpose: To explore multiple perspectives, clarify thinking, and question assumptions.

Materials: A rich text with many standout, important lines.

Group size: No more than 3 people per group. (Break up a large group into trios.)

Minimum time needed for discussion: 15 minutes.

Summary: One person reads aloud a standout line from a shared text and speaks about it for 3 minutes, uninterrupted. The next two people respond in turn for 1 minute, each uninterrupted. The round ends with the first person getting the final word for 1 minute. The process repeats with the next person.

Upside:

- Structure and parameters are given to difficult conversations, allowing everyone's voice to be heard.

Downside:

- The process involves tight time restrictions that some people aren't comfortable following.

- If a quote isn't very rich, people don't have much to say, and they just end up agreeing with the person before them.

STL Recommendations:

- Pick a strict timekeeper so that everyone has equal airtime and no one runs out of time.

Virtual facilitation tip: Pin the person talking so all focus is on that person for the full amount of time. If you want people to see the quote being discussed, share your screen highlighting the quotes each person selects.

Additional resource: School Reform Initiative, *The Final Word* (schoolre forminitiative.org/doc/final_word.pdf).

Four A's

Purpose: To analyze how a text relates to the reader and the group.

Materials: A shared text that presents new or controversial ideas.

Group size: 3–5 participants per group is ideal.

Minimum time needed for discussion: 15–20 minutes (3–5 minutes per round).

Summary: People read, noting places in the text that they *agree* with/*argue* with/notice are *assumptions* made by the author/and *aspire* to or *act* upon. Small groups can opt to discuss one *A* at a time in rounds or all together, or take rounds sharing out all four of their *A*'s. During discussion, one person makes reference to a line (and page number, if applicable) so that others can see what they are responding to.

Upside: This protocol encourages people to critically think about what they are reading or viewing.

Downside: Taking turns and only focusing on one *A* at a time can make conversation feel unnatural. Often people will want to break protocol.

STL Recommendations:

- Provide people with questions before they read:
    - What do you *agree* with in the text?
    - What do you want to *argue* with in the text?
    - What *assumptions* does the author of the text hold?
    - What parts of the text do you want to *aspire* to (or *act* upon)?
- Ask people to mark up the text with the four *A*'s as they read and add room for clarifying questions. (I know it's a *Q*, but you can't react to what you don't understand.) Invite people to annotate specific lines of the text with symbols:
    ✓ I agree with what the author is saying here.
    ✗ I disagree and can argue against what the author is saying here.
    ! I think the author is making an assumption here.
    ? I need clarity here.
    △ This is a change I want to or think I can make. I aspire to do this or act.

- When you preview the protocol (Move 4.6), give people a heads-up that as they take turns responding to only one *A* at a time, conversation might sound staccato and feel restricted, but this structure is to ensure each person thinks about the text in four ways and has a chance to express that thinking.

Virtual facilitation tip: Set up a Padlet with four categories—Agree, Argue, Assume, Aspire—so each person can contribute a "sticky note" comment and you have notes for the end of the conversation.

Additional resource: School Reform Initiative, *Four "A"s Text Protocol* (school-reforminitiative.org/doc/4_a_text.pdf).

Four Corners

Purpose: To explore multiple perspectives or points of view.

Materials: Excerpts from four different texts about the same topic.

Group size: 8+ people.

Minimum time needed for discussion: Duration varies depending on the length of the text, but you typically need 5 minutes for people to read the four excerpts and choose a text, 15 minutes to read and discuss the text in a corner, and 20–30 minutes to come together and discuss.

Summary: Present four quotes/excerpts from four different texts on one page. Teachers read all and then make one reading selection. Move to a corner of the room with others who have read the same text. Discuss. Then rejoin.

Upside: Your team can go deep with four texts about the same topic.

Downside: Not everyone reads the same text, which can cause people to summarize rather than engage in robust conversation across texts.

STL Recommendation: Select "juicy" quotes from each text that will really entice people to read more.

Additional resource: Facing History and Ourselves, *Four Corners* (www.facinghistory.org/resource-library/teaching-strategies/four-corners).

Gallery Walk

Purpose: To brainstorm ideas, or surface people's responses to various quotes or excerpts.

Materials: Multiple quotations from the same or different texts.

Group size: 5+.

Minimum time needed for discussion: Typically 3–5 minutes per quote.

Summary: Post quotations around the room on walls or tables. Allow people to stroll as if walking in an art gallery to read and think. You can add talk to this by grouping people so they rotate through quotes together.

Upside: Gallery Walks involve movement, which can elevate the energy in a room.

Downside: Because people don't have the full text, only excerpts, they might misinterpret the meaning of the text. Additionally, because there is little text to analyze, conversation can drift away from the words on the page and more into personal anecdotes.

STL Recommendations: Keep all selected quotes similar in length so that people circulate evenly. You don't want more than five people hanging out at one quote, because they won't be able to see it or engage in discussion.

Virtual tip: Use Padlet to create the gallery.

Additional resource: Gallery Walk Activity Protocol (www.uticaschools.org/site/handlers/filedownload.ashx?moduleinstanceid=273&dataid=289&FileName=Gallery%20Walk%20Activity%20Protocol-1.pdf).

Jigsaw

Purpose: To read or view different aspects of a similar topic.

Materials: Two or more texts, about the same length or viewing time.

Group size: Large groups are ideal. The number of texts determines the size of the home group.

Minimum time needed for discussion: Approximately 20–30 minutes after reading.

Summary: People sit in a "home" group and divvy up the readings so that every text is read by someone. Then they move to their "expert" groups where they read and discuss the same text with a new group of people. Finally, they return to their "home" group to report out on the text-based discussion they had in their "expert" groups.

Upside:

- People can explore a topic deeply in a short period of time.

- Participants rely on one another for learning. This builds community and trust.

- This activity creates interest and motivation in others to read/view texts they have not.

Downside: Some people share their reaction or personal anecdotes to what they read rather than highlighting key points the author made. Those who have not read or viewed the text don't leave knowing what the author said.

STL Recommendation: Save time by asking people to come prepared to your meeting already having read a text. They can immediately discuss it in their expert group, and then more time can be spent with the whole group discussing all the readings.

Virtual tip: Prepopulate breakout groups.

Additional resource: School Reform Initiative, *Jigsaw Description* (schoolre forminitiative.org/doc/jigsaw.pdf).

Mirrors and Windows

Purpose: To think about and reflect on your own point of view and explore identities, experiences, and motivations of people who are different from you.

Materials: A shared text that describes a person's experience.

Group size: Small groups.

Minimum time needed for discussion: 20 minutes depending on the text and size of the group.

Summary: Read a shared text. Each person holds a "mirror" to the text in which they reflect on their own identities, experiences, and motivations. For example: *In what ways do I identify with this character? How can I relate to this character's experience? In what ways can I understand why this character acted in the ways they did?* The participant then looks out the "window" to the identities, experiences, and motivations of others. For example: *What can I learn from reading about this character or their experience? How does reading this help me better understand what motivates others?*

Upside: People better understand their students and families, and one another. This grounds team talk about equity, race, disability, and difference in text. Small groups allow for more time to explore, listen, and be willing to show vulnerability where genuine learning can happen.

Downside: Without strong facilitation, biased comments can go unaddressed.

STL Recommendation: Literature designed for younger learners is great to use with adult learners because these texts give the child or adolescent's perspective and are usually a quick read for grown-ups. Reading nonfiction texts together can help debunk myths about cultural and learning differences, which can help teachers better understand their students.

There are so many examples of powerful literature for a younger audience that offer themes about understanding differences. Here are a few:

- *Home of the Brave* by Katherine Applegate

- *Between the World and Me* by Ta-Neihisi Coates

- *Paper Son: Lee's Journey to America* by Helen Foster James

- *Fish in a Tree* by Linda Mullaly Hun

- *Breaking Night: A Memoir of Forgiveness, Survival, and My Journey From Homelessness to Harvard* by Liz Murra

- *The Sisters Are Alright* by Tamara Winfrey Harri

- *The Reason I Jump* by Naoki Higashida and other books about autism listed at www.autismspeaks.org/blog/books-about-autism

Examples of nonfiction that help us better understand differences include these:

- *The Dyslexic Advantage: Unlocking the Hidden Potential of the Dyslexic Brain* by Brock L. Eide and Fernette F. Eide

- *What's It Like to Be a Student of Color in a Predominantly White School District?* by Tiziana Dearing and Paris Alston (www.wbur.org/radioboston/2020/07/22/july-22-2020-rb)

- *Driven to Distraction: Recognizing and Coping With Attention Deficit Disorder From Childhood Through Adulthood* by Edward M. Hallowell and John J. Ratey

Virtual facilitation tip: Conversations using this protocol can be sensitive, and connecting virtually can feel impersonal. Set up small groups of two to three people so that talk can feel more intimate than talking to a large group where everyone's face image is small.

Additional resources:

- Learning for Justice, *Window or Mirror?* (www.tolerance.org/classroom-resources/teaching-strategies/close-and-critical-reading/window-or-mirror).

- "Telling the Fuller Story: Afrika Afeni Mills," Season 2, Episode 4, of *The Science of Reading* (www.buzzsprout.com/612361/5959177-s2-04-telling-the-fuller-story-afrika-afeni-mills).

Text Rendering

Purpose: To collectively build meaning of a text.

Materials: Shared substantive text.

Group size: Small or large groups.

Minimum time needed for discussion: Approximately 20 minutes (3–5 minutes per round plus time for a read-through of the new text).

Summary: Team members read a shared text, silently marking a sentence, a phrase, and a word that they feel is critically important. This game is played in three rounds: at the sentence level, the phrase level, and the single-word level. For each round, team members individually call out direct quotes from the text. No one should paraphrase. Repetition of quotes is permitted. Someone scribes on chart paper or an electronic document what people read off. After people have shared their direct quotes, one person reads aloud the newly written rendering of the text.

Upside: This activity distills a long substantive text down to the most important standout lines, phrases, and words of the group. The act of reading aloud the newly written rendering is powerful and builds community.

Downside: Live scribing can slow down momentum.

STL Recommendation: Save time by scribing. Either (a) recruit two people to scribe on two separate chart papers (or computers), alternating back and forth (e.g., Sarah and Joe alternate writing down each comment made by a team member), or (b) request team members to write their line, phrase, and word (each on a separate sticky note). Then, when ready to share, they stick them on the wall. One person reads aloud all sticky notes in sequence.

Virtual facilitation tip: Use a shared Google Doc where each person can type.

Additional resource: School Reform Initiative, *Text Rendering Experience* (schoolreforminitiative.org/doc/text_rendering.pdf).

Three Levels of Text

Purpose: To collectively analyze a passage or line from a text.

Materials: A shared text with one or more passages that hold deep meaning.

Group size: 3–5 participants per group is ideal.

Minimum time needed for discussion: Approximately 15 minutes (three rounds at 3–5 minutes per round).

Summary: Individuals read text silently. One person reads aloud a standout passage or line from the text, making reference to the location. The group first discusses the literal interpretation of the excerpt, then moves to discuss what they interpret it to mean, and lastly, they discuss the implications to their work.

Upside: This protocol slows readers/viewers down to digest the text and think more globally about what the author is saying and how it applies to their classrooms, schools, and communities.

Downside: People need to learn how to select substantive passages or lines of text that are meaty enough to analyze.

STL Recommendations:

- This protocol is similar to one from a favorite author of mine, Kelly Gallagher (2004), in which a teacher asks students to analyze a text excerpt with three questions: *What does it say?* (literal interpretation); *What does it mean?* (infer meaning); and *What does it matter?* (why this is important).

- As the facilitator, you can select passages and lines that you want people to delve into.

Virtual facilitation tip: As a creative alternative to typing quotes in the chat box, each person can make their own Prezi presentation with the quote and include images as well as text to communicate meaning and importance.

Additional resource: School Reform Initiative, *Three Levels of Text Protocol* (schoolreforminitiative.org/doc/3_levels_text.pdf).

LEARN FROM A TEXT-BASED DISCUSSION

A successful team "builds pedagogical knowledge to learn more effective ways to reach all students" (Helen Timperley, quoted in CORE Education Digital Media, 2012). Most likely, you and your colleagues already *independently* read professional articles and books to improve your practice, but you might not, yet, do so collaboratively. Engaging your team in dialogue about a shared text can be a powerful learning experience. Most often facilitated during the *Research & Study* STL phase of collaborative inquiry, text-based discussions expose teachers to new ideas. The act of talking about a common text together furthers understanding, provokes reflection, and sets teams up to design and implement new strategies. Skillful team leaders (STLs) are intentional about the texts they select and how they will engage their colleagues in discussion about them.

STL moves:

4.8 Select a shared text.

4.9 Design the reading/viewing experience.

4.10 Prep the text, the reader, and yourself.

4.11 Build a collaborative reading habit.

What these moves promote:

Evidence-based learning. Teams ground discussion in texts and formulate new learning.

Community. Teams engage in the shared experience of reading and talking about texts together.

When to use these moves:

In preparation for a text-based discussion.

4.8 Select a shared text.

A "bad" text can turn people off to "good" ideas. I've heard people dismiss an article for numerous reasons: "The ideas are outdated," "This is about a school that's nothing like ours," "We teach high school and this is about elementary students," "The author seems biased," "The tone is condescending," "The text is too long to read in the time we have." Even teams who have established routines of reading professional texts together can encounter resistance when the text isn't a good fit. Skillful team leaders (STLs) are intentional in selecting a shared text.

How to select a shared text:

Consider at least eight factors when selecting a text for collaborative discussion:

1. *Purpose.* The text promotes learning related to our team priorities, goals, and/or inquiry. There is a compelling reason to read and discuss this text together.

2. *Date of publication.* The copyright date is current, and if not, the text holds up.

3. *Author.* The author is credible and knowledgeable. Texts consist of a range of diverse authors.

4. *Content.* The text offers worthwhile content and ideas. Any shortcomings of the text won't likely interrupt what we can glean from it. What is being said has the potential to influence our hearts, minds, words, and actions.

5. *Style.* The substance, complexity, tone, style, word choice, voice, and format of the text draw us in; none are off-putting.

6. *Audience.* We are the intended audience for this text, and if not, we will likely be able to connect to it in some way.

7. *Cultural relevance.* The text is culturally appropriate to our identities, cultures, and experiences and to the students we serve. Reading the text at this time makes sense.

8. *Length.* The length of the text is accessible or can be broken into chunks in the time we have or be adequately summarized.

In action:

STL Karen Coyle Aylward was about to lead a text-based discussion in the spring of 2021 about bolstering family engagement. She chose "Engaging Families at the Secondary Level: An Underused Resource for Student Success" by Krista L. Jensen and Kathleen M. Minke (2018). Several things went into her decision to pick this journal article:

- *The principal communicated to staff that family engagement was a school priority based on a district emphasis on culturally responsive teaching, and based on school data from an instructional learning walk, family surveys, and his own observations.*

- *Karen wanted conversation to be grounded in current research (within the last five years) so it wasn't just her sharing her own experience. The text explains that academic socialization is the form of family engagement that had the most effective impact on adolescents. The text also provides actionable ways to involve parents and caregivers in this way.*

- *Karen perceived that there was a pervasive mindset (not always obvious, but evident) in which staff saw their role as informants (i.e., communicating missing assignments or failing grades) and also partners with parents and caregivers for community social events, but few actively sought parent feedback and partnered with parents in the ways the article describes to help them influence their children's academics. Reading this research-based journal article with her colleagues had the potential to positively influence staff's mindset about family engagement and boost the school's collective efficacy, in support of their belief that their actions with parents and caregivers could impact students' academic success.*

- *Karen intentionally found a text that spoke to secondary schools because she understood that parent relationship with adolescents is different than that of elementary children, as developmentally, kids present different needs. She also understood that high school educators (herself being one) relate better to texts that speak to the age group of students they teach.*

- *Karen thought about who would be discussing the text. Many of the newly hired staff were young, inexperienced teachers who were not parents themselves and held a different perspective than those teachers who were parents or seasoned teachers. She wanted to find a reading that would bridge understanding between people with different perspectives and create a shared learning experience.*

- *Karen faced the challenge that the journal article was 25 pages long and a little dense. Her meeting time was too short to use the time to read, and she didn't want to assign such a long text to read in advance because she felt the demand would be too much on her colleagues, so she shared the link for those who wanted to read the text before or after the conversation, and created a PowerPoint presentation that would summarize key ideas and highlight key quotes for discussion.*

STL recommendations:

Share responsibility. Encourage all members of your team to find professional texts for discussion. I once worked with a team in which a science teacher on the second day of inquiry asked if he could share a reading he found. This was a clear sign that he had been thinking about his team's work and was invested. Teachers were enthusiastic to discuss what he brought, and it established a great dynamic in the group.

Offer a text set. One text may not meet all your criteria. Acknowledge what it is lacking and, if possible, present additional texts. When selecting multiple texts, check that you are looking through a diversity lens (diverse authors, diverse perspectives, etc.). You might opt for a protocol such as Jigsaw or Four Corners that allows you to discuss all texts at once, or plan to read and discuss multiple texts over the course of multiple meetings. (See Move 4.7 for text-based protocols.)

Create a text bank. Collaborate with other team leaders and share texts to which teachers always seem to respond well.

Think like a teacher:

Text selection for your team is a key component to the success of a learning discussion, just as it is in the classroom. As a teacher, you take into account key considerations when choosing texts for your students to read and discuss, particularly for an English learner population (Johnson et al., 2018). Like younger learners, adult learners can be turned off to a text that, for example, they can't relate to, or one that is outdated or culturally insensitive, and this can kill dialogue.

Find the right words:

1. Purpose. *Why should we read and discuss this text together? How will this text-based discussion further our inquiry work, priorities, and/or goals?*

2. Date of publication. *When was this text written? Is the content outdated?*

3. Author. *Does the author demonstrate credibility and seem to be an expert? What background and what experience does the author have? If we're reading multiple pieces within a text set, do we have representation of diverse authors (such as diversity of race, gender, age, political positioning, experience, or perspective)?*

4. Content. *What does the text say? What does the text not say? What are the strengths and shortcomings of this text? What potential does this text have to stimulate our hearts, minds, words, or actions?*

5. Style. *Is the language of the text digestible and the format written in a way that will engage people and not turn them off?*

6. Audience. *Who will be reading this text, and will they be able to relate to it?*

7. Cultural relevance. *Is the text culturally appropriate to our identities, cultures, and experiences and to the students we serve? Is the text culturally insensitive? What is happening around us (school, community, world) that might impact how we read this?*

8. Length. *How much time will we need to read and analyze this text? Will an excerpt or summary of this text be sufficient for a robust discussion?*

4.9 Design the reading/viewing experience.

Perhaps your local library has run a campaign where everyone reads the same book at the same time, then gathers people together to talk about it. This shared experience can be extremely powerful . . . or not. I worked in a district where administrators bought the same book for every staff member in the school in hopes that people would talk and build a common foundation. But the school never carved out time for a text-based discussion. People were left on their own to process the text and figure out how to implement the ideas in it. Sadly, neither I nor many of my colleagues gave it more than a glance. Just as important as selecting a text is deciding how your team will collaborate about it. Skillful team leaders (STLs) intentionally design an engaging professional reading/viewing experience for their teams.

How to design the reading/viewing experience:

Decide if you want your colleagues to have a shared experience in which they read or view the same text. This allows people to cross-collaborate easily, build common understandings, debunk misconceptions together, and plan to implement or apply what's learned. If, however, you want to explore different aspects or perspectives of the same subject matter, and give people choice in what they read or view, then invite people to examine different texts. Consider the number of people who will be discussing the text(s), the number of texts, the time you have, and the length of the text(s). Determine a structure that supports a conversation about the following:

- Key concepts in the text

- Shared understandings about what the author(s) presents

- Each reader's unique experience with the text

- The influence of the text and text-based discussion on the reader and/or team

- Implications for teachers, students, families, schools, and communities

- Ways to make learning actionable

You might opt to use a text-based protocol or write your own guiding questions to structure your conversation. (Sample protocols can be found in Move 4.7.)

In action:

STL Osamagbe (Osa) Osagie is about to engage her diversity, equity, and inclusion (DEI) professional learning community in a text-based discussion about the article "Growing Up Black in All the Wrong Places" by Jonathan Jackson (2020). She presents her team with six guiding questions specific to the text:

1. What are your thoughts on the concept of Black exceptionalism? Do you ever feel forced to be exceptional? How does this play out for you? How might it for others in our school community (colleagues and/or students)?

2. If you are white, what might you do differently knowing that a person of color might feel invisible in your midst? What does it mean to "work to see someone" of color?

3. How has this article shifted your perceptions about racial relations within the New England area?

4. How has this article deepened your understanding of the intersections between the twin pandemics: racism and COVID-19?

5. Because of this article, I am challenging myself to learn more about . . .

6. Given the article's provocative title, what will it take for us to create a world that is comfortable and safe for individuals who are Black, Indigenous, Latinx,* Asian, and multiracial to grow and thrive in?

—Courtesy of Carroll School, Lincoln, Massachusetts

Think like a teacher:

As a teacher, you make choices about how students will read a text in your classroom. For example, sometimes you opt for a whole-class shared read, sometimes you break a class into small groups and have the students read different texts, and sometimes you have every child independently choose what they will read. You also decide how to engage students in talking together about the texts they've read. A history teacher might have students lead a Socratic seminar, an English teacher might engage students in literature circles in which they take on different roles, and an art teacher might pose specific probing questions for students to discuss a painting. The considerations you take and the scaffolds you put in place for a text-based discussion all contribute to the experience learners have with the text.

When designing meetings in which you invite your colleagues to engage in a text-based discussion, you'll want to be just as intentional about the experience people have with the text in your meeting as you would with your students.

STL recommendation:

Structure sustainable conversations. STLs are deliberate not only in structuring a text-based discussion within a meeting, but also in thinking about how they and their colleagues will sustain talk beyond the minutes of a meeting. Conversations about DEI, in particular, are never meant to be a "one and done." Revisit ideas and language from shared texts and give the concepts time to marinate. Work with other leaders to ensure school professional development intentionally provides multiple, ongoing opportunities for learning and support in implementation.

PRIMARY INTENTION 4

Latinx is a gender-neutral term referencing people who identify with Latin American culture or ethnicity.

Find the right words:

- *Who will read what? Do we offer choices for people to read or view different texts, or will it serve our discussion better to all read or view the same text?*

- *I'm providing specific guiding questions to enrich your reading or viewing experience and set us up for a robust text-based discussion.*

- *As you read or view the text, consider the following:*
  - *What key concepts stand out to you?*
  - *What is your understanding of the author's message?*
  - *What is your initial response to this text?*
  - *In what ways is this text influencing your thinking?*
  - *What implications do the ideas of this text have for teachers, students, families, schools, and/or communities?*
  - *What are some ways we can make the ideas presented in this text (and the learning from our discussion about this text) actionable?*

4.10 Prep the text, the reader, and yourself.

If there's one key point in this book about why skillful team leaders (STLs) are successful, it's the thoughtful decision making they do before every meeting. Before teams read and collaborate about a text, STLs prep the text, their readers, and themselves.

1. Prep the text.

Have you ever sat down with learners to discuss a reading and someone says, "Oh! I think I read the wrong section"? I'm not talking about your students. Miscommunication about what to prepare for a meeting can happen just as easily with teams of adults. STLs prepare whatever texts a team will discuss so that people know exactly what to read and can easily make reference to specific passages during discussion.

How to prep the text:

Although this move is rather obvious, it's easy to forget how taking a moment in advance to prep your texts can prevent problems when you sit down to discuss. Do one or more of the following:

- *Repaginate.* If you're reading a text set gathered from different sources (e.g., multiple articles), collate and repaginate them for easy reference.

- *Delineate start and stop.* Sometimes you'll want to have people read only excerpts of a text. Make it clear with arrows or literal words to "start here" or "stop here" on the page.

- *Check e-access.* If people are going to read an electronic document, check that all share settings are on.

- *Accommodate adult learners.* For those learners with differences or disabilities, ensure text is accessible. For instance, you might need to enlarge the print, offer an audio version of a printed text, or show closed-captioning for a video.

2. Prep the reader.

Often, despite having the text in front of them, people who are not used to collaborative text-based discussions will drift to tangents about their experiences or what they think without discussing the ideas presented in the reading. STLs, regardless of the protocol, prep the reader. Informing people of expectations in advance allows them to successfully participate in a text-based discussion.

How to prep the reader:

Engage people in active reading by giving prompts before the discussion or suggesting note-taking during reading (e.g., annotating, filling out a graphic organizer, or highlighting standout lines). (If you're asking people to read on their own time before a meeting, then check that doing so does not violate any teachers' union guidelines, if applicable.) Review any protocol in advance of the text-based discussion.

STL recommendation:

Avoid overload. Providing guiding prompts while reading helps people engage in a text-based discussion, but be careful not to overload people with things to do while reading. One task, such as "highlight standout lines" or "think about what the author is saying and how you might apply it," is typically sufficient. Check the protocol you choose because some, such as Four *A*'s, prompt you to read for specific things.

3. Prep yourself.

"You never know how it's going to hit." STL Osamagbe (Osa) Osagie shared these words with me, and they could not be more true. You can be extremely thoughtful in your selection of a text, and intentional in how you collaborate about it with a team, but you cannot predict how either will affect others. STLs prepare themselves for the possibility of unexpected responses to a text from their colleagues.

How to prep yourself:

Once you have prepared the text, the discussion, and the readers, you must allow people the breathing space to take it from there. Expect that for some people, the text you chose may not resonate with them. Some may take offense at a protocol or guiding question you pose. Some may be so moved by a reading that it brings them to a heightened emotional state. Some might pose a viewpoint or belief statement so different from your own that you instinctively want to defend the author and shut the person down. You are more likely to effectively respond in the moment (even if your choice is silence) when you have thought through ways in which the text-based discussion might go and anticipate the ride.

4.11 Build a collaborative reading habit.

Not all teachers expect that they will read and analyze a text together in a team meeting. People expect to cover operations, even analyze data together, but making time to study and learn together might be a new way of working together. Skillful team leaders (STLs) build team habits to get teachers in the right headspace for text-based discussions.

How to build a collaborative reading habit:

Learn the history of professional learning at your school. Are people accustomed to using meeting time to read and discuss texts? Strengthen your collaborative muscle. Begin with frequent use of short digestible texts; then expose people to longer, more complex texts over time. Listed from least to most demanding, here are some types of text you might choose to engage your team in a text-based discussion:

- A cartoon
- A quote
- A gallery of quotes
- Video clips
- Short excerpts from chapters or article summaries
- Whole articles or chapters
- A book study
- Research studies

Mix and match these formats once your team is accustomed to reading and analyzing texts together. Once the reading discussion begins, make sure people know that it is OK to disagree with the text.

In action:

Teachers on Ruth's team read professional texts on their own all the time but have never read and discussed texts together. In the first meeting, she pulls a humorous cartoon, and people discuss how they relate to it. At the next meeting, Ruth opens with a controversial quote on their topic of inquiry and invites them to agree or disagree with it. When the team gets to STL phase of collaborative inquiry 4, Research & Study, *Ruth jigsaws passages of an article so that pairs of teachers read manageable excerpts that they can discuss deeply. Teachers also view a professional recorded video clip of the teaching strategy they are about to implement and pick apart moves they saw the teacher using. At the end of their first inquiry cycle, a new question emerges, to which Ruth pulls a related article. Reading the article raises specific questions, and the team decides to begin a new inquiry cycle.*

STL recommendation:

Reach for the summary. A popular resource written by Kim Marshall, *The Marshall Memo* (marshallmemo.com), is a weekly subscription that summarizes current articles and studies. Engaging your team in a discussion about a reading summary saves time, distills the text into key ideas, feels approachable for busy teachers, and can spark members on your team to seek out the full, original text for further learning. If you don't have a summary for a long text, you can write one; just be sure that you don't do all the thinking for your team. Summarize key points, but invite your colleagues to interpret them and analyze what they mean.

Find the right words:

- *I found this short reading that seems relevant to our discussion.*

- *Does anyone know of a text that we can read or view together to further our understanding of . . . ?*

- *I think it's important to collectively build new knowledge so we will read/view this text together.*

PRIMARY INTENTION 4

Primary Intention

5

Engage and Interact: Participation and Conflict Resolution

The premise of Part I, Chapter 2 is that skillful team leaders (STLs) do more than lead people to get along and get things done. They make sure that *what* gets done positively impacts student learning. But, what if your team's main struggle *is* how to work well together? If any of the following descriptions sound familiar, then you might need to take a step back and focus on the function of your team.

- Some people monopolize the conversation while others remain silent.

- Your meetings spin into black holes where nothing gets accomplished.

- Good ideas get lost in the mix.

- Your group frequently goes off on a tangent.

- Conflicts arise that people can't get past.

STLs lead so that all members are fully engaged, work productively, focus on what's important, and work through unproductive conflict.

Contents:

Boost engagement.

5.1 Set parameters for breakout groups.

5.2 Foster equitable airtime.

5.3 Reframe your ask.

5.4 Provide downtime.

5.5 Manage your own level of participation.

5.6 Empower others to problem solve.

Maximize productivity.

5.7 Form subcommittees.

5.8 Paraphrase.

5.9 Table the discussion.

5.10 Appoint a volunteer.

Focus talk.

5.11 Frame conversation with clear parameters.

5.12 Zoom out to the big picture.

5.13 Zoom in on a key point.

5.14 Redirect.

5.15 Pivot from teaching to learning.

5.16 Synthesize ideas.

Manage conflict.

5.17 Clarify understanding.

5.18 Interrupt negative energy.

5.19 Turn to a third data point.

5.20 Listen for the point of agreement.

5.21 Acknowledge. Assert. Move on.

5.22 Adopt a learning stance.

5.23 Clear the air as a group.

5.24 Check in 1:1.

5.25 Provide a graceful exit.

Tools and templates:

Figure 20: Iceberg Visual as Told by Daryl Campbell

Figure 21: Clear the Air as a Group: Roles and Rules of Engagement

Figure 22: Speaker and Listener Writing Prompts

BOOST ENGAGEMENT

Engagement is the Holy Grail for learning. Teachers want it for their students; team leaders want it in their meetings; schools want it for families. While there is always debate about how to engage others and how to measure engagement, there is agreement (and research to back it up) that equitable participation on a team makes collaboration better. Skillful team leaders (STLs) make moves to boost engagement so that everyone is encouraged to contribute to the conversation—particularly people who identify with traditionally marginalized populations and as non-native speakers. A few of the many moves that can boost engagement in meetings are explored in this section.

Think like a student:

I keep a 2013 article by author and consultant Jack Berckemeyer who interviewed middle school teachers and students about the best ways to engage kids. Where teachers suggested things like "technology" and "rewards and fun activities," students said they were most engaged in learning by "teachers with a sense of humor," "a classroom that looks like a middle school classroom," and "a teacher who really wants to be there." It's a good reminder that at the end of the day bells and whistles aren't really what get young learners engaged.

Transfer this idea to what engages adult learners, and the feedback I and other STLs hear from teachers includes "being treated as a professional," "being heard," "being stretched in my practice," "having time to think," and "connecting with others in meaningful ways." As you employ the moves in this section, remember that they only boost engagement when the fundamentals, such as treating people as professionals, are in place.

STL moves:

5.1 Set parameters for breakout groups.

5.2 Foster equitable airtime.

5.3 Reframe your ask.

5.4 Provide downtime.

5.5 Manage your own level of participation.

5.6 Empower others to problem solve.

What these moves promote:

Active participation. All people are encouraged to contribute.

Dialogue. STLs stimulate thoughtful dialogue between members, encouraging all voices and perspectives.

When to use these moves:

During facilitation of a meeting.

5.1 Set parameters for breakout groups.

If you've had to teach virtually, then you're likely an old pro at breakout rooms. You know how clutch the tool is in boosting engagement. Ensuring opportunity for participation, particularly on large or virtual teams, can be a challenge. Pairing people up or creating small groups helps. This move seems basic and obvious, but you'd be surprised how often leaders keep everyone together for an entire meeting. Perhaps they are concerned that breakouts will reduce their ability to manage conversation, or that people won't stay on task without a leader present to facilitate small-group conversation (a legitimate concern). Skillful team leaders (STLs) maximize participation by setting parameters for successful breakouts.

How to set parameters for breakout groups:

Consider the following:

- *Size.* Keep groups small so that people have opportunities to speak. Pairs require both people to engage. Trios can be less inclusive as one person can get left out. Quads give the option of splitting up into pairs, if desired.

- *People.* Consider what type of grouping—random or intentional, homogeneous or heterogeneous, and so on—will bring the most benefit to people.

- *Time.* Keep breakout sessions short (up to 10 minutes) unless you are leading project-based breakout groups where people are working on different aspects of a task or doing a jigsaw reading or another such activity.

- *Task.* Provide a reason for people to engage with one another. Provide one specific task for short breakout sessions. Give project-based groupings no more than three tasks. For example, (1) watch this video clip, (2) discuss how this is applicable to our work, and (3) anticipate challenges that might arise during implementation. Task choice also heightens engagement. Offer two prompts and let breakout groups choose to respond to one.

- *Task clarity.* Provide simple written directions. If the task is complex, check for understanding before moving into breakout groups.

- *Leadership.* Appoint or allow groups to self-select moderators to keep the group on task. Decide if you will manage conversation by floating in and out of groups, or be an active member of one group.

- *Reconvene as a team.* Agree to a signal in advance that indicates it is time to return to the whole group. Groups can monitor their own time, or you can offer an agreed-upon signal such as putting up hands for attention and silence.

- *Accountability.* Ask groups to report out one highlight of their conversation.

In action:

Alice: It seems valuable to break out into small groups by grade level for this discussion, and then we will come back together as a whole department. I arranged in advance for one person from each group to be the moderator. Each moderator has been given two questions for your group to discuss. Choose one person to report out on one key point from your discussion when we reconvene as a whole group. Because we are a large group, I'll use the school attention-getting signal of "give me five." If you would play along just so we don't waste time and can come back together quickly, I'd appreciate it. Thanks.

Think like a teacher:

Many of the techniques you use when you break your students into small groups can be applied to adult breakout groups. For instance:

- Intentionally group learners.

- Present directions orally and in writing to avoid confusion in the task.

- Assign group roles to keep learners accountable.

- Circulate among groups to gently facilitate and highlight common themes or questions you notice across groups.

Whatever techniques you use with adults, be cautious not to offend anyone by treating them like a student. (See Move 3.5.)

Find the right words:

- *I want everyone to have a chance to weigh in on this topic. Let's break out into small groups. I'll review the task, who is in each breakout group, how much time you will have, and what you will be expected to do when we come back together as a team.*

5.2 Foster equitable airtime.

Three things are guaranteed to kill equitable participation in a meeting: (1) pontificating, when one person speaks as if giving an on-stage soliloquy with no room for others to join in; (2) verbal ping-pong, when two people are wrapped up in a back-and-forth conversation to the exclusion of others; and (3) "othering," when team members (often unconsciously) distinguish themselves in a superior way from someone who socially or culturally identifies with a group different from theirs. People who identify with traditionally marginalized groups, such as BIPOC (Black, Indigenous, and people of color), women, LGBTQIA+, older adults, or individuals with disabilities, most often experience othering. Pontificating, verbal ping-pong, and othering each create an imbalance of airtime where some people do all the talking and others do none. Skillful team leaders (STLs) foster equitable airtime. Sometimes called "conversational turn-taking," this is not just a feel-good thing. Studies show it actually produces better learning outcomes for teams, and more well-thought-out decisions (Duhigg, 2016). In fact, when people don't get equal time to contribute to the talk at the table, the collective intelligence of the group actually declines (Becker & Smith, 2019). So when you foster equitable airtime, you are not only helping your team function better together, but also improving your group's potential impact on learning. Despite people knowing they are supposed to "share the air," as it's commonly referenced in group norms, some voices dominate conversation more than others. STLs dial down dominant voices and encourage others to speak up.

Note: Anyone on a team can have a hard time participating in conversation at a team meeting; however, it can be particularly challenging for non-native speakers and those who identify with traditionally marginalized groups. (See the shaded region that follows.).

The need for equitable airtime for non-native speakers and people who socially or culturally identify with a traditionally marginalized group.

My father, born in Uruguay, raised in Rio de Janeiro, is a native Portuguese speaker. As kids born in America, we used to giggle whenever he would say, "Let's go to the beach," as his thick accent made *beach* sound like a swear word we were not allowed to say. Non-native speakers might participate in a group less than they would if they were able to speak in their native tongue (Neeley, 2015). Those with a heavy accent or who are not fluent have an additional hardship of being understood. People might respectfully listen to a non-native speaker, but might not proactively engage with them because they are not confident that they'll be able to understand them.

Similarly, members on a team might not equitably "share the air" where there is an imbalance of representation from one race, gender, age group, (dis)ability, or religion. For example, various reports and studies found that women in business who work in a male-dominant culture experience microaggressions such as being interrupted, having their judgment or competence questioned, encountering people who are surprised by their skills, and being assigned more administrative tasks than men. Women of color or who identify with the LGBTQIA+ community experience this more than most people (McKinsey & Company, 2021).

How to foster equitable airtime:

To best create equitable airtime with teams who have an imbalanced composition of more native speakers than non-, or of more people representing the dominant culture than those who identify with traditionally marginalized populations, experts recommend that teams adopt a dial-down, dial-up approach (Neeley, 2015). Fluent speakers, for example, can dial down dominance in ways such as slowing down the pace of speech and using fewer idioms. Less fluent speakers can dial up engagement in ways such as resisting the urge to withdraw, articulating clearly so a strong accent can be understood, and regularly checking for understanding. People who identify with the dominant culture can watch that they do not impose their norms on other members of the group. And people who identify with traditionally marginalized groups can dial up engagement by remaining self-confident in what they have to offer, asserting themselves into group conversation, asking for tasks that require a high level of skill, and respectfully pointing out microaggressions as they happen.

To promote conversational turn talking with everyone on your team, you might try one of the following:

- "Serve someone the ball" by actively inviting a person who you know has something to contribute to speak.

- Interject in a verbal ping-pong match between two colleagues with a call to others in the group to join the conversation.

- Ask people to stop and jot thinking notes before you "open the floor" for talk. This gives people time to prepare what they will contribute.

- Monitor your own airtime. Contribute only when you feel it advances the conversation. Try holding back at the first urge to voice a comment or question that comes to mind, and you'll find that within minutes someone else usually voices what you were thinking. Reserve your voice to bring forward original questions or insight that no one has entertained, or to implement facilitation moves such as those highlighted in this section (see Move 5.5).

- Mix up the way you lead discourse with techniques such as "popcorning," where anyone can jump in with their voice, or round-robin, where you move from person to person giving everyone an opportunity to speak or pass.

- Use a protocol. Many, such as Final Word, have built-in time limits and sequences for people to speak, ensuring all have a voice (see Move 4.7).

In action:

In this example, Nick intervenes when two teachers engage in verbal ping-pong.

Nick: We are doing a good job teaching about the injustices of colonial times, but agree that we also want students to experience some of the different life circumstances that colonial and Indigenous children had to endure during that time. What can we do?

Teacher 1:	For a colonial life experience, we can have students loom.
Teacher 2:	Oh, I have tons of yarn from last year. And what about carving soap? That's always a big hit.
Teacher 1:	Definitely. Then there should be a station for colonial games like "cup and ball."
Teacher 2:	Nice. And I can ask the cafeteria to make food like corn on the cob.
Teacher 1:	I have a recipe for johnnycakes. Maybe the kids could make them.
Teacher 2:	Hmmm, what activities could highlight the lives of the children of the Indigenous people?
Nick:	[*Turns to Teacher 3*] I think you have begun to research a number of activities. Can you share one of those?
Teacher 3:	Thanks. Yes, we could do a read-aloud from the beginning of Chapter 3 of *Ghost Hawk* by Susan Cooper that describes 11-year-old Little Hawk's "proving time" when he must go off into the woods in winter and survive, which was a typical tradition for young boys entering adulthood. It's a very engaging passage.

Find the right words:

- (To a dominant talker) *Thank you for that insight.* (To the group) *Can we hear from other perspectives?*

- (When two people dominate the conversation) *I'm going to interrupt you both for just a moment because I'd like to bring others into the conversation.*

- (To a team with non-native speakers) *I'm grateful to have people from diverse backgrounds at our table. To make certain everyone is heard and understood, let's agree to speak slowly and clearly and avoid interrupting one another.*

Related readings:

Move 5.21, "Acknowledge. Assert. Move on." This move can be an effective response when someone needs to address a microaggression.

Moves 8.4–8.10 are intended to interrupt assumptions, bias, and unsound reasoning.

5.3 Reframe your ask.

Have you ever asked a question and heard crickets? Or, perhaps worse, you get a long-winded answer to a completely different question than the one you asked? When you hear these types of responses, you might think people are uninterested and checked out. You might be tempted to answer the question yourself or move on. But before you do, realize that people might simply not understand your question. Skillful team leaders (STLs) reframe their ask, giving their colleagues another go at it.

How to reframe your ask:

Notice when you ask a question and don't get the response you expected. Think back to why you are asking the question. Then decide how you can change your wording to elicit a different response. Consider the impact of words like *why*, which can come across in nontrusting circumstances as prosecuting (e.g., "*Why* did you do it this way?"). Remove jargon and define new terms and acronyms that people might not yet fully remember the meaning of. If you reframe and people still don't engage with your question, ask someone else to reframe for you.

In action:

Leah: What was your response to the way in which this article was written? [*Teachers look down for an uncomfortable period of silence.*] What effect did the authors' strong choice of words have on you?

Teacher 1:   I took offense at the phrase "toxic school culture." Without question all schools have things to work on, but all have positive aspects too, and I think those good elements get lost when you label the culture as "toxic."

Think like a teacher:

It's amazing how the way in which we ask something elicits different responses. I learned from Karen McCarthy (a friend and former teacher, now principal) to reframe my check-for-understanding question to students. I used to ask, "Does anyone have any questions?" but now I ask, "What questions do you have?" The first version usually resulted in crickets. The second *reframed* version sets the expectation that students have questions and I want to hear them. Suddenly, students are comfortable asking what they don't know.

Similar to your students, your colleagues might need you to pose your question in a different way.

Find the right words:

- *Let me phrase that in a different way.*

- *I don't think I was being clear. Would someone be able to reframe my question?*

5.4 Provide downtime.

I remember working with a very talented educator who shared really insightful questions with me when we were alone but was always quiet in our team meetings. When I approached her privately about this, she told me that she needed time to process group conversations. Although it feels contrary to productivity, research shows (Baird et al., 2012) that slowing down and taking time to think and even get your mind off what you are working on actually helps with creativity. Skillful team leaders (STLs) monitor the pace of team discourse, providing opportunities for downtime.

How to provide downtime:

Downtime can happen before, during, or after talk, and it doesn't have to be an awkward, sit-and-stare-at-each-other silence or close-your-eyes-and-breathe meditation (although it can be). It can take many forms. Some examples recommended in the Baird study and from other STLs include the following:

- Silent journaling
- Jotting on paper, poster board, or sticky notes
- Engaging in an art-based activity such as playing with modeling clay
- Listening to music or a podcast
- Daydreaming or doodling on paper
- Taking a stretch break or a walk
- Participating in a movement activity
- Participating in an unrelated creative activity (e.g., how many uses can you come up with for a particular random object)
- Participating in an unrelated mundane task (e.g., cleaning out your desk)

Think like a teacher:

As a teacher, you know about wait time. Ask a question. Then give students time to think before responding. If you teach elementary or middle school, you have also likely engaged students in mind and body breaks throughout a lesson. Taking time to pause allows young learners to process learning, formulate their thoughts, recharge their batteries, and see problems in a different light. Adult learners benefit from this as well.

STL recommendations:

Avoid tech tasks. There are no real rules to giving downtime to your team except that you and your colleagues should refrain from checking emails or text messaging, as this can pull someone out of downtime and into a problem that needs to be solved immediately.

Find the right words:

- *Let's pause here for a moment to jot down our thinking before we talk about it.*

- *We've had a robust discussion, so now let's sit for a moment to let it all sink in before we move to next steps.*

- *This is new and a lot to process, so we're going to take a stretch break.*

Related reading:

Move 5.9, "Table the discussion." Use this move when people need more than a few minutes of downtime in a meeting, and could benefit from picking up the conversation about a particular topic at a later date.

5.5 Manage your own level of participation.

Unlike walking and chewing gum at the same time, facilitating and participating in a meeting can be a real challenge. Beyond the coordination needed to multitask, the struggle to know just how much or how little to participate is tough. Engage actively, and you might intimidate others or dictate the learning toward your own bias. Withhold too much, and you might end up micromanaging the conversation rather than encouraging others to engage. Skillful team leaders (STLs) intentionally decide their level of participation throughout a meeting and adapt their participation based on how others respond to them. This move is particularly useful for principals and administrators who are visiting members to teams.

How to manage your own level of participation:

Here are five ways to participate in a meeting, arranged from least to most active:

Level 1—*Silent observer*. Allow others to facilitate and lead. Do not speak in the meeting, but act more as a "fly on the wall." This level of engagement allows you to view team dynamics and learning. Try being a silent observer if you are supporting a member of your team who is facilitating, or if you are a coach supporting the team leader. A word of caution: If trust is not yet strongly present on the team and your silence might feel as if you are judging people, then opt for a different level of participation.

Level 2—*Skillful contributor*. Participate strategically. Limit the number of comments you make (typically one to three in a one-hour meeting), holding back to give others an opportunity to make their points first. When you do participate, be intentional in implementing a move from this book such as redirecting (Move 5.14) or synthesizing ideas (Move 5.16). Try being a skillful contributor if you are an administrator on a teacher team, a visiting member to a team, or the facilitator of the meeting.

Level 3—*Full participant*. Act as any other team member would on the team. Participate equally. Learning alongside others. If you are both participating and facilitating the conversation, it can be helpful to outline upfront any protocols or procedures for the meeting, and invite people to share in the accountability for upholding them. This will allow you to participate more freely.

Level 4—*Co-facilitator*. Arrange in advance with others to facilitate a portion of the agenda. Guide people through protocols and procedures. When you are not facilitating, pull back to either a full participant or skillful contributor level of engagement.

Level 5—*Facilitator*. Independently lead protocols and procedures and implement moves as you see fit. Navigate between guiding people through protocols and procedures and being a skillful contributor, listening and verbalizing comments only when you feel it advances the conversation. Avoid the temptation to change the structure or time of your meeting design just so that you can squeeze in your own points. Try the role of facilitator if you are receiving leadership training (e.g., Skillful Team Leadership). Principals or school leaders should avoid this role on teacher teams unless they are modeling facilitation for the teacher leader or, of course, if it is their school leadership, school council, or specialty team.

STL recommendations:

Be transparent. Particularly if you opt for Level 1 participation, you'll want to let others know that you will not be speaking in the meeting, only observing. Briefly explain why you are showing up in this way (e.g., "This month I'm sitting in on all grade-level teams to get a sense of needs trending across the school").

Be mindful of your official title. If you are a principal or evaluator who may or may not be a regular member of a team, your presence can impact the way in which the group works together. Consult with the team leader and relay your message to the team so people know what to expect from you in a meeting. Because a principal's word carries a lot of weight, it is often best for the principal to show up as a skillful contributor (Level 2), interjecting only when helping to lay out vision or clarify purpose.

5.6 Empower others to problem solve.

Wearing the team leader hat can cause some people to naturally look to you for your opinions and advice instead of relying on themselves or their other colleagues for answers. To stick with the verbal ping-pong analogy from Move 5.2, you don't want to be the one "holding the paddle" the whole meeting. Skillful team leaders (STLs) deliberately empower others to answer questions and solve problems.

How to empower others to problem solve:

Decide if you are the only one in the room who can solve the posed problem. If you are, then of course do so. If you're not, try one or more of the following:

- *Boomerang* the question back to the person who asked it if you sense they have a solution in mind and are looking for validation. Do not do this when the answer is already decided and you know it, or people will get frustrated. For instance, if someone asks, "On what date will we give the assessment?" and a date has already been set, don't respond, "What do you think it should be?"
  - *Good question. What does your gut say?*
  - *What do you think?*
  - *It would help me to hear your thoughts first before I share mine.*

- *Invite* someone else to offer their thoughts on the problem.
  - *Ms. A, you have experience with this. What do you think?*
  - *Can someone else weigh in on this?*
  - *What do people think?*

- *Direct* the person toward a resource.
  - *You might look at . . .*
  - *I found [resource] to be very helpful in resolving that challenge.*

- *Remove barriers* for the person to solve the problem on their own.
  - *What obstacles are getting in the way of you resolving this?*
  - *How can the team and I best support you in working toward solutions?*

- *Partner* with the person to resolve together.
  - *You've hit upon a real dilemma. I don't have the answers, but I'd love to partner with you to seek them.*
  - *Are you open to meeting afterward to work on this?*
  - *Is there anyone on our team who can partner with [educator] on this?*

Related reading:

Moves 8.11–8.18, "Cultivate diverse perspectives" and "Make clear impactful decisions." Learn moves that encourage your colleagues to think flexibly about problems and make clear impactful decisions.

MAXIMIZE PRODUCTIVITY

Here's a simple riddle: No matter how strong you are, you can't hold onto it. There never seems to be enough of it. It can't be bought, earned, or sold. What is it?

Answer: Time.

Teams always look for ways to maximize what they get done in the time they have. I place productivity in the team-function category. However, when productive teams focus on the right things, they can have a tremendous impact on learning. Skillful team leaders (STLs) efficiently manage time with a variety of moves, several of which are explored in this section. Although these moves are basic, they are worth highlighting, not only for those new to leading teams, but also, for those who have been leading for years and yet, are challenged by an unproductive group.

STL moves:

5.7 Form subcommittees.

5.8 Paraphrase.

5.9 Table the discussion.

5.10 Appoint a volunteer.

What these moves promote:

Efficiency. STLs make decisions that maximize time collaborating on what matters.

Agency. Teachers have opportunities to engage in work they are passionate about through subcommittees.

Shared responsibility. Team members can implement these moves with one another.

When to use these moves:

When time is not being used efficiently.

5.7 Form subcommittees.

Sometimes what you need to get done takes more time than you have in your meeting. Whether you have a large group of people or a task that is big or complex, you want everyone to participate while remaining productive. Skillful team leaders (STLs) sometimes opt to form subcommittees. Although the concept is simple, some team leaders are hesitant to ask people to work in groups beyond the allocated time in their meetings. But the move is valuable. Not only will most people appreciate the speed at which a team can get things done when they divvy up the work and come back with parts complete, but also forming subcommittees is a tool for inclusivity. Teams can expand their reach and bring in diverse perspectives by inviting people who are not members of the original team to join a subcommittee.

How to form subcommittees:

Consider the following:

- *Purpose.* Communicate the benefit of meeting in small groups beyond team time to work on a particular task. Articulate the downside of not forming subcommittees at the given time.

- *Agreement.* Check in to make sure people on the team are comfortable with meeting outside of your designated team time and, if it applies to your setting, that you are not overstepping teacher contract union rules.

- *Membership.* Allow people to join the subcommittee of their choice. Ask subcommittee members to extend invitations to people who might not be members of their team.

- *Task clarity.* Check for understanding. Every subcommittee should know what they are charged with accomplishing—what they will bring back to the larger group, by when.

In action:

Tia: We want to write evidence-based goals for our school based on our district priorities. To use our time productively, I'd like to create three subcommittees, each focused on a different priority. You can choose your group, invite teachers who are not on our leadership team to join your group, and decide when to meet. Each group will be responsible for the following:

1. Unpack the priority. How are you interpreting it? What words do you need defined?

2. Access and analyze current data, and make note of data we don't yet have, but need.

3. Draft one goal based on the data you have with up to three action steps to reach the goal.

We'll come together in a month to report back. At that time everyone will have a chance to provide feedback and make changes to what each subcommittee puts forward.

Find the right words:

- *We are at a point where there are multiple aspects of the work that need to get done, but we don't need everyone together doing them. Please join one of the following subcommittees . . . Here's what each is tasked to do . . . by [when].*

5.8 Paraphrase.

When people struggle to articulate their thoughts or drone on, productivity can come to a standstill. Skillful team leaders (STLs) might politely interrupt and paraphrase what they hear. The move is one that you have likely done or heard others use a million times, yet not everyone is good at it. Paraphrasing actually takes skill. Too often people insert their own interpretation when paraphrasing someone else's words. And if tension in the group is high, relational trust is not present, or you have colleagues from traditionally marginalized groups who are sensitive to other people speaking for them, you will want to be intentional in when and how you paraphrase someone else's words.

How to paraphrase:

If we were to break this move down, the first three steps would be *listen, listen, listen.* Listen carefully to the essence of what a person is trying to express. Check that your paraphrase accurately captures what the person has said. If you misrepresent someone, invite them to restate it. If you can't capture their meaning, either invite someone else to paraphrase or ask the person to write their point down in the meeting notes as succinctly as they can.

STL recommendations:

Don't add interpretation. If someone is in an emotional state, listen and repeat the same language that the person used. For instance, if they say they are "upset," you can ask, "What upsets you?" But don't paraphrase their words as "What's making you so furious?" You could be putting words in their mouth, which can escalate a highly charged situation.

Ask permission. Ask for permission to paraphrase a colleague, particularly when it is a person who identifies differently from you. You never want to come across as superior or condescending.

Use with brainstorming. Paraphrasing is a great tool to use during group brainstorming when you need to capture the flow of ideas in shorthand on chart paper or in the notes of a meeting.

Find the right words:

- *You bring up so many good points. May I try to paraphrase what you are saying in order to capture it succinctly?*

- *I hear you saying . . . Does that capture it?*

- *Let me try to paraphrase what you are saying . . . Anything to add?*

- *Is there someone who can articulate, in a small sound bite, what's been said?*

5.9 Table the discussion.

Take a nap. There's a reason sleep pods are becoming popular in progressive businesses. Research shows that there is something called the "incubation effect" where complex problems deserve creative solutions and those solutions come about when people actually take a break from thinking about them (Wallas, 1926). Interestingly, when you are not racking your brain for a solution, and are instead taking a walk, cooking a meal, or taking a nap, your unconscious still works at the problem. Now you can't likely do these things at school, but you can table a discussion so that when people come back together they've had time for ideas to incubate.

This move may be familiar to most, yet I've seen many teams run talk in circles when it would have been more efficient to revisit a challenging conversation at a later date. Skillful team leaders (STLs) table a discussion when:

- A team doesn't have the facts, the necessary materials, or the right people at the table needed to make a decision.

- It's premature to make a decision due to changing circumstances.

- People are stuck thinking about a problem and can't agree on a feasible solution.

- People are emotionally charged and are no longer listening to one another.

How to table a discussion:

Communicate that the conversation is important. Make a note on chart paper (often called a "parking lot") or in the minutes of the meeting to revisit the discussion. If possible, specify a time when you will pick up the conversation. Assign tasks between now and the future date of discussion, if needed. Most importantly, follow through and return to whatever it is you tabled. Nothing erodes trust more than saying, "This is important—we'll get back to it later," and then never doing so.

In action:

Lydia leads the first parent–teacher organization (PTO) meeting in which the team is deciding when to offer meetings for the year.

Parent 1:	I predict the family survey will reveal that parents and caretakers prefer evening PTO meetings.
Parent 2:	I disagree. I know the one time we were able to offer a meeting after drop-off last year, we had a really good turnout. We should plan for more meetings at that time.

Parent 3:	Yes, but that might have been because the topic was about transitioning to middle school. Typically, for many working parents, daytime is just impossible.
Principal:	And yet, offering the meeting in the daytime actually gave an opportunity for parents and guardians who work night shifts to attend. Maybe there's some hybrid model we can try.
Parent 1:	I still think more people prefer evenings.
Lydia:	Given that we are due to get the family surveys back next week, where we will actually learn scheduling preferences of parents and caretakers, let's table the decision on when to offer PTO meetings, and shift our talk now to planning the content of the meetings. This will also give us time to think of creative solutions.

Find the right words:

Table a challenging conversation:

- *We seem to have come to an impasse. Let's table this part of our discussion to [Wednesday's] meeting.*

- *You voiced something important that we can't actually address today. I don't want to lose it, so I'll jot it down and make sure we carve out time on next week's agenda to discuss it.*

- *Understandably, this is hard to talk about. Let's table this until the next meeting.*

Table problem solving or a decision:

- *This is a complex problem with no clear solution. Let's table the discussion so that we can gain some distance from it, and then come back with fresh ideas.*

- *Given we don't have everything we need to make this decision now, let's put it off until [next month] when we will know more.*

- *Because this mandate isn't coming from me, it might make sense to have this conversation when the decision makers are with us. I meet with them on . . .*

- *As much as I know we'd love to leave here with a decision, it seems as if we don't have sufficient data to do so. Let's name what we need and then set a timeline to gather it.*

Related reading:

Move 5.4, "Provide downtime." Implement this move when you can't table a conversation but want to give people a quick recharge in a meeting or time to process what is being discussed.

5.10 Appoint a volunteer.

No doubt the title of this move sounds like a contradiction. Volunteering should be initiated by the volunteer; however, sometimes people on a team are willing to take on responsibility but don't offer unless given a direct invitation. Skillful team leaders (STLs) notice when there is a need to delegate, observe colleagues who seem willing, and appoint a volunteer.

How to appoint a volunteer:

Listen intently to the team discussion in order to identify a person who feels passionate and knowledgeable about the issue/task at hand. Actively and respectfully invite one person to take on a specific responsibility for the issue/task. If the person declines, ask them if they would be willing to accept if someone helped them. Respect their response.

In action:

Alex's team is spending too much of the meeting time outlining details of a form.

Teacher 1:	. . . We could organize the information into either a table or a narrative. If it's a table, I think we should shade the top box with column headers A, B, C, and so on. If it's a narrative . . .
Alex:	Hold that thought. I think we've gotten to a good point with this document as a team. [Teacher 1], you seem to have a good handle on the details that should be in this document. Would you be comfortable making a draft, then posting it to a Google Doc so that others can suggest small changes?
Teacher 1:	No. I'm not very good with Google Docs.
Alex:	If someone partnered with you to do the tech piece, might you reconsider?
Teacher 1:	Sure.
Teacher 2:	I'll work with you.

STL recommendations:

Consider timing. In some cases, appointing a volunteer in the moment in front of colleagues makes sense, but it can also put someone on the spot. If you do so, give them the chance to think about it. Another option is reaching out to the person privately before or after the meeting.

Watch for unconscious bias. Joan C. Williams and Sky Mihaylo (2019) suggest bias influences the roles we assign people. They suggest that housekeeping roles that require little problem solving or innovation tend to fall to those most willing, who are usually women and people from other underrepresented groups. They suggest team leaders rotate housekeeping roles and notice to whom they assign high-profile tasks.

Volunteer and recruit. If the responsibility is large or someone declines your invitation, volunteer yourself and recruit another person to join you.

Find the right words:

- *Ms. H, you have been very thoughtful about how we should unroll this initiative. Would you be willing to capture your ideas on paper for us so we can use what you write as a first draft?*

- *Mr. B, might you have the capacity to take this on with Ms. H?*

- *At our next meeting, we will need someone to . . . I thought of you because . . . Might this be something you are willing to do?*

- *I'm happy to take on the X portion of the task. Could someone help me by doing the Y portion of the task?*

FOCUS TALK

Imagine if talk on a team were characterized as group hiking. You might see some groups stop on the trail no farther than a few feet into their hike, never reaching their destination. Other groups would start on the main trail toward their destination but then take side paths that lead them away from where they are headed. And, some groups (think your Q3 low-everything teams) would wander aimlessly through the woods, bickering about which way to go. Yes, both on a hike and in collaborative learning you want exploration, but not without a sense of the destination. Skillful team leaders (STLs) notice when conversation is not advancing toward its intended purpose, and focus the conversation in the right direction.

Before you use the moves in this section, there is a caution about being too narrowly focused as a facilitator. I'll illustrate that with the following example:

I was a parent member on my child's school's diversity, equity, and inclusion (DEI) team led by STL Osamagbe (Osa) Osagie. The intended outcome for this meeting was to write a mission statement for our newly formed team. Osa showed us examples from other schools, and we brainstormed characteristics of strong statements. All was going well with just enough time left in the meeting to draft the language of our DEI mission statement, until another parent interjected with a personal story. He talked about his child's specific disability, the inequities she faced before coming to this school, the challenges that were still hard for her, and her teachers' commitment to her success. I, like others in the room, was deeply moved as he spoke. But the facilitator in me could not help but worry and wonder why Osa was letting this parent go on, pulling us away from the task at hand. She knew we had to get the mission statement written, yet she let him talk uninterrupted for about 10 minutes. When he finished his story, there was no time to write our DEI mission statement. I was frustrated—until I heard Osa's response to him.

"Thank you for trusting us with your powerful story," she said. "It embodies the purpose behind the work we must do as a diversity, equity, and inclusion team."

Hearing Osa's words, it became clear to me what I could not see that she could. This parent's story about his child was not a meaningless digression pulling focus away from our task. Rather, it was what we needed to hear in order to do our task. His story and that of many other families, mine included, drove our DEI work. We may not have left the meeting with a neatly worded statement, but we left with clarity about our mission.

Know your team's purpose, and always guide conversation toward that purpose, but mind your own assumptions and give a little time to recognize the distinction between "getting lost in the woods" and "wandering for discovery." Just know that sometimes, like me, you'll make the wrong call, and that's OK, too.

STL moves:

5.11 Frame conversation with clear parameters.

5.12 Zoom out to the big picture.

5.13 Zoom in on a key point.

5.14 Redirect.

5.15 Pivot from teaching to learning.

5.16 Synthesize ideas.

What these moves promote:

Purpose-driven talk. People take responsibility for keeping the team focused on learning, student goals, and outcomes.

When to use these moves:

- You cannot see a connection or pathway toward the purpose of the team's work.

- Other team members indicate frustration or disinterest in the digression beyond what is productive.

- The team is headed toward an idea that is bad for students or potentially low-impact.

- The conversation is too broad or aimless, or too far from student learning, and you need to focus it.

5.11 Frame conversation with clear parameters.

"I'm sorry; this isn't the place for that discussion." "We aren't going to talk about that now." These are uncomfortable things no team leader wants to say, and you won't have to if people have clarity from the start. It's not uncommon for people to come to a meeting with different understandings about what will be discussed even if they helped write the agenda. People need to know for what purpose this group is coming together and how to engage. Skillful team leaders (STLs) frame conversation so that people know the parameters within which they will be collaborating.

How to frame conversation with clear parameters:

Articulate the purpose behind the conversation or activity that people are about to engage in. Make clear the intended outcomes for the conversation. Clarify what should and shouldn't be discussed and, if needed, how people should and shouldn't engage in the meeting. Model an example, if appropriate. Keep your framing short and be matter-of-fact.

In action:

Raphael: For this 15-minute conversation we are going to make observations about the student errors on the math homework, but we are not at this time going to share our opinions about why they made these errors, or strategies we tried, or resources we know of. There will be time for that in the second half of today. For now, we are just looking at students' errors when finding ratios and unit rate. I'll start. I noticed that of the students who got the problems wrong, eight set up double number lines with the correct numbers, but incorrectly labeled them.

STL recommendation:

Use a protocol. Protocols are designed to outline clear parameters for conversation (see Moves 4.5–4.7). Data protocols, for instance, keep analysis narrowly focused on observations before inference. The Consultancy protocol dictates when people can ask clarifying questions and when they should move into probing questions.

Find the right words:

- *For this conversation, we will need to refrain from . . . because we want to be able to . . .*

- *Before we get started, let's be clear about what we are talking about and what we are not.*

5.12 Zoom out to the big picture.

Lose sight of the forest? It's easy for collaborative conversations, particularly those in which people are problem solving, to dwell on the minutiae to the point where people lose focus on what they are trying to accomplish in the first place. Details are critically important, especially when planning for implementation, but a clear vision of what you are aiming for and why gives those details context. Skillful team leaders (STLs) zoom out to the big picture, reminding the group of their purpose and desired outcomes.

How to zoom out to the big picture:

Use this move proactively when you begin conversation, or use it when people prematurely delve into details before understanding what they are trying to accomplish and why. Acknowledge that details are important. Assure your colleagues that your team will address the details after you zoom out. Prompt people to step back, get to the *why*, reconnect to what they are trying to accomplish, and focus on the big picture.

In action:

STL Karen Coyle Aylward zooms out to the reason their school instructional leadership team is about to do a virtual learning walk of the district's adoption of the Culturally Responsive Instruction Observation Protocol (CRIOP).[*]

Karen: Today we are going to dig deep into the artifacts we collected using the CRIOP tool. Each group will look at two and fill out evidence on a Google Form. Before we start this process, I want to remind everyone of the reason for delving into this observation protocol. We aren't doing this to meet some district mandate, or get good at scoring ourselves. We want to have deep, honest discussion about the ways in which our school is culturally responsive and the ways in which we need to improve. As our instructional coach brought up in our last meeting, "We don't want the *tool* of the CRIOP to get in the way of the *work* of the CRIOP."

Find the right words:

- *Ironing out these details is important, but let's not lose sight of why we are doing this.*

- *How does this connect to what we are trying to accomplish?*

- *Might someone be able to help us zoom out to the big picture before we get too far into the details?*

- *Let's step back from the planning and remember the goal of what we are doing.*

5.13 Zoom in on a key point.

Ideas are plentiful, but they are not equally good. Research points to a common team misstep: When a group strategizes, they don't discern between high-leverage and run-of-the-mill ideas. Consequently, groups don't always choose the best solutions for the problem at hand. Skillful team leaders (STLs) lift up significant[**] comments that might otherwise get overlooked and zoom in when it seems beneficial to the group.

How to zoom in on a key point:

This move requires good listening and a willingness to allow conversation to flow in a direction you might not have anticipated. Listen to group conversation

---

[*]Project PLACE. (n.d.). *CRIOP*. University of Kentucky. https://www.uky.edu/projectplace/criop

[**]Here the term *significant* refers to those comments that might present an alternate viewpoint, a key theme, an essential understanding, an assumption that needs unpacking, an effective strategy, an innovative solution, or a thoughtful question worthy of exploring.

as if you are sifting for gold. Search for ideas that you want to emphasize. Then repeat them and explore the ideas further.

To distinguish between a comment worthy of taking the time to explore in more depth and one that zooming in on would simply be a digression away from your agenda, ask yourself or the group the following:

- Is this statement worthy of highlighting?

- Is this statement in need of unpacking for understanding?

- Could exploration of this idea unlock something we have not yet considered?

- Is it worth taking time away from something else on our agenda to further explore this idea?

- Would letting this comment go without further exploring it be a missed opportunity?

In action:

In the first days of remote learning when schools had little direction as to what to do with students, Rich's social studies team had a meeting about engaging students.

Teacher 1:	I found a puzzle website that I link kids to. I'll put the link in the chat.
Teacher 2:	*National Geographic*'s web page[*] has a bunch of videos students can view.
Teacher 3:	BBC History for Kids[**] is great because it has kid-friendly videos. I've started assigning the ones about World War I.
Teacher 4:	There's a lot out there. You can put up the most awesome resources, but if kids don't use them, then what's the point? I use technology to track which students are engaging with what I posted, and that gives me direction as to what to post going forward.
Teacher 5:	Cool. My students tell me they like the Kid President videos, and there are some good ones, like "How to Disagree."[†]
Rich:	There's so much great stuff people are finding. I just want to lift up the point made by [Teacher 4] because it's really important. Not only do we want to select posts that we believe students will

---

[*]National Geographic. (2022). *Kids*. kids.nationalgeographic.com

[**]BBC. (2014). *History for kids*. bbc.co.uk/history/forkids/index.shtml

[†]RHS PBL Team. (2017, April 1). *Kid President: How to disagree* [Video]. YouTube. https://www.youtube.com/watch?v=dG5fkAgJmqc

find engaging, but we also need to monitor to see how students engage with them. Let's pause and zoom in on this point. What questions do we have about this? For instance, I'd like to know what tools people recommend for monitoring student engagement online.

Teacher 5:   I'd like to define what constitutes engagement when learning is remote. I know what it looks like live, but virtual is a whole different ball game.

Rich: That's a great place for us to begin.

STL recommendations:

Recognize your own bias. Any time you decide something is or isn't important enough to zoom in on, you are doing so from your own bias. It's fine to do this, but be conscious that what you see as a standout point might be different from what someone else sees as significant. This doesn't mean that you shouldn't use this move; it means that you should encourage others to also zoom in on points from your group conversation.

Give weight to an idea. One way to zoom in on an idea is to actually to give it weight with the backing of research or your own credible expertise.

Think like a teacher:

Something exciting happens when you are engaging students in discussion and someone brings up an insightful point. You don't gloss over it; you zoom in on it. In this way students drive the learning, and as a class you are able to explore a concept more deeply.

A key to facilitating teacher team inquiry is to be able to listen for moments when your colleagues touch the surface of a key piece of learning and zoom in on their comment to explore it more.

Find the right words:

- *I've heard us name a lot of strategies. I want to zoom in on this one . . . because . . .*

- *Let's not lose sight of the comment made by [Teacher A]. This seems worth emphasizing because . . .*

- *Do you mind if I play back something I just heard you say for a moment so we can explore it?*

- *Is there an idea you have heard that you would like to zoom in on and explore further?*

Related readings:

- Move 8.2, "Call attention to an assumption." Listen for assumptions and suspend them, as if dangling in the air, for all to examine.

- Move 8.12, "Spotlight the minority viewpoint." Give voice to opinions, perspectives, and observations that may not be popular or held by everyone at the table.

5.14 Redirect.

"All who wander are not lost" . . . but some are. It's not uncommon for someone to distract the group away from the topic at hand or outcomes the group is trying to reach. When skillful team leaders (STLs) sense talk is moving the team too far off track, they respectfully focus talk by redirecting the conversation back to what is important.

How to redirect:

Notice a comment that pulls the group away from the task at hand. Use a tone that saves face for the person who is digressing. Humor helps. Restate the purpose for collaboration or circle back to your intended outcomes for the meeting.

In action:

Teacher 1: The best way to improve attendance is to feed people. I can pick up those donuts that everyone loves. Have you ever had them? The jelly is to die for. And the glazed just melts in your mouth.

Teacher 2: Didn't you bring them in at our staff retreat?

Teacher 1: No. You're thinking of the cupcakes I got from the bakery on Main Street. But I could do those instead. The owner is a friend of my cousin, and she'll give me a good deal.

Steve: [Teacher 1], you always know the best local spots. I know families will appreciate a nice treat at the parent–teacher–student conferences, and certainly food draws people in. Now, let's continue to brainstorm ways to remove barriers to attendance for working parents. Time of day is a big challenge for many.

Find the right words:

- *Thanks. I'm going to capture what you are saying because it's important, and now bring us back to the issue at hand . . .*

- *If I may draw our attention back to the question that launched this conversation . . .*

- *I want to go back to the data. You know what is really interesting to me? Look at this . . .*

- (At the start of a conversation) *If at any point you sense us getting off track, please jump in to redirect our conversation back to focus on . . .*

Related reading:

Move 5.15, "Pivot from teaching to learning." This move redirects conversation from talk about instruction to talk about the impact of instruction.

5.15 Pivot from teaching to learning.

The most common rabbit hole conversation teacher teams fall into is talk about teaching. For example: "When do you teach this unit?" "How do you set up notebooks?" "Can you give me a copy of that assignment?" "What's your homework policy?" While these are critically important conversations to have, and teachers never have enough opportunities to find out what others are doing with students even when they teach the same subject and grade, discussion can linger too long in sharing "*what* we do," without discussion about "the *impact* of what we do." Skillful team leaders (STLs) spend collaboration time building curriculum, instruction, and assessment resources, but also know when to pivot talk from teaching to student learning.

How to pivot from teaching to learning:

Whether you spend consecutive meetings designing a unit or a single meeting planning a lesson, plant the expectation that teachers will demonstrate lessons and bring in student work throughout implementation of the design. When teachers are not in design mode, but talking about what instructional changes they made in the classroom, prompt your colleagues to examine the student response that resulted from the change. When teachers talk about learning expectations, pivot the conversation to examine how students did on assessments.

In action:

Pivot from planning to implementation:

Deena: Great. We just planned Lesson X. We plan on teaching it the week of Y. Who will bring in student work from this lesson for our meeting that week so we can see how students responded to the new design?

Pivot from talking about instruction to observing the impact on students:

Teacher 1:   This time I switched up the instructional sequence. I let students talk before they wrote so that they could formulate their thinking in hopes that it improved their writing. And it did.

Farrah: And can you show us a piece of writing from some students who you think benefited from this reverse approach?

Pivot from talking about learning expectations to examining how students did on assessments:

Michelle: It's the end of the year, so let's circle back to the five "outs" (the five essential skills/concepts) that we agreed students must leave this grade level with. Take a look at the first one.

Teacher 1:   We did that. We definitely did that.

Teacher 2:   I spent at least three weeks teaching that.

Michelle: Yes, I agree we *taught* it. Let's turn to the end-of-year assessment data we have in front of us to determine approximately what percentage of kids are actually leaving with this "out."

Find the right words:

- *We've shared a lot of great teaching strategies. Now, let's pivot to discuss how students are responding to these strategies.*

- *We have talked in depth about how to lead this practice. Let's name the outcomes we expect to see in student learning as a result of this practice.*

- *Are we ready to pivot our discussion from instructional resources we use in the classroom to talking about what groups of students are learning (and not learning yet) from these resources? Let's be evidence-based by looking at student work.*

Related reading:

Move 6.7, "(Specific) Write specific student-learning targets." Distinguish between teaching-practice goals, and goals that specify desired student outcomes.

5.16 Synthesize ideas.

If you've ever watched the Food Network show *Chopped*, then you have seen synthesis in action. The premise of the show is to take a basket of seemingly unrelated ingredients (often packaged prepared foods or bizarre foods such as giraffe weevils), deconstruct and combine them, add foods from the pantry, and race against the clock until you have transformed the parts into a whole new delicious cohesive dish. Collaborating in a team meeting isn't that much different. Everyone contributes distinct ideas to one conversation. Then a skillful team leader (STL) or other members of the team see connections and pull together ideas. The group leaves the meeting with a fresh whole new understanding.

How to synthesize ideas:

Listen or ask someone to listen for repeated ideas and points emphasized during a team conversation. Connect seemingly unrelated ideas. Combine prior knowledge with new knowledge. Lift up themes. Toward the end of the conversation, offer a newly formed understanding.

In action:

STL Karen Coyle Aylward facilitates an interdisciplinary multi-grade-level teacher study group about the role of structuring talk for students. Teachers read an article (Hurt, 2012), talk in pairs to highlight standout lines, and now share quotes and takeaways.

Ninth-Grade Teacher:	We chose two quotes "A structured protocol from the text: is the key to meaningful small group work" and "The person doing the most talking is doing the most learning." We believe a structured protocol isn't just to get kids talking. It elevates talk and helps them use academic language. Students need that structure, or talk can fall flat.
Advanced Placement (AP) Teacher:	We picked the same quote as you, "The person doing the most talking . . ." But we think the structure piece changes over time. It's more important early on, but by April, for example, structures can take a back seat once students get going.
English as a Second Language (ESL) Teacher:	We think structure is really key to get kids talking, and as teachers, we have to set that up for them.
Karen:	This is interesting because you teach ESL and you teach ninth grade. Structured talk for students at those levels is so important. But, then you both [*pointing to AP teachers*] might be seeing that maybe your students don't need the structure all the time. Now, of course, we always need to look at the individual child because some may need structures for talk regardless of age or their first language, but certainly I'm hearing from our conversation that structure is at some point essential to elevate student talk, but as students develop ownership over those structures they might not need them as much.

Find the right words:

- *We've covered a lot of ground. How can we put this all together in a way that makes sense?*

- *I've jotted down things I've heard repeated and emphasized. I wonder if what we are getting at is . . . ?*

- *Does anyone feel comfortable synthesizing all the ideas we've heard to further our understanding of . . . ?*

MANAGE CONFLICT

If you have read any other book on professional learning communities or teaming, you have likely heard that conflict is good and should not be avoided. Conflict indicates that you have a team of independent thinkers with diverse perspectives. But, a key point perhaps said best by triple Olympic crew medalist Bo Hanson is "Diversity always delivers better outcomes, but only if the team can manage the differences" (quoted in Haigh, n.d.). High-functioning, high-impact Q1 teams have learned how to manage the differences. They engage in productive conflict.

Conflict tends to fall into one of two categories: task-related or interpersonal. Task-related is most commonly caused by miscommunication, limited resources, or unclear roles and parameters. Interpersonal conflict typically stems from different ideologies, contrasting personalities and distinct work styles, generational gaps, competition, and personal grievances. Both types of conflict can be uncomfortable; neither should be left to fester. Skillful team leaders (STLs) employ various moves to manage conflict.

STL moves:

5.17 Clarify understanding.

5.18 Interrupt negative energy.

5.19 Turn to a third data point.

5.20 Listen for the point of agreement.

5.21 Acknowledge. Assert. Move on.

5.22 Adopt a learning stance.

5.23 Clear the air as a group.

5.24 Check in 1:1.

5.25 Provide a graceful exit.

Tools and templates:

Figure 20: Iceberg Visual as Told by Daryl Campbell

Figure 21: Clear the Air as a Group: Roles and Rules of Engagement

Figure 22: Speaker and Listener Writing Prompts

What these moves promote:

Communication. People have opportunities to work through miscommunication.

Respect. People learn how to disagree without personal attacks or gossip.

Harmony. Unproductive conflict is resolved so that people get along.

Morale. People work through tension and feel more positive about the team.

When to use these moves:

Most of these moves are intended to nip unproductive conflict before it escalates.

Related readings:

- Moves 2.1–2.10, "Establish expectations and responsibilities." Avoid task-related conflict with moves that set clear expectations and responsibilities.

- Moves 3.3–3.8, "Build community and relational trust through play." Implement these moves to nurture a culture of community and trust. When conflict erupts, your team will be better prepared to manage it.

- Move 8.15, "Clarify the decision-making process." Decision making can be a hot spot for conflict. When everyone has a shared understanding of how the group will make decisions, conflict is less likely to erupt about the process, and people can engage in healthy debate about the content of the decision.

5.17 Clarify understanding.

Have you ever gotten into a heated argument with someone only to realize after a couple of rounds that you actually wanted the same thing? Many conflicts arise simply because of miscommunication rather than actual differences of opinion. Tone, word choice, emotion, and assumptions can add to misunderstanding. Skillful team leaders (STLs) clarify their own and others' understanding to make sure everyone "gets" what each person is saying.

How to clarify understanding:

Before assuming that you know what your colleague is saying, structure your response in the following three ways:

1. Pinpoint what you need clarified. For example, instead of saying "I don't understand," say "I understand why you want us to do this, but I need to better understand your idea for what we should do to get there."

2. Prompt your colleague to give details or offer examples to help you better grasp what they are saying.

3. Confirm your understanding by paraphrasing and asking a closed question such as "I heard you say . . . Is this accurate?"

STL recommendation:

Remain in a learning stance. This move is about checking that you are not misunderstanding the other person's position. You may also feel the need to clarify their understanding of what you are saying, but if you do, be careful to remain in a learning stance, not a proving stance, so that they can hear you (see Move 5.22).

Grab a third party. If the stakes are high—perhaps you've had conflict with this individual before and don't want to damage relations further—invite a colleague to the conversation and ask them to mediate.

Find the right words:

- *When you say . . . what do you mean?*

- *I'm unclear about . . . Can you talk further about that?*

- *I hear you saying . . . Are you objecting to . . . ?*

- *I don't understand the part about . . . Can you give me an example?*

Related reading:

Move 5.8, "Paraphrase." Turn to this move when confirming your understanding of what your colleague is saying.

5.18 Interrupt negative energy.

Call waiting is a godsend. I have a history of the occasional heated phone conversation with a close family member. We've gotten ourselves so worked up at times to the point where neither of us can hear what the other person is saying, and the conflict will go on endlessly until something unexpected happens. One of us gets another call. That brief period of being on hold while the person clicks over to the other call is enough for both of us to calm down and reset. When we pick up the conversation again, we are usually able to resume working things out in a more civilized way, agree to talk about it later, or just let the whole thing go. When a group conflict is heightened to an emotional state where people rant, fight, panic, or even cry, skillful team leaders (STLs) intentionally interrupt the flow of negative energy in the room so that the group can move on.

How to interrupt negative energy:

Consider the following:

- *Shift from talking to writing.* Invite people to respond to the circumstances in writing. The silence can break up the bickering.

- *Change the task.* When people are at an impasse, pause and redirect attention to another less controversial task on your agenda. It should be an easy win—something everyone can agree on and accomplish. This gets people talking to one another again in a productive way. Then, return to discussing the controversial topic.

- *Get moving.* Invite people to continue the debate while walking. Change of scenery and physical movement can change the ways in which people engage.

- *Do a mindfulness activity.* Check in with how people are feeling in their bodies and try some breathing activities. (This approach can also really tick some people off, so only use it if you know your group will be receptive to it.)

- *Table the discussion* (see Move 5.9). Timing is everything. People may need to step away from the conflict before they can resolve it.

Find the right words:

- *Hold that thought for one moment. I just want to turn our attention to some housekeeping. . . . [A few minutes later] Thanks. OK. Let's revisit what we are talking about.*

- *I hear what you are saying. Let's take a moment to write down your thinking so everyone has an opportunity to weigh in on this. We'll finish our task and then have an opportunity to share out if you want.*

- *We've been discussing this while seated for a while. Let's continue the conversation as we walk to lunch.*

Related readings:

Move 8.7, "Reframe a negative association." When someone voices something negative about a person or group of people, change language to influence perceptions and the energy in the room.

Move 9.8, "Reframe talk about resistance." People often assign negative attributes to a person who shows reluctance to change. Insert different language that can get people to see the benefits of resistance.

5.19 Turn to a third data point.

In professional football, when a coach disagrees with a referee's call, they can request an instant replay. Viewing the recorded play, officials can quickly come to agreement about the accuracy of the call. When two or more parties engage in conflict on a school team, particularly if that conflict starts to devolve into personal attacks, skillful team leaders (STLs) can turn to a third data point (something other than the two people arguing in the room). This keeps the debate about ideas, not people. For example, instead of two people bickering over who is right, they turn to a shared text and say, "I disagree with your interpretation of the text."

Third data points might include a goal, a policy, assessment data or student work, or a passage from a text.

How to turn to a third data point:

Set expectations for how your team engages in disagreement. Pull back from personal attacks by redirecting the conversation to a third data point, something other than the two people talking in the room. Ask people to debate the evidence present in the third data point.

In action:

Kelsey leads a contentious individualized education program (IEP) meeting.

Parent:	I keep telling you that whatever you are doing isn't working. My child is melting down every night when he does homework.
Teacher 1:	Well, I'm doing all I can on my end. I explain the homework. I do a sample with the students. Your child never asks questions or comes to me for help. And when I walk over to him to check in that he understands, he pushes me away.
Parent:	So you're saying it's my son's fault?
Teacher 1:	No, not at all. But maybe we should look at the conditions you've set up at home for him to get his homework done. Does he have a quiet space to work?
Parent:	This is not my fault. You're the school. This is your responsibility. It's like you don't care.
Kelsey:	I'm going to interject for a moment and ask that we look at your son's most recent homework assignments that he wasn't able to complete. Maybe it will give us a better sense of how to help him, which is what we all want.

Think like a teacher:

You've likely been in a situation where two students are getting heated about what you are teaching, and you are trying to mediate, but the conflict is getting personal. There are many moves you make to de-escalate the tension, one of which is turning their attention back to the subject matter that began the debate. You might say, "Pause and let's go back into the text to see what the author is saying." Or, "If we look back at the language of the problem, then you'll see it is asking us to solve . . ."

Drawing your colleagues to an external data point can relieve conflict and help people find common ground.

STL recommendation:

Make a copy. Ensure everyone has a visual of the third data point for reference. Make copies or project it on a screen.

Find the right words:

- *I appreciate what you are saying, but when I look at [data point], I notice . . .*

- *I hear you. Can you help me better understand your point of view by referring to [data point]?*

- *This is getting personal, and I want to ground our disagreement back to a [data point].*

5.20 Listen for the point of agreement.

Two people might have completely different perceptions of the same experience, creating conflict on the surface, but underlying that disagreement there may actually be a shared value that just hasn't been made visible, yet. To illustrate this, STL Daryl Campbell, influenced by his training and work with the Interaction Institute for Social Change, uses the iceberg visual in Figure 20: a drawing of two icebergs representing two distinct opinions that, when extended, intersect. Skillful team leaders (STLs) listen for the point of agreement.

FIGURE 20   Iceberg Visual as Told by Daryl Campbell

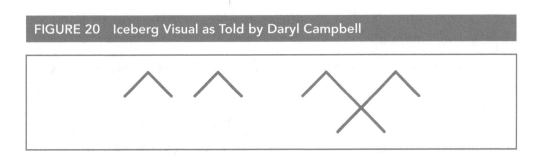

How to listen for the point of agreement:

Acknowledge that the two parties are engaged in a conflict. Validate each person's unique experience. Uncover the underlying beliefs, values, and assumptions beneath each person's opinion. Look for commonalities.

In action:

Teacher 1:   I think we have a gossip and clique problem that needs to be addressed. Said or unsaid, there is an "in" crowd, and it creates division among our staff.

Teacher 2:   I don't think this behavior is everywhere in our school. Teachers at my grade level are inclusive.

Teacher 1:   C'mon. If we are being real here, you know people talk behind one another's backs on our staff.

Teacher 2:   I don't think that's true. I'm direct with people.

Brendan: Thank you both. I'm going to interject here because it's important to note that people have had different experiences, and our purpose is not to debate to what extent those experiences are true; it's just to be aware of the hindering behaviors that might creep into our own team meetings, and set norms to avoid them. Where I see agreement between you is the recommendation for our team to be inclusive and direct.

Find the right words:

- (To both parties) *Let's look for the connection between your ideas.*

- *It sounds like you disagree on . . . but you both agree on . . .*

Related readings:

Move 8.16, "Reach agreement on group decisions." Find multiple strategies for reaching consensus with a group.

5.21 Acknowledge. Assert. Move on.

But . . . Although . . . Unless . . . Alternatively . . . On the other hand . . . To play devil's advocate . . .

This is more than a list of words and phrases. They indicate a disagreeing point of view. You want your colleagues to engage in discourse where diverse opinions are respectfully discussed. However, conflict can arise when a colleague is a contrarian, particularly if they are asserting their power or influence. It can be difficult to move a team forward. Skillful team leaders (STLs) acknowledge the person, assert what needs to happen in order for the team to move forward, and then proceed with the agenda.

How to acknowledge, assert, and move on:

1. *Acknowledge* the person who made the negative or misinformed comment by letting them know they were heard. You can do this by repeating the comment or thanking them for their contribution.

2. *Be assertive* in your response, careful not to send mixed messages. Don't lead the person on just to keep the peace. In other words, don't say, "That's a great idea. Maybe we can do that" when you know it's not good for kids or can't be done. Be explicit in what can and can't be done at that time.

3. *Move on.* Don't linger or entertain the person's negative or misinformed comment for too long. Keep the energy of the group positive and momentum going by moving on to your next agenda item.

In action:

Sharon:	We've just agreed through a vote that we will hold extended learning during winter break for a week for underperforming students who meet our intervention requirements. The next step is to identify the students and craft a parent/family letter.
Teacher 1:	Wait. I still think there are going to be families who will *say* they are sending their kids and then not send them. We'll put in all this effort, and no one will show up.
Sharon:	Yes, there's always a chance of that happening. However, we are no longer discussing whether we should or should not offer this. We have come to consensus that it is essential that we present this opportunity to families. We have designed the extended learning in a way that removes as many obstacles as we can. Now, which students from your classes can you identify would benefit from this additional support?

Think like a teacher:

A priceless tip I learned years back from a teacher who was in a behavior management course with me is to use the word *nevertheless*. Middle school students, in particular, are quick to take an opposing stance from adults. It's a part of adolescence. But sometimes pushback can put a stumbling block into the momentum of learning. Rather than trying to convince a student of your point of view or engage in an argument, you simply acknowledge the student's differing perspective (whether accurate or not) and respond with "Nevertheless . . ." For example, "I understand that you think this rule is unfair. Nevertheless, for now we will follow it." This sets an expectation without embarrassing the student and allows learning to move forward.

When working with adult learners, you might also acknowledge a person's contrarian point of view and turn to words like *nevertheless*—just be extremely mindful that you do not use a condescending tone.

Find the right words:

- *I see your point; nevertheless, for today we are going to have to live with it.*

- *I don't disagree, but given the way things are now, we just have to proceed. I hope you understand.*

- *You might be right, but we have got to work with what we have for now.*

5.22 Adopt a learning stance.

Do you have something to prove? I don't mean a personal vendetta. When two or more people are engaged in conflict, it's likely that one or both are speaking from a proving stance. It can be hard to recognize when you are in this mode, but it's certainly obvious when someone else is. They overexplain, justify, or defend their position. They aim to convince you that they are right. They might even tout their credentials, ad nauseam, in an effort to "make you understand" their side. The problem with this stance is that when a person is in it, they can't also be in learning mode. Learning mode requires listening and a willingness to be open to what you don't know. Skillful team leaders (STLs) and their colleagues adopt a learning stance when listening to one another.

How to adopt a learning stance:

Before responding to your colleague, pause to determine why you are engaging with this person. Are you authentically curious about learning what they think? Or might you be in a proving stance—even just a bit? Do you hope that if you keep talking they'll "get" what you are saying?

Edgar Schein (2013) recommends that we ask questions while remaining "curious about the other person rather than letting our own expectations and preconceptions creep in" (p. 50). Adopting a learning stance in which you humbly inquire about the other person won't only help with miscommunication and conflict, but, as Edgar Schein (2013) says, it "shows interest in the other person, signals a willingness to listen, and, thereby, temporarily empowers the other person" (p. 10). Instead of listening for the other person to say what you think they will say and waiting for your chance to prove your point, listen with an inquisitive mind, open to what you might learn from them. Resist the urge to prove. Think: "What am I learning right now? How can I stay in learning mode?" If it's just too hard to remain curious, step away from the conversation until you are ready.

The Burden of Proof

If you notice someone else is in a proving stance, resist the urge to disprove them or dismiss what they say because, "Well, that's just Judy." Aim to uncover what drives their need to prove something to you. Many people who identify with traditionally marginalized groups have had to unfairly prove their capabilities and character to other people, more so than people who identify with mainstream groups. In many cases, a person in a proving stance can feel any or all of the following: misinterpreted, misunderstood, underestimated, undervalued, unappreciated, judged, unwelcome, rejected, silenced, or even oppressed. Listen to them. Address their needs, if you can. If you can't, then ask to resume the conversation when you can. Even if that person's tone is off-putting, they are inarticulate, or they use offensive language, rely on what you know of their character. Trust that the person means well.

STL recommendations:

Be honest with yourself. "Acting defensively can be viewed as moving away from something, usually some truth about ourselves" (L. Anderson, 1997). Sometimes your need to prove something to someone else is not actually about them, but rather, it's about you. I'm not trying to get psychoanalytical, but at some point you need to check in to see *who* you are actually trying to convince. Honestly check in with your feelings. For example, if you find yourself proving to your colleagues that you know a lot, is it because *they* don't think you are qualified, or is it *you* who thinks you aren't as knowledgeable as they are?

Do not conflate advocating with proving. Although these words by definition may feel similar, there is a distinction. In both cases, you are championing a cause or standing up for beliefs, but when you advocate, you intend to engage in an exchange of ideas with another person. You communicate *with* the other person, not *to* them, and are able to regulate your emotions. When you advocate, people perceive you as thoughtful, passionate, and in control.

On the other hand, when you take on a proving stance, you engage in a conversation with the intent to *make* the other person see your side, often holding the assumption that they don't. *They don't understand; they don't get it; they don't come from my world; they underestimate me; I'm right, and they're wrong*; and so on. Your focus is strongly focused on how you think they perceive *you*, not just how they perceive your viewpoint. As a result, the conversation feels personal, and you are more likely to react. The other person perceives you as emotional and may have a harder time hearing your message.

Think like a teacher:

How would you respond as an educator to a parent or student who says, "You just don't understand"? Initially, you might be tempted to prove that you *do* understand, but at some point you would likely step back and seek to hear what they are communicating. If they were to voice that they feel misinterpreted, judged, or underestimated, you would aim to find out why and address their needs as you could.

Tap into these well-developed skills when you engage in conversation with colleagues and take a learning stance.

Find the right words:

When you are in proving stance:

- *I am noticing my need to defend my position rather than seek to understand yours. I'd like to revisit this conversation when I am ready to hear you.*

- *I'm feeling misinterpreted right now, and I am noticing myself getting defensive. This isn't how I want to engage. I'm going to pull back by being quiet without interrupting you and just listen.*

When you notice someone else is in proving stance:

- *How does this conversation make you feel—misinterpreted, misunderstood, underestimated, undervalued, unappreciated, judged, unwelcome, rejected, silenced, or oppressed? In what ways might my words or actions contribute to your feeling? What do you need from me and/or the team?*

- *Please know that I genuinely value what you say and do. I'm glad you are in this group. I need to come to understand what you are saying in my own time. Allow me the quiet space to do so.*

- *I don't want to assume I understand your objection, so can you tell me?*

- *Please don't feel the need to prove yourself with us, we know you are incredibly [capable].*

When someone puts you into proving stance:

- *I believe you are coming from a good place, but your question puts me in a role that calls on me to explain to you how my [race, religion, generation, etc.] thinks or acts, and I don't feel comfortable in that role.*

5.23 Clear the air as a group.

"Make way for elephants, dead fish, and vomit." This is a company norm at Airbnb set by leaders who noticed the culture was gossip and "back-room talk" (Gallagher, 2017). Elephants are those big things that no one wants to voice and instead they talk around. Dead fish are personal grievances or things that have gone unaddressed for a while and only get worse over time. Vomit is when people just need to get something off their chest without interruption or judgment and move on. Even with norms in place, sometimes tension is high, particularly on low-functioning Q3 and Q4 teams. There is a need to clear the air. According to Writing Explained (n.d.), "clearing the air" was evidently first named in the 1300s. I guess even back then personality conflicts, gossip, misunderstandings, and other issues plagued groups. While your instinct might be to ignore the tension and hope feelings subside, leaving things unaddressed will make things worse. Skillful team leaders (STLs) decide when the team needs to clear the air, and they do it with an emphasis on listening to learn.

Clearing the air is more of an exercise than a singular move. Its purpose is to foster empathy and understanding. This is not a resolution-seeking exercise.

How to clear the air as a group:

There is no one way to clear the air as a group; however, I have designed the following structure as an effective guide. As with any protocol, modify it to your needs.

(5 minutes) Review purpose, intended outcome, expectations, and procedure. Pass out roles and rules of engagement (see Figure 21). Answer procedural questions.

(10 minutes) Pass out prompts for speaker (see Figure 22). All silently write their individual statements. Each statement should be short enough to read aloud within one minute, but long enough to contain the content the individual wants to express.

(2 minutes) All silently review what they have written, removing or reframing assumptive language.

(1 minute per person) Team members, as they are ready, take turns reading their statements aloud. All listen. No one is permitted to respond.

(3–5 minutes) Thank people for being vulnerable. Acknowledge the mood in the room. Some "clearing the air" conversations leave people with more questions than before. Give people time to sit with what they've heard without questions and rebuttals. Allow this exercise to simply be about hearing one another, not reaching resolution. Review rules of engagement (see Figure 21)—particularly, "No conversations/email/text will be permitted after the conversation."

(5–10 minutes—optional) Some groups, particularly those who clear the air regularly, are ready to take actionable steps. End the exercise by naming overarching themes that emerge from what people shared. Decide who will look further into these problem areas and find strategies that address them.

FIGURE 21   Clear the Air as a Group: Roles and Rules of Engagement

FACILITATOR	SPEAKER	LISTENER
• Announce your intent to lead a guided conversation that will help the group move forward. Be clear that the outcome is to hear others and be heard—not resolution.	• Write a statement responding to the five prompts (see Figure 22). Write and speak in a way others can hear. Be mindful of word choice, tone, and body language. How would you want someone to tell you this?	• Hear what's hard. Don't prepare a rebuttal.
• Manage expectations that the conversation might get uncomfortable or emotional.	• Review what you wrote, reframing assumptions before you read aloud (e.g., Change "You left me out on purpose" to "I felt isolated." Or, preface an assumption with "I could be wrong, but it seems that . . .").	• Listen with the five guiding questions.
• Get agreement to roles (defined in this figure).		• No interrupting is allowed. Give no response until everyone in the group has had a turn to speak. No judgment, ridicule, or gossip is allowed.
• Get agreement to the rules of engagement. If someone cannot agree, they should excuse themselves from the circle.	• No personal grievances. No attacks, accusations, guilting, shaming, or character assaults will be permitted.	• Accept the speaker's truth and take away learning.
• Set time limits.		
• Strictly enforce rules of engagement for the psychological safety of everyone.	• Keep your statement to the five writing prompts and your time limit.	

• All: No conversations/email/text will be permitted after the conversation. Sit with what you have heard. Reflect. Process. Come to the next interaction with new learning.

> ### FIGURE 22   Speaker and Listener Writing Prompts
>
> **The Speaker's 5 Writing Prompts**
>
> 1. Name past behaviors/actions on our team that have been challenging for you.
>
> 2. How have these behaviors/actions affected you, your work, or your collaboration?
>
> 3. In what ways have you negatively contributed to, condoned, or modeled hindering behaviors and actions?
>
> 4. Convey your care and commitment to the team.
>
> 5. How can the team help you move past this challenge?
>
> **The Listener's 5 Guiding Questions**
>
> 1. Am I present as this person speaks, or in my own thoughts?
>
> 2. In what ways might my own bias and assumptions be limiting or shaping what I am and am not hearing this person say right now?
>
> 3. What am I learning as I listen to the speaker?
>
> 4. What am I feeling emotionally and physically as this person speaks?
>
> 5. What does this person need from me? How can I convey that I care?

STL recommendations:

Rename. The name of this move, "Clear the air as a group," indicates a focus on the person doing the clearing, but for this exercise to positively shape how a group works together, emphasis needs to be placed equally on the listening. In working with a thoughtful group of teacher leaders who wanted their peers to recognize that this was not meant to be a venting session, I renamed it "Hear and be heard."

Circle up. Sit in a circle to create an equal power dynamic. Having someone sit at the head of a long table can make some people feel intimidated during this exercise.

Avoid blame, sarcasm, and defense. Find truth in shame. If you adapt the protocol and decide to allow people to respond to what they've heard, invite them to only express words that convey appreciation, empathy, and learning. Avoid the following:

- Apologies that don't take personal accountability (e.g., "I'm sorry *you* feel that way.")

- Rebuttal language (e.g., "That's not what I meant.")

- Blame (e.g., "If you didn't do that to me . . . then I wouldn't have done . . .")

- Unhealthy baggage (e.g., "This is just like that time you . . .")

It's possible for listeners to feel shameful without the speaker shaming them (B. Brown, 2020). This is usually an indicator that the listener is wrestling inside with some truth that they need to face.

Set a time limit and stick to it. When people know they only have a short window to speak, they tend to treat their time as precious. Decide upfront the maximum amount of time to allocate for each person to speak, and use a timer. Don't extend beyond time, or people will feel unsafe wondering when the speaker will end. If you have a large team, then you might opt for groups to pick one representative to speak on behalf of the group. You might also opt to set a time limit for the entire exercise.

Explore why. As a team, you might want to learn from where the challenges stem. The Five *Whys* protocol described in Move 4.7 in which you ask and answer *why* five times can be a helpful follow-up protocol.

Heighten your emotional intelligence. If there is ever a time to be skilled at recognizing and managing your own and others' emotions during a conversation, this is it. Notice body language, tone of voice, pace of speech, and choice of words. Notice the emotional intensity with which people are speaking. Notice your physical responses to what is being spoken.

Make it a ritual. This exercise becomes less challenging when a team who meets weekly regularly engages in it. A good rule of thumb is once a quarter or trimester.

Find the right words:

- *We are a good team, but something is getting in the way of us reaching our potential. We are going to do an exercise in which we clear the air and listen to learn. The goal here is not to resolve conflict, but rather to leave with a better understanding of one another.*

And while you are clearing the air:

- *Thank you. I hear you.*

- *I appreciate you sharing that with me.*

- *That took courage to voice. Thank you.*

- *I have a better understanding than before.*

- *That's hard for me to hear, but I am glad you told me.*

Alternative method to clear the air as a group:

Myrna Lewis's method from her Deep Democracy work in South Africa (see Human Dimensions, 2018) aims to clear the air as a group with resolution as the goal. It boils down to four steps:

1. *Set safety agreements.* For instance: "No one has a monopoly on the truth."

2. *Say it all.* Provide structure for people to be heard and to hear what is being said; however, don't hold anything back.

3. *Mine for gold.* Lewis gives the example that if someone calls you an axe murderer, you can dismiss the name but search for the truth in that statement.

4. *Solve the issue based on the grains.* Get creative and solve beyond the issue so that everyone grows in learning.

5.24 Check in 1:1.

Meeting 1:1 with a colleague on your team is likely not a novel idea to you, but how you implement it might be. I'm sure you've had the experience of initiating a private conversation with the intent of smoothing things over, only to have things end worse than when you began. Skillful team leaders (STLs) check in 1:1 for the purpose of learning about the other person and strengthening relational trust.

How to check in 1:1:

1. Before you check in 1:1 with someone, *put your motivation in check.* Check in when you are ready to enter the conversation curious to learn about the other person's perceptions and understandings. Arrange for a private conversation with minimal to no distractions. When a conflict is personal, addressing it in front of the group raises tension or misunderstanding between you and the other person, and makes everyone else uncomfortable.

2. *Communicate what you hope to learn from the conversation.*

3. *Listen and convey genuine interest as the person talks.* Be aware of your own preconceived notions, biases, and assumptions, and listen for alternate evidence that might reshape your interpretation of what the person says.

4. *Respond in a way the person can hear.* Maintain nonaggressive body language (e.g., unclench your jaw and uncross your arms), use a nonjudgmental inviting tone of voice, and be intentional about your word choice so that you don't escalate conflict or resistance.

5. *Keep confidences.* Remember, the end game of checking in is relational trust. If confidence was requested, don't blab. Nothing erodes trust faster than a check-in 1:1 in which you convey that you care and are invested in that relationship, only to throw it all away minutes later.

In action:

Ed lets his team meeting out a few minutes early so that he can check in 1:1 with a teacher who has come 10 minutes late to every team meeting for the last month.

Ed: [*Quietly approaches teacher so others are not in earshot.*] Do you have a moment to connect?

Teacher: Sure.

Ed: I've noticed you've come late to meetings a few times, and I want to make sure things are OK and learn what you might need to get here on time.

Teacher: Well, maybe if my class wasn't in the basement and I didn't have to run up two flights of stairs, I'd be on time.

Ed: That is hard. Is it just the start time that is challenging for you, because we can talk to the team about adjusting that, or might there be something else going on?

Teacher: Well, the start time doesn't help, but then again neither do these meetings. Don't get me wrong—I like you and the other teachers; I just have so much on my plate, and these meetings feel like one more thing.

Ed: I totally get that and appreciate you telling me. Is there anything that would make the meetings more relevant to your work? And it's OK if you don't know now. You can think about it and let me or the team know later, or at the next meeting. I don't mean to sound corny, but I want you to get as much from these team meetings as we get from you being a part of them. No one wants to waste anyone's time. We can work together to make the meetings more worthwhile.

Teacher: Well, I appreciate that. Let me think about it.

Ed: Thanks. And unless you want me to ask the group to change the start time, we'll start at 10:05 as planned. Is that OK?

Teacher: Yes, I'll be there then.

STL recommendations:

Find the right time. Scheduling a check-in can add a layer of formality and sometimes give gravitas when there needn't be any. If your check-in isn't too serious, you might casually approach your colleague at the end of the day, or over lunch duty. However, if you are checking in for the purpose of working through a personal grievance that has been brewing, or if you work in a school culture where one-off side conversations might be perceived as gossip or excluding people, it's better to coordinate in advance a mutually convenient time.

Assume equal-status body language. Use your body language to make the conversation as natural and comfortable as possible so that others are open to expressing any concerns directly to you. If the person you are approaching is sitting, pull up a chair or squat down next to them. If they are walking, walk alongside them even if you are headed in a different direction. Make eye contact even if there are distractions around you.

Ask open-ended questions. Engage with questions that will get someone talking. For example, *How are you feeling about . . . ? I'm wondering what you think about . . . Tell me about . . .*

Don't overpromise and underdeliver. I've been victim to this one. When I sense someone has concerns or expresses resistance, I so badly want to help put them at ease that I risk promising changes that I don't have the authority or capacity to make happen. Be frank with what you can and can't do. Involve them in problem solving. Keep in mind that often it's enough to hear and validate a person's feelings. That being said, there is nothing more frustrating than being the one voicing concerns in search of a resolution, and instead someone nods and says, "I hear you. Thank you for telling me," and then does nothing. If you're not sure whether the person in your check-in is just venting or expects you to do something, it's best to simply ask, "Are you looking to just air your concerns, or are you hoping I can do something to change this?" Then follow through.

Take three steps back. When there is friction between you and someone else, Douglas Stone and Sheila Heen, authors of *Thanks for the Feedback* (Stone & Heen, 2015) and *Difficult Conversations* (Stone et al., 2000), invite you to "take three steps back" to better understand what could be causing the conflict. Here are a few questions to consider as you take three steps back:

1. *You and me intersection.* In what ways are our personality differences (or similarities) getting in the way of our communication?

2. *Roles.* In what ways are our roles within our workplace so different that we may not understand the other person's world?

3. *The big picture.* What other people, policies, systems, and processes or even physical environment could be impeding our ability to work together? What can we change, and what will we together need to figure out how to live with?

Think like a teacher:

The check-in is a staple in any effective teacher's repertoire. It is a tool for soliciting feedback from a student, clarifying expectations, strengthening communication, and ultimately building relational trust. Where a student might expect the check-in to be more of a corrective tool to reset a misbehavior, for example, and may tolerate a respectful "teacher voice" or instructive tone, an adult will not. Maintain the spirit of the check-in as a learning conversation between you and your colleague.

Find the right words:

- *If it's OK with you, I'd be more comfortable discussing this outside of the meeting. I am free . . . Would one of those times work for you?*

- *This conversation seems like it might need more time. Let's connect for a moment after the meeting.*

- *Would you have a moment to talk to me so that I can better understand what might be going on between us?*

5.25 Provide a graceful exit.

You might need to dig deep within yourself to implement this move, but ending a conflict in a way that allows the other person to walk away with some sense of power and their dignity intact will build more relational trust between you. The last thing you should do is try to get the upper hand or embarrass them, especially in front of other colleagues. Not only would that erode trust, but it could also cause the person seeking a power position to retaliate and shame you publicly. Skillful team leaders (STLs) provide their colleagues with the means for a graceful exit.

How to provide a graceful exit:

Acknowledge the conflict or misstep in a matter-of-fact tone. Don't beat the issue to death or hold a grudge. Allow the person to move past the moment.

Think like a teacher:

Whether the learner is a child or an adult, everyone wants to save face when a mishap occurs. As an effective teacher, you are mindful about responding in ways that preserve a child's dignity, as well as the connection you have. When I was a supervisor and a person I was evaluating felt terrible about something she did out of poor judgment, I named it a "hiccup" and we moved on. (And, I could admit my own "hiccups" as well.)

Approach problems between you and your colleagues in a way that both gives grace and lets you move forward with learning.

Find the right words:

- *You raise concerns from a place of great expertise. I want to be conscious of time now. Are you comfortable if we move on?*

- *Thank you for sharing your perspective. I feel like we have a good understanding of where you are coming from and can move forward. Would you agree?*

- *How do you suggest we move forward from here?*

Primary Intention

Lead With Purpose and Direction: Priorities, Inquiry Questions, and Goals

6

The differences between high-functioning, high-impact Q1 teams and others are apparent from the moment collaboration begins, and it's not just in the ways they interact. Nearly every expert who writes about teams will tell you that groups need to have a clearly defined purpose. Skillful team leaders (STLs) and their colleagues know where they are headed and why. They are laser-focused on getting there. I saw this firsthand in my work with teacher-led teams who successfully turned around outcomes for students in chronically underperforming schools.

While everyone agrees purpose is paramount, agreeing on a worthwhile purpose is not always easy. Part of that hurdle comes from the ways in which schools form teams. The most authentic way to group people is to say, "We've got this compelling problem. Who should be on the team to solve it?" Unfortunately, many schools don't have the resources to orchestrate the makeup of all teams by common mission. Sometimes they can put together a task force for a specific charge, such as creating common curriculum, but usually schools form teams, at best, by common role (e.g., a sixth-grade teacher team) and, at worst, by schedule (e.g., "These teachers are free at this time, so there's a team"). This approach to teaming puts the onus on the educators who are grouped together to figure out why they are collaborating and what they are working toward.

STLs and their teams set direction by aligning their work with a school priority* and asking a compelling inquiry question about a worthwhile student-centered challenge. After data analysis, they further define their focus with team goals.

Contents:

Align with a priority.

6.1 Unpack priorities for understanding.

6.2 Identify a priority-based focus area.

6.3 Maintain focus on what's important.

---

*The term *school priorities* is used throughout Priority Intention 6 to connote district, school, department, and/or grade-level priorities.

Focus on a specific student-centered challenge.

6.4 Envision possibilities.

6.5 Brainstorm student-centered challenges.

6.6 Formulate an inquiry question.

Work toward a S-M-A-A-H-R-T goal.

6.7 (Specific) Write specific student-learning targets.

6.8 (Measurable) Measure what matters.

6.9 (Attainable) Reach for a tippy-toe goal.

6.10 (Aligned) Align with priorities and individual goals.

6.11 (Heartfelt) Connect to what matters.

6.12 (Results-driven) Distinguish learning outcomes from pathways.

6.13 (Time-bound) Establish a time frame according to student need.

Tools and templates:

Figure 23: STL Tool for Developing a Priority-Aligned, Student-Centered Inquiry Question (This tool is helpful for recording decisions made when aligning with a priority and focusing on a student-centered challenge.)

Figure 24: How Committed Is Your Team to Achieving Their Goal?

Figure 25: STL Tool for Setting S-M-A-A-H-R-T Goals

ALIGN WITH A PRIORITY

Collaborative inquiry teams are teacher-driven. This makes them a powerful tool for learning and change. However, a common misconception surfaces when teachers engage in this work, especially when they do an inquiry cycle for the first time: People interpret "teacher-driven" to mean that teams of teachers can work on whatever they wish. While the spirit of inquiry is exploration and discovery, people on high-functioning, high-impact Q1 teams don't go rogue. They see power in a cohesive professional learning community aligning to school priorities (Learning Forward, 2022). Without alignment, teams in one school can resemble those little wind-up toys going off in scattered directions. Skillful team leaders (STLs) align their work with at least one school priority.

STL moves:[*]

6.1 Unpack priorities for understanding.

6.2 Identify a priority-based focus area.

6.3 Maintain focus on what's important.

Related reading:

Move 6.10, "(Aligned) Align with priorities and individual goals." Use your understanding of school priorities to write your team goals.

What these moves promote:

Clarity. Team members build a shared understanding of what is most important to the school and see their part in it.

Alignment. Teams align their work to school priorities.

Focus. Teams aim their work toward a goal.

Agency. Teachers on teams have a voice in what they collaborate about.

Cross-collaboration. Different teams work toward the same priorities and build connections and learning across the school.

When to use these moves:

At the beginning of an inquiry cycle, typically during the *Ask & Aim* STL phase of collaborative inquiry.

---

[*]STLs often make these moves in sequence. Because of this, I include one "in action" example of an STL implementing the series of moves at the end of this section (see pp. 274–276; see also prompts in Figure 23 on p. 281).

6.1 Unpack priorities for understanding.

In the first staff meeting of every new school year, my principal would show a video of our superintendent outlining our district's big-picture focus areas for the coming year. These priorities were intended to be the lynchpin for all of our professional learning and work with students and families. But, in reality, they weren't. And it wasn't because the videos that our visionary leader made were dry and hard to sit through (although that didn't help). I think it was because my colleagues and I didn't "own" the priorities. We didn't know how they came about. (We were certainly not consulted). We didn't understand why they were deemed more important than other things at the time, or how prioritizing them would require us to make shifts in our practice. I tried my best, as a new teacher, to align what I did in the classroom to what I understood these priorities to mean, but I would hardly say that they drove my work or that of our teacher teams.

This was 30 years ago. Some districts today, like mine back then, don't do the best job communicating priorities, let alone collaborating with teachers to create them, but there are many who do. (My first teaching district is now much better at this.) School leaders typically roll out three to six big-picture school priorities a year. In well-functioning schools, these are derived from data, stakeholder input, community needs, and current educational research and trends and are communicated repeatedly throughout the year to staff, families, and students. But, in order for teacher teams to fully embrace aligning their work to school priorities* skillful team leaders (STLs) take time within the first few meetings to unpack school priorities for understanding.

How to unpack priorities for understanding:

Access all priorities your district, school, department, or grade level has set. Explore the origin of and need for the priorities most pertinent to your team. For example, an 11th-grade math team might unpack department priorities, which should in some way align to school and district priorities. Convey urgency with any compelling data you may have. Collectively discover how the priority is relevant to your team and the students and families you serve. Four simple questions can guide your discussion:

1. What is our school prioritizing this year?

2. Why this?

3. Why now?

4. Why us?

---

*Throughout this book I refer to district, school, department or grade-level priorities as "school priorities."

STL recommendations:

Invite an administrator. If you are unsure of the school priorities or need to learn more about their origin, need, and urgency, invite a school leader to familiarize faculty in advance of your team setting direction for their work.

Missing priorities? Some well-performing schools skip naming broad priorities and instead define specific, measurable goals to reach. It's fine to unpack these.

If your school (or department or grade level) has no priorities, or if they are generic like the ever-popular "We prioritize collaboration," then work with school leaders to look at data from classroom observations, surveys, interviews, and quantitative reports to determine what is most important for teams across your school to focus on at this time.

Find the right words:

- *What are our school priorities? What is our understanding of them? What terms do we need defined?*

- *Why this? Why not something else? What compelling evidence informed this priority? What is the origin of this priority? Who made this a priority?*

- *Why now? Why can't this wait?*

- *Why us? Why not someone else? Why our students?*

6.2 Identify a priority-based focus area.

If you're doing a house renovation on a limited budget with everything needing an overhaul, you'll have to make some tough choices. For instance, do you update the main bedroom or go for the open-concept living room? Similarly, if you have a newborn and you find a spare hour in your day, you'll likely need to choose between self-care (like a nap!) and checking that pile of emails that has been accumulating. Prioritizing is something we constantly do in life. The Massachusetts Department of Elementary and Secondary Education noticed a key finding about successful schools: "Continuous improvement schools recognized the limited nature of time, resources, and staff willingness and strategically prioritized continued improvement efforts, whereas less successful schools tried to do it all" (American Institutes for Research, 2016, p. 7). When schools identify priorities and teams align their work with those priorities, the school becomes a coherent professional learning community ready to confront and target school-wide issues (Jacobson, 2010).

District and school priorities are intentionally written broadly. They act like floodlights illuminating a wide area. This is actually good. They give teams direction, but also wiggle room to tailor their collaboration to fit their own specific needs. But once teams have this initial direction, skillful team leaders (STLs) need a spotlight. They identify a specific focus area within the given broad priority. For instance, if a district prioritizes "literacy across all disciplines," a math team might choose academic vocabulary as their priority-based focus area. An arts team might focus on critical viewing. A science team might focus on writing claim-evidence-reasoning (CER) responses. (Sticking with the light analogy, inquiry questions and team goals act as laser pointers, pinpointing a narrow focus for the team's collaboration.)

How to identify a priority-based focus area:

Follow this four-step protocol:

1. If your team doesn't already know your school's priorities, learn and unpack them (Move 6.1).

2. Turn to data that make the case for your team aligning with this priority. This is not the time to dig deep into analyzing student-centered challenges, formulate an inquiry question, or write measurable goals. Those will come after you set an initial direction on a priority-based focus area. You're just looking to spotlight an area of focus.

3. Choose a priority-based focus area that has the potential to positively impact your practice, your students' learning, and the work of others.

4. Write it in an easy-to-understand, easy-to-remember phrase.

STL recommendations:

Put it on a T-shirt. Your team's priority-based focus area can't be that important if people can't remember what it is. An exercise that helps, and is also fun, is asking people to write their priority-based focus area in wording that would fit on a T-shirt (not a literal T-shirt, although you could). For example, a school that prioritizes equitable opportunities for all students to actively engage in and advocate for themselves in learning might reference this priority as "student agency."

Phrase your focus area in words people can get behind. I worked with an STL who initially named her department priority "i-Ready Assessments" until teachers reacted negatively to the language, feeling as if she was prioritizing testing over students. When she shifted the language to "Assessment Practices to Support Learning for All Students," teachers got behind it. It also gave teams the freedom to explore assessments beyond i-Ready (Curriculum Associates, 2022).

Align, but no need to march in step. "Does every team in our department need to have the same priority-based focus area?" This is a common question I hear, and the short answer is no. So long as you are all aiming toward a shared overarching priority, your team can narrow focus on an aspect that makes sense for you and your students. (See the "literacy across all disciplines" example in the Move 6.2 opening paragraphs.) That being said, when teams do have similar or the same focus areas, they are better positioned to cross-collaborate. (For example, two science teams each focus on different aspects of the Next Generation Science Standards Science and Engineering Practice 4 [National Science Teaching Association, 2014].)

Adopt the four why *questions.* In Move 6.1, I suggest you and your team explore four questions to unpack the meaning of district/school priorities: (1) What is our school prioritizing this year? (2) Why this? (3) Why now? (4) Why us? You may find those same questions helpful when your team is deciding between one or more priority-based areas to focus on.

Think like a teacher:

As a teacher, you have likely needed to prioritize standards. In math, for example, where standards build on one another from grade to grade, it's common to prioritize algebraic reasoning in Grades 3–5 based on the belief that it is the "gateway" to higher levels of math (Sawchuk & Sparks, 2020). That doesn't mean don't teach geometry, but it does mean acknowledging that there is greater value in spending more time on ratios than on surface area.

Pick a priority-based focus area with your team that is worth spending the bulk of your collaborative time on.

Find the right words:

- *What do we most value?*

- *What priorities emerge from our data?*

- *In what ways would this priority impact student learning beyond our classrooms?*

- *How can we write a priority-based focus area in a way that staff, students, and families will readily grasp?*

6.3 Maintain focus on what's important.

"Pick a lane!" These words, uttered by my father-in-law when we are in bumper-to-bumper highway traffic, are what I think of when I am working with a team that can't maintain focus on one thing. Teams can fall into the trap of priority switching. It sounds something like this: (First meeting) "Let's look at struggling readers in this meeting to find out what skills they need." (Next meeting) "Let's implement the grit strategies that we just learned in our last professional development session." (Next meeting) "The state test is coming up. So our priority now has to be test-taking strategies." (You get the idea.) Even the highest-functioning, highest-impact teams can be pulled in various directions. Of course, a team needs to be adaptive and reprioritize at times. (Nothing proved this more than when the COVID-19 pandemic first shook the world of education.) However, jumping from one team focus to another will cause your collaborative work to feel disjointed and have little impact on any specific problem area. Skillful team leaders (STLs) maintain focus on what's important in the face of pressure, competing commitments, and distractions.

How to maintain focus on what's important:

Once you commit to a priority-based focus area, anticipate and plan for distractions. Protect time in your meetings, as best you can, by not letting what may seem urgent trump what is actually more important (see Move 1.2). The Eisenhower matrix (not to be confused with my Team Function, Impact Matrix presented in Part II, Chapter 3, Figure 1) can help. It categorizes tasks from your to-do list into four quadrants: important and urgent, important but not urgent, urgent but not important, and neither important nor urgent (Wikipedia, 2022). A variation by Robert Glazer (2016) reframes Eisenhower's quadrants into four actions:

Urgent Important	Non-urgent Important
1. Manage crises and important pressing problems.	2. Focus on big-picture strategies and opportunities.
Urgent Unimportant	**Non-urgent Unimportant**
3. Avoid tasks that divert your attention away from what is important and are simply busy work.	4. Limit trivial tasks that might be fun and engaging but serve no purpose.

Find the right words:

- *What obstacles could distract us from our focus? How can we prepare for them?*

- *Have we or others attempted to advance this priority previously? If yes, how can we maintain the course this time?*

- *What competing priorities might pull us away from our focus?*

Related reading:

Move 8.17, "Commit to action." This move maintains focus on what a team decides it will do with actionable steps and accountability.

Moves 6.1–6.3 in action:

Note: The following reality-based script is written for the purpose of illustrating the intentional moves STLs make. Consequently, this script is heavily focused on what the STL (Alma) says and does. If this were a real full transcript, there would be much more teacher-to-teacher dialogue, and any member of the team (not just Alma) might make intentional moves to advance the conversation.

MOVES	CONVERSATION	
6.1 Unpack priorities for understanding.	Alma:	Today, we're going to set an initial direction for our team's work. To start, let's turn to our department priorities. The district wants all school teams to focus on "literacy across disciplines" this year, and our history department declared writing as a priority. Before we do anything else, I want to make sure we have a shared understanding of where the writing priority came from and why we now need to align our teamwork with it. I'll start by sharing what I know.
		A district subcommittee, made up of the department chair and teacher leaders, looked at data across schools, surveyed teachers, observed some classrooms, and talked to families to learn more about strengths and areas of need. Let me highlight some compelling data that make the case for a writing priority across our department. If you were able to attend the district-wide history meeting, this will look familiar to you.
	[Teachers look over and discuss their understanding of the evidence in a brief partner talk.]	
	Teacher 1:	I didn't even really know our department had any priorities, so this was helpful to hear.
	Teacher 2:	I better understand now why writing needs to be a priority beyond the English language arts classes.
6.2 Identify a priority-based focus area.	Alma:	Next, let's narrow our focus a bit. We won't yet draft an inquiry question or set team goals, but we can identify a small aspect of writing that we think makes sense to focus on.
	Teacher 1:	There are so many things we need to do, and they all seem important.
	Teacher 2:	I think it's high time that we get consistency on a standardized format for writing. I can't tell you how many different-looking papers I get.
	Teacher 3:	I'd be thrilled with a header that has a student's name on it.
	Teacher 4:	And a font that isn't curlicue size 20!
	[Teachers laugh.]	
	Alma:	Standardizing a format for writing would be helpful, but is it a priority? What stands out as an important focus area when looking at results from our end-of-year writing assessments?
	Teacher 1:	Construct and evaluate arguments.

(Continued)

(Continued)

MOVES	CONVERSATION
	Teacher 2: Being able to support ideas with textual evidence. **Teacher 3:** Making a claim. **Alma:** Sounds like we want to prioritize analytical writing. Why is this important to us and to students? *[Teachers brainstorm that they want students "to be critical thinkers," "to become discriminating consumers of information," "to formulate coherent arguments so that they can advocate for what they believe," "to write position papers when they get to college," and so on.]* **Alma:** In what ways would this priority impact student learning beyond our classroom? **Teacher 4:** It builds a foundation for writing in other classes. **Teacher 2:** It ultimately prepares students for higher levels of writing in college and beyond.
6.3 Maintain focus on what's important.	**Alma:** Is there any reason why we haven't been able to prioritize analytical writing before? **Teacher 1:** Well, we did. It's just that we tend to toss out our agenda when there are daily demands on our time. **Alma:** OK, so we can't always stop things that need our immediate attention, but we can choose when and for how long we will address them. Let's dedicate 10 minutes at the top of each meeting to raise a pressing issue. Let's try not to resolve the issue in this 10 minutes, but instead use the time to plan who will follow up to address it. I'll also write "analytical writing" at the top of every agenda to help remind us of our big-picture purpose. *[Next, Alma leads the team in focusing on a specific challenge for students in analytical writing.]*

FOCUS ON A SPECIFIC STUDENT-CENTERED CHALLENGE

Many would tell you that collaborative inquiry starts with a teacher team's question. I would argue that it starts with a student-centered challenge. (This is why I place those words at the core of the STL Phases of Collaborative Inquiry in Part I, Chapter 3, Figure 2.) A well-worded question will drive your team through the phases of an inquiry cycle, but it's the desire for better student outcomes that fuels your collaboration. People on high-functioning, high-impact Q1 teams notice a complex problem, difficulty, or challenge affecting students and can't help but have questions about it. They feel compelled to learn more. This sets direction for their team inquiry.

Skillful team leaders (STLs) and their teams focus on a specific student-centered challenge, but it's not always easy for a group to choose one. The moves in this section will help your team narrow focus on an important problem, difficulty, or dilemma and frame that challenge as an inquiry question that everyone is eager to pursue.

STL moves:*

6.4 Envision possibilities.

6.5 Brainstorm student-centered challenges.

6.6 Formulate an inquiry question.

Tools:

Figure 23: STL Tool for Developing a Priority-Aligned, Student-Centered Inquiry Question (This tool is helpful for recording decisions made when aligning with a priority and focusing on a student-centered challenge.)

What these moves promote:

Focus. The team aims their work on a specific inquiry question to pursue.

Ownership. The team tackles a compelling question they see as important.

Community. People learn that they are not alone in the challenges they face.

Respect. The process respects that teacher observations from lived experiences are a form of data.

Evidence-based inquiry. Once a team arrives at a compelling question, they are eager to turn to data to learn more about the student problem/challenge.

When to use these moves:

During the *Ask & Aim* STL phase of collaborative inquiry.

---

*STLs often make these moves in sequence. Because of this, I include one "in action" example of an STL using the series of moves in order to land on an inquiry question at the end of this section (see pp. 283–285).

6.4 Envision possibilities.

Soon after writing this move, my family and I will be getting a puppy for the first time. And in the spirit of real-life inquiry, I have so many questions about training that it feels overwhelming to know where to start researching and how to actually own a dog. I was surprised to learn that the first step to training is not with the dog, but with the people. DogTime (n.d.) recommends that you start with a family meeting where together you picture what you want life with the dog to be. (Eating people food from the table? No. Walking without pulling on the leash? Yes.) Although you and your team are not learning how to train a pup together, your inquiry work does benefit from an initial discussion about what you want to see for your students. Skillful team leaders (STLs) and their teams launch inquiry by envisioning student possibilities.

How to envision possibilities:

Once your team has decided on a priority-based focus area (Move 6.2), brainstorm what you expect to see from students. Refer to standards that you have. Access texts that describe what "could be." Help to create a clear picture of the team's vision by replacing jargon with examples.

STL recommendation:

Keep reality at bay. Reality does not always match up to vision. (Anyone who has ever owned a puppy knows that I can talk all I want with my family about our plan for raising one, but once our puppy arrives, some of that idealistic vision will get a hard dose of reality.) Nevertheless, keep this conversation focused on what could be. Move 6.5 will give people an opportunity to name the challenges that students exhibit.

Find the right words:

- *Given the school priority we are aiming to advance, what do we envision for students?*
- *Let's turn to professional texts and standards for what is recommend for students.*
- *Please provide an example so that we can envision what you are saying.*
- Try the following sentence frame: *If [insert school priority], then [insert the benefit to students].* For example: *If students were strong, independent readers, then they would have the stamina to read long passages of complex text.*

6.5 Brainstorm student-centered challenges.

Have you ever sensed something is wrong, but not had the hard evidence to prove it? Educators, parents, patients—we all have gut feelings that we listen to. Conzemius and Morganti-Fisher (2012) call this "intuitive data," and it's worth paying attention to as a team. Make no mistake: There is an absolute place in collaborative inquiry for analyzing surveys, student work, and standardized tests. (In fact, it's the premise for STL phase of collaborative inquiry 2, *Assess & Analyze*.) But before combing through spreadsheets and surveys, skillful team leaders (STLs) encourage their colleagues to launch a "gut dialogue" about student-centered challenges. In fact, starting with intuitive data actually gets your team invested. Team members become ready and eager to turn to assessment data to learn more about the student centered-challenge.

How to brainstorm student-centered challenges:

Follow this three-step protocol:

1. Make a two-column chart with the first column labeled "strengths" and the second labeled either "areas for growth/change" or "challenges." (Going forward, I'll refer to this column as "challenges.") Brainstorm student strengths, then challenges, within your priority-based focus area.

2. Within each brainstorm, invite your colleagues to draw from their everyday observations. Delay examining quantitative data; it will come next. Encourage your colleagues to describe student strengths and challenges in terms of specific concepts, skills, knowledge, habits, and mindsets. Refer back to the expectations your team outlined when they envisioned possibilities (Move 6.4) and pull language from standards, if available. Invite people to think broadly about patterns they notice across all students, as well as specific student populations such as English learners or those with specific learning disabilities. Prompt your colleagues to reflect on what *they* have observed, and also on what they hear from students and parents.

3. Look for themes, and choose one specific student-centered challenge that, if resolved, would make a significant difference for student learning and teacher practice.

STL recommendations:

Know your school's data culture. Launching inquiry with a "gut dialogue" is beneficial and even refreshing to teams in which school culture places a heavy focus on data. But if educators in your building are new to data analysis, have relied a bit too much on intuition, and are not, yet, in the habit of making decisions based on evidence, you're better off skipping this move and starting with the numbers and student work to see what student challenges become evident through data.

Keep the conversation student-centered. Be careful when naming challenges that talk does not drift toward what teachers do or need to improve. Although your inquiry work will ultimately address teacher practice, a better entry point is to focus on students. Teachers will be more comfortable speaking about students than about themselves, and if you are leading a low-functioning Q2 or Q4 team, your colleagues will be less defensive because they won't feel as if they are in the hot seat.

Write with a marker. Offer to record ideas on visible chart paper. The sensorimotor component of writing on paper helps the brain take in and process information (University of Stavanger, 2011). For a facilitator, this helps make connections between brainstormed ideas, which is useful when a team is ready to narrow focus on a standout student-centered challenge.

Be cognizant of your own bias. When you seek themes from a group brainstorm, you might steer the conversation toward what you see as an important focus based on your own preferences. Be mindful that you are open to all key challenges raised by your colleagues even if you don't see them as challenges yourself.

Having trouble narrowing down to one student-centered challenge? Turn to another move. If narrowing down to one student-centered challenge is difficult for your group, then modify and apply the four *why* questions from Move 6.1 to the challenge you are considering:

1. What is the student-centered challenge we are considering?

2. Why this?

3. Why now?

4. Why us?

Or, modify the questions that helped you identify your priority-based focus area from Move 6.2:

- What, according to the data, is an important area of specific student challenge?

- Why is this student-centered challenge important to us?

- How could this student-centered challenge positively impact our practice, student learning, and other teams?

If your group is having trouble agreeing on which of many student-centered challenges to focus on, move ahead to formulating an inquiry question (Move 6.6). Use the criteria checklist on page 283, and it will be clear which challenge is a good focus for your team inquiry.

Find the right words:

- *Within the parameters of our priority focus area . . .*

  - *What do our students know/do well? What concepts, skills, knowledge, habits, or mindsets do they exhibit?*

  - *What are students' areas for growth? What obstacles stand in the way of our vision for success? What dilemmas do we face?*

  - *What questions emerge for you in your practice as you think about student strengths and areas for growth?*

FIGURE 23 STL Tool for Developing a Priority-Aligned, Student-Centered Inquiry Question

From start to finish, this tool can help a team craft their first priority-aligned, student-centered inquiry question using Moves 6.1–6.6.

Intent: Align with a priority

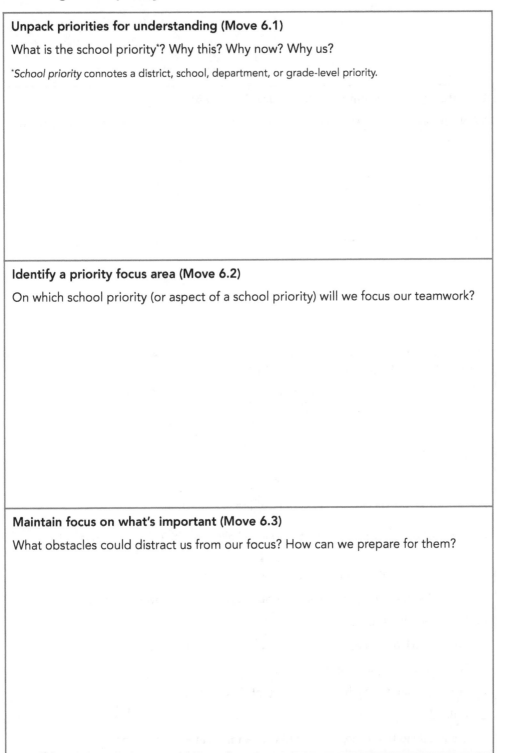

Unpack priorities for understanding (Move 6.1)

What is the school priority*? Why this? Why now? Why us?

*School priority connotes a district, school, department, or grade-level priority.

Identify a priority focus area (Move 6.2)

On which school priority (or aspect of a school priority) will we focus our teamwork?

Maintain focus on what's important (Move 6.3)

What obstacles could distract us from our focus? How can we prepare for them?

(Continued)

(Continued)

Intent: Focus on a student-centered challenge

Envision possibilities (Move 6.4)

What do we expect to see from students in academics, social-emotional skills, and habits of mind?

Brainstorm student-centered challenges (Move 6.5)

What student strengths and challenges within our priority-based focus area do we notice?

What is one specific student-centered challenge that we are eager to work on?

Formulate an inquiry question (Move 6.6)

What initial question do we have about this student-centered challenge?

Are we set up for success? Check that our inquiry question:

☐ Is based on an evident student learning challenge within a priority-based focus area

☐ Presents a "real" dilemma for everyone on our team

☐ Is substantive enough to drive an inquiry cycle, but not overwhelming

☐ Starts with *What* or *How*

☐ Presents a learning opportunity for everyone on our team

☐ Necessitates research and study

☐ Feels relevant to teachers' practice (not theoretical)

☐ Is timely

☐ Is something that is best explored with a team rather than alone

6.6 Formulate an inquiry question.

Nancie Atwell (2017) tells adolescent writers when choosing an essay topic to find the itch and scratch it. One could take a similar approach to adult team inquiry. Find a compelling question about a student-centered challenge and pursue it. Skillful team leaders (STLs) and their teams set direction for their work with a strong inquiry question. Once they have this, they are able to advance through the STL Phases of Collaborative Inquiry, which are described in detail in Part I, Chapter 3.

How to formulate an inquiry question:

Formulate one or more questions using the following checklist criteria:

- ☑ Is based on an evident student-learning challenge within a priority-based focus area

- ☑ Presents a "real" dilemma for everyone on our team

- ☑ Is substantive enough to drive an inquiry cycle, but not overwhelming

- ☑ Starts with *What* or *How*

- ☑ Presents a learning opportunity for everyone on our team

- ☑ Necessitates research and study

- ☑ Feels relevant to teachers' practice (not theoretical)

- ☑ Is timely

- ☑ Is something that is best explored with a team rather than alone

Examples of strong inquiry questions include the following:

- *How do we teach students to write with structure but not formulaically?*

- *How do we encourage students to pursue their own learning interests, but also teach them essential content?*

- *How can students write challenging personal academic goals that don't negatively impact their personal wellness or social and emotional goals?*

- *What are the five "ins and outs" students should enter and exit each grade level with, and how do we respond to students who have not yet mastered these?*

STL recommendations:

Expect to start broadly. It's perfectly normal to exit the *Ask & Aim* STL phase of collaborative inquiry with a broad inquiry question that could be the subject of a dissertation (e.g., "How do we stimulate student motivation?"). Remember, you are only trying to give your team a general direction to aim toward. You'll narrow your focus in the *Assess & Analyze* and *Target & Plan* STL Phases of Collaborative Inquiry. And throughout the course of your team's collaboration more specific inquiry questions will come up organically.

Don't ask something that can be Googled. This is the advice that leaders at The Teacher Collaborative, based in Boston, give to their teachers who participate in their Co-Labs, where teachers come together across public, charter, and independent schools in small collaborative groups to explore specific issues affecting teachers and students (see theteachercollaborative.org). Collaborative inquiry empowers teams to tackle complex problems that pose real dilemmas for educators. Tap into the complexity of the student-centered challenges that you are working to solve. Highlight or call on others to surface the push and pull of a dilemma.

Reframe a teacher dilemma. If your team generates a teacher-centered implementation question (e.g., "How do I teach X?" "How do I facilitate Y?"), flip it to student-centered language. Simply invite teachers to name what they expect to see from students. For instance, you can change "How do we facilitate accountable talk?" to "How do we help students cite relevant evidence from text through accountable talk?" Or shift "How do we implement restorative justice Talking Circles in the classroom?" to "How do we effectively implement Talking Circles so that our fourth-grade students learn how to communicate with each other and work through conflict?" (See Move 5.15 for more detail on how to shift focus from teachers to students. See also Bintlif [2014] for a discussion of Talking Circles.)

Start with What *or* How. Avoid questions that begin with *Why* as these can get theoretical. Try the following sentence stems:

- *How will we help students be able to Z?* or *We want students to be able to Z.* (Note: You might name a student subgroup.)

- *How do we reduce [or increase] students' ability to Z?*

- *How do we help students overcome X in order to do Z?*

- *What effect does Y have on students?*

- *How do we teach Y so that students know how to Z?*

Take a moment to celebrate. It can be difficult to find a meaningful direction for your team's collaboration. Many teams struggle to do that efficiently and also in a way in which every member of the team is genuinely invested. Once you have an inquiry question or aim, by no means do you need to throw a party, but it is worthwhile to acknowledge the accomplishment.

Find the right words:

- *What concern keeps tugging at you? What student-centered challenge "keeps you up at night"?*

- *What student-centered challenge, when resolved, would make a difference to students, families, and us?*

- *What student-centered challenge stirs up questions that we don't know the answer to, but feel compelled to try and resolve together?*

- *What student-centered challenge sparks our curiosity to turn to data to learn more about the problem?*

- *Which student-centered challenges present the most learning and growth for each of us as professionals?*

Moves 6.4–6.6 in action:

STL Karen Coyle Aylward has aligned her high school team's work to the district priority of culturally responsive teaching and her school priority of family engagement. Her school prioritized family engagement because of what they learned from a school learning walk and family surveys. To advance the school priority, teachers on Karen's team are now learning about academic socialization, a research-based effective means to involve parents in conversation with their children (Jensen & Minke, 2017).

STL MOVES:	TEAM EXAMPLE:	
6.4 Envision possibilities.	Karen:	[*Reads from a journal article (Jensen & Minke, 2017, pp. 171–172).*] Academic socialization is "defined as communication-based behaviors from parents that convey the importance of education, their aspirations for the adolescent, and plans for the future. . . . Of the three types of parent engagement examined, academic socialization had the strongest association with adolescents' achievement." The article suggests schools can bolster family engagement through academic socialization by (1) making the parent a true partner; (2) being an empathetic listener; (3) informing parents that talking about school together, sharing dreams for the future, and talking about educational goals together does have a big impact; and (4) reassuring parents that offering support and encouragement to their child is working. What do we envision each of these actually looking and sounding like?
	[*Teachers share out.*]	
6.5 Brainstorm student-centered challenges.	Karen:	We are focused on academic socialization at home and have envisioned how we hope parents will engage with their children. Next, let's begin to narrow down to a more focused inquiry question by discussing what's working for kids and families and what obstacles/areas for growth exist.
	[*As teachers talk, Karen fills in a T-chart with + and Δ columns indicating student strengths and challenges.*]	

(Continued)

(Continued)

STL MOVES:	TEAM EXAMPLE:	
	Teacher 1:	I am now realizing that at the end of a parent–teacher meeting, parents are more likely to engage with their children when I explicitly give parents something they can do—a specific conversation they can have with their child. So instead of saying, "Your child didn't finish their project," I'd ask, "Would you be able to help your child make a schedule to complete their project?" Parents need to have something they can grasp that they can get done. I'd like to learn more ways to do this.
	Teacher 2:	Students in my class need to engage their parents for some assignments, but only some of them do it. I have been tempted to stop requiring this type of engagement because I recognize that some students don't have a caretaker with whom they can do the activity, but I now see that it's important. But what do I do with the kids who couldn't do the assignment when we talk in class about the conversations some kids had?
	Karen:	So it's not just how do we get parents and caretakers to engage, but how do we empower students to lead these conversations at home, particularly when they can't or maybe don't want to? It's challenging, too, because as the article said, teenagers naturally want to pull away from their parents at this age, and we are asking them to engage with their parents instead.
	Instructional Coach:	There's something powerful in routines and rituals. When you have things that happen at the same time at the same clip, then folks can opt in when they are able. I like the idea of maybe once a term we do a family project or every week a discussion question goes home and if you don't do it you're not going to get in trouble, but it's there every week and so when parents and caregivers and kids feel ready to do it, they take it on and share with us.
	Karen:	And now back to that metaphor of the iceberg in the article because academic socialization is not always visible. We may never know what effect these conversations are having, but the idea of keeping a ritual and holding that space for discussion might spark a conversation between parent or caregiver and child that we never even hear about.
	Teacher 1:	And even the parent might not see the impact of their engagement with their child.

STL MOVES:	TEAM EXAMPLE:
	Karen: Right, and we don't want them to get discouraged. Based on what I heard, I jotted down in a chart what's working for students and families in the plus column, and obstacles or areas for growth in the delta column. The areas for growth that we have discussed pose real dilemmas that we can now zero in on in the form of an inquiry question.

+ **STRENGTHS:** **WHAT'S WORKING?**	Δ **CHALLENGES:** **WHAT OBSTACLES GET IN THE WAY? WHERE ARE THE AREAS FOR GROWTH?**
• Parents/caretakers are responsive to explicit tasks and specific recommendations from teachers. • Parents/caretakers participate when our school makes engagement opportunities routine. • Students engage with their parents/caretakers when there are no penalties for not participating.	• Not all parents/caretakers can engage with their students. • Developmentally, adolescents don't always want to engage with parents/caretakers. • The impact of engaging conversations isn't always visible. • Parents/caretakers need reassurance that what they are doing makes a difference.

STL MOVES:	TEAM EXAMPLE:
6.6 Formulate an inquiry question.	**Karen:** I'm hearing a few inquiry questions emerge from the challenges we shared: 1. What specific tasks can we assign to students and parents so that they engage with each other? How do we respond to students and caretakers who can't or don't do these tasks? How might we implement rituals to increase engagement? 2. While we want parents and caretakers to persist, how do we reassure them that they are having an impact when they don't feel like they are? 3. How do we engage parents with their high school–age children when it's developmentally appropriate for teenagers to not want to spend as much time with their parents and begin to disengage? These are complex questions, and we will likely explore them all at some point, but to launch our inquiry, let's start with one. *[Karen shares the list of criteria for a good inquiry question. Teachers choose the first question as something that captures a real dilemma that they are curious about, and know they need each other to research and aim to resolve it.]*

WORK TOWARD
A S-M-A-A-H-R-T GOAL

If you've ever set professional goals for yourself, your team, or your school, you are likely familiar with the acronym SMART—used to describe goals that are specific, measurable, attainable, results-driven, and time-bound. The SMART criteria can help you move from a wish to a realized outcome. For example, "I hope to make cum laude" becomes "By the end of the third quarter, I'll raise my GPA by 0.3 point to be cum laude. I won't skip class. I'll join a study group, do all assignments, and go to office hours once a week." SMART goals have become commonplace in schools and can serve a team well. But, as I'm sure you've seen, simply having them does not guarantee impact on student learning. While this can be attributed to poor implementation of a goal, in many cases the problem lies within the written goal itself.

Q2 and Q3 teams (both low impact) tend to write what I call "seemingly SMART" goals. Explained in detail in my first book, *The Skillful Team Leader* (MacDonald, 2013), these are goals that technically meet each criterion of the SMART acronym, but when goals are reached, nothing much has changed for student learning. For instance, a team might set a goal that is seemingly specific in that it specifies what teachers will do (e.g., *We will collect resources for teaching writing in history and English*) but it does not specify the anticipated improved outcomes in student learning (e.g., *Students will differentiate relevant from irrelevant textual evidence to defend a position*). Make no mistake: Sharing teaching practices is worthwhile, but unless teachers identify where learning breaks down and set goals for specific students for whom learning is a struggle, impact is left to chance.

Skillful team leaders (STLs) and their teams don't settle for seemingly SMART goals. Instead, they deliberately aim for small, equitable student-learning targets that align to bigger priorities and goals. They write goals that are specific, measurable, attainable, aligned, heartfelt, results-driven, and time-bound, or S-M-A-A-H-R-T—intended to be pronounced with a Boston accent as a fun homage to my colleagues and to my Revere, MA-raised husband. (Imagine Matt Damon in *Good Will Hunting* telling you to make your goal S-M-A-A-H-R-T!)

Side note: Some schools have stepped back from the infamous SMART acronym for reasons such as misguided enforcement of goals, creating a culture of intimidation, or too heavy a focus on only those goals that can be measured with assessments schools have. You don't need to use the acronym if you think people will adversely react, but you should intentionally engage your team in dialogue about the aspects of goals that can improve your chances of impact.

Other factors influence goal attainment.

There's more to achieving a team goal than ensuring it's written as specific, measurable, attainable, and so on. Research shows that people are more likely to reach their goals when they have a desire to achieve the goal, intent to implement the goal, and the perception that they have control in attaining the goal (Bagozzi et al., 2003). Attention to the language you use to write your team goal, coupled with the belief that you intend to and will achieve the goal, is what gets your team across the finish line. Figure 24 in Move 6.11 can help you get a sense of how invested people are in reaching the goal.

STL moves:

6.7 (Specific) Write specific student-learning targets.

6.8 (Measurable) Measure what matters.

6.9 (Attainable) Reach for a tippy-toe goal.

6.10 (Aligned) Align with priorities and individual goals.

6.11 (Heartfelt) Connect to what matters.

6.12 (Results-driven) Distinguish learning outcomes from pathways.

6.13 (Time-bound) Establish a time frame according to student need.

Tools and templates:

Figure 24: How Committed Is Your Team to Achieving Their Goal?

Figure 25: STL Tool for Setting S-M-A-A-H-R-T Goals

What these moves promote:

Evidence-based analysis. Teams look toward data to determine desired student-learning outcomes.

Accountability. Teams determine measures by which they will evaluate progress.

Alignment. Selected team goals advance school* priorities.

Agency. Teams focus on goals that they are deeply committed to achieving and can reach.

---

*Note: School priorities include district, department, and grade-level priorities.

When to use these moves:

During the *Target & Plan* STL phase of collaborative inquiry.

What is a skillful, intentional approach to goal setting with a team?

Before you lead the moves in this section, remember that your approach matters. Be careful not to get so caught up in acronyms or wordsmithing that you forget what goal setting is really about—getting on the same page about where you are headed and why. Skillful team leaders (STLs) use whatever approach works for their team. They think through key considerations of setting a goal using S-M-A-A-H-R-T as a guide, not a straitjacket.

Avoid seemingly SMART goals, those that are technically specific, measurable, attainable, results-driven, and time-bound but won't likely bring about the impact you are seeking. Play with the moves in this section without feeling married to the sequence of the acronym, and pick an approach that doesn't feel cumbersome or forced.

STL recommendations for working toward a S-M-A-A-H-R-T goal:

Use a question guide. If you want to make sure you don't have a seemingly SMART goal, then refer to the checklist in Figure 25 at the end of this chapter. There's no need for your whole team to go through every checkbox together; instead, you can simplify the list by focusing only on the S-M-A-A-H-R-T criteria that you think need to be addressed.

Fill in the blank. There's nothing wrong with using a linguistic frame for SMART goal writing, such as this one: *Evidence [name sources] shows that students [describe current reality]. By [date], students will be able to [expected learning results] as measured by [assessment tool]. This goal aligns with [priorities]. This goal matters to us and students because . . .*

Bullet. If plugging your goal into a linguistic frame or answering questions in a checklist is too much for you or your team, simply bullet the student outcomes you want and the teacher outcomes you expect on your draft plan (see Figures 12–14 in Move 4.1). Then, accompany it with a simple narrative explaining the rationale for the decisions you have made, such as how this goal aligns to priorities and your plans to measure the goal.

Use the moves, but shake up the sequence. As convenient as acronyms are, you don't have to follow the sequence of letters. Start where it makes sense. Usually, the best place is to start by aligning to priorities (*A*). Then, analyze data and name the specific learning outcomes you want to achieve for students (*R*), write the specifics (*S*) of the goal, and check that everyone on your team is strongly committed to achieving it (*H*). Later, you can ask how students are doing, which will prompt your team to put some progress-monitoring assessments in place for whatever you are assessing (*M*). After you've studied some strategies, you can make a timeline (*T*) for implementation. And, if you were overly ambitious in your initial goal, you can always adjust at any point to make it more attainable (*A*).

Assess readiness. If you're having trouble naming a S-M-A-A-H-R-T goal, it might be because your team isn't ready to do so. Perhaps you don't yet have data that show which students are affected in what ways by a problem, and you first need to assess. Perhaps you don't yet have progress-monitoring tools to tell you how effective your actions are on student outcomes, and you need to take a step back and create them. Or, maybe you are in the initial stages of just trying to name a student-centered challenge that your team wants to pursue, and you need to refine your collaborative inquiry question.

6.7 (Specific) Write specific student-learning targets.

Joan Benoit Samuelson, winner of the first Olympic women's marathon and many running accomplishments thereafter, shares one strategy she uses to reach the finish line in record time: She sets visual targets throughout the race (*get to the street light, pass the person in the red shorts, etc.*). Each goal is something she can literally see (Balcetis, 2020). I have seen this approach applied successfully by teacher team leaders with whom I have worked in extraordinary turnaround schools across the nation. Although they don't necessarily set visual markers, skillful team leaders (STLs) write specific student-learning targets. They specify which students will make what incremental gains, by when and by how much, based on data.

How to write specific student-learning targets:

In the early phases of your team's inquiry cycle, set direction for your team with a specific student-learning goal. Examine state, district, or school assessment data you have. If you need a more narrow view of specific student-learning challenges, use a teacher-created assessment (see Moves 7.1–7.4). Refer to benchmarks that students are expected to reach. Notice specific areas of need for specific groups of students who are not yet at the specified benchmarks. Specify targets for groups of students. Check that your goal is inclusive so that 100% of students have a goal. In other words, it's OK to specify 80% of students will reach X benchmark, but don't forget to also set a goal for the remaining 20% of students. Check the other criteria of a S-M-A-A-H-R-T goal to make sure you have specified all the details you need to start working toward the goal.

In action:

A second-grade math team decides the specifics for their initial student-learning goal.

District Data:	Over the past three years, we noticed that the number of students entering remedial math classes in ninth grade has increased by 30%. District data show gaps in proficiency in the foundations of math as early as when students exit fifth grade.
School State Test Data:	At our elementary school, as early as third grade, we noticed approximately 25% of students show low scores in understanding math concepts.
Second-Grade End-of-Year Benchmark Data:	Approximately 1 out of every 3 second-grade students is not at proficiency in the computational fluency standard.
Initial Specific Student-Learning Goal:	By May, 11 second-grade students who are not yet proficient will demonstrate computational fluency. Students will demonstrate understanding of multi-digit numbers (up to 1,000) written in base-ten notation, recognizing that the digits in each place represent amounts of thousands, hundreds, tens, or ones (e.g., 853 is 8 hundreds + 5 tens + 3 ones).

Note to the reader: This goal is *specific.* Next steps will be for the team to decide the other criteria of a S-M-A-A-H-R-T goal. With this, the team will have an initial direction. Once team inquiry begins, the team will assess students and analyze data to a greater extent, and can target this goal further. An example of what that could look like follows.

Team Question: Where is understanding breaking down for kids? Are they able to notate a double-digit number in base-ten notation? Are they able to add double digits applying the strategy of pulling out tens and ones?

Design the Formative Assessment: In school, we will administer a teacher-created six-question assessment.

Task: For the first three questions, students will need to write double-digit numbers in base-ten notation. For the second three questions, students will need to add double-digit numbers and explain the strategy they used to get the answer.

Criteria for Success: *What we want to see: number talk strategy.*

> *22 = 10 + 10 + 2*
>
> *I pulled out the tens and the ones.*
>
> *11 + 14 = ?*
>
> *10 + 1 + 10 + 4 = ?*
>
> *10 + 10 = 20, 1 + 4 = 5, 20 + 5 = 25*
>
> *I pulled out the tens and the ones.*

Analysis:

We observe: 15 out of 30 kids applied the "counting on" strategy to all math addition problems.

Sample student work 1: 11 + 14 = 25 I started at 11 and added 14 cubes.

Sample student work 2: 11 + 14 = 23 I started at 11 and counted on with my fingers 11, 12, 13, 14, and so on.

We infer: These students are over-reliant on the "counting on" strategy. It is inefficient when adding double digits, slows kids down, increases errors, and indicates that they may not understand units of 10.

Target Goal: Fifteen identified students will demonstrate understanding of units of 10 by using the number talk strategy, in which they pull out tens and ones, to add double-digit numbers. These students will rely less on the "counting on" strategy.

Teacher Pathway Goals: We will create supplementary teaching resources to target the identified skills. . . . We will develop push-in supports for specific, identified students. . . . We will learn strategies from Kathy Richardson's "Developing Number Concepts" book series.

STL recommendations:

Toss out the random percentage goals. You've seen it and maybe even written it—a goal like *80% of students will get a proficient score in English language arts on the state test by May.* As written, this goal is specific, but it is seemingly so. It leaves many unanswered questions: Is 80% a number that came from data? Can whoever set this goal identify which students are in that 80%? What do students need to learn in order to get a proficient score? What about the remaining 20% of students; what goal do they need? The details of this goal don't provide the team with a small enough data-informed focus. (See Move 6.8 for further learning about how to measure a goal.)

Start with an aim. If you don't yet have all the data you need to target a goal and get as specific as I am suggesting, start with an aim such as *80% of students will get a proficient score,* but write it with the intent of revising your goal as soon as you have the data you need to make targeted decisions.

Tweak the language. The language of your team goal is for your team—not an administrator, not parents—it's for you and your colleagues. Write the specifics in a way that gives clarity and direction to everyone tasked with achieving the goal. Don't worry about fitting it into a neat, one-sentence format. Write it so that it makes sense to your team.

Find the right words:

- *What specific student-centered problem, challenge, or need shows up in the data?*

- *What do we expect students should be able to understand, know, and do? Which students? How soon can we hit this target? What additional targets must we set for other groups of students?*

- *What details do we need to decide on so that we know where we are headed?*

Related reading:

Move 7.13, "Target and plan for student success." Once your team has a direction for your work and you are in the *Strategize & Design* STL phase of collaborative inquiry, target goals for small groups or individual students and decide plans that you can implement immediately. A plan might include reteaching to a small selected group of students or designing an intervention.

6.8 (Measurable) Measure what matters.

At the most basic level, the measures you specify when writing a goal tell you when you have achieved your goal. Classic example: *I plan to lose 10 pounds as measured by a scale.* It gets wonky when the measures you choose don't give you the information you need when you need it. I call these seemingly measurable goals.

These types of goals don't serve your team. They typically fall short for one of the following reasons:

1. *Numbers and percentages are baseless or arbitrary.* "80% of students will . . ." "Students will provide 3 pieces of evidence that . . ." There's nothing wrong with putting these numbers in your goal, *if* they are informed by data. Skillful team leaders (STLs) are intentional about how they arrive at the numbers articulated in their goals. They count kids.

2. *They collect data on levers that affect learning rather than measuring the learning itself.* "We will increase the participation rate in the math extended school year (ESY) summer program by 50% . . ." "We will reach a 90% attendance rate . . ." "Students will read 10 books . . ." "Teachers will collaborate 3 times a week . . ." Every one of these goals is measurable, and all are worthwhile, but none of the "measures" mentioned, actually measures the impact that hitting these marks is expected to have on student learning. In other words, it's good that you are measuring the participation rate in your ESY summer program, but what measures will you use to track math learning growth of the students who participate? STLs measure indicators of learning.

3. *They rely on measures that don't give data in real time.* High-achieving schools systematically target goals for specific groups of students,

regularly progress-monitor those students with formative assessments (see Move 10.4), and respond immediately. They base team data analysis on what they see in the data. In comparison, low-achieving schools focus mostly on discussing teaching practices (Timperley, 2008). STLs and their teams have frequent rapid access to data to regularly monitor the progress of students.

How to measure what matters:

When monitoring your goal, consider the following:

- Which students will receive the instruction/intervention, and what will it be?

- What learning target or student-learning outcome do we expect as a result of the instruction/intervention? What benchmarks, if any, do we expect students will likely reach?

- What will instruction/intervention look like in core instruction, small group, and/or intensive 1:1 intervention? Who will deliver the instruction/ intervention? How often will the instruction/intervention be delivered? By when will the instruction/intervention finish?

- (During progress monitoring) How are we responding to student needs? What new goals do students need?

STL recommendations:

Don't avoid SEL goals. We know social-emotional learning (SEL) skills, mental wellness, and habits of mind are linked to academic skills (Zins et al., 2004). The good news is measurement tools are constantly being developed. For instance, I learned of a website with free and paid-for psychosocial data collection tools from a presentation by John Crocker, director of school mental health and behavioral services for Methuen (Massachusetts) Public Schools, called School Health Assessment and Performance Evaluation, or SHAPE (www.theshapesys tem.com). If your school does not have system-wide measures, prompt your colleagues to name qualitative indicators of what they intend to see and hear from students, and what they don't. For example, "We aim to improve students' self-advocacy. We expect students will ask for help on assignments. We expect to receive fewer emails with questions about assignments from parents because students will be self-advocating for what they need."

Be wary of lagging indicators. Measures that provide results later than the team needs to view them are considered lagging. Standardized state tests are a typical example because you don't usually get data back until after students have left the grade level that they were in when they took the test. It's fine to include a lagging indicator as one measure of the success of your goal, but you'll also want to include formative assessments and likely a summative assessment at the end of your study and intervention.

Remember: The measure is not the goal. Take an everyday example: "I'll weigh myself on a scale at the end of my diet to show that I have lost 10 pounds." The goal is weight loss, and the measure is 10 pounds on the scale, but other measures could include dropping one clothing size or being able to run without becoming winded for a specific amount of time. Similarly, school team goals should be more than a percentage achievement on a test (e.g., *80% of students will get a proficient score in English language arts on the state test by May*). There is nothing wrong with including in the language of your goal specific scores or levels of proficiency. This is, in fact, a measure of success and should be articulated, but the goal can't only be about scores. Scores don't often tell the full story of learning. STLs go a step further in naming "look-fors" in learning—indicators of what teachers will (and won't) see and hear from students.

Related reading:

Move 7.2, "Choose an assessment based on the view of data you need." When writing your team's student-learning goal, turn to this move to intentionally select an assessment that will measure your goal.

Move 10.4, "Monitor student progress." Regularly track how students are doing given the changes you are implementing through progress-monitoring tools.

6.9 (Attainable) Reach for a tippy-toe goal.

In a PBS interview with Charlie Rose (2017), Ursula Burns, the first Black CEO of a Fortune 500 company, used the term "tippy-toe experience." She defined it as "higher than I thought I could do it, a little bit beyond my reach, but if I jumped really high I could grab it, and I was able to just continue to grow." Skillful team leaders (STLs) and their high-functioning, high-impact Q1 teams reach for attainable tippy-toe goals.

How to reach for a tippy-toe goal:

Identify with your team a just-above-reach challenge that each group of students needs. Use standards, performance expectations, and frameworks to guide your decision. Accompany your student-learning tippy-toe goals with professional goals that will stretch you but not cause burnout as you try to achieve them. Make a list of resources needed to attain the goal to determine if it is within reach. Then, mark what you have, what you can get (perhaps with some creative thinking and effort), and what is truly impossible to access at this time.

STL recommendations:

Don't dismiss a goal due to limited resources. While it's understandable that no one wants to set a goal for which there are insufficient resources or insurmountable obstacles, often these are the problems that most need ambitious goals. Get creative. I've seen schools change their schedules in order to make time for an intervention/enrichment block for all students, partner with local colleges and community programs to bring in students and retired specialists as tutors, write grants for extra time for teachers to meet, and allow teacher teams to merge classes when substitute teachers were not available to allow teachers to observe one another. Although it doesn't involve a teacher team, one of the most stunning examples I've heard of not allowing setbacks to hold you back from attaining your goal comes from the Topeka (Kansas) Public Schools where Superintendent Tiffany Anderson creatively provided Wi-Fi access via parked school buses to those in the community who were not able to get online during the COVID-19 pandemic (Taglang, 2021).

Consider school culture. If you notice yourself or your colleagues shying away from tippy-toe goals, it is worth examining why. The answer may lie in your school culture. Do school leaders encourage risk and allow for failure and reflection? Or, is there such pressure on teachers that if they don't hit their goals they will be criticized, penalized, or dismissed? Engage in honest conversations about setting and meeting high expectations. Collaborate with school leaders to develop healthy responses to missed goals that give teachers support, as learners, but don't lower the bar for students.

Find the right words:

- *What goal is within reach but still a stretch for students?*

- *What strategies do we intend to implement to reach this goal? Are they sustainable, or do they have the potential to burn us out?*

- *Are limited resources keeping us from setting an important goal? If yes, what support and resources do we have or can we creatively get? If our resources deplete, can we still attain our goal?*

- *We did not attain our goal, but what can we learn from the outcome we got?*

6.10 (Aligned) Align with priorities and individual goals.

Moves 6.1–6.3 delve into how and why teams should align their teamwork with school priorities, but when possible, S-M-A-A-H-R-T goals also align with other goals that teachers are working toward. Skillful team leaders (STLs) are cognizant of the many, many goals teachers are responsible for achieving. They work with their colleagues to find connections between team goals and others, particularly individual professional practice goals.

How to align with priorities and individual goals:

Your team goal will not line up with every goal your colleagues are responsible for achieving, but it helps if you can find common themes between a few so people don't feel pulled in different directions. Begin by learning what goals teachers are already responsible for achieving outside of your team meetings. Aim to find organic connections. (If all teams are aligned to one of several school priorities, it should not be too hard.) If it makes sense to your colleagues, make the team goal and individual professional practice goal the same. This ensures that there will be little competing for teachers' time. If teachers prefer to individualize their professional practice goal, then the team goal can specify specific student-learning outcomes, and each person can set their own goals for learning in order to reach those outcomes.

Examples of alignment:

Align with a priority.

All teams in an elementary school have prioritized improving students' executive functioning.

- A kindergarten team sets a goal to improve students' self-regulation.

- The Grades 3–5 English language arts team sets a goal to improve student organization in writing.

- A special education team analyzes data that indicate a subgroup of students with learning differences needs to improve working memory. They make this their team goal.

- A fifth-grade team decides to better prepare their students for middle school. They aim to build up students' abilities to independently organize their materials, manage their homework responsibilities, and set personal goals.

Although each team in the school is working on what they see as relevant and important, all are helping to advance the school's larger priority of executive functioning.

Align aim/goals.

Jamaal is a member of multiple teams. All the goals that he is responsible for are focused on helping students who are negatively impacted by trauma.

School leadership team aim: To identify students for whom trauma is negatively impacting their literacy, attendance, and social-emotional functioning, such as self-regulation. The school will improve literacy by X% and decrease truancy rates by Y% by providing these students with services they need for social-emotional wellness and academic success.

Interdisciplinary grade-level team aim: To increase a sense of belonging at school among students negatively affected by trauma by establishing predictable routines across classes and prioritizing relationship building.

Content grade-level team aim: To advance the reading skills of students who have been negatively affected by trauma. X% of students are reading below grade level. The team sets measurable goals to reduce the number of students receiving Tier 3 instruction, thereby increasing the number of students receiving Tier 2 instruction. To reach this goal, the team sets individual student fluency goals to reach by midyear and end of year.

Individual professional practice goal: Jamaal will study Don Meichenbaum's (n.d.) research on reading as a resilience factor for children who have experienced trauma, and implement strategies.

STL recommendations:

Deviate. Sometimes a team will discover a need not yet identified as a priority by school leaders, and want to work on a goal that addresses that. Should your team desire to pursue a goal unrelated to the other things teachers in the school are working toward, confirm that data support the decision. Know that this focus will redirect resources (most notably teachers' time) away from the school priority that everyone is responsible for advancing. Proceed, but also communicate why you are choosing this path.

Find the right words:

- *In what ways would reaching our team goal advance a school priority?*

- *Are we comfortable making our team goal and our individual professional practice goals the same? If not, can people align their individual professional practice goals to our team goal so that no one feels that these meetings pull them away from their "real" work?*

6.11 (Heartfelt) Connect to what matters.

I observed a team meeting in which a teacher said, "I really hope we get our kids to this goal." The team leader quickly responded, "We can't just *hope* to get kids there. We *will* get them there. These kids are depending on us."

This conversation happened to be about students who were multiple grade levels behind, and the urgency to get them back on track was palpable. However, even if this were not the case, there is no doubt that this team, and others who set heartfelt goals like them, would attain their goals. Heartfelt goals are worthwhile. People feel strongly about them and intend to accomplish them. Intentions connote commitment. They encompass at least some form of partial planning, and this makes them more powerful than a goal that is simply wished for. This isn't just semantics. Bagozzi et al. (2003) found from their research that intent to act is "directly connected to a multitude of activities and outcomes related to the choice of means for action implementation, impediments to action, and temptations to perform other actions or consider other goals"; see also Bagozzi (1992). In other words, once you set an intention, you're more likely to implement it no matter what comes your way. (Now you see why I named this book *Intentional Moves*.) Skillful team leaders (STLs) and their teams choose heartfelt goals, those that matter to their students and to them.

How to connect to what matters:

Identify what goal, when achieved, would make a notable difference to students and to you and your colleagues' practice. Once you get to the stage where you are ready to implement an action plan, check in with your colleagues on their desire and intent to implement the plan. Ask any of the survey questions from Figure 24 intermittently throughout your course of collaboration to get a sense of how heartfelt the goal is and how comfortable people are with the decisions made about the goal.

STL recommendation:

Write goals from a diversity, equity, and inclusion (DEI) lens. STL Osamagbe (Osa) Osagie recommends that leaders notice the impact that mindset, cultural experiences, norms, bias, and other preconceived notions have on people's commitment to achieving a goal. For example, if teachers believe external factors will prevent them from reaching a student goal, then they are less likely to reach their goal unless they grow their mindset.

Find the right words:

- *What student-learning problems keep us up at night?*

- *What goal would make a real difference to our students, families, and us?*

- *What focus area might not be a struggle for all children, but will be significant for some?*

- *If we were to fast-forward several months, what would we be most proud to have accomplished for students?*

- *Let's choose a goal that matters to students and to us.*

Alternative use:

You'll want to check that your team has a heartfelt connection to all that you do in your team, not just to goals. You can use the questions in Figure 24 to check that people are committed to team norms, an inquiry question, any implementation plan you design, or any decision you make.

FIGURE 24   How Committed Is Your Team to Achieving Their Goal?

Research shows that desire, intent, perceptions of worthiness, perceptions of control, and feelings about decision making affect people's success rate in reaching a goal. Together these things indicate a level of commitment. The following choice of prompts and questions can help you determine if someone's "heart is in it."

COMMITMENT TO A GOAL	
Worthiness	• I feel our goal is worthwhile to explore as a team. (Scale: 1 [*strongly disagree*], 2 [*disagree*], 3 [*neither agree nor disagree*], 4 [*agree*], 5 [*strongly agree*])
	• If given the choice to pursue something different, what would you choose? Explain.
Desirability	• How strongly do you wish to achieve this goal? (Scale: 1 [*no wish at all*], 2 [*slight wish*], 3 [*moderate wish*], 4 [*strong wish*], 5 [*very strong wish*])
	• If we didn't reach this goal, how would you feel? Explain.
Intent	• I intend to reach this goal. (Scale: 1 [*no chance at all*], 2 [*highly unlikely*], 3 [*neither unlikely nor likely*], 4 [*likely*], 5 [*highly likely*])
	• If you rated 4 or above, what drives your intent to reach this goal?
COMMITMENT TO IMPLEMENTATION OF A GOAL	
Perceived control	• How much control do you have over performing the action steps needed by [*specify a time frame*]? (Scale: 1 [*no control*], 2 [*moderate control*], 3 [*significant control*])
	• Are these action steps doable? Is anything outside of your locus of control? If so, explain why.
Desirability	• My overall wish to implement action steps can be summarized as follows: 1 (*no wish at all*), 2 (*slight wish*), 3 (*moderate wish*), 4 (*strong wish*), 5 (*very strong wish*).
	• Do you want to take these action steps? If not, why not?
Intent	• I intend to perform the action steps by [*specify time frame*]. (Scale: 1 [*no chance at all*], 2 [*highly unlikely*], 3 [*neither unlikely nor likely*], 4 [*likely*], 5 [*highly likely*].
	• Is it your intention to implement these action steps regardless of what comes your way?
COMFORT AND CONFIDENCE WITH GROUP DECISION MAKING	
Comfort	• I feel comfortable with the decision-making process we used to set this goal/arrive at this plan. (Scale: 1 [*strongly disagree*], 2 [*disagree*], 3 [*neither agree nor disagree*], 4 [*agree*], 5 [*strongly agree*])
	• In what ways did our decision-making process work for you? In what ways should we improve the process?
Confidence	• I feel confident with the decisions made by our team to set this goal/arrive at this plan. (Scale: 1 [*strongly disagree*], 2 [*disagree*], 3 [*neither agree nor disagree*], 4 [*agree*], 5 [*strongly agree*])
	• Are you confident that we are making the best decision given the information we have at this time? Explain.

Source: The language of the questions is influenced by recommendations made by Richard P. Bagozzi et al., "How Effortful Decisions Get Enacted: The Motivating Role of Decision Processes, Desires, and Anticipated Emotions," in *Journal of Behavioral Decision Making*, no. 16 (2003): 273–295.

Related readings:

Move 6.6, "Formulate an inquiry question." Start with a meaningful inquiry question and examine data to learn more, and these will likely lead you to a heartfelt goal.

Moves 8.15–8.18, "Make clear impactful decisions." When making any group decision, the questions in Figure 24 can help determine how comfortable people are with the decision-making process and how confident they are in the agreed-upon decision. Their comfort and confidence affects how likely they are to implement the decision with fidelity.

6.12 (Results-driven) Distinguish learning outcomes from pathways.

Realtor Tim sets a goal for 50 people to attend an open house in the first weekend. He advertises the open house, sends invitations to potential buyers he knows, has homeowners spruce up the curb appeal, and puts a sign on the front lawn. Sixty people show up. Tim has exceeded his goal. No one makes an offer on the house. Is the realtor successful?

Reaching the open house quota might be worthwhile, as it could increase the likelihood of a serious buyer, but it's not the end goal. Tim has to sell the house. The sale is the desired outcome; the open house goal is a strategy or pathway to get there.

It's not uncommon for teacher teams to conflate strategy or pathway goals with desired learning outcomes. "Open house" goals, as I call them, describe what teachers will implement or what activities students will do, rather than name the student-learning outcomes that they expect to see as a result of what they do.

Imagine three different teams set three different writing goals:

> **Teacher team A goal:** Students will write three claim–evidence–reasoning (CER) paragraphs by the end of the month.

> **Teacher team B goal:** All teachers will model how to write a CER paragraph.

> **Teacher team C goal:** Students will generate and interpret data as evidence to support a claim. They will achieve this by engaging in more writing practice (three practice CER paragraphs a month) and explicit instruction, in which teachers model writing for students.

Goal C defines the desired student-learning outcome, while goals A and B are pathways to reach that outcome. Let me be clear: Open house goals are worthwhile. They define strategies and pave a path to desired outcomes. But, as stand-alone goals, they are insufficient in three ways:

1. *They create a false sense of accomplishment.* For instance, Tim the realtor could think hitting his open house quota means a sale is in the bag when it isn't. Similarly, teacher teams A and B might assume that they are successful because of the efforts they and their students put in, without actually seeing improved writing results.

2. *Achieving them doesn't guarantee the ultimate outcome you want.* For instance, the realtor can hit the open house quota and still not sell the house. Similarly, teacher team A can model writing a CER paragraph, and teacher team B can get students to write more, but neither might result in students being able to generate and interpret data as evidence to support a claim.

3. *They limit your team approach.* When you name a pathway or strategy as a goal, without naming the desired student-learning outcome, you limit your team to one approach. On the contrary, name the outcome you intend to get, and you can use multiple strategies to get there. For example, Tim will sell the house in three weeks by posting the listing online, staging the home, hosting buyers' realtors at the home, having the home featured in the local paper, and getting 50 people to the first weekend open house.

Skillful team leaders (STLs) and their teams might set strategy or pathway goals, but not without also naming the student-learning outcomes they are aiming to reach.

How to distinguish learning outcomes from pathways:

Option 1: Name the impact you want to have on three things: student learning, teacher practice, and (if it makes sense) school culture and climate. One concrete way to lead results-driven goal setting is to draw a horizontal line on chart paper. Above the line, name the student-learning outcome you desire to reach. Then, below the line, list all of the strategy or pathway goals needed to reach the above-the-line goal.

In action:

Jairo: We've noticed that on this assessment, most students didn't recognize the bias in these different authors' accounts of the same historical event. Let's explore the problem.

Teacher 1: I think it goes beyond this assessment. They only read or watch what they want, and consequently they aren't getting exposed to diverse texts written from various points of view.

Teacher 2: Even I notice that my social media feed is biased and, if I'm not actively seeking alternate sources, I get a one-sided view of things.

Teacher 1:   That's one of the problems. Most kids won't actively seek out other sources as you would.

Teacher 3:   I think they don't realize that bias exists in what they read and view or that it's a big deal.

Jairo: So, if we were to write this as an initial goal, what student-learning result would we expect to see?

[Teachers discuss and decide: "Students would recognize bias in texts and how bias affects the reader/viewer." Jairo writes this above the line on chart paper as the basis for their goal.]

Teacher 2:   I think our goal should be to create a multimedia mini-unit about where bias is found and its impact on students.

Jairo: That is a good strategy goal. So I will list it below the line, along with a few others I heard from our conversation.

[Jairo writes below the line: "Increase exposure to texts written from various points of view. Heighten our own awareness of bias in the media we access and how we recognize it."]

Option 2: Alternatively, if your team has named a strategy or pathway goal, shift your colleagues to name the student-learning outcome they want to result from implementing the strategy. Here's a process to do so:

1.   Write a strategy/pathway goal in a text box on chart paper/whiteboard/ SMART board.

2.   Ask, "Why is this goal important?" and write responses on lines radiating from the box.

3.   On sticky notes, write down responses to the following question: "If this is done well, then what outcomes should result?" (Limit one response per note.)

4.   Sort the sticky note outcome responses into two groups: (1) teaching/ teacher-learning outcomes and (2) student-learning outcomes.

5.   Tease out more student-learning outcomes by going through each teaching/ teacher-learning outcome and asking, "By doing this, what should result for students and their learning?"

6.   Group the sticky notes and give the outcomes an overarching name.

7.   Prioritize and include the most desired student-learning outcome(s) in the second iteration of your goal.

Go to www.elisamacdonald.com for additional examples.

STL recommendations:

Learn from the outcome you get. I place a lot of emphasis in this book on measuring success by reaching your student-learning goals. But one day I was watching CNN when a friend of Dr. Frank Gabrin, the first emergency room doctor who died of coronavirus in 2020, shared words of wisdom: "It's not (always) about the outcome. You don't get to save every patient. But it's about what you do with the outcome (you get)" (Cuomo Prime Time, 2020). Your team might not reach the goal you set for student learning, but what can you and your team learn from the outcome you get so that you can do better next time?

Find the right words:

- *What learning outcomes do data show students need? What professional practice goals do we need to set for ourselves so that we can produce those student-learning outcomes?*

- *What influence do we expect to have on student learning? On teacher learning and practice? On climate and culture?*

- *We've named a strategy as our goal. What are our students going to be able to understand, know, and do as a result of this strategy?*

- *Our current goal is to create/implement [a curriculum unit, a lesson plan, a policy, a strategy]. What do we ultimately want for students' learning?*

Related reading:

Move 1.2, "Allocate time to examine learning outcomes." Make time in your meeting to talk about the impact of the practices and policies you implement.

Move 5.15, "Pivot from teaching to learning." When facilitating talk becomes too heavily focused on what teachers do, shift focus to what students are learning.

6.13 (Time-bound) Establish a time frame according to student need.

If you desire a job that requires a certification that you don't yet have, you likely won't give yourself 10 years to get certified. Timelines give us an end point by which we must achieve something, but too often schools allow schedules and calendars to dictate the "by when" instead of the urgency of the goal. Realistically, you must consider calendars and availability of resources in order to set your timeline, but skillful team leaders (STLs) to first establish a time frame according to student need.

How to establish a time frame according to student need:

Start with an ideal date by which students need to achieve a goal. Anticipate roadblocks that could slow down your timeline. Determine which can be worked around and which are immovable. Then, set your end date and include progress checkpoints.

In action:

A third-grade team is planning a goal for intervention.

Henry: We're near the end of the year, and there are a group of students that we are just now identifying as needing reading support. We need to accelerate our goal for them so they are more prepared for the reading demands of fourth grade.

Teacher: We only have so many in-school days between now and then.

Henry: Right, but they needed this goal "yesterday." So let's not limit ourselves by the calendar. Of course, we can't deliver intervention on any religious holidays, but what if we rethink spring break, which is still two months away? Let's consider in-person or remote learning options so we can keep students on track toward their goal. We'll need to problem solve for funding sources and personnel and talk with school leaders about how to make it happen, but let's at least try to make the case for why this timeline is important.

STL recommendation:

Think beyond the school year. We have a tendency to set the parameters of a goal between the start and end of a school year. Sure, it makes sense to set some goals within this time frame, as students are only in a particular grade level for a given period, but some goals take longer than 10 months to reach. Starting a new goal every fall, particularly when the first goal wasn't achieved, can leave people feeling disheartened. You have the option to set ambitious goals beyond the confines of one school year. Set checkpoints to monitor progress, as you would with a one-year goal, but be comfortable with the decision that the end result might not be reached for two to three years.

Find the right words:

- *By when do students need to achieve this goal?*

- *How much time do we need to teach and assess this goal? Might it be longer than one school year?*

- *What might get in the way of our timeline, and how can we stay the course?*

- *What timeline checkpoints should we schedule to monitor progress?*

FIGURE 25   STL Tool for Setting S-M-A-A-H-R-T Goals

You have a goal. Is it S-M-A-A-H-R-T? Or seemingly so? Check it against the following criteria:

Specific	Our goal . . .
	• is targeted. It specifies which group of students will make what gains, by when, and by how much.
Measurable	Our goal . . .
	• is informed by data. Numbers and percentages are not baseless or arbitrary.
	• measures learning outcomes.
	• relies on formative assessments to guide our decisions.
	• provides indicators of learning beyond performance on a single assessment.
Attainable	Our goal . . .
	• is within reach, but also the stretch students and teachers need.
	• can be accomplished without burning people out.
	• is not dumbed down because of limited resources or unhealthy aspects of our school culture. We plan to creatively get what we need to attain the goal.
Aligned	Our goal . . .
	• aims to advance school priorities.
	• connects to our everyday "real" work with students.
	• does not compete with other goals.
Heartfelt	Our goal . . .
	• matters to us and would make a difference to students/families. We intend and are committed to achieving our goal.
Results-driven	Our goal . . .
	• articulates student-learning results we expect to see. If we fall short on student outcomes, important educator resources and learning will still result.
	• (if academic) targets a high-leverage standard or skill and attempts to dismantle inequities.
	• will ultimately have a positive influence on our district-school-department climate and culture. We know that these results can take time to show up.
Time-bound	Our goal . . .
	• is designed to be accomplished within a time frame set first and foremost around student need, not calendar logistics or restrictions. We are intentional about what we desire to accomplish at different checkpoints (by the end of 6 weeks, by the end of 12 weeks, etc.), and we know we can set goals that extend beyond one school year.

Primary Intention

Promote Intentional Data Use:
Assessment and Analysis

7

//

One afternoon I observed a team examine a teacher's student work together for the first time. The team leader used an abridged protocol and facilitated each step as written. All team members participated and showed gratitude to the teacher who presented her data. When the protocol was over, the team leader debriefed the process. Teachers were candid.

"I wasn't quite sure which assessment or student work to pull for this team meeting. So I just grabbed what I hadn't yet returned to kids," the presenting teacher said. "And, to be honest, this conversation didn't tell me anything I didn't already know."

The presenting teacher did not seem annoyed or frustrated when she said this. She even offered to bring in student work again if the team leader wanted her to (an indication that this team had relational trust). But she did not walk away from the process with any new understanding or action steps that she hadn't already thought to do. The team functioned well, but looking at student work samples together had no impact on the thinking or practice of the presenting teacher or anyone else.

Although poor facilitation of a protocol can be to blame, problems that surface during collaborative data analysis often take root even before the team comes together—during preparation. Skillful team leaders (STLs) and their teams are intentional about which assessments they choose to give students and analyze, knowing that a poorly written assessment or the wrong view of data can bring talk to a halt. They thoughtfully prepare data and engage colleagues in an evidence-based process of analysis that results in targeted action plans.

Contents:

Select (or design) a meaningful assessment.

7.1 Specify the reason for assessing.

7.2 Choose an assessment based on the view of data you need.

7.3 Examine (or design) assessment tasks/questions.

7.4 Optimize assessment conditions for students.

Prepare data to examine.

7.5 Select student work samples (student data) to examine.

7.6 Organize student data.

7.7 Make data accessible.

7.8 Plan teacher work to examine together.

Facilitate data analysis.

7.9 Maintain a healthy data culture.

7.10 Prompt for evidence-based observations.

7.11 Prompt for evidence-based reasoning.

7.12 Analyze student errors.

7.13 Target and plan for student success.

Tools and templates:

Figure 26: Three Lenses to View Data

Related readings:

Moves 4.5–4.7, "Structure tasks and talk." Learn protocols for analyzing data collectively.

SELECT (OR DESIGN) A MEANINGFUL ASSESSMENT

Mark any of the following comments that resemble something you have heard at one point during team analysis of data:

☐ *I see students got the wrong answer, but I don't know why since we don't have the test question.*

☐ *I taught kids how to X, but this question requires them to Y. I haven't taught Y yet.*

☐ *This question is asking so much of kids. I can't decipher where this student is having trouble.*

☐ *There's only one question on the test that asks that, so I don't think we have enough to go on.*

☐ *It's unclear if the students struggled with the concept or the wording of this question.*

☐ *I'm not sure if the student left the last set of questions blank because they didn't know the answers or because they just lost stamina since the assessment was so long.*

☐ *I don't know if students had enough time to answer the question.*

Each time someone makes one of these comments, data talk comes to a standstill. But the problem isn't with the people making the comments; it's most often with the assessment. Before analyzing data, skillful team leaders (STLs) and their teams examine the assessment, keeping in mind that they might need to create something new.

Disclaimer: The moves in this section may feel more like "what good teachers do" rather than "what skillful team leaders do." I include them because collaborative data analysis hinges on well-designed assessments. You'll find essential understandings and practical advice; however, if assessment is a real area of need for teachers on your team, you should further your learning beyond this section by turning to the extensive books and web resources referenced throughout.

STL moves:

7.1 Specify the reason for assessing.

7.2 Choose an assessment based on the view of data you need.

7.3 Examine (or design) assessment tasks/questions.

7.4 Optimize assessment conditions for students.

Tools and templates:

Figure 26: Three Lenses to View Data

What these moves promote:

Focus. People determine which assessments are best suited for a data dialogue about the student-centered challenge.

Critical thinking. People learn to recognize the limitations of an assessment, which can drive them to seek or create an alternate assessment.

Investment. Creating assessments generates an eagerness to examine data together.

Student understanding. People closely analyze questions and tasks to better understand the cognitive demand on students and potential student errors during analysis.

Evidence-based discourse. A team must establish success criteria, which lays the foundation for data talk grounded in evidence.

When to use these moves:

Throughout the course of inquiry. For example:

- *Assess & Analyze* STL phase of collaborative inquiry. Choose assessments to find student-centered challenges worth investigating.

- *Target & Plan* STL phase of collaborative inquiry. Get small with targeted assessments to learn more about a student-centered challenge.

- *Act & Evaluate* STL phase of collaborative inquiry. Progress-monitor with assessments that give you data in real time as you try out new strategies.

7.1 Specify the reason for assessing.

My friend's daughter was recently diagnosed with diabetes, and until now I had no idea of the different types of testing available and the reason for each test. A doctor seeking to catch diabetes early will *screen* a person to see if they meet specific high-risk criteria with a glucose test. If ready to *diagnose* type 1 or gestational diabetes, the doctor will ask an individual for symptoms and give the person a random blood sugar test or a fasting blood sugar test and possibly a urine test. If the doctor is looking to *predict* the likelihood of a woman who has gestational diabetes getting diabetes later in life, they will test for the presence of specific metabolites. If *diagnosing* type 2 diabetes, the doctor will give an individual a hemoglobin A1c test, which measures blood sugar over the past three months. If the test returns positive, the doctor will *prescribe* insulin and suggest lifestyle changes. To *monitor* a patient's progress, the doctor will periodically give the person the hemoglobin A1c test and take blood and urine samples. If a patient participates in an intervention such as an exercise study, the doctor will *evaluate* the effect of the program on the patient's diabetes and health (University of Toronto, 2016). Bottom line: Doctors give particular tests based on what they seek to learn from data that result.

Although the work of teacher teams is not as technical and complex as working with diabetic patients, skillful team leaders (STLs), when selecting assessments, decide the reason for turning to data, then choose an assessment (or design one) that serves this purpose.

How to specify the reason for assessing:

Discuss with your team what you hope to learn from assessing students. What don't you yet know that data can help illuminate? Some distinct purposes for collecting and analyzing data are listed as follows:

- Describe what the student-centered challenge/concern is, who it affects, and how often it occurs over time. (Describe)

- Determine which students are at various levels of risk. (Screen)

- Predict outcomes based on historical data. (Predict)

- Determine probable causes for a challenge/concern. (Diagnose)

- Name solutions/interventions for consideration. (Prescribe)

- Monitor intervention treatment. (Progress-monitor)

- Determine the effectiveness of a completed intervention. (Evaluate)

In action:

(To describe) Abdi's team selects classroom observation records to describe a student's challenging behaviors and when they happen.

(To screen) Barbara's kindergarten team uses the state guidelines to select an appropriate, research-based screening assessment so that they can identify students at risk for dyslexia.

(To predict) Christine's team selects a student's recent reading assessments to predict how the student will perform in a Tier 1 setting without classroom pullout support.

(To diagnose) A child's parents and teachers fill out Vanderbilt surveys* so that the neuropsychologist can gather data to diagnose the child with attention deficit hyperactivity disorder (ADHD) or rule it out.

(To prescribe) Dwayne's team reviews a student's quarterly grades to pre-scribe summer skill building, if needed.

---

*American Academy of Pediatrics & National Initiative for Children's Health Quality. (2022). *NICHQ Vanderbilt assessment scales: Used for diagnosing ADHD.* https://www.nichq.org/sites/default/files/resource-file/NICHQ-Vanderbilt-Assessment-Scales.pdf

(To progress-monitor) Hao's team explicitly teaches Vietnamese students how to use English linking verbs, since these verbs are not used in their native language. Teachers assess students' progress every week for four weeks, with a cloze passage in which they have students fill in the verb or leave it blank (e.g., "He ____ tall").

(To evaluate) Candace's inclusion team chooses a post-assessment to evaluate a six-week program intended to improve performance on working memory challenges for students receiving an intervention.

Find the right words:

- *What are we specifically curious about that an assessment could shed light on?*

- *What do we want to do/learn from the assessment we administer?*

- *What is our reason for assessing students at this time? To describe a problem? Screen students for risk? Predict results? Diagnose existing challenges? Prescribe solutions? Monitor student progress? Evaluate the effectiveness of something we have implemented?*

7.2 Choose an assessment based on the view of data you need.

You know to choose assessments based on *when* you need to see data. If you decide to monitor progress of an intervention, then you opt to give regular formative assessments. If you intend to evaluate the effectiveness of an intervention when it's complete, then you administer and analyze a summative assessment. But there's another consideration skillful team leaders (STLs) make when selecting an assessment to analyze—*what* data you need to be able to see. Not all assessments are designed to provide you with the view of data that you need.

For example, a standardized test designed by someone other than you, whether formative or summative, might give you student scores but might not provide test questions. If you intend to engage in error analysis with this assessment, you won't learn too much. Much like photographers decide on the shot they want, then choose a lens that will give them that shot, STLs determine the view of data they need, then choose (or design) assessments that deliver this view.

How to choose an assessment based on the view of data you need:

Sticking with the photographer analogy, we can view assessment data through three different lenses: a wide lens, a zoom lens, or a super-zoom lens (see Figure 26). Decide what view you need, then select an assessment that will provide you with this view. If you discover that the assessment you have does not present data in a way that you need, you may need to organize data (Move 7.6) or choose an additional assessment.

FIGURE 26 Three Lenses to View Data

	WIDE LENS	ZOOM LENS	SUPER-ZOOM LENS
Description	A wide-lens view of data is most helpful when you are interested in contextualizing a problem. When you want to find out how epic a learning problem is across the district, observe trends in one school over time, or discover how your country, state, district, or school compares to others, then select an assessment that gives you a wide-lens view of data. **Example:** How have our reading proficiency scores as a nation improved over the past five years? Let's turn to the National Assessment of Educational Progress (NAEP) reading assessment.	A zoom lens permits you to drill down into data to examine specific standards and skills and how particular subgroups of students performed on the assessment. When you want to learn which of the many problems makes the most sense to focus on and prioritize, then view assessment data through a zoom lens. This lens will help you identify which test items proved challenging and what level of proficiency students are at. And, depending on how the assessment is written, teams can sometimes see students' wrong answer selections. A zoom lens of data helps you decide where to invest your time and resources. It provides a more detailed view of student learning than a wide lens, but not as granular a view as a super-zoom lens. **Example:** Which English language arts standard did our students receiving a special education struggle with most? Let's examine the state test.	A super-zoom lens lets you view specific questions, prompts, and tasks and also see individual student responses and errors. A super-zoom lens is most useful when a team needs to diagnose, understand, or problem solve for specific students. This view promotes insight into where understanding breaks down and why. It assists teachers in targeted goal setting. **Example:** What are the most common misconceptions students still hold about the sun, earth, and moon that we need to reteach? And which students should we put in the reteach group? Let's give students free-response questions and analyze their responses.
Assessment data most often viewed through this lens	Most often summative. **Examples:** College entrance exam data, Advanced Placement data, state testing data, graduation and dropout rate data, teacher attrition data, and district benchmark data.	Most often summative but can be formative. **Examples:** State test data, district benchmark data, grade-level placement test data, course remediation data, counseling referral data, student or family or teacher survey or interview data, and teacher-created common benchmark assessment data.	Most often formative but can be summative. **Examples:** Unit test, quiz, and exit slip data; student notebook, classwork, and homework data; student or family survey or interview data; and student portfolio data.
Teams who typically turn to this lens	National, state, district, and school leadership teams.	School instructional leadership, department, and grade-level teams.	Teacher teams.

In action:

Administrator:	Let's examine the district-designed third-quarter assessment. It is already created and aligns to the standards. It's a simple multiple-choice test, so it won't take too long to administer, and the district organizes the data for us, so all we need to do is analyze it.
Linda:	It's a good assessment for evaluating students' proficiency in the standards; however, we want to learn what misconceptions remain for specific students so that we can group students and reteach what's needed in the last quarter. The district assessment tells us the standard assessed for each question. However, it does not let us view the actual question or student thinking. It only lets us see if a student got the question right, missed it, or skipped it. I think the district assessment is too limited a view of data for our needs. We might learn more from giving students our own open-response questions where they are required to explain their thinking.

Additional decision points when choosing an assessment to give and analyze:

Should we give common assessments?

Common assessment—All teachers give the same tasks/questions to their students.

Benefits:

- All teachers are familiar with the assessment, reducing time needed to review tasks/questions during collaborative analysis.

- Assessment data reveal patterns and trends across classrooms.

- It can foster conversation about best practices when one teacher's students performed better than another teacher's students on a task.

- All teachers have invested interest in analyzing student work because it is the work of the students they teach.

Challenges:

- Teachers who teach different content areas (math, English, world languages, etc.) cannot make common assessments, because of the different subject matter, unless assessments measure social-emotional skills or habits of mind.

- Some teachers cannot agree on what should be asked on an assessment.

STL recommendation:

- Write common assessments before teaching content. Engage in discussion at that time about student-learning expectations and learning indicators.

Do we need to give a pre-assessment?

Pre-assessment—An assessment administered before implementation of new practices and/or academic intervention.

Formative assessment—An assessment administered throughout implementation of a new teaching practice or student intervention.

Post-assessment—An assessment administered when intervention is complete.

Benefit:

- Administering pre- and post-assessments can give your team a window into student progress after you intervene.

Challenges:

- When pre- and post-assessments are the same, it is difficult to know if improvement is attributed to learning or to students' familiarity with the assessment tasks/questions.

- When pre- and post-assessments are different, it is difficult to make the tasks/questions comparable.

- Pre-assessments can be a waste of time when used to gather data that reveal information you already know. (Case in point: You can ask chemistry students to explain Le Chatelier's principle before you teach it, but you probably won't be surprised by the number of "I don't know" responses you get.)

- Students, particularly those who have learning differences, can get frustrated or discouraged taking a pre-assessment on content that has not yet been taught.

STL recommendation:

- Like a beauty makeover, giving both pre- and post-assessments can reveal improvement. However, if you have clear standards and expectations to measure progress against, then you likely only need post-assessments.

Should we ask a few tasks/questions on the assessment instead of many?

This is sort of like the Goldilocks dilemma—too short, too long, just right.

Benefits:

- An assessment with only a few tasks/questions requires less time to collaboratively analyze than a lengthy one.

(Continued)

(Continued)

- Depending on how time-consuming the task is, fewer tasks/questions could potentially take less time to complete than a lengthier assessment.

- Although many factors contribute to stamina, an assessment with a few questions tends to hold students' attention longer than a lengthy one.

- Students with learning differences, attention challenges, or emotional challenges might be less anxious about taking an assessment that is short in length than one with many tasks/questions (see Move 7.4).

- What you don't learn from a few questions on an assessment you can get from administering different, follow-up tasks/questions.

Challenges:

- Ask too few questions and you might not get reliable data.

- Even if you only ask a few tasks/questions, if they are poorly written, are too complex, or demand too much of students, you may see students perform poorly.

STL recommendations:

- Keep the length of the assessment short by limiting the concepts or skills you want to assess. Decide if one question is sufficient to determine if a student has mastered the target. Bailey and Jakicic (2011) recommend assessing one learning target with three questions to increase the likelihood that students getting the question or task right or wrong is not a fluke.

- Cut back on what you analyze together. You can opt to give a lengthy assessment to students, but you don't need to examine every response to every task/question in order to take away learning. Reduce the number of student work tasks/questions you will comb through to a manageable amount so that people are not overwhelmed and there is enough time in a meeting to discuss observations and draw conclusions. Decide what to look at and what to set aside based on your inquiry question or team goal.

Should we give multiple assessments?

Multiple assessments—Two or more different types of assessment that measure the same content (e.g., students' proficiency in understanding vocabulary words is assessed through a fill-in-the-blank definition quiz, vocabulary slides homework, and a reading comprehension passage).

Benefits:

- Findings become clear when analysis of multiple assessments reveals the same results.

- A single assessment may not be sufficient to give you the view of data you need.

- Students have more opportunities to show what they know when multiple assessments are in different formats (e.g., multiple choice, student interview, and homework notebook entry).

Challenges:

- Teacher teams might struggle to find or create one assessment, let alone three.

- Analyzing multiple assessments together is time-consuming.

STL recommendation:

- Don't view assessment as "one and done." There is no such thing as a perfect assessment. Questions might not ask what you want to find out, and you may not know the questions you have until you see what students can do. Begin with one assessment. Analyze it. Surface teacher questions that can't be answered with the data you have. Pursue additional assessments to further your learning. It could be as simple as asking a follow-up question on an exit ticket. Caution: Don't overload students with tests just to get the complete data view you need, either.

Find the right words:

- *What assessments will give us the view of data we need? Can we use an existing assessment, or do we need to write one?*

- *We want to put our student-learning concerns in context. Let's look at assessment data through a wide lens to learn how we are doing as compared over time or to other schools.*

- *We want to prioritize problems on which to focus. Let's look at assessment data through a zoom lens to learn where there is the greatest area of need or what we should investigate further.*

- *We want to target a specific challenge for a specific group of students. Let's look at assessment data through a super-zoom lens to identify where understanding is breaking down for specific students and learn why, so that we can aim our inquiry work toward addressing this.*

Related readings:

Move 6.8, "(Measurable) Measure what matters." When writing a team goal, be intentional about the measures you select to indicate success.

Move 10.4, "Monitor student progress." Regularly track how students are doing given the changes you are implementing through progress-monitoring tools.

7.3 Examine (or design) assessment tasks/questions.

"The answer is . . ." These are the infamous words uttered by the late game show host, Alex Trebek, on *Jeopardy*. Most will tell you the key to what made the quiz show exciting wasn't the answer (in the form of a question) that contestants had to come up with; it was the clues themselves. According to Billy Wisse, a head writer on the show, tremendous thought goes into crafting these—for example: writers ensure there's only one possible answer to a clue; name categories for a set of clues in a way that guides the contestants; intentionally sequence questions; cleverly word clues; and vary the level of difficulty so that Final Jeopardy is the hardest (Wenz, 2018).

Of course, writing a student assessment has a different purpose than making a quiz show; however, skillful team leaders (STLs) and their teams are just as intentional in their design of tasks and questions. There's so much that goes into writing assessment tasks and questions. I can't include everything in this small section, but I do highlight key considerations that STLs make. (Note: If the assessment is already designed by someone else, STLs and their teams examine the tasks/questions *before* collectively examining student responses.)

How to examine (or design) assessment tasks/questions:

Consider the following:

- *Test what you taught.* What's wrong with the following scenario?

   Students are taught how to determine the theme of fantasy text and analyze its development over the course of the text. When it comes time to assess their ability to independently meet this standard (see corestandards.org/ELA-Literacy/RL/7), the teacher requires students to write a fantasy story with a specific theme.

Did you catch it? The teacher taught students *how to read* for theme in a fantasy text, not *how to write* one—a different set of skills. Writing a fantasy story isn't going to tell the teacher if students can determine and analyze the development of theme in a given text. Unfortunately, it's more common than not for students to be evaluated on something they weren't explicitly taught how to do. Not only is this unfair to them, but it also produces data that are not useful to teachers. When examining data for the purpose of evaluating learning (not a diagnostic assessment), check that the task or question is something students were taught to do. If it isn't, adjust the task or question.

- *Measure one thing.* On a scale of 1 (*not at all*) to 5 (*extremely*), how satisfied are you with the quantity and challenge of homework in this class? Not only would a student be confused about answering this question, but a teacher would not know what to make of a student's response. This is because it is a double-barreled question, one that asks someone to select only one response to a question that asks two different things. Joe Feldman (2018), in his book *Grading for Equity*, recommends that teachers "disentangle" questions so that they only measure one thing. Break apart compound questions that force students to pick one response.

- *Choose a format that gives you what you need.* You get what you give. Give a question that asks for a one-word answer, and you'll get a one-word answer. The task/question format you choose dictates how much or how little students will show what they know. Common formats include multiple choice, true/false, matching, fill-in-the-blank, short answer, sequencing, extended free response, problem solving, and audio or video prompts. When creating assessment questions, fast-forward to how you plan to analyze the data. If you're looking to get into the minds of students, extended free response might be more valuable than true/false. But, if you're looking to do a quick sort to find out which students know what facts, true/false might be just the format to use.

- *Don't compromise quality for creativity.* Both Universal Design for Learning (UDL) and differentiated instruction (DI) recommend that teachers vary product assessments and give students choice when possible. Creative assessments are great for students, but not if they limit students from demonstrating all that they know and can do. For example, a student who chooses to write a poem about their understanding of the Greek gods might be constricted in showcasing all they know by the need to rhyme with *Poseidon*.

- *Evaluate the demand of the task/question.* Examine the rigor each task/question demands of students. Norman Webb (1997) created a framework called Depth of Knowledge (DOK), which categorizes tasks into four levels. Each level requires greater learning and thinking (cognitive demand) than the one before it. STLs look at the cognitive demand of tasks/questions on assessments. Collaborative data analysis is more robust when teams analyze tasks/questions that demand the use of concepts, skills, and basic reasoning (DOK Level 2 questions), strategic thinking from students (DOK Level 3 questions), or extended learning (DOK Level 4 questions) than analyzing tasks/questions that demand simple recall (DOK Level 1). You can still ask DOK Level 1–type questions on an assessment, but your team might not gain too much from analyzing the responses together.

- *Plan to experience the student experience.* Don't just look at assessment questions and tasks; do them. This will help your team gain clarity on the demand of the task and better understand what could be challenging for students.

- *Predetermine learning indicators.* "How do you know that students have learned?" Every educator asks this question, but not everyone on your team will have the same answer. It's difficult to have a robust discussion about data if people have not first agreed on the different levels of proficiency in what is being assessed. Use standards and subskills to write criteria for success when assessing content. When assessing things that seem harder to measure, such as social-emotional skills, name "look-fors" and provide examples. For instance, students who show metacognition in the way we expect would identify specific points of confusion. Instead of saying, "I don't get it," a student might say, "I know to use a number line to solve this addition problem, but I am not sure which number to start at."

- *Build test-taking confidence.* Ben Clay (2001) published a short guide to writing test questions, and he suggests that teachers design an assessment where the first question is a "softball" or even contains humor to put any anxiety kids may have at bay.

- *Be as intentional about offering wrong answer choices as you are about including the right one.* You can learn just as much from an incorrect answer selection on a multiple-choice test as you can from a correct selection. Be intentional about writing distractor choices and other wrong answers. You should be able to say during error analysis, "Students who chose wrong answer C did so because they got distracted by X." If you are using a multiple-choice question prepared by someone else, take time to examine incorrect answer choices to determine why a student might pick each option.

- *Examine assessment tasks/questions (or write them) for clarity.* A poorly worded task/question, or one that has challenging vocabulary, can raise questions during data analysis like "Did this student get this question wrong because they don't know the answer or because they didn't understand the question?" Preview assessment questions for clarity. If using a predesigned assessment, anticipate language that might confuse students. Reword misleading questions or tasks, if possible, or ask a follow-up question to ascertain what you want to know. When writing your own questions and tasks, think ahead as to how a student might interpret the wording of the question. If your team plans to repeatedly give an assessment to different students over time, you can tweak questions each time.

Find the right words:

- *Does this task/question measure what we taught?*

- *Does this task/question measure more than one thing? If yes, how can we break it apart?*

- *How should we format the task/question so that we get the view of data we need?*

- *What are criteria for success for this task/question? If students are proficient at the task/question, then we should expect to see/hear . . .*

- *What do the incorrect answer choices tell us about the student's misunderstanding or confusion?*

- *Is the wording of the task/question clear so that students know what they are expected to do?*

7.4 Optimize assessment conditions for students.

I was a terrible standardized test taker as a child. I'd watch the second hand on the wall clock steadily march forward. I'd read a passage again and again not knowing what I read. I'd panic as I heard other students' pencils scribbling and pages turning. (I don't know that I'd be any better had I to do it now, either.) Even with the most well-written assessments (standardized or not), if a student has a negative testing experience, you can get an inaccurate picture of what some students can and cannot do. In addition to examining assessment questions, take note of how an assessment was, or will be, given to students, as this could affect performance. Skillful team leaders (STLs) and their teams optimize assessment conditions for students.

How to optimize assessment conditions for students:

Do one or more of the following:

- *Go small and frequent.* Assess students often with short formative assessments. They will view them as routine, and taking the assessment will not feel like a burden and can establish a less anxiety-producing experience.

- *Give feedback.* Share what you learned right away. After you and your team have analyzed the formative assessment and made instructional goals and instructional decisions, tell students, for example, "Two days ago you took a quiz and I learned X. So today we are doing Y."

- *Offer retakes.* If the object is to see what students know and can do, then retakes provide equitable opportunities for students to do this. Feldman (2018) recommends that retakes be targeted so that students need only retake the portion they got wrong. Key point: Retakes only work if the students are given time and teacher support to help them relearn the material, understand misconceptions from the first take, or participate in intervention or tutoring; otherwise, the retake is a "fruitless exercise for the student" (Feldman, 2018, p. 169) and, I would add, potentially damaging as it reinforces to the student that they couldn't do it the first time and now they can't do it again.

- *Provide individual and universal accommodations.* Individual education programs (IEPs) specify test-taking conditions for particular students in special education. State testing gives the option for accommodations for these students as well, and offers universal accommodations from which all students can benefit (e.g., an untimed test). Consider conditions that will help get the best performance out of all students. For instance, my daughter has a medical eye condition that can cause eye fatigue when there is too much visual clutter on a page. Her global studies teacher had been assessing students' geography skills using a prefabricated computer program that had a lot of information written in very small, crowded text on a map and did not allow for a student to modify the screen view. She was having a hard time deciphering countries, capitals, and physical features. When her global studies teacher shifted to providing enlarged-print maps with more white space on the page and larger text, she performed much better. Seeing this marked improvement for my daughter, the teacher offered the option of taking the assessment in this format to other students, too.

Find the right words:

- *How can we optimize conditions so that students do their best on this assessment?*

- *How can we design and/or administer an assessment that reduces performance anxiety for some students so that they are able to show us what they know?*

- *Are there universal accommodations that could benefit all students? What test-taking accommodations do some students in special education have in their IEPs?*

- (As you review student data) *Were special education accommodations provided at the time the student took the assessment? If not, how did conditions affect the student's performance?*

PREPARE DATA* TO EXAMINE

Why are home-meal delivery services like HelloFresh and Blue Apron so popular? They prepare everything you need to make a delicious meal. Whether you subscribe to one of these services or do your own dinner prep, there's no question that thoughtfully assembling everything you need before you start cooking makes a difference. (Nothing like starting that chicken stir-fry only to realize halfway in that you forgot to defrost your chicken.) Similarly, some assessment data are prepared for you to easily access, and others need to be organized before people can make sense of them. Skillful team leaders (STLs) prepare data to examine.

STL moves:

7.5 Select student work samples (student data) to examine.

7.6 Organize student data.

7.7 Make data accessible.

7.8 Plan teacher work to examine together.

What these moves promote:

Focus. Data are prepared so that your team can make observations and draw conclusions related to the team's inquiry work.

Clarity. Data are organized in ways that people can make sense of them.

Productivity. Data are easily accessible so that time is not wasted with people trying to find things in the meeting.

When to use these moves:

Before you analyze data as a team.

7.5 Select student work samples (student data) to examine.

Random acts of kindness? Good. Random samples of student work? Not so much. Looking at student work or other types of student data can be one of the most powerful learning experiences for a team, but only if a team makes thoughtful choices about the work to examine together. Skillful team leaders (STLs) check that student work samples are authentic, relevant, and current before leading data analysis.

---

*Data may include results/responses from quantitative tests, student work, and/or data collected in an observation.

How to select student work samples
(student data) to examine:

Select student work samples that follow the ARC of robust data analysis:

- *Authentic.* Select student work samples (student data) that bring up a real concern, dilemma, or question for you (or the presenting teacher or the team). You might have an inkling of what is going on, but something in the student work/student data should leave you scratching your head, creating a need for you to analyze it with others.

- *Relevant.* Spending 40 minutes looking at someone else's student work samples (student data) is a tough sell when people don't see how group analysis of these samples is relevant to their own teaching and students. Choose data to examine that connects to your team's inquiry question and goals. (In other words, if your goal is to improve student writing with textual evidence, then don't bring in spelling tests.) If possible, let different people share their own student data. Whether everyone is looking at one teacher's student work or their own, the selected data should make people say, "This feels important. I want to talk about this with my colleagues."

- *Current.* Consider the time lapse between when students take an assessment and when the team analyzes data that result from it. Lagging data (data that are available weeks or sometimes months after students have been assessed) are helpful for identifying trends over time or setting long-term goals, but formative or benchmark assessment data make for a better data dialogue if you are trying to determine how students are performing now and want to decide next instructional steps.

Additional decision points when choosing student work samples (student data) to examine:

How many teachers should bring in samples?

Everyone on your team can bring in student samples when using a common assessment. If you are a multi-grade or multidisciplinary team with individualized and distinct assessments, teachers can take turns bringing their student work into each meeting.

How do teachers examine someone else's individualized assessment data when they are not familiar with the topic?

Not being a science person, I learned from my science colleagues that just because a person teaches biology doesn't mean they can confidently analyze student data from an Advanced Placement chemistry exam. I saw multi-linguistic world language teams face a similar challenge. (It's tough to weigh in on why a student performed poorly on a Mandarin test if the student wrote in Mandarin and you don't speak Mandarin.)

Support the presenting teacher by having them provide models and indicators of success so that anyone can analyze the work on the team without needing content expertise.

How many samples do we need to examine?

Review as many work samples as needed to gain an understanding of a student-centered challenge or teaching dilemma. Some teams opt to examine representative samples. For example, a teacher brings in one representative sample that is above expectations, one that meets expectations, and one that is below expectations. If work samples are short—perhaps they are exit tickets with only one question—you can likely examine many in the time you have. If you are problem finding or problem solving for one student, you might opt for samples from different subjects so that you can see how the student performed across disciplines. Keep in mind that most data analysis protocols have time limits where everyone examines the same student work samples and discusses them. If you choose a protocol like this, you'll need to limit the number of samples people have time to look at. The length of each student work sample will also determine how many samples people can read in a fixed amount of time.

In action:

Presenting teacher:	I signed up to bring in student work on Friday. I have 120 five-paragraph student essays that I just collected on Monday, but that seems a bit much to bring in.
Peter:	Yep. Let's narrow it down. What dilemma do you have that makes you want to examine them with our team?
Presenting teacher:	I want to figure out which skills to reinforce for my English learners in my next writing unit.
Peter:	I think people would be invested in looking at work from that student population since it is a growth area for all of us.
Presenting teacher:	My upper-intermediate English learners need work in grammar and word choice, and I'm not sure where to start. It would be helpful to have our team examine samples from them.
Peter:	OK, maybe examining a representative sample would be best: Sift through these students' essays and select just three, since they are long. The first can represent something close to what you want to see in a student essay, perhaps from an advanced English learner. This will help the teachers know what you expect to see. The second can showcase student errors that you would like support in addressing. And, the third sample can be from an upper-intermediate English learner whose writing is far below expectations.

STL recommendations:

Create a sign-up. Using meeting time to focus on one presenting teacher's student work samples (student data) is extremely valuable, but sometimes getting people to volunteer can be tough as it requires vulnerability-based trust. Distribute a sign-up list in the first few days of meeting, as if it were a housekeeping task, explaining that no one needs to know, yet, what data they will bring in or from which students. They only need to agree to a date in which they will bring something in. If people are particularly reticent, bring in your own student work samples (student data) the first week, and then put out the sign-up sheet.

Make a checklist. To help your colleagues select their own student work, customize a criteria checklist. The following is an example from STL Michelle Fox's science team.

> *Directions: We are going to examine student work samples to further uncover challenges they had in explaining phenomena through the use of models. Select student-created models (e.g., diagrams) that meet the following criteria:*
>
> ☐ The student-created model raises questions for me about student understanding and/or next instructional steps.
>
> ☐ The student-created model falls into one of three categories:
>   - The student-created model is clear, but the science is inaccurate (e.g., the student diagram of cause and effect is set up correctly, but the student named the wrong effect).
>   - The student-created model is insufficient or inaccurate, but the science is accurate (e.g., the student diagram reverses the relation between cause and effect, but the student accurately labeled the scientific cause and effect).
>   - The student-created model is insufficient or inaccurate, *and* the science is inaccurate (e.g., the student diagram shows multiple causes and no effect, and the causes are inaccurate).

Don't ask people to bring in student work samples and then never look at them. Nothing kills morale faster than asking people to take time outside of a meeting to prepare for an upcoming meeting and then not using what they prepared.

Ask the tough questions. You'll quickly know if someone brought in student work to examine that does not reflect an authentic dilemma because data talk will fall flat. The National School Reform Faculty (2017) recommends we pose some tough love to our colleagues by asking, "'Do we strut our stuff by bringing the student work that shows how successful we can be?' Or 'Do we mine our mistakes, by bringing the work that didn't meet our expectations?'" Aim for the latter.

Find the right words:

- *Do these student work samples shed light on an important student-centered challenge or teaching dilemma that we have?*

- *Is examining these work samples together a relevant task for everyone on the team? Can everyone potentially walk away from data analysis with a takeaway that will help their practice or student learning?*

- *If there is a time lapse between when the assessment was given to students and when we are examining it, will it get in the way of what we hope to learn and do? Is there a more recent assessment that makes more sense to analyze together?*

Related readings:

Move 4.5, "Choose a protocol," and Move 4.7, "Facilitate a protocol." Once you have selected the student work samples you want to analyze, turn to these moves to choose a looking at student work protocol and facilitate it.

Move 7.6, "Organize student data," and Move 7.7, "Make data accessible." Prepare student work before analyzing it as a team (e.g., remove student names from work samples; type illegible student responses).

7.6 Organize student data.

One day I observed a grade-level content team discuss the results from one teacher's test. The teacher passed out a blank template of the multiple-choice assessment he had designed and given to students. He had gone to great effort to calculate and handwrite in the margin next to each question the percentage of students across his three classes who had gotten each question correct (e.g., Question 1: 60%), but as teachers engaged in discussion about the data, questions arose that no one could answer and the conversation stalled.

> *"The vocabulary in Question 9 seems challenging. How did your English learners do on that one?"*

> *"You said 24% of students got Question 4 right. What was the most commonly selected wrong choice for that question?"*

> *"Only 10% of students got Question 6 wrong. I wonder who those students are and what tripped them up."*

Teachers were eager to participate in data analysis, but they could not further their understanding of the student challenges because the assessment data they examined weren't prepared in a way that could answer their questions.

Many assessment providers like i-Ready, IXL, Achievement Network, and DreamBox organize data for you, but when you examine data from an assessment your team has created, or when you look at student work together, the organization of data is on you. Skillful team leaders (STLs) organize student data (or delegate to someone who can) so that all can make sense of them.

How to organize student data:

Consider the following.

- *Disaggregate, if needed.* Aggregated data can be misleading without being broken down. A 2021 Facebook study concluded that a large percentage of teenagers *are not* being negatively harmed by Instagram; however, when data were disaggregated, it was found that aspects of Instagram *are* very harmful to middle school girls (Bursztynsky & Feiner, 2021). When preparing a zoom lens view of data (see Move 7.2), you can disaggregate data by student race/ethnicity (country of origin), age group, mobility, gender, grade, English learner designation, special education and/or disability placement, and honors or Advanced Placement—whatever you can't see in the aggregate that could shed light on what you are aiming to learn.

- *Make visual displays.* When you compare two or more variables, it's helpful to put data into tables, graphs, or charts so that people can notice relationships between them. Use color to help people make sense of data, as shown in the following examples:

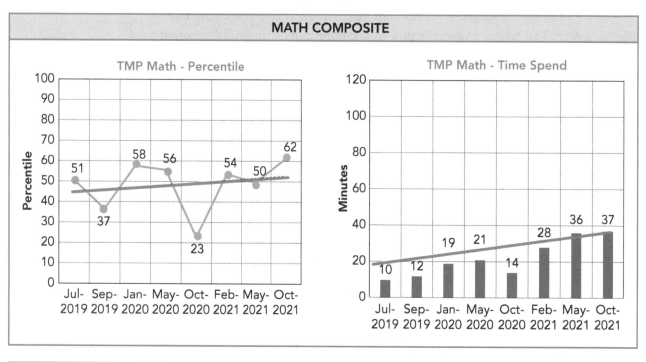

(Left) A chart illustrating a student's percentile correct on test questions over time, compared with (Right) a chart indicating time the student spent answering questions. The side-by-side graphs show that when this student spent more time on questions, the percentile of questions correct increased.

Photo courtesy of the Carroll School.

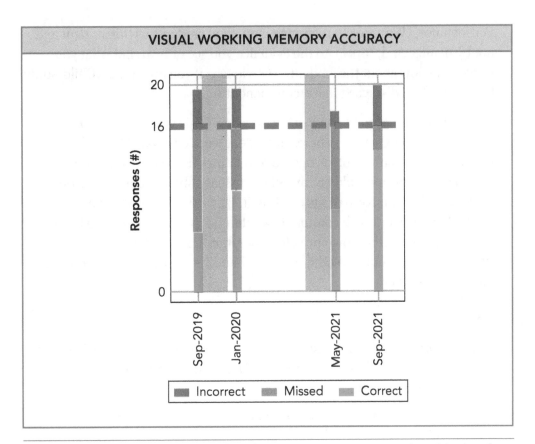

VISUAL WORKING MEMORY ACCURACY

Responses (#)

20

16

0

Sep-2019   Jan-2020   May-2021   Sep-2021

Incorrect   Missed   Correct

Chart of a student's correct, missed, and incorrect responses over time. It's clear from the stacked graph that this student's visual working memory accuracy increased from September 2019 to September 2021.

Photo courtesy of Carroll School.

- *Write titles.* If including a specific graph in a PowerPoint presentation, jot down a header to help draw out important information not to be missed (e.g., "All students performed above 60%").

- *Number pages.* Paginate or even number paragraphs so teachers can quickly reference and flip to specific sections of the student work.

- *Pair with criteria for success.* If you select an assessment to examine that no one has seen before, be sure to include details such as the task and criteria for success along with the work so people can thoughtfully examine it.

- *Initially withhold student names.* "I know that this student was retained in third grade, so this score is good for him." It's easy to let our biases influence our interpretations of student data. You can minimize the likelihood of bias when you are organizing student work samples by removing student names. Block out students' names on papers and substitute with easy identifiers such as Student A, Student B, and so on; Student 1, Student 2, and so on; or Student Green, Student Blue, and so on. If the student work is audio or visual, it might be difficult to keep the student's identity anonymous, so set an agreement when you structure data talk to help keep bias in check.

For instance, "We agree to reference individual students as *this student* and not by name." And, "Speak to the evidence you see or hear, not what you think you know about the student." (Obviously, if you are doing a Child Study [see Move 4.7], disregard this recommendation.)

- *Return hard copies to the presenting teacher.* (This is a recommendation for after you analyze paper copies of student work or data.) Although it is recommended that you block out student names from the work whenever possible, educators should be careful not to leave student data where other students, educators, or parents can find it, particularly if teachers have marked up the work with comments. Certainly, a team can agree to keep all student data in their own private folder, but the easiest way to make sure it doesn't get out into other people's hands is to just give it back to the presenting teacher.

Find the right words:

- *Have the data from this assessment already been prepared for us in a way that allows us to make observations and inferences? If not, what visuals should we prepare to make analysis easier?*

- *What support do you need in interpreting data tables, graphs, charts, and so on?*

- *How can we best organize data so that we can maximize our productivity when analyzing it together?*

- *How can we prepare data to minimize bias during analysis? Should we remove student names, or are they an important part of the dialogue? Can we provide criteria for success or student samples to give people a point of comparison during analysis?*

7.7 Make data accessible.

Nothing interrupts productivity more than when people arrive at a meeting unable to log in to view data, or when they have to wait for someone to pass them a student work sample before they can make a comment. Skillful team leaders (STLs) make data accessible in order to remove obstacles that can hinder analysis.

How to make data accessible:

Consider the following.

- *Check that everyone has the necessary passwords and login information* to access electronic data in advance of your meeting.

- *Test video links* of student interviews or observations that you plan on analyzing as a group.

- If your team is going to examine student work together, *ensure that samples are legible.* If student work samples are illegible, either choose different samples or type the student responses. I know it is laborious, but people can't discuss what they can't read. (Side note: My son has dysgraphia, so I am always looking for tools to help make his writing legible. Kami and SnapType are two useful tech tools. You take a photo of a worksheet, for example, and a student can type their responses directly on the uploaded PDF instead of having to handwrite them.)

- *Scan or take digital photos and post electronically.* Prepare a slide show or go "old school" and provide photocopies of student work samples (student data). Environmentally, paper is not the best option. However, depending on how comfortable and tech-savvy people are (not to stereotype, but many Gen Xers and Baby Boomers prefer hard copies) and how user-friendly and flexible the technology is, highlighting, cutting, sorting, and so on might be easier done with actual paper. If you opt for paper, offer to make photocopies. It puts more responsibility on you, but it pays off when you have the peace of mind that the student work samples are prepped in the way the team needs to view them, and you know you won't arrive at your meeting only to find out from the presenting teacher, "Sorry. The copier was broken." It will also give you an opportunity to preview the work, which is particularly helpful when you are playing the dual role of facilitator and participant.

- *Check for data literacy.* Access goes beyond being able to view data; it includes being able to understand it. Not all team members have the same level of data literacy. Review graphs and what they represent. Provide safe conditions and an opportunity for people to ask questions that will help them make sense of data.

Find the right words:

- *What do we need to access data (passwords, log-in information, etc.)? Who will provide access, and by when?*

- *How can we best interact with the data and have a robust data analysis conversation about it? Electronic data or paper copies?*

- *What do we need to do before the meeting so that everyone can access the data we will examine? Are student work samples legible?*

7.8 Plan teacher work to examine together.

Collaborating about curriculum and instruction is comfortable for teacher teams. As teachers, we are always looking for ideas, resources, and effective strategies, and who better to turn to for those things than our colleagues? But high-functioning, high-impact Q1 teams do more than exchange tools and tips. Together they *critically examine* curriculum, instruction, and assessments—what I call looking at teacher work (LATW). LATW is the companion practice to looking at student work (LASW). When teams engage in both types of collaboration, they can have a great impact on teacher learning and student outcomes. Examples of teacher work may include curriculum maps, units, lesson plans, mini-lesson designs, teacher models, and assessment questions and tasks. Skillful team leaders (STLs) plan teacher work to examine together for feedback.

How to plan teacher work to examine together:

Plan, organize, and make teacher work accessible, much the same as you would with student work (see Moves 7.5–7.7).

- The teacher work represents an authentic dilemma for the presenting teacher(s) and a relatable problem for everyone else on the team.

- The teacher work seems relevant to the inquiry work and goals on which the team has chosen to focus.

- The teacher work is current. It is something someone plans to use in the near future.

- Someone prepares the team with essential background knowledge about the teacher work.

Find the right words:

- *How can we best prepare teacher work that will be examined so that everyone on the team is able to make sense of the [lesson plan, assignment, policy, parent letter, etc.] and give feedback?*

FACILITATE DATA ANALYSIS

Consider the following hypothetical mini-dialogue:

Facilitator:	Next on our agenda is looking at student work. Ms. P brought in student responses from a recent quiz. What do people notice?
Teacher 1:	I notice some student answers are completely off topic.
Ms. P:	Agreed. Some kids don't give me anything I ask for.
Facilitator:	What might be going on?
Teacher 2:	I've been teaching this for 10 years. I think the responses are typical.
Teacher 1:	And some of these questions are hard.
Facilitator:	What might be a next instructional step?
Teacher 1:	I've found a lot of ideas on this website. [*Shows site.*] You should check that out.
All:	That's fantastic. What a great resource!
Facilitator:	Thanks, everyone. Ms. P, hopefully that gives you some ideas. Moving on to the next thing on our agenda . . .

Data talk is the engine that drives inquiry teams, and yet, so often, like the above condensed dialogue, it resembles a routine safety inspection at a gas station. "Lights, fluids, wipers, tires—check." While the tone of this meeting is good-natured and people are talking on topic, there are a number of challenges for the team: No one makes specific reference to student work samples or the criteria for success on the task. Conversation moves prematurely into problem solving. No one leaves with a deeper understanding of which students need what support. No one examines their own teaching. No one delves into the nuances of implementing strategies. Teachers collaboratively "look" at data and talk instruction, but the problems students have before the team meets are really no closer to being resolved after the meeting adjourns.

It is common for teams to get caught in "activity traps" (Timperley, 2008, p. 69) in which teams have data meetings that look more like a "ritualized enactment" (Little, 2012, p. 151) than anything that could potentially transform learning. High-functioning, low-impact Q2 teams, in particular, get caught in these traps, which is why the symbol I use for their teams is a hamster wheel—running fast and getting nowhere. Skillful team leaders (STLs) facilitate analysis in a healthy data culture where people ground observations and interpretations in evidence and set next instructional steps.

STL moves:[*]

7.9 Maintain a healthy data culture.

7.10 Prompt for evidence-based observations.

7.11 Prompt for evidence-based reasoning.

7.12 Analyze student errors.

7.13 Target and plan for student success.

What these moves promote:

Evidence-based discourse. People engage with data, citing evidence to inform their claims.

Competency. People sharpen their data literacy skills.

Critical thinking. People interpret data and plan for teaching and learning.

When to use these moves:

Data analysis most often happens during the *Assess & Analyze, Target & Plan,* and *Act & Evaluate* STL Phases of Collaborative Inquiry.

7.9 Maintain a healthy data culture.

Data in raw form have no meaning, and yet working with them can certainly elicit strong and varied reactions from people. Go to one school and teachers fervently embrace data: "Look at our data walls. Time for our Grade 10 data meeting. Our team makes collective data-informed decisions. Data drive our instruction. Students are tracking their own data. Parents, please request a data meeting." Go to another school and teachers accept using data as part of the job but see it as a solo act. Go to a third school and simply say the word *data* and teachers cringe, roll their eyes, worry, or feel that their work is reduced to a numbers game. The difference between these examples comes down to data culture. Skillful team leaders (STLs) maintain a healthy attitude toward data on their teams.

How to maintain a healthy data culture:

Harvard University's Data Wise (Bocala & Boudett, 2015) suggests teams establish healthy habits of mind around data by using the acronym ACE:

---

[*]Moves 7.10–7.13 are sequenced to follow the structure of most data protocols: observe, analyze, target a goal, and make a plan. For this reason, I provide one "in action" example of an STL implementing the series of moves at the end of this section (pp. 344–345).

A = Shared commitment to action, assessment, and adjustment. This means teams routinely engage in cycles of data inquiry where they implement strategies, monitor through formative assessments how well students respond to interventions, and adjust their next steps to get better outcomes for all. The key here is routine.

C = Intentional collaboration. If this book is advocating for anything, it's certainly this. STLs implement intentional moves to help the team function as a group and achieve their desired impact on educator and student learning. With their teams, they set direction and purpose where they investigate problems that would make a difference to students, families, and their own teaching. They are intentional about what data they analyze, how they interpret the data, and what they do with the information they learn from analysis.

E = Relentless focus on evidence. It's the "relentless" part that speaks to the habit of mind here. In healthy data cultures, teams constantly collect and examine evidence to inform their decisions.

STL recommendation:

Adopt a ground rule. Before analyzing one another's student data together, remind yourself and your colleagues: *Behind every number is a student who is trying. Behind every student is a teacher who is trying.*

7.10 Prompt for evidence-based observations.

Adults are problem solvers (see Part II, Chapter 5). When people come together to analyze data, they often want to jump quickly to name problems and offer solutions. However, doing this before taking time to closely look at and discuss what everyone actually observes in the data at hand can cause people to jump to conclusions. Skillful team leaders (STLs) linger in observation mode based on data.

How to prompt for evidence-based observations:

Invite your colleagues to observe quantifiable things such as number of questions correct or incorrect and patterns and inconsistencies. Give directions to your team to cite a specific place in the student data when they make an observation. Model this (e.g., "This student started every sentence with *I* in paragraph one"). When someone makes an observation that does not seem to be supported by evidence, encourage people to ask, "Where do you see that in these data?"

STL recommendations:

Ban "because". Nancy Love (2008) suggests holding off on using the word *because* during the observation period. You might also consider banning phrases such as *I think . . . , I wonder . . . , Why . . . ,* and *What if . . .* as these lead people to make inferences before fully naming what they objectively observe in data.

Adopt a norm. To keep in observation mode without slipping into interpretation, adopt the norm of *talking about what you see before you talk about what you think.*

Find the right words:

- *How many questions/which parts of a question or task did student(s) get correct? Get partially correct? Get incorrect?*

- *If multiple sources of data are available, what patterns do we notice? What inconsistencies in performance do we observe?*

- *What performance data are available for subgroups of students (students of color, students with language-based learning differences, English learners, LGBTQIA+ students, etc.)?*

- *What did student(s) report as challenging?*

- *What words does the student use repeatedly in their response? How many times?*

- *What do we expect to see in the student response that is not present?*

Related reading:

Move 5.11, "Frame conversation with clear parameters." Set up your team for data talk that focuses on observations by setting parameters upfront so people understand how they should and shouldn't participate at this time.

7.11 Prompt for evidence-based reasoning.

Harvard University's Data Wise (Bocala & Boudett, 2015) recommends teams form a habit of relentlessly focusing on evidence, and yet, countless times I've seen teams have actual paper or electronic data in front of them but never reference them in dialogue. Research shows that even with data in hand, teams in low-achieving schools tend to talk about what they think without examining the evidence (Little et al., 2003). Skillful team leaders (STLs) prompt for evidence-based reasoning.

How to prompt for evidence-based reasoning:

Invite your colleagues to give explanations for and interpretations of data. Give directions to your team to connect their reasoning to what they notice in the data. Model this (e.g., "I don't think the student knows the formal tone expected in an analytical essay because her first paragraph is riddled with the first-person pronoun *I*"). Watch for reasoning based on bias and assumptions (see Moves 8.1–8.10 that address this).

For an example, see "Moves 7.10–7.13 in action" on page 344.

Find the right words:

- *What do we see/hear in the data that indicates student(s) falling below, approaching, meeting, or exceeding objectives and expectations?*

- *Based on what you see, why do you think this student responded this way?*

- *Why do you think X percentage of students responded incorrectly to Y?*

- *Why do you suppose students could do this [point to evidence] and not that?*

- *This . . . shows that . . .*

7.12 Analyze student errors.

You can't determine what interventions students need unless you closely and thoughtfully examine the errors they make. I'll use my son as an example.

When he was 10 years old, a state standardized reading assessment showed him one grade level behind in reading comprehension. The seemingly logical response was to put him into a comprehension intervention, but error analysis of additional formative assessments proved that this would have been a mistake. My son showed no comprehension errors when he read aloud while tracking with his finger under each word, or when someone read to him, but he was reading very quickly, skipping words, and inaccurately guessing at multisyllabic words. This caused him to lose the meaning of the text, which explained why his comprehension was low on the state test. Through close examination of his errors, his reading tutor and I suspected fluency (rate and accuracy) was his challenge, and we turned to fluency assessments to learn more.

Skillful team leaders (STLs) pinpoint confusion in student work (student data), engaging their colleagues in error analysis. Common types of error (although not a comprehensive list) include the following:

Task/question confusion. Students are confused by the wording/vocabulary of the question or task. For example, a child learning to tell time is asked to set the hands on the face of a clock so that it reads five minutes to 9. She mistakenly places the hour hand a little before the 9 and the minute hand on the 5. She misinterprets *to* to mean *before*, and thinks the "five minutes" tells you to put the minute hand on the number 5.

Lack of conceptual understanding. Students don't have a depth of understanding of the concept needed to do the task. (See the "in action" example beginning on page 340.)

Weak computational skills. Students get tripped up when computing, diagramming, or labeling. They make procedural errors. For example, a student mislabeled

East and *West* on a geography task and consequently made an error when asked to name a country to the east of the United States.

Struggle with written expression. Students struggle to communicate an accurate response. For example, a student makes a strong argument verbally in a writing conference, but did not capture her sophisticated ideas on paper.

Weak habits of mind. Students make errors due to low stamina, persistence, self-discipline, confidence, or other habits of mind. For example, a student's rate of accuracy decreased after the first 30 questions due to loss of stamina.

How to analyze student errors:

Review what students are expected to know and do on the assessment task/question. Start with what students do well, then focus on errors. Discuss the type of errors made. If confusion persists beyond error analysis, then ask the students to explain their thinking or have them redo a task, live, so you can observe the choices they make and ask them about their choices.

In action:

A math team examines the work of a student who used the "Big 7 strategy" for division but arrived at the wrong answer. (View the student work before reading the dialogue.)

Singh:	Let's find out where the student is making errors and why.
Teacher 1:	I see he can estimate multiples of landmark numbers because he chose to multiply the divisor by 100, then 10, then 20. And he multiplies correctly.
Teacher 2:	He also knows the procedure because he did all the right steps, but it looks like he subtracted incorrectly more than once.
Teacher 1:	Yes, and I'd go a step further and say that he doesn't get the concept of place value.
Teacher 2:	Well, yes, he doesn't line up his ones, tens, and hundreds.
Teacher 1:	I agree, but that doesn't actually get in the way of his calculation. The real issue is that he didn't regroup. See here the student said, "123 − 60 = 143." He did 3 minus 0 for the ones column, but then when he got to 2 minus 6 for the tens column, he reversed the digits and did 6 minus 2. Perhaps he doesn't understand that 123, which is 1 hundred, 2 tens, and 3 ones, can be regrouped as 12 tens and 3 ones. If he understood that, he would have solved 12 − 6.

Singh: It also points to a challenge with number sense because he should know that you can't subtract 60 from 123 and get a bigger number.

Teacher 1:   Looks like he has the same regrouping and number sense issues when he solves 23 minus 18 further down.

For another example, see "Moves 7.10–7.13 in action" on page 344.

For another example, see "Moves 7.10–7.13 in action" on page 344.

STL recommendations:

Discuss when errors are not present. This recommendation might sound odd. How do you do error analysis when the student did not make any errors? However, some students make choices to avoid making errors. For example, if a student is being evaluated on spelling, they may avoid including words they can't spell in their essay. If a student in a world language class is evaluated on speaking with accurate verb tense, they might only speak with words they know how to conjugate. If your team sees no errors on an assessment, decide if you need an additional assessment to confirm what the student does or doesn't know.

Find the right words:

- *What is the target/learning expectation for the task or question?*
- *What errors has the student made? Is there a pattern?*
- *If we don't see/hear errors, did the student avoid a task to avoid making errors?*
- *What type of error is it? Why did the student make the error?*
- *Is the student aware of the error? Are we able to ask the student to elaborate on the error? If yes, what can we learn from the student?*

Related reading:

Move 7.3, "Examine (or design) assessment tasks/questions." Preview or design assessment questions with error analysis in mind. Check for clarity and intentionally create incorrect answer choices in multiple-choice assessments so that your team can understand student errors.

7.13 Target and plan for student success.

Like shooting an arrow toward a target, skillful team leaders (STLs) and their teams aim for small, specific, targeted goals for students. In truth, I am not proposing a new move here. It is essentially the same as Move 6.7 except the timing for using this move happens later in an inquiry cycle, teachers tend to use formative data, and the STL intention behind using the move is a little different.

Move 6.7 is part of setting a S-M-A-A-H-R-T goal, which typically happens at the start of team inquiry in the *Assess & Analyze* and *Target & Plan* STL Phases of Collaborative Inquiry. STLs use this move to give purpose and direction to the team. Like the example in Move 6.7 illustrates, a team starts "big" with district- and school-level data and zeros in on a specific student-learning challenge, which becomes the basis for a cycle of inquiry.

Once the team has a direction for their work and they are further along in the cycle in the *Strategize & Design* and *Act & Evaluate* STL Phases of Collaborative Inquiry, teachers regularly test out new strategies, assess student response, tweak the strategy, assess student response, and so on. Throughout this time, STLs target and plan for student success, typically using formative data. They aim for small specific learning targets, often for small groups or individual students, and decide plans they can implement immediately. A plan might include a reteach to a small selected group of students, or the design of an intervention.

Distinguishing between these moves is not as important as putting into practice the principle underlying both: analyzing any data as a team at any point in a team's inquiry cycle should result in specific goal setting and action planning.

How to target and plan for student success:

Identify criteria for success. With this, examine your formative assessment data, first making observations (Move 7.10) then inferences (Move 7.11). Decide the next incremental goal for the student(s) to reach. Create a short-term plan, effective immediately, to reach the target. Love and colleagues (2015) recommend in their FIRME model that after analyzing formative assessments, teams select one or more of the following responses: reteach/reengage/regroup, move on, and/or extend learning.

In action:

STL Daryl Campbell and his co-teaching partner analyze student work for the purpose of providing feedback and next steps for a student. (View the student work before reading the dialogue.)

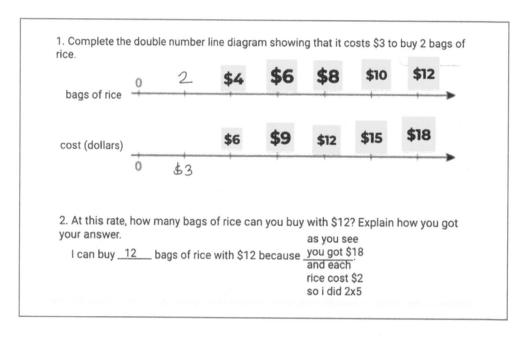

Daryl: This student's work highlights for me what has come up a couple of times in that something is more solid in her procedure than in her understanding and explanation of the concept. She is at mastery level in skip counting correctly on both number lines (even though she gave all numbers dollar signs). She knows that procedurally you are supposed to look at what numbers line up vertically on a double number line, in this case numbers 12 and 18. We can give her that positive feedback. However, she doesn't yet understand how the number lines relate or how to use the double number line to answer the ratio question.

Co-teacher: Right, and if she conceptually knew what she was doing, she would have (a) realized her mistake in labeling the top numbers with dollar signs and why bags of rice cannot also be cost and (b) selected the $12 on the bottom number line knowing that that line represents cost.

Daryl: I understand how she arrived at 12 bags for $12. She picked the 12 on the top number line, and because she mislabels it as dollars, she thinks the cost is $12. But where I'm not sure I'm clear is in her explanation. She says, "As you see you got $18 and each rice cost $2 so I did 2 × 5." Where is she getting 5?

Co-teacher: I believe she counted 5 places on the number line from 2 bags of rice until she landed on 12, which she mislabels again as dollars instead of bags.

Daryl: OK, I see. So let's get to specific feedback for the student.

Co-teacher: We tell her to reread the problem and notice what two things are being compared—in this case cost to number of bags, not cost to cost. Label each number line correctly—in this case remove dollar signs from the top number line.

Daryl: And then as a next step we need her to be placed in our math reteach group using the double number line to answer ratio questions.

For another example, see "Moves 7.10–7.13 in action" on page 344.

STL recommendation:

Involve your students. Whatever target is set and whatever the plan is to reach it, communicate (or even co-create it) with students so that they can actively work toward reaching it.

Find the right words:

- *Let's shift from data analysis to a targeted goal and next steps.*

- *We have a good understanding of what we are seeing in the data, so now let's decide what we can do about it.*

- *Based on evidence we see and our interpretation of it, what does this student/these students need, and what's our plan to deliver it?*

Related reading:

Move 6.7, "(Specific) Write specific student-learning targets." Explained in detail above, this is a move you would make toward the beginning of your inquiry cycle. You would analyze data in order to target a goal for the purpose of setting direction for your team.

Moves 7.10–7.13 in action:

The following example illustrates a team leader facilitating data analysis by using Moves 7.10–7.13.

In action:

Marty structures data talk as his team looks at a student response to the prompt, "Why should we celebrate Juneteenth?" The student's written response is as follows:

> *I used to think the fourth of July was great, because it was a day of freedom. But now I understand that it was a day of war and fighting. We should instead make juneteenth a big holiday. **THAT** was a day of Freedom and justice to the people! We should not be celebrating war and fighting, we need to celebrate love and compassion and of course **FREEDOM**. That is what I think. And I am **VERY** glad that the slaves are free. I just wish it didn't take so long. but we still have more fighting to do, we can't stop protesting **until all are equal.** So I think that as much as I love seeing the fireworks, that we need to move all of that to juneteenth, because that was the real day of freedom.*

7.10 Prompt for evidence-based observations.	Marty:	What do you notice in the student's writing?
	Teacher 1:	She uses the word *freedom* five times in the paragraph.
	Teacher 2:	In the fourth sentence she describes Juneteenth as "a day of freedom and justice to the people," but she does not specify which people.
	Marty:	Is anything else missing from her response that we would expect to see?
	Teacher 3:	I notice there is no mention of General Granger issuing an order to free the slaves that still existed in Galveston Bay, Texas, over a year after the Emancipation Proclamation was issued.

7.12 Analyze student errors.	Marty:	Let's examine this student's misunderstandings and begin to make sense of them.
	Teacher 2:	It seems she answers the prompt but makes a weak argument as to why we should celebrate Juneteenth.
7.11 Prompt for evidence-based reasoning.	Marty:	What does she write that supports your thinking?
7.12 Analyze student errors.	Teacher 2:	Her argument is mainly that we should celebrate freedom, and she even goes so far as to say we should no longer celebrate the Fourth of July. In line 5, she writes, "We need to celebrate love and compassion and of course FREEDOM." Juneteenth should be a "big holiday" "instead" of the Fourth of July.
	Teacher 1:	I don't think she knows what happened on June 19.
7.11 Prompt for evidence-based reasoning.	Marty:	What makes you conclude that?
7.12 Analyze student errors.	Teacher 1:	She understands we celebrate because slaves were freed because she says four times "day of freedom," but she doesn't show understanding of the historical events that took place on that day.
	Teacher 3:	I'm wondering, too, if she is unclear about when Juneteenth took place.
7.11 Prompt for evidence-based reasoning.	Marty:	What does she write that makes you say that?
7.12 Analyze student errors.	Teacher 3:	In the eighth line, she writes, "we can't stop protesting UNTIL ALL ARE EQUAL." Nowhere in the reading did it mention protests on Juneteenth, but in our current events discussion on a different day we were talking about protests in Black Lives Matter. I'm wondering if she made this error because she is conflating the two.
7.13 Target and plan for student success.	Marty:	OK, so next steps for this student and others who need further learning?
	Teacher 1:	Do a close read of the text that explains Juneteenth and have them fill out a graphic organizer with key details such as what happened before this day and what happened on this day.
	Teacher 2:	And to help clarify time and drive home the significance of the day, have students create a timeline placing "Lincoln issues Emancipation Proclamation" on January 1863 and "Union troops march into Galveston Bay, Texas, and decree slaves there are free" on June 19, 1865. This will help them see the significance of the date.
	Marty:	OK. Then we reassess.
	Teacher 1:	Let's ask a more specific question this time: What significant event happened on June 19, 1865?

Primary Intention

Engage in Analytical Thinking, Creative Problem Solving, and Clear Decision Making: Unbiased Reasoning and Diverse Perspectives

> *"Mental models" are deeply ingrained assumptions, generalizations, or even pictures or images that influence how we understand the world and how we take action. Very often, we are not consciously aware of our mental models or the effects they have on our behavior. (Senge, 1990, p. 8)*

If you are a high school science teacher, you have likely heard your share of misconceptions about why and how things happen. It's not just children who form mental models based on generalizations and assumptions to make sense of the world and take action; adults do it, too. It's normal. However, when unsubstantiated assumptions, bias, and unsound reasoning make their way into data analysis and problem-solving conversations, our perceptions are distorted and poor decisions get made.

At the heart of collaborative inquiry is a commitment to diversity, equity, and inclusion (DEI), as well as social justice. Skillful team leaders (STLs) and their colleagues seek diverse perspectives in order to build new mental models, particularly about students who have experienced some disadvantage. They engage in flexible ways of thinking that deepen their understanding of problems in order to arrive at creative solutions. When decisions are made, everyone on the team is satisfied with the process used and clear on and committed to what has been decided.

Contents:

8.6 Explore alternate reasoning.

8.7 Reframe a negative association.

8.8 Contrast with a high-expectations belief statement.

8.9 Capitalize on a learning moment.

8.10 Address deficit thinking.

Cultivate diverse perspectives.

8.11 Exercise flexible thinking.

8.12 Spotlight the minority viewpoint.

8.13 Invite dissent.

8.14 Advocate with humility.

Make clear impactful decisions.

8.15 Clarify the decision-making process.

8.16 Reach agreement on group decisions.

8.17 Commit to action.

8.18 Communicate a changed decision.

Tools and templates:

Figure 27: Ladder of Inference Example

SUSPEND AN ASSUMPTION

One day I was at the beach with my twins when my two-year-old son saw a dog digging a hole in the sand. My son picked up his toy shovel and gave it to the dog. He made what seemed to him like a logical assumption: *When I dig a hole in the sand, I use a shovel. This dog is digging a hole in the sand; therefore, he must need a shovel.* My son's assumption was harmless. However, when people make assumptions about students, families, and educators, the consequences can be significant.

Peter Senge and colleagues (1994) recommend that leaders and their teams suspend assumptions—that is, intentionally detach from what people perceive as true in order to examine it objectively. "We have found it useful to mention Bohm shares a useful metaphor—"assumptions suspend in air before us, as if hanging on a string a few feet before our noses" (Senge et al., 1994, p. 379). In doing so, an individual becomes both the observer and the observed. Skillful team leaders (STLs) intentionally suspend their own and others' assumptions.

STL moves:*

8.1 Spot an assumption.

8.2 Call attention to an assumption.

8.3 Inquire into an assumption.

Tools and templates:

Figure 27: Ladder of Inference Example

What these moves promote:

Self-awareness. People become conscious of assumptions they make.

Humility. People learn that they have much to learn. They recognize the limitations of their individual perspectives.

---

*STLs often make Moves 8.1–8.3 in sequence. Because of this, I include one "in action" example of an STL implementing these moves at the end of this section (see pp. 356–357).

8.1 Spot an assumption.

I notice my baby is crying in his crib. What does he need? He just woke up, so he must be hungry. Yes, he needs to be fed. If I feed him, then surely the crying will stop. I give him a bottle.

Nothing here seems out of the ordinary, and if you've ever cared for a baby, you've likely done this a million times without giving it a moment of conscious thought. Chris Argyris explains our meaning-making process as moving up a "ladder of inference" (see Senge et al., 1994, p. 243). Figure 27 shows the parent in this example moving up the ladder. (Begin reading from the bottom of the ladder.)

FIGURE 27   Ladder of Inference Example

LADDER OF INFERENCE	PARENT
7. Action	I give the baby a bottle.
6. Belief	Crying will stop if I feed the baby.
5. Conclusion	Baby needs to be fed.
4. Assumption	Baby just woke up, so he must be hungry.
3. Addition of meaning	Baby needs something.
2. Data selection	Baby crying.
1. Data	Baby's bedroom. Toys on floor. Noise from TV. Baby crying. Baby woke up.

It seems like sound reasoning that a parent would hear their baby crying, assume the baby is hungry, and conclude that the baby needs to be fed. But what if the parent's assumption is wrong? This is when, instinctually, a parent will go back and look for data that might have been missed and come to a different conclusion. ("Yuck! Smells. The baby must have a dirty diaper and need to be changed.") Most parents will just keep trying until they figure out why the baby is crying. But, when we make mistaken assumptions during data analysis about student learning, we can end up taking actions that negatively impact our students. Skillful team leaders (STLs) spot assumptions.

How to spot an assumption:

We move up the ladder of inference in an instant, almost unnoticeably. It can be hard to recognize when you or a colleague has made an assumption, particularly when engaged in student data analysis. The following "look-fors" don't automatically indicate someone is making an assumption; however, paying attention to these things can help you detect when one is present.

- *Listen for argument setups.* Arguments involve premise–conclusion language, and if an assumption is present, the reasoning won't make sense. For example: "Given that the child is not paying attention and children with attention deficit hyperactivity disorder, or ADHD, do not pay attention, the child must have ADHD." This argument houses an assumption in the conclusion. Here are some additional examples of argument setups:

    - Since [premises] . . . it must mean that [conclusion] . . .
    - Due to [premises] . . . it follows that [conclusion] . . .
    - Given [premises] . . . it is clear that [conclusion] . . .
    - This is true [premises] . . . so therefore this is true [conclusion] . . .
    - These data indicate [conclusion] . . . because [premises] . . .

- *Notice questionable logic.* You don't need to be an expert in the distinction between deductive and inductive reasoning or sound and unsound arguments to recognize when someone uses false premises to make a false claim (e.g., "This class can't handle field trips because adolescents are incapable of self-regulation").

- *Notice when someone embeds an assumption in one of the following types of arguments (The Princeton Review Canada, 2015):*

    - Causal assumptive argument: A person claims that there is only one cause. Example: "The other elementary school changed their math curriculum, and students are performing better. Therefore, if we want to improve our scores, we need to change our curriculum."
    - Sampling assumptive argument: A person makes a claim about a large group that is based on a small sample. Example: "When I was in middle school, I stayed organized with a Mead Trapper Keeper binder. Therefore, we need to get Trapper Keeper binders for all students."
    - Analogy assumptive argument: A person makes a false analogy between two things and claims that if the first is true, the second must also be true. Example: "Students already know how to write one paragraph. So they shouldn't need any support when writing a five-paragraph essay."

- *Listen for extreme language.* Notice when you or others speak in absolutes or generalizations (e.g., "This *must* be true." "*Every* student . . ." "*All* families . . .").

- *Be mindful of assumptions disguised as humor.* You've likely heard (and maybe even made) a side comment for a quick laugh or a moment of commiseration (e.g., "I want Sandra to be able to write a good topic sentence. But who are we kidding? I'd be satisfied if she would just remember to write her name on the page!"). When tossed out casually with no ill intent, these comments are seemingly benign. But when you listen to what's actually being said, you notice that these comments usually signal low expectations and are based on assumptions. Even though the moment may get a quick laugh and the team might brush past the joke, STLs will spot the hidden assumption (see Move 8.1).

- *Tune in to the emotional response in the room.* When someone else voices an assumption, particularly about difficult subjects like race or politics, notice your own emotional response toward them and put it in check. On the flip side, if people have a strong reaction to something you have said, pause. You might have made an assumption.

For an example, see "Moves 8.1–8.3 in action" on page 356.

Think like a teacher:

Both children and adults make assumptions. Here are some everyday examples:

Students and adults can draw conclusions due to unsound reasoning.

- A kindergartener knows the cafeteria serves pizza every Friday. The week of Thanksgiving they serve it on Wednesday, and the child assumes it is Friday.

- A new teacher tries literature circles for the first time. Chaos ensues. The teacher assumes this class can't handle group work.

Children hold an egocentric view of the world that shapes their conclusions; adults can make decisions from their narrow, often self-centered perspectives.

- A young child reasons, "I follow the tradition of dressing up for Halloween; therefore, every kid must do this too."

- A team leader prefers meeting on Fridays and assumes the teachers on the team do, too. The leader changes the schedule without checking in with team members.

Students and adults can make assumptions when they are learning.

- A student writer leaves out description and detail because the student assumes the reader already has an understanding of the material.

- An adult learner participates in professional development led by someone who teaches elementary students. The learner assumes the strategies presented could never work with high school students.

8.2 Call attention to an assumption.

If a colleague made a mistaken assumption about you, would you call it out or let it slide? What if the assumption was about your colleague? Your student? What if the assumption was about an entire group of people? Judith Warren Little (2008) studied group conversations and discovered that it's not uncommon for teachers on a team to ignore assumptions made by others or deflect them with humor. Instead of calling attention to the assumption, they would normalize problems, reassuring each other that "this happens to all of us," then suggest a quick-fix strategy and move on. On the contrary, effective groups examined their own problems and assumptions, pressing people to say more about their beliefs and practice. These teacher teams were able to engage in "learning-rich conversations" (Little, 2008, p. 55).

Skillful team leaders (STLs) call attention to assumptions that should not be ignored.

How to call attention to an assumption:

Calling attention to an assumption can go very wrong and even turn into conflict, if not done well. But making this move with the following key components can keep conversation productive:

- *Establish trust.* No matter how careful you are with your words, calling attention to someone else's assumption can embarrass or offend the other person. You have to build relational trust. (Some trust-building moves and games are explored in Primary Intention 3.) Express gratitude for the safe relationship you have with each other that allows you to be candid with one another and call attention to assumptions made.

- *Clarify understanding.* Not to blow your mind here, but are you making an assumption about the person who you think just made an assumption? You might be climbing up your own ladder of inference about this person. Make sure that you are not misinterpreting what others are saying.

- *Respectfully push back.* Advocate for values without shaming the person whose assumption contradicted your values.

- *Describe the impact.* Without judgment of those who made an assumption, and trusting that their intentions are good, let them know how the comment affected you and/or the implications of acting on such an assumption.

For an example, see "Moves 8.1–8.3 in action" on page 356.

STL recommendations:

Decide whether to call out or call in. "Call out" and "call in" are two similar moves you may have heard of that call attention to an assumption. "Call out" is directive and confrontational. That's not necessarily a bad thing, but you need to be very certain you are not jumping to conclusions about what the person is saying, and also be ready for the other person's potentially negative response. Most adults don't like when a colleague corrects or chides them. For example, telling someone "I feel obligated to tell you that your comment isn't OK" can escalate tension.

"Call in" is when you are genuinely curious about where the person's assumption has come from without judgment. You and the other person seek to understand one another. You are both learners in the dialogue. It is more in line with Senge et al.'s (1994) inquiry-based approach to suspend assumptions (see Move 8.3).

Don't police people. You don't want to gain a reputation as someone who is just waiting for others to say or do the wrong thing so you can "right their wrongs." Doing so unintentionally contributes to a culture of fear. Instead, call attention to an assumption, but aim to preserve the dignity of the other person so as not to damage your relationship.

Don't gang up on people. This recommendation comes from Brené Brown's (2021b) *Daring Leadership* podcast. If you intend to call out individuals on their behavior and want them to hear you, then don't create an "us vs. them" climate in which you and other team members talk about certain members behind their back. And don't, then, send one person to approach the individual and say, "We've all been talking about you. We need to tell you that you are doing X and it bothers us." The person will feel threatened. Don't gossip and plot. If you notice a behavior worthy of a callout, then speak as an individual directly to the person who is exhibiting the bothersome behavior.

Find the right words:

STL Osamagbe (Osa) Osagie recommends a great resource from Seed the Way for language you can use to "call out" vs. "call in." Visit www.racialequityvtnea .org/wp-content/uploads/2018/09/Interrupting-Bias_-Calling-Out-vs .-Calling-In-REVISED-Aug-2018-1.pdf for more on interrupting bias.

Clarify for understanding:

- *Just to clarify, are you concluding X based on Y?*
- *Would you mind walking us through how you came to that conclusion?*

Respectfully push back:

- *I disagree with the assumption you are making.*
- *I need to address the assumption behind your comment.*

Describe the impact:

- *I need to tell you how that comment landed on me.*
- *If you were to act on that assumption, [students/families/others] would be impacted in this way . . .*

Related reading:

Move 3.11, "Practice compassion." To strengthen vulnerability-based trust, practice compassion toward another person instead of judgment. Approach colleagues who make assumptions that trigger you, with empathy and a beginner's mind, remembering what it was like when you were first learning about any highly charged topic.

8.3 Inquire into an assumption.

In the crying baby scenario described in Move 8.1, it is second nature for the parent to inquire into the made assumption: "I assumed the baby was hungry because he was crying. But then, the crying continued. Why did I make this assumption? What did I miss? Could I have misinterpreted the meaning of his crying? Of course. Let me try again."

It's easy to step back and examine a low-stakes assumption like this. But, when we feel certain that the assumption we made was correct, when we feel so passionate about our point of view that we don't want to let go, or when we make assumptions about highly charged topics (race, politics, sexism, ageism, etc.) and get uncomfortable when others question us, then inquiry gets hard. Skillful team leaders (STLs) dangle their own and others' assumptions in front of everyone and create a space where it is safe to ask difficult questions.

How to inquire into an assumption:

Whether you are inquiring into your own or someone else's assumption, remain curious. Detach from your point of view as much as you can, "loosening the grip of [your] certainty about all views, including [your] own" (Senge et al., 1994, p. 361). Expect that you could be wrong. Ask questions that explore the different rungs on the ladder of inference (Figure 27), specifically relating to data that you used to come to your conclusion and data you may have overlooked. Consider alternate reasoning. Pull from Moves 8.4–8.10 as needed.

For an example, see "Moves 8.1–8.3 in action" on page 356.

STL recommendation:

Linger in discomfort. When assumptions are suspended, conversation can get uncomfortable. Senge (1994) tells us that this "crisis of suspension" is necessary for group learning. Crisis shakes things up. Ultimately, when a group embraces the crisis that suspending assumptions brings, the team is stronger for it. Key point: Feeling discomfort because you are wrestling with your own assumptions, preconceived notions, or unconscious bias is good. Feeling uncomfortable because you feel judged is bad. The latter weakens vulnerability-based trust.

Take action. Suspending assumptions requires you and your colleagues to recognize assumptions, slow down the conversation long enough to call attention to them, and inquire into them. But Aiko Bethea reminds us to go one step further. Once you uncover unconscious bias, ask questions about how to put new learning into practice (see Brown, 2020). Even if our assumptions about sensitive topics, particularly race, are mistaken, it's not enough for us or someone else to point it out. As Bethea says, we have to find a "path of correction."

Find the right words:

- *I want to explore that remark further because I think it's based on an assumption that needs to be unpacked.*

- *Let's step back and look at where that assumption comes from. What would happen if we thought about this differently?*

- *Now that we've learned new things as a result of suspending this assumption, what are we going to do differently?*

Moves 8.1–8.3 in action:

Ezra leads a district-level team made up of parents and school representatives. He suspends assumptions using all of the moves in the preceding section.

MOVES	CONVERSATION	
	Ezra:	65% of families in the district responded favorably on a survey question that asked whether the school welcomed their opinions.
	Teacher 1:	That's not great. That means 35% don't think their opinions are welcome!
8.1 Spot an assumption.	Parent team member:	I bet the dissatisfied families are mostly those who have children in special education.
8.3 Inquire into an assumption.	Ezra:	What makes you think that?
	Parent team member:	I see on the parent group Facebook page all the time posts from people complaining about the school. My daughter has an individualized education program (IEP), and at her prior school I often had to advocate hard for her. At times, I felt like no one was listening. I hear stories of contentious IEP meetings. I know of two mothers who feel frustrated with the responses they have received from the school about services for their children who are neurodiverse. Families of students in special education in this district don't feel like their voices matter.
8.2 Call attention to an assumption: Clarify understanding.	Ezra:	[*Repeats.*] "Families of students in special education in this district don't feel like their voices matter." Did I hear you correctly?
	Parent team member:	Yes. I think teachers and administrators care about kids, but they don't want to hear from parents.
8.2 Call attention to an assumption: Respectfully push back.	Ezra:	[*Pauses.*] We have worked together for a while now, and I feel safe saying that my gut reaction when I hear you make that assumption is to defend my staff.

MOVES	CONVERSATION	
8.2 Call attention to an assumption: Describe the impact.	Parent:	I didn't mean to insult any staff members.
	Ezra:	I know. Whether a parent makes a generalization about staff, or a staff member make a generalization about parents—either way, it does not strengthen relationships, and ultimately that's what we all want.
8.3 Inquire into an assumption.	Ezra:	[*Pauses.*] But, the experiences you describe are real. They inform your point of view. And my experiences, different from yours, are also real and shape my point of view. Is either one of our experiences sufficient to conclude one way or the other how the majority of families in our district feel? Probably not. One way we can further inquire into this assumption is to refer back to the data.
		[*The team disaggregates responses by subgroups such as families of special education students. The data show families of special education students responded that they were more satisfied than any other group.*]
	Parent team member:	I'm shocked. That makes no sense to me. Parents must have misread the question.
	Ezra:	Let's stay in inquiry mode and try not to hold tightly to our points of view. How could we make meaning of this new view of data?
	Teacher 1:	Parents of students receiving a special education have regular access to a team of teachers in ways that other families don't. We give them weekly updates. Co-teachers view them as essential partners in their children's education. We create IEPs together. They have lots of opportunities for their opinions to be heard.
	Parent team member:	I didn't think of it that way, but I can see how that could make sense.
	Ezra:	And I can see how you could make such an assumption before seeing the disaggregated data. Given the experiences you shared, I'm convinced there are some families of students receiving a special education who don't feel heard. We can always do a better job.

INTERRUPT ASSUMPTIONS, BIAS, AND UNSOUND REASONING

With a growing body of literature about culturally relevant teaching and all-inclusive education, we are now much more aware than ever before of our implicit biases (though there is always more to learn). It is human to view the world from our varied biased perspectives.

Here are some examples of different types of biases that we bring to our everyday interactions:

- *Affinity bias.* We gravitate toward people with whom we share similar traits and features (e.g., gender, race, age, appearance, or upbringing).

- *Attribution bias.* We attribute characteristics to a person based on the person's membership in a particular group (e.g., race, gender, age, or sexuality) as opposed to viewing the person as an individual. Name bias, where we make assumptions about individuals we don't know based on their names, is similar. (This happens frequently in hiring practices when employers sift through résumés.)

- *Confirmation bias.* We seek data that support our already established ideas and beliefs. This is the reflexive loop Argyris talks about in the ladder of inference (see Move 8.1 and Senge et al., 1994).

- *Conformity bias.* We conform to group beliefs even if it means going against our own. This is most evident in groupthink, described in Part II, Chapter 4.

- *The halo effect.* We assume positive characteristics about someone who is attractive or impressive. Conversely, we are also biased when we assume negative characteristics about someone who fails to impress us. This is referred to as the horns effect (Howard, n.d.).

"Research shows that implicit biases can be reduced through the very process of discussing them and recognizing them for what they are" (U.S. Department of Justice Community Relations Service, n.d., p. 2). Skillful team leader (STL) Daryl Campbell first introduced me to a powerful text by Margaret Wheatley titled *Willing to Be Disturbed.* Wheatley (2002) writes, "We have to be willing to let go of our certainty and expect ourselves to be confused for a time. . . . Change always starts with confusion; cherished interpretations must dissolve to make way for the new" (pp. 34–37). STLs and their teams are willing to interrupt assumptions and unsound reasoning, particularly that which harbors bias about race, ethnicity, gender, poverty, and politics, even when it means feeling disturbed.

STL moves:

8.4 Seek alternate evidence.

8.5 Confront bias with success criteria.

8.6 Explore alternate reasoning.

8.7 Reframe a negative association.

8.8 Contrast with a high-expectations belief statement.

8.9 Capitalize on a learning moment.

8.10 Address deficit thinking.

What these moves promote:

Rigorous discourse. A concept I explore in my first book, rigorous discourse occurs when data talk is "evidence-based, dialogic, culturally proficient, reflective, and actionable" (MacDonald, 2013, p. 103).

Competency. These moves build up a team's data analysis skills.

When to use these moves:

Throughout a team's course of inquiry and learning, particularly in data analysis conversations during the *Assess & Analyze, Target & Plan,* and *Act & Evaluate* STL Phases of Collaborative Inquiry.

8.4 Seek alternate evidence.

Think about how most people in the polarized political climate of the early 2020s accessed news on social media. They clicked on posts that confirmed their biased views. They dismissed anything that might cause them to think otherwise and ended up more committed to their positions than before.

The world is full of observable data, and we learn to select what we think is important. We make meaning and form beliefs from these data. But at some point, the belief we have formed starts to dictate both the data we select and the data we overlook. In short, we unconsciously seek evidence that proves us right. Chris Argyris describes this phenomenon as a "reflexive loop" (see Senge et al., 1994, p. 244). This behavior lays the groundwork for group polarization and groupthink, two divisive pitfalls for teams (see Part II, Chapter 4). Skillful team leaders (STLs) intentionally interrupt this reflexive loop by seeking alternate evidence that can, in turn, influence what people believe.

How to seek alternate evidence:

Notice the data you and your colleagues attend to and also what you are over-looking. Recognize the conclusions you reach with this limited view of data. Go back and revisit the evidence you have before you, intentionally exploring what you may have unconsciously filtered out.

In action:

Will notices a teacher regularly arrives late to meetings. He assumes the teacher doesn't want to collaborate. Thereafter, in every interaction he has with the teacher, he looks for indicators that confirm this belief. For instance, he notices that the teacher is quiet during meetings—further evidence, he feels, that she really doesn't want to be there. One day, Will notices the teacher is on her computer throughout an entire meeting. Will is initially frustrated and annoyed. But, he decides to seek alternate evidence before again jumping to his same earlier conclusion. Over the next few meetings, he intentionally notices things he hadn't before, such as she takes copious notes during meetings, she signed up twice to do a demonstration lesson for the team, and she sent an email link to an upcoming workshop about the topic of the team's inquiry. Noticing these things helps Will see the teacher differently. Now, without assuming that she doesn't want to collaborate, he reaches out to her about arriving late and can engage in a learning conversation with her about what she needs to be able to join meetings on time.

Think like a teacher:

You don't jump to write a referral for intervention when a student misses a few homework assignments. You seek a more complete picture of the evidence you have. You look at what homework the student has turned in. You talk with the student to learn what may be going on that you don't yet know. You check the student's performance on classwork and tests, behavior in the class, and social interactions with peers. Only after seeking alternate data, and only if there is sufficient evidence pointing to the possible need for targeted support, do you write a referral.

Bring this approach to your team when they are collecting data in order to avoid making decisions based on insufficient evidence selected from your own biased points of view.

Find the right words:

- *What evidence might we be missing?*

- *What data might tell an alternate story?*

- *If presented with different observable data, would my/our thinking shift?*

- *How might our assumptions be influencing the evidence we are looking for?*

- *Are we relying too heavily on self-reporting and recollection data? If yes, what student work, class video, or transcribed conversations might we have access to?*

8.5 Confront bias with success criteria.

When scoring students' analytical papers, college professors tend to favor perspectives similar to their own (Steinke & Fitch, 2017). To counter this bias, researchers recommend that teachers focus on the quality of the argument and the effectiveness of a student's reasoning, rather than the position the student is taking. This may sound obvious, but it's not so easy to do when you are scoring papers of students you know. The same bias can show up when K–12 teams are talking about students and collaboratively examining their work. Skillful team leaders (STLs) intentionally counter bias by making team decisions for students based on success criteria. (For example, when reviewing analytical writing, they would score based on clear expectations about what makes a strong argument and reasoning, not what they know about the student or the position they take.)

How to confront bias with success criteria:

Notice when you or your colleagues make instruction and assessment decisions based on what you know of the student or your own personal preferences. Redirect conversation to criteria for success.

In action:

Alejandra's team in support of English learners is examining student position papers in which students are asked to take a stance on America's Deferred Action for Childhood Arrivals (DACA) immigration policy. Teachers are surprised by the position one student takes.

Teacher: Knowing what I do about this student's Latinx background, I don't understand how this student could take a position like this. I would mark the student poorly on interpretation of facts.

Alejandra: While we might disagree with the student's interpretation of the facts and conclusions, according to our rubric, students deserve a proficient score if they "cite evidence to defend and support their interpretation of facts." Let's look specifically at the evidence cited. Does this student's writing meet that expectation?

Find the right words:

- *How did the student perform with respect to the expectations outlined in the standard/criteria for success?*

- *Let's look at the language of the standard/criteria for success to evaluate this student's work sample.*

- *Putting our opinions aside, what evidence do we have that this student did or did not meet the performance expectations on this task?*

Related reading:

Move 7.3, "Examine (or design) assessment tasks/questions." Determine criteria for success before analyzing an assessment.

8.6 Explore alternate reasoning.

Some cats are black. I have a black pet. Therefore, I must have a cat.

You don't need to ace the LSAT to recognize invalid reasoning. In the preceding example, each premise is true, but the conclusion is false. (Move 8.1 provides more examples of premise–conclusion language that are based on assumptions.) When problem solving with a team, skillful team leaders (STLs) recognize invalid arguments and intentionally explore alternate reasoning.

How to explore alternate reasoning:

Before accepting the first conclusion people make of data, invite your colleagues to think of interpretations beyond what they immediately thought. Ask probing questions. Point out when reasoning doesn't hold water.

In action:

Teacher 1:   Fifty-two percent of the parents who took our survey responded favorably when asked if we did a good job of discussing current events with students. So, almost half think we can do better.

Teacher 2:   That feels so off. I feel like especially, given this year, with so much going on in the world, we've gone out of our way to process it with students. We've even changed our curriculum. I guess we could do more, but if we did, that would take time away from learning other content.

Mariana: Before we change our curriculum, let's seek alternate reasoning here. I notice when we drill down to the way parents answered this question, we see what most of the 48% actually marked off "I don't know how well my school is doing at discussing current events." So we might be doing a good job with kids, but maybe we need to improve communication to parents about what we are doing with their children.

Teacher 2:   OK. Maybe communication is the real issue. That would make sense because I think a lot of middle school kids don't tell their parents what we do in school. So, of course, parents are going to say we don't do a good job talking about it.

Parent:	I bet the group that marked "I don't know" are parents of boys. Because my daughter tells me everything, but getting my son to share with me what he learned in school is like pulling teeth.
Mariana:	Maybe, but we can't assume that. Let's explore additional reasons why parents report that they are not informed.

Think like a teacher:

While we may think we know what's going on with certain students when they act up in class, our immediate conclusions aren't always right. One of the most influential theories for my practice when I was a classroom teacher was *Positive Discipline*'s "Four Mistaken Goals of Misbehavior" (Nelson, 2006). The Mistaken Goals are based on Dreikurs's (1968) research finding that children need to feel a sense of belonging. When children don't feel as if they belong, they "misbehave." And they do so because they are seeking one of four things: attention, power, revenge, or avoidance of failure/feeling inadequate. More interesting than learning about why children act in these ways is realizing how often teachers misinterpret a child's goal of misbehavior. A child who refuses to participate in class might not be acting oppositional, but instead may be trying to avoid failure. When we explore alternate reasoning for behavior through a culturally responsive lens, we sometimes realize that "misbehavior" isn't really a "miss" at all—just different from what we are accustomed to. When we don't jump to conclusions, we better understand what our students need.

When interpreting data with your colleagues, don't settle for the first explanation; explore alternate reasoning.

Find the right words:

- *We've identified a few potential reasons for what we are seeing in the data. Are there others?*

- *What if the causes we have identified are not the root of the problem? What else might be at play?*

- *I thought that as well, but then I noticed the data show . . . and I came to a different conclusion. Can we explore that together for a moment?*

8.7 Reframe a negative association.

"Black students are loud and disruptive" vs. "African American students are enthusiastic and energetic." Zaretta Hammond (2015b) shares this as an example of reframing a negative racial association in a way that presents an alternative interpretation. Reframing is about more than semantics (Hammond, 2015a). It is about interrupting our default ways of thinking and speaking. When a comment lands on the table laden with assumptions based on stereotypes, racism, or disinformation, it can be hard to know how to respond. Skillful team leaders

(STLs) do not let these comments go unaddressed. They intentionally and clearly reframe negative associations.

How to reframe a negative association:

Notice biased comments. Refer to page 358 "Interrupt assumptions, bias, and unsound reasoning" section, which describes many types of bias. Specifically, listen for attribution and negative impression bias. Attribution bias occurs when we attribute undesirable behaviors to someone, simply because they are a member of a particular identity group. A teacher might attribute a student's not wanting to read, for example, to "laziness." Negative impression bias occurs when we feel harmed by someone else and exaggerate negative associations with that person or group. "I can't believe my colleague left me off that email," a teacher might say. "She is so cliquey."

Reframe language to offer a different perspective. To the person who presented an attribution bias, you might say, "Perhaps the student is not lazy, but is actually struggling with the text, which leads to avoiding reading." To the person who presented a negative impression bias, you might say, "Perhaps my colleague left me off that email in order not to burden me with the problem."

Remember to be mindful of your own biases and ask others to reframe your language when needed.

In action:

Teacher:	That's a good answer for that student because she has ADHD and is normally spaced out. [*Laughter.*]
Katie:	Or, she is wonderfully imaginative with so many ideas that can draw her attention away from the task.

STL recommendations:

Interrupt racial bias. Patricia Devine suggests that implicit racial bias is a habit and developed a research-based intervention to break it. In a 2018 article, she writes, "The necessary ingredients to break the prejudice habit include motivation, awareness, strategies and effort." Hammond (2015b) highlights in her blog a few interventions from Devine's work:

- *Stereotype replacement:* Recognizing when one is responding to a situation or person in a stereotypical fashion, and actively substituting the biased response with an unbiased one.

- *Counter-stereotypic imagining:* Detecting one's stereotypical responses and visualizing examples of people who are famous or known personally who prove the stereotype to be inaccurate.

- *Individuating:* Gathering specific information about a person so that the particulars of that person replace generic notions based on group membership.

- *Perspective taking:* Adopting the perspective of a member of a stigmatized group. (This strategy can be useful in assessing the emotional impact on individuals who are often being stereotyped in negative ways.)

- *Increasing opportunity for positive contact:* Actively seeking out situations that expose us to positive examples of stereotyped groups.

Shake off Pollyanna syndrome. Jumping in to reframe a negative association can make it seem like you are putting a positive spin on everything. Don't worry about coming off as Pollyanna. Be confident in presenting a new association. If you need to follow up and explain why you are not comfortable with the negative association someone has presented, do so. For instance, if Katie in the "in action" scenario gets a few eye rolls from her statement, then she can add, "Associating ADHD with 'spacing out' does us and the student a disservice. We know ADHD is complex. And we know that 'spacing out,' as we are calling it, can be the result of many things—a student's imagination, a boring or confusing lesson or task, or even the student taking time to process what we've just taught. Let's just be mindful of how we are connecting the two."

Practice. Like all the moves in this section, reframing a negative association once won't likely immediately stop people from making biased comments. However, when you and your colleagues intentionally do it repeatedly over time, you become aware of and interrupt the unconscious implicit biases that you have.

Find the right words:

- *Alternatively . . .*

- *Or, it might be that . . .*

- *That statement associates X with Y. Instead, let's associate X with Z.*

- *Who can lead us in reframing what was said in a way that conveys the high expectations we have for these students?*

- *I think your intent is to . . . but the impact of your statement on me is . . .*

Related readings:

Move 5.18, "Interrupt negative energy." When conversation enters a black hole of negativity, pull people out with a task that will reset the group.

Move 9.8, "Reframe talk about resistance." People often assign negative attributes to a person who shows reluctance to change. Insert different language that can get people to see the benefits of resistance.

8.8 Contrast with a high-expectations belief statement.

Ever go to a paint store to pick out a white? Look at a swatch in isolation and it seems just right, but then contrast it with another and, suddenly, your "crisp white" looks more like a dull yellow. Comments that harbor low expectations can go unnoticed when presented in isolation as a joke or a casual side comment. Skillful team leaders (STLs) help make them visible by intentionally contrasting them with high-expectations belief statements. This is also known as "'counter-stereotyping,' in which individuals are exposed to information that is the opposite of the stereotypes they have about a group" (U.S. Department of Justice Community Relations Service, n.d., p. 2).

How to contrast with a high-expectations belief statement:

Listen for a low-expectations assumption made about students, families, or educators. People might laugh at the comment, reassure the person who said it that it's OK, or not even notice it was said. Pause conversation and present your contrasting belief statement in a matter-of-fact, nonjudgmental way. Beyond voicing a contrasting statement, you might also counter-stereotype with data/evidence to help your colleagues actually observe the high expectations that they do not yet see.

In action:

Teacher 1:   The day these kids write in complete sentences is the day I can retire!

Teacher 2:   Well, don't buy that lake house just yet. [*Light laughter.*]

Ronaldo: [*Smiles.*] I think you can go ahead and at least buy your retirement boat because not only will students write in complete sentences, but they will also write convincing arguments based on evidence by the end of the year. We just need to come up with the instructional plan to get them there. Let's start.

STL recommendation:

Preempt with norms. It can be hard to be the one who responds to an off-color comment when everyone else in the room brushes it off as lighthearted and funny. If you are about to engage in a difficult conversation, or any conversation about looking at student data, set a norm so people know that humor at the expense of others is not acceptable. For example: "Speak as if parents were in the room." "Make jokes, but not at the expense of others."

Preserve the dignity of others. Your goal in using any of these moves is neither to embarrass anyone nor to puncture the energy in the room, but you should not let slide, comments that harbor low expectations about students and families, even when those comments are framed as a joke. Respond just as casually as the person who made the joke (no need to get indignant), and be mindful of your tone. Clearly convey high expectations in your words. Then nimbly redirect to the task at hand.

PRIMARY
INTENTION 8

Find the right words:

- *There might be truth to that, but . . . [offer a high-expectations belief statement]*

- *[repeat low expectations comment] . . . yet students are . . . [name high expectations comment]*

- *I know we are making light of this, but let's raise our expectations.*

8.9 Capitalize on a learning moment.

Here's a familiar scenario: You're deep into a lesson when a student makes an off-color comment that causes the class to erupt into laughter. Rather than get mad, you use this as a teachable moment. Skillful team leaders (STLs) don't necessarily "teach" their colleagues (as this can create an unhealthy power dynamic, particularly in cultures with low trust), but they do intentionally capitalize on learning moments. I don't intend to split hairs with language here, but a *learning* moment, as opposed to a *teaching* moment, is one in which you invite your team to reflect on what's been said and then together formulate new learning.

How to capitalize on a learning moment:

Recognize when a comment contains antiquated thinking, bias, or negative assumptions. Pause the conversation and bring forward new learning.

In action:

Teacher 1:   I wonder if your student noticed the word *not* in question 4.

Teacher 2:   I'd be lucky if he noticed there was even a test in front of him! [*Light laughter.*]

Len: All kidding aside, it's common for students to miss the word *not*. That type of question is designed to assess if students are close reading. Given the student missed the word, do you think he needs help in this area?

STL recommendations:

Watch your tone. Be careful not to offer up new learning to your colleagues in a way that appears condescending or paints you as a know-it-all. This does not need to be a pedestal moment.

Refer to a credible source. Some people are more receptive to learning moments when you ground the information in research or cite a professional author they might recognize or even a well-respected colleague in the building.

Find the right words:

- *All kidding aside, this tells us . . .*

- *Let's use this as a learning moment and revisit what we know about X . . .*

- *Your remark makes me think that this is a good opportunity for us to further learn about X.*

- *I used to think that also, until . . .*

8.10 Address deficit thinking.

The heart of collaborative inquiry is working through students' real problems, but this does not mean flooding a discussion with evidence of what students cannot do. It's understandable that teachers might talk about students' shortcomings (or those of their parents), and even well-intentioned educators sometimes speak of students who are homeless; who experience extreme poverty; who have a history of trauma, violence, or chronic stress; who have physical disabilities or learning differences; or who experience some other hardship, as victims who must be saved. However, this deficit thinking does no one any good. Skillful team leaders (STLs) recognize and address deficit thinking.

How to address deficit thinking:

When you hear deficit thinking, shift talk so that your team sees the whole child—talents, gifts, and strengths, as well as areas for growth. Aim to build off the many strengths that these students have. Do not let disadvantages lower your standards or make you doubt your team's collective efficacy.

In action:

A high school instructional leadership team led by STL Karen Coyle Aylward discusses how to implement academic socialization when students with certain disadvantages may not have access to their parents as often as other students do.

Teacher 1:   I get that we want to give assignments that get kids talking to their parents, but I'm worried we might single out a student who doesn't have a parent at home or a good relationship with one. And, if we assign tasks like this that disadvantaged kids can't do, aren't we penalizing them for something that's not their fault? Maybe it's better not to do it.

Karen: I hear you and appreciate you highlighting that segment of our student population, but I think it is important to remember with something like this that the goal is improvement, not perfection. So, if I were giving a student assignment including six reflection questions and question 5 involved having a conversation with a parent or caretaker—say, about post-graduation plans and steps the student can take now to get there—and the student completed all of them except for question 5, I wouldn't deduct any credit. So no one is being penalized for their circumstances.

Also, I think, we need to think in terms of what students *do* have. The research didn't say this, but I think academic socialization could happen with any trusted adult; it doesn't have to be a parent. Adolescents who may face challenges at home likely still have access to a trusted adult with whom they can have a talk about school and their goals, hopes, and dreams for the future. The goal is for them to have the conversation.

Teacher 2: I don't even use the word *parent*. I say *family member* or *older friend*.

Teacher 1: I like that. And reframe the prompt to say, "If you have access to a trusted adult . . ."

Karen: And finally, let's not lose sight of all those students who *do* have parents in their lives and *can* meet these expectations, and those parents who are looking to us for ways to engage. The benefits to them are worth us assigning the task. Our principal is always urging us to interpret "equity work" not as setting the bar low so that everyone can reach it, but as raising the bar and finding innovative ways for all kids to access it. So instead of dismissing good ideas like this because some students have a disadvantage, let's implement them, play to what students do have and can do, and simultaneously seek ways to support those students who may not have this support at home.

Find the right words:

- *Does this viewpoint affirm any negative stereotypes about students/ families?* (STL Osamagbe [Osa] Osagie recommends this question.)

- *Let's name the strengths that we see in students before we address the deficits.*

- *I've noticed that we voiced the problems that students are showing. What strengths do we see?*

- *I'm concerned that the challenges we have named might be overshadowing the incredible gifts that our students bring. Let's dive into those for a moment and see how we can capitalize on them.*

- *We are focused on students with great needs. Let's also think about those students who don't have such needs. Are there beneficial decisions we can make or actions we can take for those students as well?*

Related reading:

Move 1.7, "Leverage strengths in disability." Discuss any learning differences, disabilities, or disadvantages that you or your colleagues have experienced that might better help you understand students.

CULTIVATE DIVERSE PERSPECTIVES

If you assemble a team consisting of a white 60-year-old woman born in the South, a Black 32-year-old man from New York, and an Asian non-binary 25-year-old from California, can you be assured that you have assembled a diverse group? Educational psychologist Brooke Carroll would say, not quite. She astutely points out, "You can have a very diverse group of people based on their social identifiers who really are very homogeneous in the way that they think." On the flip side, she says, "You can have diversity of thought within a very homogenous group of people. They can have very different ways of thinking" (see Cort, 2020). It is always a goal to bring together educators who identify differently by race, gender, age, region, and so on. (This typically starts with hiring.) But assembling a group of "diverse-looking" people does not guarantee that people will hold widely divergent perspectives, which is important in group problem solving and decision making (Adams, 2021). The good news is, however, that diversity of thought, as it is known, can be cultivated. Through engaging others in flexible thinking exercises, skillful team leaders (STLs) encourage diverse perspective taking.

STL moves:

8.11 Exercise flexible thinking.

8.12 Spotlight the minority viewpoint.

8.13 Invite dissent.

8.14 Advocate with humility.

What these moves promote:

Learning outcomes. Better group decisions are made when people engage in flexible thinking.

Self-awareness. People recognize the mental modes in which they are stuck.

Productive conflict. People engage in exercises in which it is safe to voice opposing opinions.

When to use these moves:

Throughout a team's course of inquiry and learning, particularly during the *Strategize & Design* STL phase of collaborative inquiry when people are generating and planning to test out solutions.

8.11 Exercise flexible thinking.

I was born on my mother's birthday, yet we approach problems and decisions very differently. We joke that instead of me being "the apple that doesn't fall far from the tree," I somehow dropped down as a cantaloupe. I'm a hyper-analytical "head" person, and she is "all heart" led by feelings and intuition. When we are fixed in these ways of thinking, conflict can ensue, but when we are able to flexibly think beyond our go-to modes and assume the other person's way of thinking, we develop a better understanding of each other and the problem at hand.

Collaborative inquiry is about uncovering problems and testing out solutions to achieve better outcomes. But our success can be limited by our fixed mental modes of thinking. (As the infamous Einstein quote goes, "We can't solve problems by using the same kind of thinking we used when we created them.") Like a muscle that needs to be worked in different ways, thinking needs to be stretched (Cort, 2020). Skillful team leaders (STLs) intentionally create safe and structured opportunities for people to practice voicing diverse ideas respectfully, and encourage individuals to go beyond their own mental modes by engaging in flexible thinking.

In this section, I present three team exercises that can help you and your colleagues practice flexible thinking and cultivate diversity of thought:

1. **Agree/Disagree**—an exercise where a group airs diverse perspectives to further their understanding of a complex decision or issue and, when possible, consensus.

2. **For vs. Against**—an exercise that requires people to argue from a perspective that is not their own.

3. **Edward de Bono's (1999) Six Thinking Hats**—a group process for engaging in flexible thinking to arrive at well-thought-out decisions.

1. Agree/Disagree

In this exercise, group members air diverse perspectives to further their understanding of a complex decision or issue and, when possible, come to consensus.

Group: One or more groups of 4–7 people.

Prep: Write 3 to 5 position statements about a specific topic, issue, or decision that needs to be made. Make 3 signs in 3 different colors or with 3 different symbols: Agree (green ☑), Disagree (red ☒), and No Consensus Yet (yellow ☐). Each group should have their own set of 3 cards. (For example, if you have 4 groups, you will need a total of 4 sets of cards, totaling 12.)

Minimum time required: 2–3 minutes per statement plus a 3- to 5-minute debrief at the end of the exercise.

(Continued)

(Continued)

How to lead:

1. Form table groups of 4–7 people.

2. Flash and read aloud one position statement on your screen or somewhere that everyone can see.

3. Give table groups about 2–3 minutes to discuss whether they agree or disagree with the position statement as it's written.

4. Aim for consensus. If the team unanimously agrees with the position statement, they hold up the Agree card. Likewise, if they unanimously disagree, they display the Disagree card. If a group cannot come to consensus within the time limit, ask them to hold up the No Consensus Yet card.

5. If all groups display the same opinion (e.g., all 4 table groups hold up Agree cards), then move on to the next position statement. If there is discrepancy between groups, lead a whole-team discussion to understand where different perspectives exist.

6. Debrief as a group about any struggle you experienced when trying to come to consensus as a team. Were you able to explore diverse ways of thinking, but still come to consensus? If not, why not? How flexible were you in your thinking?

Upside:

- Encourages diversity of thought.

- Works well with any size of group.

- Immediately engages a group in discussion.

- Provides an opportunity to visually see where everyone stands in a short amount of time.

Downside:

- It can be challenging for a leader to select a few key position statements that can be viewed from multiple perspectives and are worthy of discussion.

STL recommendations for Agree/Disagree:

Avoid right and wrong position statements. The success of this exercise really depends on the position statements selected. Choose statements that are nuanced and complex and get people thinking on both sides of an issue or decision. For instance, if you are making decisions about transforming your grading policy, don't pose the statement "Mistakes are necessary for learning" because who would argue with that? Instead, present a statement where you anticipate diverse positions such as "Effort should be factored into a grade." This is a position statement that could be argued both ways. It takes multiple perspectives and group discussion to arrive at an agreed-upon response.

Start with a "softball." Choose a fun controversial position statement such as "Our home team will make it to the Super Bowl this year." This helps people learn how the exercise works and gets people comfortable expressing diverse positions in a low-stakes way.

"It depends." This is a phrase you will likely hear uttered by one of your colleagues about a position statement that seems vague or that could be interpreted more than one way. They might look to you to clarify the statement. Unless it's a wording error on your part, it's best to allow the group to interpret each position statement as they see it, because discussing the gray areas in a statement allows diverse ideas to come forward.

2. For vs. Against

I created this exercise because I wanted people to do more than listen to a viewpoint different from their own; I wanted them to try it on. In this exercise, individuals participate in "boxing rounds" in which they argue on behalf of a viewpoint assigned to them, even if it's different from what they actually believe.

Group: 6 or more people. Large, even-numbered groups are ideal.

Prep: Write 3–5 position statements, similar to the statements in the game Agree/Disagree.

Minimum time required: 2–3 minutes per statement plus a 3- to 5-minute debrief at the end of the exercise.

How to lead:

1. Invite people to stand with a partner. Do not show the position statement at this time.

2. Before seeing the position statement that they will debate, partners decide who will argue *for* the statement and who will argue *against* the statement.

3. Once partners have chosen sides, flash on the screen or somewhere that everyone can see, and read aloud one position statement.

4. Give people 1 minute each to argue their preassigned side.

(Continued)

(Continued)

5. Play music to indicate the round is over. (A boxing bell can be fun.) When they hear the signal, people find a new partner and repeat the exercise with a new position statement.

6. Lead 3–5 rounds. Keep the exercise to under 15 minutes.

7. Debrief as a group about any struggle you experienced when arguing or listening to a position that you didn't believe. How challenging was it to flexibly think from another person's perspective? How did doing so help you understand better an opposing position to your own?

Example: For round 1 of the game, Marisol decides she will be "for" the position statement and Ishaan agrees to be "against" it. Next, they read the statement: "Children are motivated by failing grades." In real life Marisol does not agree with the statement, but because she chose the "for" position, she must defend this statement.

Upside:

• Encourages empathy and flexible thinking.

• Works well with any sized group.

• Energizes a group when led as a movement activity.

• People enjoy (and feel challenged by) the unexpected twist in having to defend or argue for something they disagree with.

• Works well as an icebreaker or community builder because participants engage with different people for each round.

Downside:

• If you choose to play this exercise as "boxing rounds," each round should be short, which doesn't give time for long deep discussion if some people want that.

STL recommendations:

Stick to your side. Remind partners that regardless of what they really think about the position statement, they must stick to the "for" or "against" position that they chose *before* seeing the statement. For instance, I wrote a position statement about Deflategate as a warm-up in a workshop for some New England team leaders. (You may remember this was a controversial story about whether or not the Patriots football team, with then quarterback Tom Brady, cheated by deflating the football.) I had to remind pairs that in this game, the partner who chose "for" in advance of seeing the statement would need to argue in favor of the belief that Brady *did* deliberately deflate the football, even if they were a die-hard Patriots fan who believed Brady would never do anything wrong. Talk about requiring flexible thinking.

3. Six Thinking Hats

This is a technique designed by Edward de Bono (1999) for teams to examine a complex problem or decision from diverse perspectives. Six Thinking Hats helps team members avoid function hurdles such as indecision, poor decisions, aimless conversation, and miscommunication. It nudges people to think flexibly beyond their default mode and bring cohesion to a team. It's particularly useful to a team in which there is push and pull between wanting to make visionary decisions—what could and should be—and the need to leave the meeting with practical here-and-now decisions. The following is a guide to the Six Thinking Hats symbols:

- **Blue hat:** Manage the process (state the goal, decide the order of hats, plan action steps, debrief the decision-making process and collaboration).

- **Red hat:** Express gut instincts, interpretations, and emotions without a need for justification.

- **White hat:** Examine data and facts. Identify what data you need.

- **Green hat:** Generate creative innovative ideas, brainstorm possibilities, and explore alternate options.

- **Yellow hat:** Highlight the plusses and benefits and maintain optimism.

- **Purple hat:** Anticipate hurdles, analyze risk, evaluate, and constructively criticize.

Note: De Bono (1999) originally calls the purple hat the black hat. A very important hat for a group to wear, it is used when people evaluate potential solutions and voice concerns and risks that could get in the way of successful implementation. But some people associate the hat with obstructing thinking and take offense to the color, assuming negative connotations about race. A number of facilitators have thus changed the color of the hat to purple, as I have done in this chapter. Know your group. If the name of any color will get in the way of people accepting the exercise, change it. You could give the hats numbers or animal names—whatever works for your team.

Group: Any team, any size.

Prep: Handout describing the thinking for each hat.

Minimum time required: If led as designed by de Bono (1999), this process could take up to one hour in one sitting.

How to lead:

1. Select a timekeeper and a facilitator.

2. The facilitator begins the discussion with the blue hat:
   - Explain how the team will use the Six Thinking Hats process.
   - Articulate succinctly the complex decision to be made by the group.

(Continued)

(Continued)

3. Name the intended outcome for the conversation. The facilitator navigates discussion in which the whole group spends a set amount of time "wearing" the same thinking hat before moving on to a new thinking hat. The facilitator can lead discussion in any sequence; however, often the facts (white hat) precede creative problem solving (green hat), and yellow and purple hats (pros and cons to a solution) follow the green hat.

4. The facilitator ends the discussion with the blue hat:
   • Clarify the reached decision and next steps.
   • Debrief the process.

Upside:

• Encourages flexible thinking.

• A group typically arrives at creative solutions people feel ownership over.

• Efficient use of time. Discussion does not wander in circles or linger in one mode. If you lead the full process, it is a big time investment upfront; however, it actually saves the group time from revisiting the problem later.

Downside:

• Best led by a skillful, intentional facilitator.

• Takes a few times for the group to get used to only thinking with one hat on, and for some this restriction can feel frustrating.

Note: Six Thinking Hats is a lengthy process. Including a team example in this book would extend over multiple pages. Go to the Resources page at www.elisamacdonald .com to read an example.

Additional resource:

• Brainy Dose. (2018, August 25). *The Six Thinking Hats technique for problem solving* [Video]. YouTube. https://www.youtube.com/watch?v=PASrBGtcrdU

Think like a teacher:

Tweens and teens tend to have strong one-sided opinions. It can be a challenge to get them to see a different person's perspective or a different way of doing something. And so as a teacher you engage students in exercises that require them to flex their thinking. I've seen teachers have students write a persuasive essay from two people's perspectives, debate two sides of an issue, read narratives from people who were at the same historical event but experienced it differently, or create a piece of art with everyday objects that require them to think flexibly about how those objects are used. Each time you do things like this as a teacher, you are helping students get unstuck from one way of thinking.

Adults have had a lifetime of experiences that, for better or worse, sometimes keep them fixed in their opinions. They can benefit from practicing flexible thinking. Where younger learners might need more scaffolding (e.g., relying on sentence starters or management strategies like tossing a ball to speak so that they don't talk over one another), adults typically don't. In fact, your colleagues are likely to be turned off if you use these aids. However, offering structures such as the ones in this section can encourage flexible thinking without being condescending to adult learners.

8.12 Spotlight the minority viewpoint.

You can almost feel the momentum when ideas take flight and every member of your team is on board. It's an energy that high-functioning Q1 and Q2 teams especially experience and don't want to lose. Momentum works in favor of majority-supported ideas, but isn't so great for giving airtime to hear minority viewpoints. I cite Myrna Lewis in Move 3.1, but her words bear repeating here: "There is wisdom in the minority" (see Lewis, 2016; Lewis & Woodhull, 2018). The "minority view" references that which isn't the widespread view of the majority. Skillful team leaders (STLs) intentionally spotlight the minority view so that people hear the less popular view and give it the attention it deserves.

How to spotlight the minority viewpoint:

Listen for tiny moments where someone voices a perspective that might not be held by the majority of people in the room. The voice might come from some-one who is part of or speaking on behalf of an underrepresented group. Give your support to the person who said it. Make time and invite your colleagues to understand the minority viewpoint.

In action:

Jemma and her English language arts team are deciding on a focus for their team inquiry.

Jemma:	We are aiming to improve students' skills to access complex texts. Today we are narrowing our focus to name what we see as areas of much-needed growth for students.
Teacher 1:	Definitely the need to infer. It's a high-level skill, and complex texts are full of inferences.
Teacher 2:	And when kids make an inference, they don't always know how to back their claim up with evidence from the text.
Teacher 3:	I completely agree.
Teacher 4:	Me too. This inquiry focus works perfectly with our upcoming poetry unit.

Teacher 5:	And the state test always asks kids to make inferences, so that's another plus.
Special educator:	The students I serve could certainly benefit from improving their inference skills, but I also see vocabulary development as key. Often I see students with specific language disabilities struggle with a complex text because they don't have exposure to the vocabulary and lack strategies to attack unknown words. But I'm happy to go along with whatever the group wants to do, and actually the vocab focus might only affect my kids and might not be a pressing need for the whole team to address.
Jemma:	It might not be a big problem across the board, but if it is a big problem for those students, we should not overlook it. Let's write down inferring as a possible focus, but now talk about the vocabulary needs these students have.

Find the right words:

- *Let's not gloss over that point. It might not affect everyone, but it's important to explore.*

- *I'm so glad you brought that up because I wasn't even thinking about it from that perspective.*

- *It's so easy to focus on what impacts the majority of students, but we can't forget that the work we do for the few can be just as important.*

- *I welcome it if anyone wants to bring up a less popular viewpoint.*

8.13 Invite dissent.

The 1978 packaging for Pepperidge Farm® Goldfish® crackers showed a school of tiny fish all swimming in the same direction, except for one. I don't know why they changed it to have them all swimming together. I think the little guy who boldly took a different path represented an important aspect of teams (even if he was just a cracker)—specifically the concept of diversity of thought. Skillful team leaders (STLs) intentionally invite dissent. They create a space where people are expected to push back on ideas, challenge positions, share opposing viewpoints, and disagree.

How to invite dissent:

Show genuine appreciation for people who voice their perspectives or opinions. Then, give the floor to others who hold a different position. Even if no one initially voices a different point of view, invite someone to take the devil's advocate position, if for no other reason than to shed light on what might not have been considered.

In action:

Teachers speak in enthusiastic support of ideas presented in a professional reading.

Teacher 1:	I don't mean to sound contrarian, but I don't agree with what the author is saying.
Mike:	Not at all. I'm so glad you are expressing a different point of view. What in the reading do you disagree with, and why?

STL recommendations:

Discourage self-censorship. Notice when colleagues self-censor. This could look like people prefacing their views with a disclaimer, such as "This is probably a dumb idea, but . . . ," or dismissing their own idea before they finish speaking. Ask them directly to continue voicing their idea. If people self-censor frequently in front of you or another leader, it might be that they feel intimidated. Be hyper-aware of your response (or another leader's response) to someone who voices dissent.

Don't abandon your norms. STL Osamagbe (Osa) Osagie reminds her teams that voicing dissent doesn't mean neglecting the norms to which everyone has agreed. Encourage your colleagues to voice disagreement without personal attacks. Insist that people deliver opposing viewpoints in a way that others can hear.

Find the right words:

- *Are you open to someone pushing back on that idea?*
- *In what ways do you disagree?*
- *I don't hold the same position as you. Here's what I think and why . . .*
- *I welcome anyone who has a different perspective to speak.*
- *The concerns you raise are valid and worth exploring here.*

Related reading:

Part II, Chapter 4, "The Psychology of Groups." Learn how social influences can impact a person's willingness to dissent from the group.

8.14 Advocate with humility.

Teachers and advocacy are not unrelated. In fact, many teacher leaders speak up for teachers and students at the district and policy level, and thank goodness they do. Effective teacher leaders understand that controversial issues are often complex and nuanced. They do not charge at people with their positions; they engage in dialogue. They advocate from a place of moral values, fighting for equity and social justice, but do so in a way that does not erode trust, shut people down, or polarize people. In their advocacy work, they remain open to learning what they might not know. Skillful team leaders (STLs) advocate with humility.

How to advocate with humility:

Before you advocate for your position, reflect on the following:

- *Timing.* How will others respond if I speak out now? Are others in the right mindset to hear my position? Is there a better time for me to advocate?

- *Source.* Am I the best person to deliver this message? Would my message be better received coming from someone else?

- *Motive*: Am I advocating from a place of values and principles, or am I speaking up because I am primed for a fight?

When you advocate for your position, consider the following:

- *Be confident.* Don't hem and haw around your position. Voice it clearly so there is no ambiguity about where you stand.

- *Communicate values.* People might disagree with your position, but if they learn of the values on which it is based, they may more likely be open to dialogue.

- *Watch your volume, emotions, and tone.* Saying your position loudly, forcefully, or through tears might get people's attention, but it can also turn some people away.

- *Adopt humility.* Holding strong to your position because you believe in it is admirable, but be mindful that there is always the possibility that you are missing something that others see. Seek to understand alternate perspectives with an openness to be influenced. You may not flip sides, but at best you'll gain a nuanced understanding about your position and the other person's differing position.

STL recommendation:

Self-monitor. Notice how frequently you advocate. Too much might give you a reputation as someone who is just about the fight. Too little can give others the impression that you are willing to do whatever anyone wants and don't act from your own principles and values.

Find the right words:

- *I am advocating for . . . And here's what led me to this position . . . I want to better understand those who disagree with me.*

- *I feel strongly that . . . Because . . . Help me understand your different point of view.*

- *Here's where I stand . . . This position comes from my belief that . . . I'd like to hear from opposing positions.*

- *I'm not changing my position, but I see now where you are coming from.*

- *In listening to you I now realize I was advocating so hard for this that I overlooked . . .*

MAKE CLEAR IMPACTFUL DECISIONS

It's the first week of my freshman year of college. I don't know anyone and become "friends" with everyone on my dorm floor. This means a very large group of 18-year-old girls jointly deciding what time to go to dinner and which dining hall. Nightmare.

Group decision making can be challenging, even beyond choosing between the place with the salad bar or the one with the taco bar. People are subject to social influences such as groupthink and group polarization (explored in Part II, Chapter 4), and that can result in poor decision making. If anyone perceives that the process a group uses to reach a decision is flawed, then they are less likely to want to implement the decision (Bagozzi et al., 2003). And, for low-functioning Q3 and Q4 teams, it's not uncommon for people to leave a meeting unsure of next steps.

Skillful team leaders (STLs) intentionally design and communicate a decision-making process that people can feel confident in. There is no ambiguity about how decisions are made or who ultimately has the authority to make them. They bring forward diverse voices so that the team can arrive at a thoughtful decision, and ensure people leave the meeting with clarity about next steps.

STL moves:

8.15 Clarify the decision-making process.

8.16 Reach agreement on group decisions.

8.17 Commit to action.

8.18 Communicate a changed decision.

What these moves promote:

Clarity. There is no ambiguity about how decisions are made.

Harmony. People are able to come to a thoughtful decision without causing team function issues.

When to use these moves:

During any moment when a team needs to make a decision. Teams make a multitude of decisions during all STL Phases of Collaborative Inquiry.

- *Ask & Aim:* Teams decide on which priority to focus and what inquiry questions to explore.
- *Assess & Analyze:* Teams decide what assessments to give.
- *Target & Plan:* Teams decide goals and a plan to reach them.
- *Research & Study:* Teams decide what research and texts to study.

- *Strategize & Design:* Teams decide how to implement something new and how to assess progress.

- *Act & Evaluate:* Teams decide what they might do differently during the next inquiry cycle.

Related reading:

Move 6.11, "(Heartfelt) Connect to what matters." Gauge your team's comfort and confidence in the group decision-making process for generating a team S-M-A-A-H-R-T goal that matters.

8.15 Clarify the decision-making process.

If Dante were seeking suggestions for a 10th circle of hell, I'd vote for it to be "ambiguity." Uncertainty, coupled with a lack of clarity, at best feels unsettling and at worst feels paralyzing. We learn to tolerate ambiguity when we don't yet know what *outcomes* we will achieve, but we should not accept ambiguity in the decision-making *process*. Even if people aren't keen on how much say they have in a final decision, people appreciate having clarity about their role in making the decision upfront. Skillful team leaders (STLs) intentionally clarify the process.

How to clarify the decision-making process:

The following questions, organized into five categories, can help you clarify the decision-making process for everyone on the team:

1. *The decision.*
   - What decision(s) have already been made that are non-negotiable?
   - What decision(s) needs to be made?
   - Why does this decision need to be made?
   - Who will this decision affect?

2. *Roles in decision making.*
   - Who is responsible for making the final decision, and what role do others play in it? Which responsibility "bucket" does this decision fall into? (See the shaded box on page 384 for an explanation of buckets.)
   - If making the decision as a group, then what level of agreement do we need—majority rule, consensus, unanimous enthusiastic agreement, or another level?
   - How many steps are there in the decision-making process? Will people's involvement be the same throughout the process?

3. *Decision logistics.*
   - What needs to be prepared/done in order for this decision to be implemented?

- Who will do what's needed to prepare?
- By when will preparations get done?

4. *Decision accountability and evaluation.*

- Who is responsible for implementing this decision, and how will they be kept accountable?
- Who will evaluate the implications of this decision, and when?
- (Post-implementation) What modifications, if any, should be made to this decision?

5. *Reflection on the group decision-making process.*

- How satisfied were people with the decision-making process?
- How can we improve our collaborative decision-making process for future decisions?

Decision-making buckets

I worked with a principal, now superintendent, who told me how she used the concept of buckets to explain her decision-making approach. I have adapted it slightly and provide relatable family-life examples to help distinguish between the buckets. (Note: In no way are these examples meant to compare school leaders to parents, or teachers to children. They are simply a way to demonstrate how the approach would work between people who hold different levels of authority.)

BUCKET	DESCRIPTION	REAL-WORLD EXAMPLE
1. **"Me"**	An individual is *the* decision maker. This person's role is to communicate the decision clearly. Neither debate nor feedback is sought. Those affected by the decision have no say in the decision. (Note: Typically the deciders have information that others are not privy to.)	Parents decide their teenager will not go out Saturday night. They communicate and explain this to the teenager. The teenager asks questions to understand the decision, but cannot influence the decision and has no choice but to accept it.

BUCKET	DESCRIPTION	REAL-WORLD EXAMPLE
2. **"Me with input"**	An individual is *the* decision maker but seeks feedback from other stakeholders such as teachers, students, and families in order to influence the final decision.	Parents have not yet decided if the teenager will be permitted to go out Saturday night. They invite the teenager to give her opinion. After genuinely listening, the parents decide the teenager can go.
3. **"Us"**	An individual collaborates with others, and together they come to a decision, typically through consensus (an agreement that everyone can live with) or majority rule (a vote) or unanimous decision (an agreement is not reached until everyone enthusiastically agrees or disagrees).	Parents and the teenager sit together to discuss the pros and cons of the teenager going out Saturday night. They take a vote (2:1 in favor of the teenager going out).
4. **"You"**	One person or group, typically an authority figure, fully empowers another person or group to make the decision. The authority figure accepts whatever decision is made. Note: STLs only put decisions into this bucket when they feel confident that the decision makers share the same mission, vision, and values as they do.	The teenager is empowered fully to decide if she will go out Saturday night. The teenager decides she will. Her parents must accept her decision.

STL reflection questions: Look at the decisions you have made over time. Do most fall into one bucket? If yes, is this intentional? What might it say about your leadership style if all your decisions are made by you alone (bucket 1?) Is making every decision by consensus (bucket 3) the most efficient way to lead? Be deliberate when you involve others in decision making and to what extent.

STL recommendations:

Get the roles right. There are a variety of acronyms that can help clarify roles in decision-making. Here is a popular one:

RAPID is a organizational tool developed by Paul Rogers and Marcia W. Blenko (2006) to help clarify responsibilities. Note: The five words represented in the acronym do not follow the exact sequence of letters in RAPID, but the designers wanted a word for people to remember the roles.

Person(s) who **recommend** a course of action based on evidence.

Person(s) who must **agree** to move forward and have the ability to change the course of action.

Person(s) who will give **input** into the decision.

Person(s) who will ultimately **decide** the course of action and commit the team to it.

Person(s) who will **perform** the decision.

If you're looking for more details, the authors include a primer in their article "Who Has the D?" (Rogers & Blenko, 2006).

Manage expectations. Establish the expectation that not every decision will be made collaboratively. Some are better made by one person or a small group of people.

Communicate the why. If your team is used to making every decision collaboratively, presenting a decision you must make alone can make people feel left out. Express your appreciation for others, but communicate why this decision must be made by you alone. The reverse is true as well. If your school culture is such where one person typically makes most decisions and others are not involved, people might initially be mistrustful when you invite them to collaboratively decide.

Find the right words:

- The decision: *Here's the decision that must be made . . . because it will affect . . .*

- Roles: *This is the [first] step in the decision-making process. This decision falls in bucket [1, 2, 3, or 4]. (If it is a collaborative decision) We will reach agreement through . . .*

- Logistics: *Let's be clear about what each of us needs to do to implement this decision and by when.*

- Accountability and evaluation: *Let's circle back by [date] to report on how this decision is affecting others and tweak it if needed.*

- Process: *On a scale of 1 to 5, 1 being least satisfied and 5 being most satisfied, please rate your satisfaction with our decision-making process and make one recommendation for future group decision making.*

8.16 Reach agreement on group decisions.

How do couples on the HGTV show *Love It or List It* decide whether to stay in their newly renovated house or move to a new one? The premise of the reality show is that the couple can't agree from the start, yet by the end, after a spiffy renovation and several home searches, they come to a unified decision. Whether the show is actual reality or designed by producers to hold viewers' interest, one thing is real: Group decision making is not easy. Skillful team leaders (STLs) intentionally use a range of methods to help a group make collaborative decisions to which everyone can commit.

How to reach agreement on group decisions:

A few popular methods are described as follows.

Distill the *what* from the *how.*

If you and your partner are raising children together and find yourselves in a heated moment over how to parent, you're likely more on the same page than you think. Joined together by shared values and goals, you both want what's best, but may have differences of opinion about how to reach them. Teams engage in this same struggle when trying to make a decision, causing people to think they are further apart than they really are. One way in which STLs reach consensus is by distilling the *what* from the *how.*

How to distill the what *from the* how:

Aim to find agreement in what your group values and is trying to accomplish. Then, determine if you also need to come to consensus on strategy.

Find the right words:

- *Can we come to consensus on what we are trying to accomplish for [students/families] first, before looking for agreement in how to get there?*

- *Let's first agree on what we value and the outcome we are looking for. Then let's decide if we need to come to consensus on strategy.*

Agree to content, not wording.

Wordsmithing (editing the language of something for clarity and style) is a useful move when language matters, but when it stands in the way of consensus on a decision, STLs agree first to the content of what is being written, then to how it is phrased.

How to agree to content, not wording:

Before you get lost in bickering over verbs, boil down to the essence of what is being said. Find agreement in the substance. Celebrate the group for accomplishing what they have thus far, and then decide who will revise the wording at a later date. You might couple this with Move 5.10 to get someone to volunteer to wordsmith outside of the meeting.

Find the right words:

- *If we can't yet agree on the wording, can we agree on the substance of the document?*

- *We agree on what the decision should be. On your own time, go into our shared doc and make suggestions for the word choice and tone of how we will communicate the decision.*

- *We have some disagreement on the right language to use. Ms. Z, you have expressed some important opinions on how it should be worded. Are you open to revising it on your own, and then bringing it back to our next meeting for final tweaks?*

Conduct an inverse poll.

Watch any movie in which two people are getting married, and you'll likely hear, "If anyone can show just cause why this couple *cannot* lawfully be joined together in holy matrimony, speak now or forever hold your peace." This is an example of an inverse poll, where you ask for objections instead of agreement. Asking for agreement can result in compliance, but inviting objections calls on people to reconcile what they can and can't live with, and makes it OK for them to speak up. STLs use this move to intentionally bring forward objections and reach consensus.

How to conduct an inverse poll:

Think of a regular poll question (e.g., "Who agrees?") and ask the inverse using words such as *not* (e.g., "Who does not agree?"). (Note: If an inverse poll feels like it might stifle someone from voicing disagreement, you can always take a regular poll.)

Find the right words:

- *Is there anyone who can't live with this?*

- *Would anyone like to voice a reason as to why we should not move forward?*

- *Who here is not in agreement with this decision and would like to voice their reasons to the group?*

Offer a binary choice.

When you have to choose between many options, analysis paralysis can set in. STLs are sometimes able to narrow a decision down to two options and give people a binary choice.

How to offer a binary choice:

Encourage people to state their reasons for one choice over the other and the supports they will need if the decision does not go in their favor.

STL recommendation:

Whittle down options. Although offering a binary choice can make coming to agreement easier, it can also be limiting. Voting down to preferences (the next move) might be a better choice.

Find the right words:

- *Share your reasoning for your choice.*
  - (To those who chose the minority position) *What would it take for you to come along with the majority?*
  - (To those who chose the majority position) *What value do you see in the position few or no one has selected?* (Lewis & Woodhull, 2018)

- *Both of these choices have pros and cons. In a moment I'm going to take away one of these two choices. [Pause to let people think.] Which choice were you wishing I would keep? Please voice your reasons why.*

Vote down to preferences.

It's our family holiday tradition to have a Yankee Swap gift exchange every year (also known in some regions as White Elephant or Dirty Santa) but, we up the stakes with a wrapping contest. Family members anonymously lay out on a table their wrapped masterpiece for a vote. Each person gets three sticker dots, equivalent to three votes, and is permitted to place the dots on the wrapped presents that they think should win a prize. Players can allocate the dots as they wish—all on one wrapped present if they feel it, and only it, should win, or spread them among up to three presents. The three presents with the most stickers each win a prize. When teams don't need to come to completely agree on a single choice, STLs vote down to preferences.

How to vote down to preferences:

Lay out the options on chart paper or index cards. Give people a limited number of sticker dots to circulate through the choices and place dots on all the options they can live with. Start by eliminating those options with no dots. Then invite people to discuss options with the fewest dots to confirm that people are OK discarding those choices. Be sure anyone who did place a dot on the option has an opportunity to speak in case they see something others don't. Continue this process until you have consensus on the cards with the most dots. You might need to do a second round with cards that remain before coming to consensus on a few options.

Dipstick for consensus.

You might be closer to consensus than you think. STLs gauge where a group is at by inviting colleagues to indicate if they can live with a decision, have reservations about it, or are fully opposed to it.

How to dipstick for consensus:

Similar to the dipstick method used to check for understanding with students, you can ask teachers to indicate their level of agreement using thumbs: "Give a thumbs-up if you can live with the decision whether you are enthusiastic about it or not. Give a thumbs-down if you cannot live with the decision for now."

If you don't have a thumbs-up agreement from everyone, give people an opportunity to explain their reservations or opposition, then dipstick again, or change from consensus to majority rule. If you have a complex decision to make as a team, you may need to dipstick parts so that you can identify specific areas of disagreement.

Find the right words:

- *Please give a thumbs-up if you can live with this decision for now, and a thumbs-down if you absolutely cannot.*

- *This decision has many parts. We'll dipstick and discuss each until we can come to consensus.*

Related reading:

Move 2.1, "Co-construct norms through consensus." Reach agreement on norms for your team.

8.17 Commit to action.

I see it again and again—an incredible, energizing exchange of ideas and creative solutions between team members . . . with no commitment at the end of the meeting to implement any of them. Sure, some people might try out something on their own, but there's no intentional decision or plan for what to tackle before the next meeting and the support people might need to take action. This challenge causes many high-functioning teams to become low-impact (Q2) teams. Skillful team leaders (STLs) intentionally close meetings with a commitment to action.

How to commit to action:

Because your team will want to keep one another accountable to what has been decided, it's important to gain clarity about what people are committing to before anyone takes action (Bregman, 2016).

- *Nail down details.* Specify who will do what, by when.

- *Clarify expectations.* Discuss what following through with a commitment looks like. What outcome(s) are people expected to deliver?

- *Check that each person has the capability and capacity (e.g., time) to follow through* with commitments before adjourning the meeting. Offer resources or support, if needed.

- *Gain verbal commitment.* Don't assume agreement. Get confirmation.

- Carve out time on the next agenda to *circle back* and allow people to give an update on the action they committed to doing.

- *Be transparent about any consequences*, natural or imposed, that will occur if someone does not follow through.

STL recommendations:

Announce. A sign that people are committed to an action is for them to tell students and families that they will do that action. If a person resists, they may not be fully committed to the plan, and you might need to listen to what needs they have in order to feel ready to commit.

Chart responsibilities. Include a simple table in your notes for the meeting that specifies who will do what, by when. For example:

WHO	WHAT	BY WHEN

Find the right words:

- *Let's be explicit about next steps and commit to one another to follow through.*

- *Who will do what, by when?*

- *By committing to this, you are expected to . . .*

- *Is there anything you need to be able to follow through with this commitment?*

- *I want to be upfront about consequences, should anyone not follow through with their commitment.*

Related reading:

Move 4.4, "Close a meeting to establish next steps for learning." Commit to action each time a group decision is made, and review expectations and next steps at the end of a meeting.

8.18 Communicate a changed decision.

If you've ever had the experience of discovering someone undid a decision that you had a part in making, then you likely understand the connection between decision making and trust. Whenever a communal decision gets changed, skillful team leaders (STLs) are intentionally transparent about what changed and why.

How to communicate a changed decision:

You don't need to convince others that the change to the decision was worthwhile. Do not open up conversation for negotiation or solicit input if you have no intention of switching back the decision, as this will further erode trust. Simply announce the change, state the impetus for the switch, validate any reactions people might have to hearing the change, show appreciation to them, and set up supports people might need to accept the change.

In action:

Stephanie: I know we had planned to design a lesson today to introduce the next unit; however, upon looking at the data from the last assessment, I see clearly that a handful of students need a reteach. So, instead, we will plan for them and also create an enrichment lesson for those students who do not need the additional review. I understand that this switch might feel unsettling because it is not what you had expected. I appreciate your flexibility. To get us started, I have drafted a reteach lesson plan that we can tweak.

Find the right words:

- *I had to make a change to a decision we made, and here's the thinking that went into it . . . I understand this can cause people to feel . . . Thank you for adapting.*

- *I know we agreed to do . . . but upon talking with . . . I learned . . . and this led me to change course. It's expected that you would have feelings about this last-minute switch-up; nevertheless, this is how we need to proceed. Thank you for your flexibility.*

- *This will look different from what you saw last. Let me explain the reason for the changes. You may or may not welcome this change. That's OK. I appreciate you moving forward with it.*

Primary Intention

Implement New Learning: Change, Peer Observation, and Accountability

I once co-facilitated a multi-grade team of competent, dedicated teachers who voluntarily met after school once a week for six weeks with the aim of improving students' responses to reading. Teachers combed through student notebook entries, read professional texts together about reading for adolescents, and engaged in thoughtful high-level discussion about the role metacognition plays in literacy. We produced a detailed continuum intended to assess students and set goals with them. Our team was so enthused by what we had learned and produced that teachers presented our learning to the whole department, complete with an engaging role-play. It was well received.

By all standards, our team's collaborative inquiry was successful—all standards except one: implementation. In the weeks thereafter, I met with teachers who were on the team and teachers who saw the presentation, and asked how use of the continuum was going. While a few people mentioned they tried it once or twice, no one was using it now. People continued teaching and assessing the way they had before our inquiry group. This caused me to rethink my success as a team leader.

Although a hallmark of professional learning teams is learning (hence the name), skillful team leaders (STLs) do not view collaborative inquiry as a grad-school study group. Teams research and study, but they also learn from doing. When they reach the *Act & Evaluate* STL phase of collaborative inquiry (see Figure 2, page 26), teams routinely observe one another, test out new strategies, and collect and analyze data to see how students respond. This type of collaboration calls for a culture in which people embrace change and are willing to be vulnerable with one another. STLs recognize that not everyone is comfortable with this. They set up accountability so that implementation is expected and people are supported.

Contents:

Lead peer observation.

9.1 Set a focus for peer observation.

9.2 Design a peer observation.

9.3 Choose an observation method.

9.4 Decide a means for collecting student data.

9.5 Debrief a peer observation.

9.6 Strengthen vulnerability-based trust for peer observation.

Navigate resistance to change.

9.7 Spot reluctance to change.

9.8 Reframe talk about resistance.

9.9 Address implementation questions.

9.10 Address the emotional side of change.

9.11 Remove technical barriers to implementation.

9.12 Surface competing commitments.

9.13 Focus on student impact.

9.14 Give time and space.

Invite accountability.

9.15 Partner for accountability.

9.16 Go to an authority figure.

Tools and templates:

Figure 28: STL Peer Observation Planning Template

LEAD PEER OBSERVATION*

Don't you love when you can pop across the hall and tell your colleague how your lesson went? How much more would you get out of that conversation if your colleague had actually observed your lesson? Research has found that showing, not telling, has a greater impact on learning. Judith Warren Little (2008) noticed that in high-performing schools, teams are in and out of each other's classrooms regularly, discussing peer observations. Daniel Willingham, a cognitive scientist interviewed on the *Science of Reading* podcast (Amplify Education, 2020), found that showing provides more accurate data than telling because telling involves retrospective data, which requires memory, and memory is fallible. Telling is also problematic because it means self-reporting data. It's human nature to want to present yourself in a positive light, and therefore you select data that do that (Baumeister & Hutton, 1987). Peer observation allows for teachers to show their colleagues what they are implementing, not just tell them about it.

Before teachers head into one another's classrooms, skillful team leaders (STLs) plan details that include a clear purpose for observation, thoughtful design and data collection, and a means to collaborate about what was observed. Above all else, they establish a trusting culture.

STL moves:

9.1 Set a focus for peer observation.

9.2 Design a peer observation.

9.3 Choose an observation method.

9.4 Decide a means for collecting student data.

9.5 Debrief a peer observation.

9.6 Strengthen vulnerability-based trust for peer observation.

Peer observation is a well-recognized term describing when teachers conduct live or recorded classroom observations of teaching. If your school culture, or teachers' union, bristles at the language out of concern that it indicates teachers evaluating other teachers (which it does not), you might opt for a less teacher-centric term such as *classroom or lesson observation, demonstration lesson,* or *student observation.*

Tools and templates:

Figure 28: STL Peer Observation Planning Template

What these moves promote:

Data collection. Peer observation produces observational data.

Trust. Teaching in front of colleagues requires vulnerability. Trust builds when observation is met with a positive response from colleagues.

Community. Teachers engage in a shared learning experience.

When to use these moves:

Plan peer observation during the *Strategize & Design* STL phase of collaborative inquiry. Facilitate peer observation during the *Act & Evaluate* STL phase of collaborative inquiry.

Related reading:

Part II, Chapter 6, "The Upside (and Downside) of Being a Peer Leader." Use your peer status to your advantage by demonstrating a lesson or strategy with your students. Learn about other advantages you have as a peer leader in this chapter.

Note: Moves 9.1–9.5 help you plan and debrief a peer observation. Figure 28 provides a template where you can record the decisions your team makes.

FIGURE 28   STL Peer Observation Planning Template

Use the following prompts before you lead a peer observation.

Overarching team inquiry question or team goal: _____

Focus for this observation: _____

Observation date/time/room: _____

Demonstrating teacher: _____

Student(s) being observed:

Observation method (select one):

Live*   Prerecorded video   Dry demo (without students)

*If live, name observation ground rules. (How will we show up in the classroom? As silent observers? Coaches to students? Facilitators of small groups? How will we communicate our role to students?)

_____

Description of what will be demonstrated (attach plans):

Relevant background knowledge/context: _____

Method for collecting data or guide for observation (attach recording sheets, checklists, etc.):

_____

_____

_____

_____

_____

_____

_____

Debrief of Peer Observation

Use the following prompts after you have participated in a peer observation:

Debrief date/time: _____

Observations: _____

Inferences/wonderings: _____

Implications for learning: _____

9.1 Set a focus for peer observation.

Have you ever walked into someone's classroom and become flooded with ideas that you can't wait to bring back to your room? This is wonderful. However, if you're in a classroom to participate in a peer observation lesson, what's around can distract you from your purpose for observing. While there's always good stuff to take away from seeing other classrooms, skillful team leaders (STLs) and their teams intentionally set a clear focus for peer observation that further advances their inquiry work.

How to set a focus for peer observation:

Teams often opt to participate in peer observation during the *Act & Evaluate* STL phase of collaborative inquiry. Once your team has researched and studied strategies to reach a goal, you are ready to test them out. Ask the following:

- What benefit do we hope to gain from having someone demonstrate an instructional practice?

- What can we learn from a peer observation that we might miss if we weren't seeing instruction as it unfolds?

- If one person is demonstrating instruction, what feedback are they looking for?

In action:

Matthew: We want to implement Responsive Classroom[*] and are reading about strategies for Interactive Modeling (IM). But we all agree we need to see the strategy with kids. David has agreed to open his classroom for us to observe. Before we work out logistics, let's review the Responsive Classroom Assessment Tool for Teachers so that we can know what to look for once we're in the room. The tool provides criteria for 10 practices, but for this observation we'll only focus on IM.

STL recommendation:

Design guiding prompts or rubrics. Some people can focus better when they are given (or co-create) questions/prompts or rubrics for a specific observation that name what to look for. For example, a peer observation guiding prompt might be "I want people to notice what indicators of engagement and disengagement you see from my students."

[*]Responsive Classroom. (2013, June 2). *What is Interactive Modeling?* https://www.responsive-classroom.org/what-interactive-modeling/

Responsive Classroom. (2017). *What is the Responsive Classroom Assessment Tool for Teachers?* https://www.responsiveclassroom.org/wp-content/uploads/2017/10/Becoming-an-Responsive-Classroom-Teacher.pdf

Find the right words:

- *Just a reminder that we are observing this class for the purpose of noticing X, Y, and Z.*

- *I love going into classrooms because I get so many ideas for my own students, but for the purpose of this observation, let's agree to name now what we will look for once we are in the room.*

Related reading:

Move 5.11, "Frame conversation with clear parameters." Articulate clearly the dos and don'ts of dialogue and observation.

9.2 Design a peer observation.

What will your team observe? A mini-lesson to the whole class? A teaching strategy in action? A guided reading group led by a teacher? A Socratic seminar led by students? A morning meeting? A teacher–student conference? Whatever the subject for peer observation and analysis, skillful team leaders (STLs) take time to intentionally design what someone will demonstrate. (This is often referred to as a demonstration lesson—or "demo lesson," for short—which does not have to be a full-period lesson; demo lessons can be as brief as a teacher modeling a five-minute strategy).

How to design a peer observation:

- *Begin with your student-learning target* (what you desire for students to know, understand, and do by the end of a lesson).

- *Decide upfront how you will assess student learning* of what is being taught in the demonstration, such as using a student exit ticket or classwork.

- *Use any new learning* from your team's *Research & Study* STL phase of collaborative inquiry to inform your instructional design.

- *Finalize logistics,* making decisions about the following:

  - On what day and time will the observation take place (or be recorded)?

  - Which teacher will implement the practice for observation? (Remember: Teachers can demo with another teacher's students.)

  - Which students will be observed (e.g., a whole class, a subgroup, or a single student)?

  - For how long will the observation last? Does it need to be a full class period, or will observing a specific portion of the class period meet our needs?

  - In what room will the observation take place?

STL recommendations:

Plan 1:1. If you anticipate that planning a lesson from scratch in your team meeting will be too time-consuming, or if you have a low-functioning Q3 or Q4 team and are concerned you won't get the lesson designed in time for observation, set learning targets and criteria for success with the whole team, and later meet privately with the demonstrating teacher to work out design decisions. In this way, everyone has a role in naming the objective for the demonstration lesson and is clear about what to look for when observing it in action.

Use a Tuning protocol. Your team might opt for someone to bring in an already planned lesson for demonstration, rather than designing it together. Structure the conversation with a Tuning protocol (see Move 4.7) so that people can give warm and cool feedback on the plan before the teacher implements it with students.

9.3 Choose an observation method.

Typically, when you think about demo lessons for peer observation, you imagine a group watching someone teach live. Live observation, however, is only one means of seeing instruction. Sometimes teams use prerecorded videos of classroom instruction. Sometimes teams choose to demonstrate a lesson for colleagues in a team meeting before bringing the lesson to students. I call this a "dry demo" and explain this terminology on page 403. Each method has its pros and cons. Skillful team leaders (STLs) are intentional about choosing the method that best serves their team's learning goals.

How to choose an observation method:

When deciding which method to implement, consider the school culture you are working in, the experience you are looking for, and logistics that could aid or hinder learning. Each method is described in the following section.

Methods for Peer Observation

Live Observation

Description: Live observation brings team members into a classroom to observe a demonstrating teacher lead an instructional mini-lesson, strategy, or practice with students. The team decides in advance if teachers will interact with students. The team uses observational notes to debrief the observation immediately afterward or in a subsequent team meeting.

Upside:

- Educators engage in a full observation experience in which they can view instruction and materials, interact with students, and feel the energy in the room.

- Students benefit from extra hands on deck when teachers agree that they are permitted to interact with students during the observation.

- Virtual live-stream lessons allow for teachers to observe and cross-collaborate across sites without being physically in the room.

- Opening classroom practice becomes part of school culture.

Downside:

- Live observation can be a tall task to schedule. Finding common time for multiple teachers to observe a classroom is challenging. Some schools get creative with teacher coverage, but even if you can do this, you have to weigh the costs and benefits as taking teachers out of their classes might cause more disruption to learning than benefits.

- Interruptions (a fire drill, classroom delays, etc.) can disrupt viewing.

- Teachers can lose sight of the purpose of an observation and pay more attention to things such as interesting bulletin boards than the demo lesson.

- Teachers and students might not be accustomed to many people observing, particularly in school cultures where it isn't common practice.

- Labor union guidelines might prohibit live observation.

- Even with a schedule that supports teacher coverage, it doesn't mean you will see what you planned. I remember getting coverage for a team of teachers for 20 minutes—just enough to observe a mini-lesson—but when we arrived in the classroom, the presenting teacher was still reviewing homework. Because observing teachers had to return to their own classrooms, we never got to see the planned demo lesson.

STL recommendations:

Break up your team. To alleviate scheduling challenges, you can split up a team and pair teachers for observations. Teachers lead a demo lesson with combined classes, and no substitute teachers are needed. You can also schedule post-observation debriefs of live demo lessons during a regularly scheduled team meeting time, so long as there isn't a large gap between observation and meeting.

Agree to ground rules. Together and in advance, determine how observers should or should not interact with students and each other, and how technology should or should not be used. Here are a few examples of classroom observation agreements:

- Refrain from discussing the observation while we are in the classroom.

- Be a "fly on the wall." Do not interrupt the demo lesson or engage with students.

- Record what you notice without judgment.

- Use cell phones/technology for taking photos or notes, not personal use.

- If recording, opt for audio or use video but do not record students' faces without permission.

(Continued)

(Continued)

Let the kids in on it. I was once a part of a classroom observation in which we were looking to identify how students handled struggle when the teacher did not immediately assist. We all agreed we would not talk with students and instead silently observe the lesson. But the demonstrating teacher forgot to tell the students how we would show up in the room. One student who knew me kept asking me for help, and although I tried to explain why I could not assist, he kept asking why. It was awkward for the student and me. Make sure you let the students know why people are in the room and in what way they have agreed to participate.

Prerecorded video observation.

Description: Video-recorded observation involves a teacher recording a demo lesson with students for the team to view in a subsequent meeting.

Upside:

- Team members can edit, view the demo lesson more than once, pause, and debrief particular moments just as coaches might analyze plays of a football game.

- Educators can share a recorded demo lesson in a professional development session, with other teams, or with people not able to attend.

- The demonstrating teacher and students can self-record, allowing teachers to see multiple things going on at once.

- Students can view the demo lesson with teachers and participate in the post-observation debrief of it if a team wants their feedback.

- A team can typically view the recording and debrief what they observe in one team meeting with no lag time in between.

- Video-recorded demo lessons can be a relief to teachers because if something goes very wrong and they are not comfortable showing it to others, they don't have to.

Downside:

- Educators can observe only what the camera records.

- Tech issues (user error, poor audio or light, etc.) can impact video quality.

- Editing, if desired, can be time-consuming.

- Students not accustomed to being recorded might present atypical behaviors.

- Labor union guidelines might prohibit video-recording.

- The demonstrating teacher might be uncomfortable with being recorded or fear the recording will get into the wrong hands and be used as an evaluative tool.

STL recommendation:

Get a good recording. Use recording devices that capture sound for group work. Position the camera so that it doesn't face a bright window. Avoid constant zooming in and zooming out as this can make the viewing experience nauseating. If recording with a phone, lean it on a surface so that the recording is still. If using a platform like Zoom, enable live transcript if you have the option.

Dry-demo observation.

Description: The dry-demo observation occurs when teachers "workshop" an instructional practice on colleagues without students present. (I took the name from theater—the director and tech designers do a "dry tech" in which they run a show for lighting and sound cues without the actors present.)

Upside:

- To test-drive instruction in a lab-like setting before implementation with students permits educators to anticipate and work out problems and fine-tune instructional moves.

- Teachers are in the students' shoes. They experience the lesson as learners.

- Dry demos are a low-stakes way to try a strategy for the first time, particularly when people are nervous or guarded.

- There are no labor union restrictions.

- Dry-demo observations and post-observation debriefs are a logistical breeze as they require no changes to schedule and both can occur during regular meeting time or outside school hours.

- It's a great baby step for teachers who aren't comfortable with trying out something publicly with students. Doing so with supportive colleagues can help them work out the kinks before bringing the lesson to students.

Downside:

- Teachers don't get to see the actual student response to the instruction. This is why dry demos are usually followed by a live or video-recorded demo observation.

- Teachers who are more comfortable with children than adults might actually have more anxiety testing out a lesson on colleagues than on students.

STL recommendation:

Discourage bad acting. It might happen that someone on your team will think acting as a student learner in your dry demo is their moment to overact. This might include talking in a childish voice, interrupting your demo, modeling extreme behaviors like falling off of a chair—essentially taking on an overexaggerated representation of a student. Remind your colleagues upfront to experience the demo lesson as a learner and think about how a student might receive the lesson, but always act as themselves.

STL recommendation for all methods of peer observation:

Push past mistrust. If you work in a school or on a team where trust is low, it can be tempting to avoid any type of peer observation with the excuse that people aren't ready or willing. Make small moves to overcome reluctance to participating in peer observations. It could mean offering to do a demo lesson yourself or beginning with a dry demo and then working up to a live demo. You can also ask people to sign up for their students to be the subject of the demo lesson, but indicate that the teacher does not have to lead the demo lesson—anyone on the team can do it. Once you do the first observation of a demo lesson and you lead the debrief in a way that is *not* evaluative, trust builds, and more people open up their classrooms and offer to demonstrate lessons and be observed by their peers. (See Move 9.6.)

9.4 Decide a means for collecting student data.

Observing does not mean watching. Skillful team leaders (STLs) and their teams are more intentional than that. They decide in the planning phase how observers will collect evidence of learning during the demonstration lesson.

How to decide a means for collecting student data:

Collect student-learning artifacts from the lesson such as exit tickets, snippets of student dialogue, or student notebooks. In addition to student work, observation notes can act as a great source of data for your discussion. Decide, in advance, what and how observers should transcribe the qualitative data they collect. A few methods for live data collection and transcription include the following:

- Take photos of student work (e.g., snap photos of student work that show students solving a math problem differently).

- Video- or audio-record students (e.g., record a student Literature Circle).

- Record observations in a chart with two columns: Teacher Actions and Student Responses (e.g., Teacher turned around/Student put head down).

- Listen to and write out a conversation verbatim like a stenographer (e.g., capture, as best as you can, quotes from a very short student-to-student Turn and Talk).

- Jot on sticky notes in-the-moment observations (e.g., jot down, each on a different sticky note, questions you hear students ask. During analysis, sort them by type of question).

- Tally (e.g., tally how often individual students raise their hands).

STL recommendation:

Bite off what you can chew. If you observe a whole lesson or a long teacher–student interaction, consider collecting and transcribing data for only a portion of the time. If you are video- or audio-recording, this is easy because you can capture the whole lesson and then play back in the debrief only what is relevant. If you are using a method where you and your colleagues are actually scribing what is spoken or actively taking observation notes, decide in advance who will capture which parts so people don't get so caught up in documenting that they miss the experience of the observation.

Find the right words:

- *In what way will we collect evidence of learning?*
- *How will we record our observations?*
- *Let's agree to collect data in the same way so that we can compare findings during our post-observation debrief.*

9.5 Debrief a peer observation.

Two people can watch the same movie but leave with different interpretations. The power of collaborative peer observation is in the conversation that follows. Skillful team leaders (STLs) intentionally debrief the observed demo lesson.

How to debrief a peer observation:

Make the focus of your post-observation debrief the same as the focus of the peer observation. Unexpected learning will emerge, but aim to keep discourse focused on the student-learning challenge or concern you were investigating. Examine student artifacts and teacher notes to infer what led to student success and what caused some students to struggle. Lead your post-observation debrief as you would any data analysis conversation.

STL recommendation:

Withhold judgment. Acknowledge the courage of the demonstrating teacher(s) and set up a judgment-free zone with an agreement such as "Put yourself in the demonstrating teacher's shoes."

Time it right. Schedule time to debrief the observation on the same day or within the same week so that the experience is fresh in people's minds and implications for learning can be applied right away. Some teams who do instructional rounds in which they observe classroom after classroom take 10 minutes in the hallway to debrief before heading into the next classroom. Some teams utilize a regularly scheduled team meeting to do a live demo lesson or watch a prerecorded video lesson for the first half of the period, then debrief what they see and hear for the latter half of the meeting.

Related readings:

Move 4.7, "Facilitate a protocol." Choose a data analysis protocol to examine the data collected from the peer observation.

9.6 Strengthen vulnerability-based trust for peer observation.

You'll do many things with your team that require psychological safety, but none more so than conducting peer observations and examining student data together. Moves 9.1–9.5 suggest ways to help prepare your team for the technical aspects of leading peer observations, but at the heart of successful observations is a trusting group culture. Skillful team leaders (STLs) strengthen vulnerability-based trust between team members so that they are willing to open their class-room doors and examine data together.

How to strengthen vulnerability-based trust for peer observation:

Do one or more of the following:

- *Design together.* When possible, design together the lesson or assignment that your team plans to examine so that there is not only a shared understanding of it, but also a shared responsibility for it. This minimizes a blame culture in which one team member, the person who designed the practice, feels responsible if something goes wrong.

- *Mix and match.* If you're doing a peer observation, keep in mind that any teacher can demonstrate instruction with anyone's students. This can be a helpful move to use when teachers are reticent to try a strategy or don't believe it can work with their students. Suggest that you or another colleague demonstrate the strategy with another teacher's students.

- *Go first.* Even if your group is the most high-functioning, supportive team, it's normal for people to be hesitant about showing vulnerability in their practice. Be intentional about when you take a turn, whether for bringing in student work, modeling a lesson, or even just a team game, knowing that opting to go first can pave the way for others to follow. Remember, it's actually good to express any reservations you may have about going first as it will normalize fears others might have when it's their turn.

- *Suggest self-recording.* Often it's the anticipation of doing a live demo lesson that raises teachers' anxiety, causing them to hold back from wanting others to come into their room to observe. Self-recording a demonstration lesson can reduce that anxiety. When teachers self-record a lesson, they can make the decision afterward whether to share it with colleagues or try the lesson again and rerecord. Most of the time, teachers opt to share the first recording even when things didn't go well. If a demo lesson involves group work, students can be charged with recording their groups so that teachers can capture multiple student-learning conversations. (Check with school leaders to make sure this is permissible.)

- *Focus on students, but make a connection to teaching.* If teachers are self-conscious or worried about being observed or having their student data examined by the team, keep focus as much as possible on students, not the teacher. Key point: Teams in high-performing schools focus on students, but also do not shy from making connections to what the teacher does or doesn't do during analysis of the data in order to improve instruction (Timperley, 2008).

- *Pair a debrief with student work.* Specifically for peer observations, when it's time to debrief the observed lesson, don't just talk about what you saw and heard. Refer to student work in addition to any observational notes you took. You might opt for a looking at student work (LASW) protocol (see Move 4.7).

- *Seek the flop.* Student data are perceived as a reflection on the teacher, so it's not uncommon for someone to feel pressure to deliver the perfect demo lesson. Remind your team that examining student data that result from peer observations is intended to be a learning experience. Capitalize on the opportunities that come from mistakes and missteps.

- *Start small.* Judith Warren Little (2008) reminds us that we don't have to open our classrooms to the whole team to begin gaining the benefits of de-privatizing practice. If your team is ready for that, go for it. But if not, don't forgo peer observations. Encourage each team member to start by inviting just one partner they trust (even someone not on the team) to observe their implementation of a new practice and provide feedback.

- *Hop around.* Lesson study, a Japanese professional learning practice (Doig & Groves, 2011), encourages multiple educators to try the same lesson and be observed. Each time that someone new demonstrates it, others observe, collect and analyze data, give feedback, and tweak the lesson before the next person tries it. This is particularly beneficial in creating a collaborative culture where everyone is vulnerable and all take responsibility for the impact of the demo lesson on students.

- *Conduct routine learning walks.* Instead of observing one lesson in one teacher's classroom, observe teaching and learning throughout the school. Work with school leaders to conduct whole-school, departmental, or grade-level *learning* walks. These are different from "walk-throughs," which are intended to evaluate. Set a focus for peer observation (Move 9.1), but expand your view of teachers and classrooms you are observing. If mistrust is present or people are guarded, hold off on observing instruction and suggest teachers first observe classroom spaces after students have gone for the day.

- *Make peer feedback the norm.* Teach people how to give warm and cool feedback based on agreed-upon criteria when examining student work and observing classroom teaching and learning. Establish a team (and school-wide) routine of observation with feedback so that it becomes normalized. For example:
    - *Warm feedback:* "I notice this classroom has a student book talk wall where students share titles they have read and engage in a sticky note dialogue with one another about shared books they have read. This is a strong example of student voice."
    - *Cool feedback:* "I notice this classroom has a list of rules on the wall that state, 'No talking while the teacher is talking' and 'No getting out of seat.' I wonder if students had a say in crafting these agreements."

Related readings:

Moves 3.9–3.11, "Strengthen a culture of vulnerability-based trust." Distinguish between vulnerability-based trust and relational trust by reading the introduction to Primary Intention 3 and implementing moves that encourage people to share challenges.

NAVIGATE RESISTANCE TO CHANGE

I could be wrong, but if you are new to leading teams, I'm going to guess that you flipped to these moves first. Most team leaders can quickly grasp (and, with practice, execute) the moves at the beginning of this book. Preparing a team to collaborate by attending to room details (Move 1.5), for example, is not hard to implement, but leading adult learners who seem resistant to change is. It's hard with younger learners, too. In fact, 38% of teachers say managing resistant behavior ranks in the top 10 leading causes of stress (Organisation for Economic Co-operation and Development, 2020). I can vividly remember my first weeks of teaching in a Boston public middle school, when I hadn't gotten my sea legs yet, my anxiety level rising with each flight of stairs I climbed on the way to pick up my eighth-grade class, knowing the challenges I was about to face. It seemed as if they did not want to learn and fought me every step of the way, until I learned (with the support of the assistant principal and colleagues) that my approach to resistant behavior had to change before they would.

Adult learners might not talk back, slam a door, or put a tack on your chair, but they can exhibit strong feelings of resistance toward change just like younger learners can. The mistake many team leaders (and novice teachers) make when faced with these behaviors is following the instinct to make them go away. That's understandable. You might try to convince people to change. Sell them with hope. Cheerlead them in a "you can do it," Adam Sandler–movie character way. You might resort to pressure, bargaining, or anything else that might get them on board. Or, you might want to avoid any confrontation and just hope that everything will resolve on its own.

The primary intention of a skillful team leader (STL) is to navigate resistance, not overcome it. STLs don't interpret resistance to change as a bad thing. They expect it. And they even encourage people to voice their reservations and concerns throughout implementation of a new practice. They work to understand and address what might hinder someone from fully adopting a change.

STL moves:

9.7 Spot reluctance to change.

9.8 Reframe talk about resistance.

9.9 Address implementation questions.

9.10 Address the emotional side of change.

9.11 Remove technical barriers to implementation.

9.12 Surface competing commitments.

9.13 Focus on student impact.

9.14 Give time and space.

What these moves promote:

Empathy. These moves foster understanding about what causes people to resist change.

Continuous improvement. Resistance is an expected part of change that, once addressed, can bring forth growth and improvement.

Momentum. Although resistance is to be expected, it can drag a team down. Navigating resistance can help maintain momentum for advancing toward goals.

Vulnerability-based trust. People let their guard down and invite their peers to help them navigate the challenges of change.

Growth mindset. STLs believe that all adult learners, even those who show resistance, have the capacity to grow and learn.

When to use these moves:

Throughout a team's course of inquiry and learning.

9.7 Spot reluctance to change.

If resistance to change always showed up as outright refusal—sounding like "No! You can't make me"—you would know what you were up against and could address it head-on. However, when resistance is less obvious, it can go unnoticed until one day you realize no one is fully adopting a change. Skillful team leaders (STLs) pay close attention to the subtle signs of reluctance.

How to spot reluctance to change:

Signs that a person is unlikely to implement new learning can sometimes look and sound like the following:

SIGN OF RELUCTANCE TO IMPLEMENT NEW LEARNING	EXAMPLE	POSSIBLE SUBTEXT: "I won't fully implement this change because . . ."
Deems that particular obstacles cannot be overcome.	"I'll try the new approach, but without parental support I don't see how this can work."	I can't be successful at this change.
Expects failure to result from implementation.	"I don't see how this will be any different from everything else we've tried that didn't work."	I can't be successful at this change.

SIGN OF RELUCTANCE TO IMPLEMENT NEW LEARNING	EXAMPLE	POSSIBLE SUBTEXT: "I won't fully implement this change because . . ."
Possesses low self-efficacy in which the individual believes that regardless of their efforts, they cannot change outcomes.	"This is a systemic problem well beyond anything we can do to fix it."	I can't be successful at this change.
Delays implementation.	"I think we should wait to implement until next year when things calm down."	I'm not ready to implement this change.
Assumes that they don't really need to change what they are doing.	"I've done this new method for years. So it's no problem for me to implement the change now."	I don't understand this change.
Voices low expectations for students.	"I'm all for it. I just think it won't work because the kids aren't ready, yet."	I'm not ready to implement this change.
Uses humor or sarcasm to avoid adopting a change.	"I have a kid who would lose his head if it were not attached to his body, and you now want me to stop organizing his folder for him so he can learn independence? [*Sarcastically*] Sure, I'll give that a go."	I don't know how to implement this change.
Agrees to implement, but only because of a directive or mandate.	"I guess I'll give it a try. It's not like I have a choice."	I disagree with this change.

Find the right thoughts:

Because this move is about noticing, it's less about what you say and more about what you think:

- *I hear what my colleague is saying. Might this individual be expressing a reluctance to implement a change? If yes, what might be behind their words?*

9.8 Reframe talk about resistance.

We love our cheerleaders and those who are open and willing to change from the minute someone says, "Go." But, we also need the people who resist fully adopting a new practice. These colleagues hold wisdom that helps us anticipate possible challenges in implementation of a change and actually, in the long run, lead to better outcomes. And yet, it can be hard to embrace those who show resistance.

Look at the following two lists of words used to describe the same person.

LIST A	LIST B
• Difficult	• Thoughtful
• Obstinate	• Invested
• Stubborn	• Concerned
• Immovable	• Contemplative
• Inflexible	• Devoted
• Headstrong	• Valuable
• Resistant	• Visionary

Let's be honest. If I asked you or your colleagues to think of one person on your team who is demonstrating resistance to implement a change that you all agreed to do, you might gravitate toward a few descriptive words from column A. Adjectives such as *immovable* and *inflexible* indicate that at some level there exists a belief that this person is not going to come on board with a change. This, in turn, can fuel a mindset that nothing you or anyone else can do will influence the person. Before long, your team starts to work around or dismiss the person who is digging their heels in the ground.

Skillful team leaders (STLs) maintain a growth mindset about their colleagues, starting with the language used to describe those who are resistant to implementing a change.

How to reframe talk about resistance:

Notice the language you use when you talk about, or think of someone who demonstrates, resistance to change. Choose words, like those in column B, that portray the individual as thoughtful, wise, capable, and willing to change. This isn't just semantics. As you speak of the person differently, you'll likely start to see them differently. Instead of, for instance, seeing someone as stuck in their old ways, you'll begin to see the person as someone who takes pride in how things used to be done.

Find the right words:

- *You have given a lot of thought to this change.*

- *I appreciate your devotion to the way we used to do this.*

- *You are clearly invested in the outcome of this decision and have reservations that I would like to better understand.*

- *I hear you apologizing for being "difficult," but I actually welcome the pushback. You hold a valuable perspective that we need to explore.*

- *I see you not as a "negative nelly" but as someone who is anticipating challenges. We don't want to proceed full-steam-ahead without pausing at various points to plan for what can go wrong.*

Related readings:

Part I, Chapter 1, "Skillful Intentional Leadership." Maintaining a growth mindset about the adults we lead, not just our students, is part of taking a skillful approach to team leadership. Read more about it why it's important to believe that your colleagues can change.

Move 5.18, "Interrupt negative energy." When conversation enters a black hole of negativity, pull people out with a task that will reset the group.

Move 8.7, "Reframe a negative association." When someone voices something negative about a person or group of people, change language to influence perceptions and the energy in the room.

Move 8.13, "Invite dissent." Those who show resistance might be thinking differently than others on the team. Invite them to share their opinions in an effort to encourage diverse perspectives about a specific change.

9.9 Address implementation questions.

If you've been used to doing something one way for a long time, and now you must do it in a new way, you're going to have a lot of questions, even if the change was your idea. Many questions about change are predictable. Wagner and Kegan (2006) have identified four "arenas of change," also known as the four *C*s (context, conditions, competencies, and culture), that can be helpful to schools or individual teams undergoing a change initiative. Skillful team leaders (STLs) and their colleagues make or communicate decisions within these categories. Doing so before expecting people to implement a change can satisfy questions from those who are reluctant to jump on board.

How to address implementation questions:

I have adapted questions within the four *C*s that are relevant to teams implementing changes to teaching and learning. You might explore these questions during the *Ask & Aim, Strategize & Design*, and/or *Act & Evaluate* STL Phases of Collaborative Inquiry. If you are a member of a school leadership team, then you might explore these questions as a school-wide or department-wide team before launching a change initiative.

- *Context*—Organizational systems and goings-on that surround this change.
  - What is the change? Who initiated this change? Why this change? Why us? Why now? (See Move 6.1.)
  - What does our school prioritize, and how does this change initiative align?

○ What else is going on? What demands/mandates/changes are we experiencing beyond this initiative?

- *Conditions*—Resources.

  ○ What conditions do teachers need to be successful in implementing this change?

  ○ Which current policies and practices are conducive to successfully implementing this change? Which are not?

  ○ Which conditions do we have control over? Which do we not? (e.g., time, space, money, materials, staffing)

- *Competencies*—Knowledge and skill.

  ○ How skilled and confident are teachers now in implementing this change successfully?

  ○ What understanding, knowledge, and skill do teachers need to acquire?

  ○ What access do people have to gaining the competencies they need?

- *Culture*—Values, beliefs, mindsets, assumptions, bias.

  ○ What values, beliefs, mindsets, assumptions, and biases do people hold about this change?

  ○ What shifts in mindset and in "ways of doing" might need to occur in order for the change initiative to be successful?

  ○ What aspects of our school/team culture might help us successfully implement this change, and what aspects might hinder it?

STL recommendations:

Lead a Gallery Walk. See Move 4.7. This can be facilitated as an interactive activity in which you hang four posters around the room, one for each of the four *C*s. Include or display guiding questions for each category. Rotate groups around the room, brainstorming on chart paper plusses (+) (things that will help implementation of the change) and deltas (Δ) (things that could hinder implementation and need to be addressed).

Get personal. Hall and Hord's (1987) Concerns Based Adoption Model, explained in their book and *The Skillful Team Leader* (MacDonald, 2013, p. 134), can help identify what individuals need to implement new learning. Leaders can ask, "What personal *concerns* do you have about implementing this change?"

Find the right words:

- *As we get ready to implement this change, let's explore questions people might have:*

  1. *What's the **context** within which we are initiating this change? (What's happening?)*

2. *What* **conditions** *do we have that support this change, and what don't we have yet?*

3. *What* **competencies** *do we have, and what do we need to acquire?*

4. *How does our school* **culture** *support this change, and in what ways does it not?*

9.10 Address the emotional side of change.

Anyone who has ever sat in on their child's graduation, even just from kindergarten, knows that there is an emotional side to change. Different people have different responses to change, whether the change is self-initiated or not. Skillful team leaders (STLs) are attuned to the varied emotional responses that people can have to change and get people talking about them.

How to address the emotional side of change:

There are many ways to implement this move. Here are a few effective options to facilitate communication:

- *Lay out magazine photos* (or picture postcards) and ask each of your colleagues to choose one that represents their emotional response to the upcoming change.

- *Invite people to form a human continuum* where they stand side by side in a line. Those who are eager and excited to embrace the upcoming change stand more toward the right; those with reservations, or anxious feelings, stand toward the left. Anyone with a mixed response to the change stands toward the center of the line.

- *Lead a Color Emotions activity* (see the description that follows).

PRIMARY INTENTION 9

Activity: Color Emotions

This is a movement activity to surface varied emotional responses toward something new.

Groups: Color Emotions works particularly well with large diverse groups, such as a whole faculty who teach different grade levels and subjects, because there is more of a likelihood that people will have different responses to the change that is about to take place.

Prep: Create a slide of the color quadrants (demonstrated as follows). Also get pieces of paper or a sticky note in each color to place on different walls.

(Continued)

(Continued)

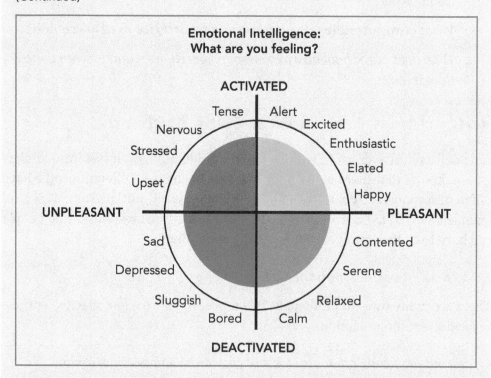

Minimum time required: 15–30 minutes depending on the size of the group.

How to lead:

1. Stick one red, yellow, green, and blue sticky note in different locations of the room as stations.

2. Present the color quadrants with adjectives.

3. Name the change that people are about to implement.

4. Ask people to stand at the color quadrant that best matches their dominant feeling toward the change.

5. Invite people to talk with others who chose the same color about the similar feeling they have toward the change.

6. Ask people to notice where other colleagues are standing. Prompt their observation with questions such as these: At what color are the most people standing? At what color are the least people standing? Are your colleagues from the same groups to which you belong standing at the same color? (For example, "I notice teachers from my content team are split between blue and red.") Are your colleagues from groups to which you do not belong standing at the same color as you are? (For example, "I notice the administrative team is at yellow, while my content team is at red.")

7. Invite people to cross the room to connect with someone standing at a different color quadrant to learn about their different emotional response to the change. (Before people do this, set a ground rule: "Don't try to convince anyone to change the way they feel. Aim to understand where they are coming from.")

8. Debrief the diverse emotions people hold about the change you are about to undertake as a school or team. Take time to listen to people at each color. Don't make decisions at this time, but record next steps if they come up.

STL recommendations for Color Emotions:

Balance voices. Listen to the people standing at the red and blue positions without letting their less desirable views of the change overpower the other voices in the room. Acknowledge and validate their concerns, but do not solve them now. Give equal time to people standing at the yellow and green positions. Don't let their more accepting views overshadow others. Encourage dialogue.

Debrief an imbalanced result. You might do this activity and discover everyone on your team stands at the same color. For instance, everyone stands at yellow, eager to embrace the change. Ask questions to reveal emotional nuances. For example, "I notice we are all standing at yellow. Did anything make you consider moving toward a different color, and if so, what?"

Expect emotions to fluctuate. Emily Becker, friend and former principal, asks the question, "How are you doing in this moment?" (personal communication, November 18, 2021). It encourages people who feel overwhelmed to focus on their present emotional state. Normalize that a person can start in the yellow position, feeling eager to embrace a change, and when implementation gets hard, shift into blue where they are feeling insecure and discouraged. You can lead this exercise at several points throughout the duration of the change to dipstick where people are at and what supports they need in a given moment.

9.11 Remove technical barriers to implementation.

"What do you want me to do, Elisa, carry the books on my back?" This was the response I got from a very frustrated, seasoned teacher when she learned that she was supposed to have a classroom-based library even though she traveled from classroom to classroom to teach. Is it possible that this teacher was not ready to implement this new initiative? Maybe. But, it was also possible that she just needed a cart. I understood that this teacher could not implement anything until I addressed her personal concern. I got her a cart. Skillful team leaders (STLs) recognize that technical concerns can get in the way of implementation. They do what they can to intentionally remove obstacles.

How to remove technical barriers to implementation:

Be clear on what everyone is expected to implement. Listen for technical concerns about things such as space, schedule, and materials and work with your colleagues to resolve issues that you can control. Here are a few solutions to common technical problems that arise during implementation of a new instructional practice:

- *Space:* Arrange a new room setup; borrow furniture; put in a work order to get something fixed; show an example of what the space should look like; communicate changes you had to make in your own classroom; reorganize an existing space.

- *Schedule:* Advocate for a small schedule change such as swapping out lunch duty for bus duty; offer to cover or find coverage for a class so that the teacher can observe someone else; offer time-management strategies; co-plan a lesson to make time for the new practice.

- *Supplies and materials needed for implementation:* Access books, technology, and supplies; provide templates, models, and sample language/phrasing to use with students.

In action:

STL Osamagbe (Osa) Osagie leads colleagues in how to hold conversations about diversity, equity, and inclusion (DEI) with students, specifically in the politically and racially divided pandemic year of 2020. The following conversation is had days before the presidential election.

Osa: We are living in a massive pressure point. It's especially hard for folks who work in schools where we wonder, "What can I say? When should I say something? What should I say? Will something I say conflict with a family's belief system?" Questions like these are challenging and may even feel overwhelming; however, it's important that we acknowledge and name those nuances so that we can create opportunities for learning, provide support where needed, and continue to build a healthy culture within our community. So now that we've identified the multiple layers at hand, the question then becomes, "How do we implement this approach?"

A few weeks ago, I was listening to Jen Cort's *Third Space* podcast, and there was a quote that stood out to me; it's been a great guide as I continue to think about that question. [*Shows slide: "I hope that you will be politically ambiguous (but crystal clear on our values and morals)."*] What I appreciate about this statement is that it's a reminder that our role as educators isn't necessarily to share our political values or candidate of choice with our students, but rather, this is an opportunity to communicate to students that we have a baseline of how we've agreed to treat people within our school community.

Teacher 1: What are some DEI responses you could give to students if they ask you if you voted, or who you voted for?

Osa: Great question. There is a resource I'll post that offers some language that you can use to respond to a question like that. One that comes to mind sounds something like "Who I voted for is a personal choice that I'd like to keep private. I don't really feel comfortable sharing that piece of information with you, but what I will tell you is that I was really excited that I was able to exercise my right and share my opinions by participating in the electoral process. Another highlight for me was that I witnessed a big moment in American history." So basically shift the conversation away from the candidate and the party to the process of voting and the power in using your voice.

Director: This is a good time to highlight our commitment to our school values (empathy, respect, inclusion, and kindness, or ERIK). Don't shy away from relating what's going on in the world to the pledge that they took. You might create with them a list of words and actions that might demonstrate these values particularly this week and beyond. I have a template for this that I will post to our shared resources page.

Osa: And to piggyback off the director's point, I've collected some sentence stems that you can use when you see or hear things that don't align to our school values. [*Shows slide.*] These are tried and true whether it is a DEI-related situation or just a kid jumping up and down the hallways [*smiles*] and you're like, "That's not what we do in the hallway. That behavior is inappropriate because . . ."

Find the right words:

- *What obstacles do time, space, schedule, supplies, or materials present that we can access or problem solve?*

- *What resources would help you implement this?*

- *In anticipation that people might have concerns about . . . [e.g., materials], I prepared . . .*

Related reading:

Moves 1.1–1.5. Just as you would remove technical barriers in order to help someone implement new learning, you would also do so in a team meeting during collaboration about that change.

9.12 Surface competing commitments.

Imagine a father tells his teenager daughter that she is now able to make decisions on her own, but then, he micromanages her every decision. The father's behavior contradicts the commitment he has made to her. A close look reveals what's getting in his way: He wants his daughter to make the *right* decisions so that she doesn't get hurt. These two commitments, (1) allowing the daughter to make her own decisions and (2) making sure she makes the right decisions, become competing when the father assumes that his daughter cannot make the right choices on her own.

If you notice someone commits to doing something but does not follow through, it's possible that competing commitments are at play (Kegan & Lahey, 2001, 2009). This occurs when a person commits to a goal requiring a behavioral change but some internal, hidden commitment to something else prevents the person from reaching their goal. Skillful team leaders (STLs) surface competing commitments to help people implement changes they want to make.

How to surface competing commitments:

Kegan and Lahey (2001, 2009) recommend people surface their competing commitments by thinking through four things:

1. Name your visible commitment (the change you want to see).

2. Describe the ways you act now (and the ways in which you don't).

3. Identify your hidden commitment (that which competes with the change you want to see).

4. Discover your underlying assumptions (beliefs you've formed that are getting in the way of you fully adopting the change).

Use the following chart as a reflection tool when you notice you or your colleagues are not yet implementing new learning. Model your own example first.

VISIBLE COMMITMENT	DOING/NOT DOING	HIDDEN COMMITMENTS	HIDDEN ASSUMPTIONS

In action:

Teachers aim to give students more responsibility for learning in the classroom. Rob's team is charged with implementing peer-to-peer feedback;

however, no one seems to be doing it consistently. Rob models his own competing commitments that he has uncovered:

VISIBLE COMMITMENT	DOING/NOT DOING	HIDDEN COMMITMENTS	HIDDEN ASSUMPTIONS
I am committed to giving students more responsibility over their own and each other's learning. I am committed to implementing peer-to-peer feedback in student writing.	I write all the feedback to students on their writing. I only let students give each other feedback on their writing once.	I'm an English teacher, and I'm committed to making sure my students receive accurate and specific feedback in order to be strong writers.	I don't believe that my students can give quality feedback to each other as effectively as I can. I believe peer-to-peer feedback will promote bad advice, and then I'm going to have to "fix" all the bad writing habits that result.

Rob: Let's unpack my assumption—where it comes from. How can you help me so that my hidden commitment does not need to compete with my visible commitment?

Find the right words:

- *You seem committed to this goal, yet something keeps holding you back. What do you think that might be? I'd like to explore this together so that we have a plan to move forward.*

- *Is there something else you want that competes with this goal?*

- *What assumptions might be holding you back from implementing this change?*

9.13 Focus on student impact.

What if, in order to get people to adopt a new behavior, you told them the benefits that adopting the change would have on them, answered their questions, removed whatever barriers to implementation you could, offered them incentives to change, and gave consequences to them if they didn't, but they still didn't change? This was the dilemma that a Boston hospital faced when trying to get doctors and nurses to consistently wash their hands between treating patients in order to reduce the spread of infectious disease. But an experiment revealed one tactic that got more doctors and nurses to increase their handwashing more than any other—emphasizing how implementing the change would affect others. When doctors and nurses were reminded of the benefits that handwashing had for the patients they served, as opposed to the implications for themselves, they washed their hands more frequently (Grant

& Hofmann, 2011). Similarly, when colleagues don't fully implement a new practice, skillful team leaders (STLs) turn focus away from teaching toward the impact on student learning.

How to focus on student impact:

In actuality, this is less its own move and more a reminder of the multitude of moves in this book that aim to keep an eye on the impact of teams on student learning. These moves include the following:

- Move 5.15, Pivot from teaching to learning.

- Move 6.2, Identify a priority-based focus area.

- Move 6.5, Brainstorm student-centered challenges.

- Move 6.7, (Specific) Write specific student-learning goals.

- Move 6.12, (Results-driven) Distinguish learning outcomes from pathways.

- Move 6.13, (Time-bound) Establish a time frame according to student need.

- Move 7.4, Optimize assessment conditions for students.

- Move 7.5, Select student work samples (student data) to examine.

- Move 7.12, Analyze student errors.

- Move 7.13, Target and plan for student success.

- Move 9.4, Decide a means for collecting student data.

- Move 9.5, Debrief a peer observation.

- Move 10.4, Monitor student progress.

9.14 Give time and space.

When I was a literacy coach, I set up a small resource room with an old 48-slot mailbox shelving unit that I stocked with readings and templates that teachers could grab when they wanted, as needed. Teachers who were in an eight-week collaborative inquiry cycle with me typically took resources and implemented templates based on what we were studying. But, I remember one teacher who didn't. It was surprising to me because she was very agreeable and enthusiastic in our meetings. We had a good relationship. And she cared very much for her students. Nevertheless, despite my efforts, she would not read these resources and implement the strategies like her colleagues did. Then, six months later, I walked into the resource room to find her sitting at a table sifting through a pile of readings she had pulled off the shelves. She smiled at me and said, "I wasn't ready to take this in during our cycle, but now I am."

Skillful team leaders (STLs) give their colleagues a little time and space, trusting that they will adopt the change when ready.

How to give time and space:

Consider the following:

- *Personal need.* Is this a person who has expressed to me or shown that they benefit from time to process and experiment with this change independent of me?

- *Equity.* Will giving this person time and space give them an unfair advantage or privilege over others?

- *Urgency.* Will any harm come from slowing down the implementation of this change?

- *Follow-up.* What is a reasonable amount of time for me to step back and let this person navigate this change on their own?

- *Accountability.* What are my next steps if they do not implement the change in the time and space provided?

Think like a teacher:

Very early in my teaching years, I had a middle school student who, to put it mildly, "tested my limits" in our first week of class. I'll call her Jeanne. I'd say, "Line up." Jeanne would stay seated. I'd say, "Take your seat." Jeanne would stand. I'd announce, "Open to page 12." Jeanne would close her book. Each time I successfully employed a teacher move, like quietly but directly repeating the expectation, Jeanne would show opposition. There was no specific exchange between us that prompted her resistance to me, or to the norms of our classroom. This was, as my colleagues told me, how she acted when she first met teachers she didn't yet trust.

Then one day my class entered the room and silently started their opening writing activity as they always do. Jeanne did not. Instead, she put a soda can on her desk, popped it open, looked at me, took a slow sip, and then rested the can on the corner of her desk. Not going to lie—it took everything I had not to lose my cool. I very slowly walked around the room, looking at students' writing, making my way toward her desk. As I got to her, I bent down and almost inaudibly whispered, "I like that you are starting your journal entry. Now, I need you to put your soda can at the back of the room on my desk. Thank you." Then I slowly continued walking around the room, looking at other students' work. She didn't move. I did not know what to do at that point, and now the class was intently watching this standoff between the student and me, waiting for me to do something—call the office, yell, cry. I walked to a lectern at the front of my room and began dramatically writing on a piece of paper, probably something like "I hate my job" (which wasn't true, but I was really mad). As I took almost a full two minutes scribbling random words on this paper, something unexpected happened. Jeanne very slowly stood up, soda can in hand, sauntered to the back of the room, and placed the can on my desk. Then she went back and started her work. This was the turning point for her and me.

This is an extreme example of resistance, and it is unlikely that you will encounter such behavior from your colleagues, but make no mistake—even adults can show resistance to change in unexpected ways that try your patience and your team's. Asserting power might not be someone's motivation for resistance, but the need to be in control may be at play. Use time and space as a means to put the person back in the driver's seat and regain your own composure.

STL recommendations:

Weigh readiness against student need. This "give time and space" move can be controversial. While you want to empower people to decide when they are ready to make a change, sometimes there is urgency around the change. Waiting for grown-ups to implement change in a slow-drip-coffee kind of way might eventually lead to powerful results, but it also might not be in the best interest of students who need the change now.

You can't predict how much time and space people will need to own the change, but you can gently nudge them with support. For instance, in my example to open this move, I could select one short reading that I thought the teacher could relate to, add a note about it, and drop it in her mailbox. Our team could agree to read one text and discuss it in a meeting. I could model a strategy with her students and then point her to the reading that describes what I did so she could do it on her own. And, if a particular change was mandated by a particular deadline and the teacher was still reluctant to implement it, I could bring in an authority figure to make the expectation and consequences for not doing so clear (see Move 9.16).

Related reading:

Move 1.3, "Foster collaboration between meetings." Encourage team members to continue collaborating after a team meeting so that they have time to process what's been discussed before coming together the next time.

Move 5.9, "Table the discussion." When conflict arises and resolution seems a long way off, give people time and space to process what they've heard others saying and regulate their emotions, if needed.

INVITE ACCOUNTABILITY

Ask & Aim–Assess & Analyze–Target & Plan–Research & Study–Strategize & Design–Act & Evaluate. While the wheels could fall off at any point throughout these STL Phases of Collaborative Inquiry, they won't when teams feel a sense of obligation to one another to follow through with commitments. Accountability is often associated with a hammer. Elected officials don't keep their promises? They're going to hear from the voters. Schools chronically fail their high-needs student population? The state is going to get involved. Principals don't deliver results? They will have to answer to parents. With this "I'm watching you" approach, it makes sense for team leaders to be unsure what role they have, or want to have, in accountability of their peers. And yet, without accountability, teams can end up living in low-functioning, low impact Q3.

Skillful team leaders (STLs) view accountability not as a "gotcha" but instead as a shared responsibility for doing what's needed to reach the team's intended outcomes. They foster a team culture where no one wants to let anyone else down. If a person does not follow through on their commitments, STLs and their colleagues engage in honest discussion about challenges and offer support. On the rare occasion that a team member is reluctant to implement change and also refuses to be accountable to their peers, STLs involve a principal or school leader to help.

STL moves:

9.15 Partner for accountability.

9.16 Go to an authority figure.

What these moves promote:

Accountability. As the title of the chapter suggests, these moves are intended to keep teams accountable to what they agreed to implement.

Community. People take responsibility for supporting one another in implementation.

When to use these moves:

Throughout a team's course of inquiry and learning.

Related reading:

Move 8.17, "Commit to action." People need clarity about what they are being held accountable to doing. Ensure expectations, capabilities, and consequences are clear.

9.15 Partner for accountability.

I remember watching a competition on television when the winner expressed her gratitude to her "accountability group." She explained that this was a team of like-minded, supportive friends who encouraged her to compete. Her group made sure she followed through with the steps she needed to reach her goal. Skillful team leaders (STLs) create opportunities for team members to act as accountability partners.

How to partner for accountability:

Whether you are simply trying to uphold a norm like "Be on time" or you have committed to implementing a new teaching strategy and need someone to keep on top of you so you don't fall back to your old methods, an accountability partner can help you do what you say you will do. Agree on partner responsibilities. Examples might include the following:

- Regularly meet for progress check-ins.

- Observe and provide feedback to one another during implementation of a new practice.

- Troubleshoot barriers to success.

- Listen with empathy but nudge your partner toward commitments.

Think like a teacher:

Students tend to listen to their peers. As a teacher, you use this to students' learning advantage every time you partner or group students for a task to which they are all responsible to one another for a project. You are likely thoughtful about how you pair students, or ask them to pair, so that they hold each other to high standards, are supportive of one another, and work well together. You can take a similar approach with your colleagues.

Find the right words:

- *Choose someone you trust to keep you accountable to the work of our team. Give this person permission to nudge you, check up on you, and problem solve with you.*

9.16 Go to an authority figure.

"Can I speak to your manager?" These are pretty much the six words every sales representative dreads to hear from a customer. Going above someone's head is not the first thing anyone wants to do. It is usually a last-resort move, but if you are a peer team leader, there are just some things you should not have to hold your colleagues accountable to. School-wide policies for attendance and punctuality at meetings, for example, should not fall under your list of responsibilities to enforce. You can certainly find out why someone consistently arrives late to meetings, and see if there is something you or the team can do to adjust or help. But, if a teacher is breaking a school-wide expectation, it needs to be brought to the attention of an administrator. Skillful team leaders (STLs) use this move deliberately and sparingly.

How (and when) to go to an authority figure:

At the end of the day, you have to continue working with the person you "report." First, decide if your colleague's behavior warrants involving an authority figure or if it is something you can address. If you decide it's beyond your jurisdiction or capabilities, then be transparent and tell your colleague the reason you plan on going to an authority figure. They may not like it. They may be mad at you. But, they'll appreciate that you are not going behind their back.

GO TO AN AUTHORITY FIGURE WHEN . . .	DO NOT GO TO AN AUTHORITY FIGURE WHEN . . .
• Any person(s) might be in harm's way. • The person presents a regulatory or legal risk. • The person is not upholding a district- or school-wide policy. • You are seeking leadership advice and agree to preserve the person's anonymity.	• You have a personal grievance. • The person breaks a team-specific norm. • You are looking to get the person in trouble.

Think like a teacher:

You don't immediately run to the principal or a parent the moment a student shows resistance. You consider the most effective way to reach the student. You must decide if going to an authority figure will undermine your authority or relationship with the student, or if the circumstances warrant it.

When you are a peer leader, you are sometimes faced with a similar difficult decision: when to involve a "higher-up" and when to work to resolve the conflict on your own. Weigh the circumstances as carefully as you would with a student in your classroom.

Find the right words:

- *This extends beyond the scope of my role. I will need to bring this to the principal.*

- *I'm not sure how to handle this. I think it's in both of our best interests to bring an administrator into the conversation.*

- *I've tried to support you in the ways I know how, but I think it's time to get support directly from a school leader.*

- *I am going by our school policy. If you have a different agreement with the principal, I just need word from them, and I'm fine with whatever decision the principal makes.*

Related reading:

Part II, Chapter 6, "The Upside (and Downside) of Being a Peer Leader." Explore the advantages you have as a peer leader.

Primary Intention

Assess: Feedback, Reflection, and Growth for Teams and Leaders

//

Teacher collaboration is now widely accepted as an important priority among districts. The challenge for most schools is no longer how to schedule team meetings. It's knowing whether or not they are effective. If everyone is collegial, if time is used efficiently, if people communicate well, and if tasks get done, *then* can we say that the team's collaboration is effective? Not quite. These are important measures of how a team functions together, and if a team doesn't do these things, collaboration may be difficult. However, as explored extensively in Part I, Chapter 2, ultimately, teacher collaboration needs to have a positive impact on student learning.

It can be hard to draw a direct line between what teachers do in a meeting and the learning outcomes they get for students. Impact is most visible when teachers observe student progress toward goals, but there are additional signs within each meeting that a team is on their way to making a measurable difference for students. Skillful team leaders (STLs) notice specific indicators and reflect on the strengths and areas of growth for their team. In addition to observation and reflection, they solicit feedback from their colleagues. Even when feedback is hard to hear, STLs listen and use it to better lead their teams. As they work hard to support team growth, they also look inward toward developing what it takes to be a skillful, intentional team leader.

Contents:

Solicit feedback.

10.1 Design feedback questions.

10.2 Hear what's hard.

10.3 Make feedback public.

Assess team function and impact.

10.4 Monitor student progress.

10.5 Reflect on a meeting.

10.6 Publicly celebrate impact.

Develop as a leader.

10.7 Self-assess.

10.8 Set leadership growth goals.

10.9 Admit missteps.

10.10 Practice mindfulness.

10.11 Build capacity.

Tools and templates:

Figure 29: STL Meeting Reflection Tool

Figure 30: STL Team Inquiry Summary

Figure 31: STL Self-Assessment Tool

Figure 32: STL Self-Assessment Tool Examples

SOLICIT FEEDBACK

About four years ago, I had what then seemed like an odd experience but today would be quite ordinary. I bought a snack at a gas station, and as soon as my credit card went through, two smiley faces popped up on the screen (well, one smiling, the other frowning). "How was your experience today?" the screen asked.

Soliciting feedback has been standard practice for teachers since long before my gas station experience. And it goes beyond clicking on a happy or sad face. Teachers routinely give students surveys or exit tickets, or check in 1:1 to learn how a lesson went. Skillful team leaders (STLs) use similar methods with their colleagues to learn how a team meeting went.

While you might be tempted to skip asking your team for feedback at the end of a meeting, perhaps because time is short or you are concerned that it will feel like a burden to your colleagues, please don't. Feedback creates opportunities for people to reflect and speak out. It gives you a feel for how things are going. STLs establish a habit of giving and getting feedback, during and after meetings, so that people come to expect it as part of the collaborative process. They are thoughtful about what they ask and how they ask it. They make the feedback public and share with their colleagues how it will shape their next leadership moves.

STL moves:

10.1 Design feedback questions.

10.2 Hear what's hard.

10.3 Make feedback public.

What these moves promote:

Reflection. Soliciting feedback invites your colleagues to reflect on how they and others participate in team meetings and what they need in order to further advance team goals.

Voice. These moves give people an opportunity to voice what is and is not working for them as learners.

Communication. Feedback slips and surveys are not the best means for working out problems. However, they can be used to indicate there is a concern for follow-up.

Awareness. People reflect on their team's collaboration and their contributions to their team's function and impact.

When to use these moves:

Solicit feedback throughout a meeting and more formally at the end of every team meeting or when a course of inquiry has moved through a full cycle.

10.1 Design feedback questions.

Have you ever led a meeting or workshop for your colleagues where you sensed that something was off, but when you asked people for feedback afterward, they told you that everything was "fine"? In some cases, people withhold candid feedback because they are not comfortable giving it. But in other cases, it's the question that stifles their response. Skillful team leaders (STLs) are intentional about how they design feedback questions.

How to design feedback questions:

Consider the following before writing your feedback questions:

- *Purpose: What do I (or my team) want to learn from or about my colleagues?* Be clear about what you need to find out in order to improve the function and/or impact of the team. Imagine how people will respond to your question. If you already think you know the answer, it is probably not worth asking unless you are looking for confirmation.

- *Type: Specific or broad?* A specific question such as "How satisfied were you with our team decision-making process today?" can focus the feedback you get. Doug Stone and Sheila Heen (Talks at Google, 2014) recommend that you write a question about one specific thing, and that you give people permission to be honest and invite them to be specific. That said, a more general question such as "What worked today?" can give people free rein to shed light on something you didn't think to ask. Both types of questions are worthwhile.

- *Time: How much time do people realistically have to give feedback?* If you are short on time, try feedback slips, polls, or a Google Form, or request one comment jotted on a sticky note.

- *Bias: Do my feedback questions contain bias? How can I rewrite questions so that I don't influence responses?* Remove language that reflects your own position. For instance, instead of asking, "How much do you agree with the following statement? 'School administrators have no regard for teacher voice and obstruct our instructional decisions,'" ask, "How much do you agree with the following statement? 'We are able to make instructional decisions.'"

- *Processing: How easily will I be able to read through feedback, make sense of it, and use it to shape future decisions?* Open-ended questions (those that cannot be answered with a yes or no or single answer choice) on a feedback form can give you a good understanding of what everyone is thinking. However, they will only be useful if you have the capacity to read through everyone's comments, interpret them, and format them in a way that allows you to then share them with the team. Sometimes closed questions are preferable for this reason.

STL recommendations:

Don't ask for two things at once. Because you are looking for specific feedback, you should avoid asking a question that won't tell you clearly what you need to know. It's common to want to keep a survey short and combine two questions into one, but this will only result in ambiguity when you are reviewing responses. If you want to know two things, ask two questions. Also, avoid double-barreled questions when designing student-learning assessments (see Move 7.3).

Be consistent when possible. Reduce the burden of answering feedback questions. Ask the same open-ended questions consistently at each meeting. Or, if giving a survey, keep the same rating scale for every question (e.g., "Rate on a scale of 1 [*strongly disagree*] to 5 [*strongly agree*] how much you agree with each of the given statements"). When you do that, people will know what to expect and won't need to take time to process the questions.

Give people adequate time to think. Save a few minutes at the end of a meeting to ensure that people have time to give feedback. You may not find out what you need if people are rushing out the door.

Invite personal responsibility. Feedback forms are not meant to serve as a complaint file. Yes, you want to know what isn't working, but your role as leader is not to solve everything for everyone. Make your colleagues part of the solution. After soliciting feedback, empower people to think about what they can do to move themselves and the team forward. Include a question such as "What are your next steps?"

Think like a teacher:

Feedback from students helps teachers learn what to stop, start, continue, and tweak. As an effective teacher, you regularly solicit feedback from students. Some of the nonverbal methods used during a lesson might include the following:

Dipstick—Learners indicate understanding or approval with a thumbs-up, thumbs-sideways, or thumbs-down (see Move 8.16).

Fist to five—Learners indicate understanding or approval with their fingers. One finger indicates a low favorability or understanding, and up to five fingers indicates greater favorability or understanding.

Sticky notes parking lot—Learners write feedback on a sticky note and "park" it on a piece of chart paper hanging on the wall for the teacher to read.

Color-coded cards—Learners place a red card on their desk if they are stuck and need immediate help, a yellow card if they have a question that is not urgent, and a green card on their desk if they are all set.

It's fine to incorporate quick feedback opportunities like these in your team meeting, but be cautious about treating adults as students. Level up language (see Move 3.5) if you use any of the above. And don't let quick checks throughout a meeting substitute for methods of collecting more meaningful feedback on things such as exit tickets, surveys, and focus groups.

Find the right words:

- Take any specific prompt from the STL Meeting Reflection Tool (Figure 29) and frame it as an agree/disagree statement. For example:
  - *On a scale of 1* (strongly disagree) *to 5* (strongly agree), *how much do you agree that our team . . . ?*
- Generic sentence prompts:
  - *Something that worked is . . .*
  - *Something that would have made this meeting better is . . .*
  - *My question/concern is . . .*
  - *My next steps are to . . .*

Related readings:

Move 6.11, "(Heartfelt) Connect to what matters," Figure 24. This tool provides survey questions that you can ask your colleagues when you are setting direction for your team. They will give you a sense of people's commitment to the team goal, the likelihood that they will implement actions to achieve that goal, and their comfort and confidence in the group's decision-making processes.

Move 8.16, "Reach agreement on group decisions." Methods such as dipsticking and conducting an inverse poll explored in this move can be used to solicit feedback about individual understanding or favorability among choices.

10.2 Hear what's hard.

As Douglas Stone and Sheila Heen point out in their book *Thanks for the Feedback* (2015), you can't control what feedback people give you or how they express it; you can only decide what to let in, how you will interpret it, and whether or not to change because of it. This empowers you, but also requires you to have the discipline not to dismiss feedback that is difficult for you to hear. Skillful team leaders (STLs) intentionally choose to hear what's hard because it makes them better leaders.

How to hear what's hard:

I recommend this move throughout this book, but here I describe how to actually do it. I know, from firsthand experience, it's not easy. Listen to the hard-to-hear feedback. If your immediate response is to dismiss it or respond to the person who gave it, don't do that just yet. Recognize your reaction as normal, press pause, and reflect on the following four things:

1. *Affect.* Am I having an emotional response to the feedback given to me? Am I reacting to the person who delivered this feedback or the feedback itself? Is my reaction influenced by the timing or manner in which they gave me this feedback? How is this emotion affecting my body, mental state, and spirit?

   - Body: Tension, nausea, shortness of breath?
   - Mind: Rationalizing, defending, self-doubting?
   - Spirit: Injured pride, isolation, depression, fight-freeze-or-flight mode?

2. *Understanding.* What do I understand the feedback to mean? Do I need clarification?

3. *Truth.* What truth might this feedback hold? Am I ready to hear it? If not, why not?

4. *Action.* In what ways can I use this feedback to improve our collaboration or myself as a leader?

In action:

Helena looks through her team's feedback forms with her leadership coach at the end of her meeting and sees one from her colleague that says, "I know you mean well, but I feel like you are talking at us too much."

Helena: [*Body*] As I initially read this feedback, I feel sick to my stomach. I notice my jaw clenching and my shoulders tightening each time I reread it.

Helena: [*Mind*] As I reflect, I realize I had to talk a lot in this meeting because I was explaining a strategy that I've used successfully and everyone was supposed to implement. Other people on the team gave positive feedback; so maybe this was just this one person's experience. Someone is always going to complain about something. I might be rationalizing my actions.

Helena: [*Spirit*] I feel deflated. There's a part of me that wonders if it would be better to step down to let someone else lead the next meeting.

Helena: [*Understanding*] What is this person trying to communicate to me that I'm having a hard time hearing? The person saw me as someone who was telling them what to do instead of collaborating with them. They wanted more voice in our conversation.

Helena: [*Truth*] I designed the meeting in a way that would give my colleagues opportunities to collaborate, but I recognize that in the meeting, I micromanaged the conversation. I think this is because I was afraid that they would leave the meeting not knowing how to do the strategy. Possibly, too, I see myself as the one needing to teach them how to do it.

Helena: [*Action*] When the next opportunity presents itself, I will set a time limit for me to do my explanation and then pose a question about the work that I really don't know the answer to. That will give everyone I'm leading an opportunity to contribute.

STL recommendations:

Give yourself time. This move is about listening and learning, not about how to respond to the person who gave you the feedback. If you have an immediate, strong emotional response to what's been said, you may need to let the feedback marinate before being able to absorb it. That's OK.

"Let it go." When Elsa sings this song in Disney's *Frozen*, I can certainly relate. Stone and Heen (2015) write about a person's "sustain time" and "recovery time" from the point of receiving feedback. Sustain time is the amount of time you dwell on feedback. In other words, how long do you celebrate after hearing positive feedback? Recovery time is the amount of time you perseverate (maybe even come down on yourself) after you receive negative feedback. (Confession: I've got a short sustain time and too long a recovery time. I continue to work on hearing what's hard, without being hard on myself. Let it go.)

Seek feedback from those you trust. STL Daryl Campbell shared that he received a piece of critical honest feedback that ultimately shaped who he is now as an educator, but at the time he found it hard to hear. He says it's easier to see the truth in hard-to-hear feedback when that feedback comes from someone you trust and consider credible. You know they care about you and want you to succeed. If you don't have a relationship with the person who is giving you the hard-to-hear feedback, seek someone whom you do trust to help you process what's been said.

10.3 Make feedback public.

I know that you have at one time in your life as a partner, parent, or educator taken extensive time and been thoughtful before giving someone feedback, only to wonder if they actually took it in. Not only do skillful team leaders (STLs) solicit feedback after team meetings; they also intentionally share it with their colleagues so that their team members know that they have been heard.

How to make feedback public:

With your team, either share direct quotes from feedback received, or share common themes among what people said. Be transparent about how you are using their feedback to influence your decisions. Invite your colleagues into problem-solving conversations.

In action:

Craig: I'm just going to take a moment before we start today's agenda to highlight feedback from our last meeting. [*Craig shows a slide with summarized comments and numbers next to each.*] I chose five common themes from your feedback. Beside each is a number indicating how many people expressed the same sentiment. You'll notice that people experienced our last meeting differently. Some reported that our pacing was too fast, and others thought it was just right. Let's agree to speak up if the pace is not working for anyone and to make decisions in the moment about when we need to slow down as a group or table something so that we can return to it after people have had a chance to process.

STL recommendations:

Respond in a timely manner. If you have a significant lapse of time in between meetings, connect with any individual who has expressed on a feedback form a time-sensitive need or concern.

Implement changes. Follow-through is one of the key means to building trust. So if you say, "I heard you. I'm going to make this change based on what you said," then go do it.

Think like a teacher:

The best way to let someone know you "heard" their feedback is not to tell them, but to make the change they suggested. We do this with students all the time. When I first taught middle school theater, I did not have a whiteboard on the wall, so I purchased a small portable one to write daily homework assignments on and leaned it against the wall at the front of the room. At the back of my classroom was a platform stage for acting. On our acting days, students would walk in to find all the desks facing the back-of-the-room platform. One day I asked students what would make the class better, expecting them to say things like "Play more drama games!," but one boy caught me off guard and said, "Move the homework board to the back of the room on days when we are facing the platform so we don't have to turn our heads around to copy the homework." This simple feedback was an indication that I was viewing the room from my perspective, not that of my students. From that day forward, I moved the homework board depending on which way the students were facing.

While you and your colleagues won't be able to make every change someone on your team suggests, when you can, do it. And when you can't, acknowledge the suggestion and give an explanation if it will foster understanding of why the change cannot be made.

Find the right words:

- *In reviewing the feedback from our last meeting, I noticed many people found X helpful. Some voiced concerns about Y. Based on that, I tweaked today's agenda . . .*

- *I graphed responses from the surveys and want to highlight feedback from question 2. What do you think our next steps should be in order to address this?*

- *You'll notice that we are doing things differently today. This is because of the feedback I received from our last meeting . . .*

- *I appreciate the suggestion . . . however, given X, we can't do that at this time.*

ASSESS TEAM FUNCTION AND IMPACT

I can remember a wonderfully enthusiastic first-year teacher coming into my literacy coaching office practically skipping when he felt like he had had a great lesson. I would always mini-celebrate with him and then ask, "How do you know it went well?" In the first few months of his teaching, his response was always something like "It just felt great. The energy in the room was terrific. I felt 'on.'" By the end of the year, however, his response to that question had changed: "The kids totally figured out that the author was trying to say . . . Look what Darius wrote about why this character said . . . And Ashley's group asked the most insightful question at the end of the lesson." He had learned to see indicators that his teaching was having an impact on students' learning.

For team leaders and those who support them, the indicators of team impact on learning can at first be just as misleading as they were for the new teacher. I'll use myself as an example here. When I began leading teams, I felt like it was a good meeting if the conversation was lively and collegial with a few laughs and a good exchange of ideas. A typical meeting might be one where we read about a successful teaching strategy. If my colleagues wrote on an exit ticket, "Loved the strategy—I want to try it," that was cause for a mini-celebration. I saw it as a sign that I was having an impact. And I was, but to what degree? Our purpose for collaborating has to be more than just connecting with each other and gaining a few ideas in our toolbox in the classroom. We are coming together to facilitate improved learning for all students. "Conversation research has revealed that in many cases, participants themselves are not aware of many of the subtle signals and patterns that are most critical for an effective team to result" (Scribner et al., 2007, p. 73). The STL Meeting Reflection Tool (Figure 29) names specific indicators that team leaders can look for in order to assess how team meetings are going.

STL moves:

10.4 Monitor student progress.

10.5 Reflect on a meeting.

10.6 Publicly celebrate impact.

Tools and templates:

Figure 29. STL Meeting Reflection Tool

Figure 30. STL Team Inquiry Summary

What these moves promote:

Reflection. The STL Meeting Reflection Tool prompts the person who is filling it out to candidly reflect on specific aspects of function, impact, and leadership of the meeting.

Mindfulness. The STL learns what they and their team need to work on. They can be mindful of those particular areas when leading the next meeting.

Focus. Use of the STL Meeting Reflection Tool can focus the STL and their team on specific areas for improvement.

Evidence-based thinking. The STL Meeting Reflection Tool requires anyone filling it out to reflect and discuss specific moments in a meeting.

Growth mindset. STLs and their colleagues believe that each educator on the team has the capacity to grow and improve.

Collective efficacy. Teams believe that, through effective collaboration and implementation, they can positively impact all learners and positively shape school culture.

When to use these moves:

You can use the whole STL Meeting Reflection Tool to assess your team's collaboration at the beginning, middle, and end of your collaborative inquiry cycle. Or, if you decide to assess meetings regularly, you might prefer to focus on a few specific primary intentions so that you are not overwhelmed by the tool. Celebrate wins throughout a team's inquiry cycle and learning.

10.4 Monitor student progress.

Thanks to Response to Intervention (RTI) as a part of a Multi-Tiered System of Supports (MTSS), progress monitoring is a staple for teacher teams. It's common for elementary teachers and reading specialists to regularly gather student-reading data to measure student progress, determine next instructional steps in Tier 1 or student placement for intervention in Tier 2 or Tier 3, and evaluate the effectiveness of an intervention. Skillful team leaders (STLs) and their teams of all grade levels and content areas also use this move to track student progress toward any academic, behavioral, and social-emotional learning (SEL) goals, as well as habits of mind, such as persistence. It's not always easy to know what indicators of progress to look for, but frequent monitoring using a template can help you and your team keep track.

How to monitor student progress:

Many good templates are available depending on what you are monitoring. For example, Positive Behavioral Interventions and Supports (PBIS) offer ways to use Direct Behavior Ratings (DBR), systematic direct observation and intervention-based measures to monitor students' responses to behavioral supports (Bruhn & McDaniel, 2016). Intervention Central offers a template with seven steps for progress monitoring in reading, writing, math, and behavior at www.interventioncentral.org/blog/assessment-progress-monitoring/how-structure-classroom-data-collection-individual-students. Crafting Minds has a detailed organizer on their Resources page (craftingmindsgroup.com/site/resources) for data collection to make determinations for Tier 2 or Tier 3 placement in reading. And there are many others.

Regardless of what tool you use, most contain much of the same information:

- Student(s) names

- Notable student context (e.g., individualized education program [IEP], English learner [EL], student special interests)

- Family contact information

- Current performance on specific assessment measures

- Specific learning target(s)

- Type(s) of intervention (Tier 1, 2, or 3)

- Intervention program description

- Dates of intervention

- Periodic recordings of evidence of progress on specific assessment measures

- Team response/next steps

In action:

In my ASCD article "A School on the Move" (MacDonald, 2015), I give an example of a school that considers team progress monitoring one of several key practices in achieving their rapid, sustainable success. Principal Mairead Nolan and her teacher leaders regularly monitored the progress of reading growth for individual students and intentionally intervened with supports for students who were not progressing as needed. (The article, which includes the progress-monitoring tool they used, is available at www.ascd.org/el/articles/a-school-on-the-move.)

Related readings:

Move 6.8, "(Measurable) Measure what matters." Determine how you will monitor progress of your S-M-A-A-H-R-T goal right from the start.

Move 7.2, "Choose an assessment based on the view of data you need." Select measures that tell you what you need to monitor progress toward your goals.

Move 7.13, "Target and plan for student success." Don't just collect data and monitor progress. Engage in data analysis that leads to targeted goals for specific students and action steps for the teacher team to take.

10.5 Reflect on a meeting.

How do you know your meeting went well? How do you know you're on your way to impacting educator and student learning? The STL Meeting Reflection Tool (Figure 29) provides prompts for you to reflect on a single meeting through the lenses of function and impact. Indicators that a team is collegial, engaged, communicative, productive, and efficient are listed in the High Function column. Indicators that a team is (or is likely to be) achieving, performing, and effective, and that the team will reach learning outcomes and make a measurable difference, are listed in the High Impact column.

How to reflect on a meeting:

After a meeting, move through the following four steps using the STL Meeting Reflection Tool (Figure 29).

1. *Choose.* Decide which meeting(s) you will assess and with whom. Print or use an electronic version of the STL Meeting Reflection Tool (Figure 29). Select one or more partners to reflect with about a meeting or a series of meetings over a short period of time.

2. *Focus.* Decide which of the 10 STL Primary Intentions you will reflect upon. Think back to your intentions in the meeting. Unless you are doing a full audit of a team, don't assess all 10 STL Primary Intentions in one sitting. Instead, choose up to three areas of focus. (Another way to scale the tool back is to only assess function or only assess the impact of your meeting.)

3. *Cite evidence.* Reflect with examples. You and your partner(s), independently, read through the "Observable Indicators of High Function" and "High Impact." Check the box of each indicator with a highlighter in one of three colors:

   Green = Evident in this meeting.

   Yellow = Partly evident in this meeting.

   Orange = Not evident in this meeting, but should have been.

   No highlight = Not applicable. (For instance, skip "Accommodations for adults . . ." if none of your team members has any specific learning differences or disabilities or preferences.)

4. *Discuss.* After you and your partner(s) have independently reflected on the meeting and highlighted evidence, compare your responses. Determine areas of strength for the team and decide on an area to watch or improve for subsequent meetings. If you find an area for improvement, turn to the corresponding primary intention chapter in this book and see if any of the moves can help your team.

STL recommendations:

Reflect. Don't evaluate. This tool should *not* be used to evaluate any person or team. It is meant to give leaders and team members a snapshot of how they are doing and guide them to make changes in future meetings. Anyone who attended the meeting can take part in this meeting assessment tool and reflection dialogue.

Type evidence. You can modify this tool by leaving blank the two columns that provide indicators for function and impact. Instead, type next to each prompt specific evidence from your meeting. See the following example:

10. Assess	
Solicit feedback.	*Evidence:* 80% of my team completed my Google Form in between meetings.

Collect over time. If you opt to use this tool multiple times throughout the course of your team's collaboration, you will likely start to see patterns of strength and trouble spots.

FIGURE 29 STL Meeting Reflection Tool

Date of team meeting: Team leader(s):

Team: Debrief partner(s):

Context about the team or meeting:

EVIDENT	INTENTION	OBSERVABLE INDICATORS OF HIGH FUNCTION Reflect on team dynamics (collegiality, engagement, communication, productivity) and collaborate about teaching.	OBSERVABLE INDICATORS OF HIGH IMPACT Reflect on team performance and collaborate about student-learning outcomes.
	1. Optimize learning conditions.		
	Maximize collaborative time.	☐ Started and ended on time. Minimal or no interruptions to meeting time. ☐ Time spent collaborating about teaching vision, desired goals, design, or plans (e.g., "We revised a lesson together").	☐ Collaboration between meetings contributing to a culture of ongoing inquiry. ☐ Time spent collaborating about student-learning outcomes that result from implementation of plans (e.g., "We analyzed exit slips to learn which students met the lesson targets").
	Enhance the learning space.	☐ Accessible location and seating. Good acoustics and visibility. Personalized space. Organized and ready-to-use meeting materials.	☐ Strategic use of space to foster collaboration (e.g., flexible groups, interactive movement for large groups, intentional seating).
	Promote equitable access to team learning.	☐ Accommodations for adults with differences, disabilities, or preferences.	☐ Opportunities for adults with disabilities and differences to showcase their strengths.
	2. Establish expectations and responsibilities.		
	Facilitate a group norm-setting process.	☐ Clear understanding of how to interact in meetings.	☐ Unanimous commitment to behave in ways that help the team reach their goals.
	Institute social norms that maximize team impact.	☐ Agreement on adopting team norms. ☐ Sensitivity to cultural differences when working in a group.	☐ Lived norms through words and actions. ☐ Appreciation for cultural differences when working in a group. ☐ Honest dialogue when tacit (unwritten) norms or broken agreements impeded collaboration.
	Share responsibility through roles.	☐ Clear understanding of team leader's and team members' responsibilities. ☐ Shared responsibility for meeting tasks (e.g., timekeeper, note-taker, data organizer, food).	☐ No one assigned a role based on social and cultural identifiers (e.g., race, gender, age). ☐ Shared responsibility for collaborative learning (e.g., bring in student work; revise a lesson; lead a demonstration lesson; facilitate a text-based discussion).

3. Nurture group culture.

Foster inclusivity.	☐ People respected and included one another. Everyone felt welcome. No one felt excluded, ridiculed, or "less than."	☐ New members and people from traditionally marginalized groups felt a sense of belonging.
Build community and relational trust through play.	☐ People enjoyed working together (e.g., energy, laughter, joy). Sense of optimism and possibility. ☐ All understood purpose and directions for, and participated in, icebreakers or games.	☐ Relational trust, sense of community, and connection were present, not only during icebreakers and games, but also during learning conversations throughout the meeting.
Strengthen vulnerability-based trust.	☐ People were dependable, supportive, and respectful.	☐ Vulnerability-based trust/psychological safety was present. People voiced or modeled challenges, missteps, confusions, and struggles and listened without judgment.

4. Design and plan learning.

Plan purposeful meetings.	☐ A clear reason for meeting—everyone understood the purpose for each agenda item. ☐ Meeting tasks were sequenced and designed for a positive collaborative experience. ☐ Everyone clearly understood what needed to get done in the meeting.	☐ The reason for meeting was worthwhile. ☐ Meeting tasks were designed and facilitated to help advance the team toward its goals. ☐ The team achieved what it set out to accomplish in the meeting.
Structure tasks and talk.	☐ Clear task directions—all knew what was expected of them. ☐ Tasks did not overwhelm or underwhelm team members. ☐ Any protocols or templates provided scaffolding for conversation without stifling it.	☐ When appropriate, tasks required higher-order thinking skills (i.e., apply, analyze, evaluate, and synthesize) and demanded strategic or extended thinking. ☐ Any protocol(s) or template(s) helped bring about new learning.
Learn from a text-based discussion.	☐ Accessible, relevant, culturally sensitive text(s). ☐ Sufficient time and non-stifling structure provided for reading and discussion. ☐ People engaged with the text(s) and each other.	☐ Readings prompted new learning and insight into thinking and practice. ☐ A team culture of reading/viewing and learning together.

5. Engage and interact.

Boost engagement.	☐ Equitable opportunities to participate. No individual dominated the meeting. ☐ No one distracted or off-task in the meeting or in breakout groups.	☐ Less dominant voices were empowered to speak. ☐ Active participation (e.g., presenting, questioning, researching, problem solving).
Maximize productivity.	☐ Productivity tools kept the meeting moving (e.g., subcommittees, delegating tasks).	☐ Produced outcomes that benefited students.
Focus talk.	☐ On topic and on task. If the team wandered, it was worthwhile to do so.	☐ Attention to levers that influence student learning. ☐ Attention to both the big picture and important details.
Manage conflict.	☐ People engaged in respectful disagreement of ideas. No one personally attacked.	☐ Conflict resolution was reached and resulted in new understandings of one another, and helped shape a collaborative community.

(Continued)

(Continued)

EVIDENT	INTENTION	OBSERVABLE INDICATORS OF HIGH FUNCTION — Reflect on team dynamics (collegiality, engagement, communication, productivity) and collaborate about teaching.	OBSERVABLE INDICATORS OF HIGH IMPACT — Reflect on team performance and collaborate about student-learning outcomes.
		6. Lead with purpose and direction.	
	Align with a priority.	☐ A shared understanding of school priorities. ☐ Agreement on what is important. ☐ Connections to inquiry work. (Meeting did not feel out of place.)	☐ Sustained focus on school priorities. Distractions did not derail the team. ☐ Decisions driven by what is important. ☐ Connections to priorities, professional development, and/or individual professional-learning goals.
	Focus on a specific student-centered challenge.	☐ Agreement on a vision for what students are expected to know and do. ☐ Inquiry into **teaching** challenges that team members don't yet have answers to. ☐ Dialogue focused on teaching resources and practices that could potentially help students.	☐ A high-expectations vision for student learning regardless of students' social and cultural identities. ☐ Inquiry into **student-learning** challenges that team members don't yet have answers to. ☐ Dialogue focused on evidence of student-centered challenges and progress.
	Work toward a S-M-A-A-H-R-T goal.	☐ Team satisfaction with the goal-setting process. ☐ Agreement on team goal(s), action steps, timeline, and measures. ☐ Clarity around what to do to reach goal(s).	☐ A data-informed process for goal setting and action planning. ☐ Targeted student-learning goals with strategic action steps, a time frame based on student needs, and measures that assess student progress. ☐ A teacher practice goal is viewed as a pathway to reach a student-learning goal, but is not the end goal itself. ☐ Strong desire, intent, and perceived feasibility to reach goal(s).
		7. Promote intentional data* use. (* Data may include student work samples, test scores, survey responses, etc.)	
	Select (or design) a meaningful assessment.	☐ Clarity about which students will be assessed, with what type of assessments, and for what purpose. ☐ Agreement on questions/tasks to give students.	☐ Student work samples/assessment data were current, authentic representations of what students can do, and relevant to the team's inquiry question(s) and/or goal(s). ☐ Well-designed questions/tasks (e.g., test what was taught, measure one thing, format to get data you need, evaluate task demand, predetermine learning indicators, build student confidence, intentionally design answer choices).
	Prepare data to examine.	☐ Data prepared and organized in a way that all can access and make sense of (e.g., charts, tables, graphs, spreadsheets, use of color).	☐ Student data or teacher work (e.g., lesson plans) prepared in a way that facilitated evidence-based analysis (e.g., removed student names; presented different levels of work; included standards, models, task/test questions, and rubrics).
	Facilitate data analysis.	☐ Willingness to analyze data together. ☐ Adhered to the steps of a data protocol or routine.	☐ A healthy team attitude toward data analysis. (No blame, no shame.) ☐ Insight gained from data discussion. ☐ Targeted planning for student success.

8. Engage in analytical thinking, creative problem solving, and clear decision making.

Suspend an assumption.	☐ Willingness to examine one's own assumptions.	☐ A culture where team members called attention to one another's assumptions.
Interrupt assumptions, bias, and unsound reasoning.	☐ Non-judgmental tone and language when inquiring into assumptions.	☐ Inquiry into implicit bias, negative assumptions, or fixed mindsets, particularly about people's social and cultural identities (race, gender, ability, learning profile, age, etc.).
Cultivate diverse perspectives.	☐ A respectful exchange of diverse ideas. ☐ A diverse team working cooperatively to problem solve.	☐ Empathy for others' perspectives. ☐ Flexible thinking about problems and solutions. (Get beyond fixed ways of thinking.) ☐ People were not intimidated to voice less popular opinions.
Make clear impactful decisions.	☐ Clarity around decision making (e.g., who decides, who gives input, next steps).	☐ Decisions positively impact staff, students, families, and/or community.

9. Implement new learning.

Lead peer observation.	☐ Productive planning of a peer observation (e.g., purpose, method, logistics).	☐ A culture of trust where team members implement new practices for peer feedback.
Navigate resistance to change.	☐ Strong team relationships withstood any individual's reluctance to change.	☐ Evidence of adopting a change and making progress toward team goals (or intent to implement new practices).
Invite accountability.	☐ Clear expectations. ☐ Shared feelings of commitment toward one another.	☐ Clear consequences for lack of follow-through. ☐ Shared feelings of commitment toward student-learning goals.

10. Assess.

Solicit feedback.	☐ Regular opportunities for feedback. ☐ 100% of team members give constructive feedback.	☐ Feedback, even that which was hard to hear, informed next steps for the team and the leader.
Assess team function and impact.	☐ Produced teaching resources or plans to change practice. ☐ Team worked well together.	☐ Implemented changes to practice resulting in improved outcomes for students. ☐ Team made progress toward collaboration goals.
Develop as a leader.	☐ Strong relationships and clear communication with colleagues. ☐ Productive, efficient, engaging facilitation skills.	☐ A skillful approach to leadership grounded in values, growth mindset and efficacy, emotional intelligence, responsiveness to hurdles, and intentional implementation of leadership moves.

Note: This tool captures many indicators of function and impact in a team meeting, but there are always others. Elisa edits this tool from time to time as new learning about teams becomes available. Go to www.elisamacdonald.com for updates.

10.6 Publicly celebrate impact.

Slight wins are still wins. When a team is on a quest to build stamina in students who are reluctant to write so that they ultimately produce a five-paragraph essay and the team sees their first five-sentence paragraph, that is something to celebrate. When a team explores the impact of a visual arts lesson on student achievement in science and does not yet see an improvement in scores but does notice that an activity helped English learners (ELs) envision phenomena that they were not able to directly observe, that is a win (Brouillette & Graham, 2016). Regardless of what a team has set out to problem solve, even if they do not yet see the full impact of their efforts, skillful team leaders (STLs) take time to recognize progress by celebrating incremental wins with others. This builds morale within the team and also a lively collaborative community.

How to publicly celebrate impact:

Here are two ways you might celebrate modest or substantial impact with others:

1. *Data walls and portfolios*: The nice thing about writing measurable goals is that you are collecting data as you implement new learning. This makes sharing wins easy. Make a visual display of growth on a bulletin board. Create shared folders with students so they can track their own progress on a spreadsheet and share them with caregivers at a conference. Host grade-level celebrations when all classes meet or exceed learning targets for nonacademic goals such as attendance, punctuality, or persistence at challenging tasks.

Lisa Lineweaver, former director of accelerated improvement and Teach Plus coach at Blackstone Elementary in Boston, and current principal of Kelly Elementary School in Chelsea, Massachusetts, made the following recommendations in a 2012 professional development training:

- *Clearly publicize a simple story.* Don't overwhelm the wall with every piece of data you have (e.g., "This graph shows our growth in X over time" or "This visual table tells the story of how our students have made gains over the district").

- *Label data properly so that it is understandable.* If comparing two things (e.g., grade point average and attendance), label them appropriately. Define acronyms and jargon. MOY (middle of year) and ORF (oral reading fluency) don't sound like something to celebrate.

- *Make growth visible to all.* Reporting that a third-grade student moved from reading Level F to reading Level M is impressive, but a more relatable way to show growth might be to say, "This student was reading the phonics-based Pete the Cat series and is now reading Junie B. Jones chapter books!" Parents and educators who are not reading specialists, as well as the students themselves, will instantly realize the significance of the child's accomplishment and the team of teachers who got the child there.

- *Remove identifying information.* Use student ID numbers or symbols to convey student-level data while maintaining privacy. Exception: Use names for noteworthy accomplishments, such as improved attendance and honor roll.

2. *Publicize an inquiry work plan.* Use the work plan template (Move 4.1, Figure 13) to capture the details of your team inquiry cycle and share it with others. If this is too much detail, simply fill in and share the STL Team Inquiry Summary in Figure 30.

FIGURE 30   STL Team Inquiry Summary

Dates of our team inquiry cycle:
Team with member names:
Inquiry question(s) and/or S-M-A-A-H-R-T goal:
Research/resources studied:
Strategies implemented:
A hurdle we faced:
Findings:
Emerging questions:

DEVELOP AS A LEADER

You did not become an effective teacher overnight. You made deliberate moves to become the practitioner you are. You owned every misstep. You persisted through challenges. You associated with colleagues who inspired you to get better at your practice. You set goals to be better. Like teachers, skillful team leaders (STLs) intentionally aim to improve at what they do. Whether this is your first year leading a team or your tenth, you will always encounter hurdles. Regular self-assessment, leadership goal setting, and the moves in this book will help you lead the team you have, and help you develop into the leader you want to become.

STL moves:

10.7 Self-assess.

10.8 Set leadership growth goals.

10.9 Admit missteps.

10.10 Practice mindfulness.

10.11 Build capacity.

Tools and templates:

Figure 31: STL Self-Assessment Tool

Figure 32: STL Self-Assessment Tool Examples

What these moves promote:

Self-awareness. STLs develop an awareness of their own strengths and areas

Agency. STLs direct their learning by setting leadership-growth goals.

Growth mindset. STLs see themselves as ongoing learners who are expected to make missteps and persevere despite them.

Community. STLs work with colleagues, school administrators, and other team leaders to support one another in their growth and development as leaders of adult learning.

When to use these moves:

Every day.

10.7 Self-assess.

A meeting or two will not define the type of leader you are, but meetings can be a good source of data for you to reflect on as a leader. As described in the first chapter of this book, a skillful approach to team leadership is rooted in your (1) values, (2) mindset and efficacy, (3) emotional intelligence, and (4) responsiveness to hurdles; and the intentionality with which you lead. Skillful team leaders (STLs) reflect on specific leadership moments within these categories. They celebrate successes and uncover areas for growth.

How to self-assess:

After a meeting, move through the following three steps using the STL Self-Assessment Tool (Figure 31).

1. *Choose.* Decide what to reflect on and with whom. Print or use an electronic copy of the STL Self-Assessment Tool (Figure 31). Reflect on one meeting or several meetings over a period of time. (If you self-assess regularly, then focus either on the statements within only one category or on one statement from every category. If you self-assess one to three times a year, then reflect on all the statements in one sitting.) It is advisable to talk with a trusted partner(s) about your self-assessment.

2. *Cite evidence.* Aim to think of specific examples in which you did or did not demonstrate the statement. Mark *Y* for yes, *S* for somewhat, or *N* for not yet. If the statement does not apply, leave it blank.

3. *Celebrate and reflect.* Discuss with a partner. Celebrate leadership moments when you were skillful and intentional. Focus in on one area for which you would like to set a leadership growth goal (Move 10.8).

FIGURE 31   STL Self-Assessment Tool

Am I leading my team with a skillful intentional approach?

CATEGORY	DESCRIPTION	YES	SOMETIMES	NOT YET
Intention	1. I optimized learning conditions for collaboration.			
	2. I established group expectations and responsibilities for collaboration.			
	3. I nurtured a group culture of trust and community.			
	4. I designed and planned learning experiences for my team meeting.			
	5. I engaged others in learning and fostered positive interactions with and among my colleagues.			
	6. I led with purpose and direction.			
	7. I promoted data use to advance learning.			
	8. I engaged others in analytical thought, creative problem solving, and clear decision making.			
	9. I facilitated implementation of new learning.			
	10. I assessed the function and impact of our team.			
Values	11. I made decisions based on my core values (e.g., about equity) and personal values (e.g., transparency).			
	12. I modeled our school's core values through my words and actions.			
	13. I aligned teamwork to research-based, widely accepted principles about teaching and learning.			
Mindset and efficacy about students	14. I acted on the belief that all students, regardless of cultural or social identity (i.e., race, gender, ability, etc.), can learn and reach high expectations.			
	15. I sought to understand why students might reduce effort or give up. I pursued strategies to engage them.			
	16. I acted on the belief that our team can positively influence outcomes for all students and families.			

CATEGORY	DESCRIPTION	YES	SOMETIMES	NOT YET
Mindset and efficacy about adults	17. I acted on the belief that all team members can learn and achieve high expectations for students.			
	18. I sought to understand why colleagues might reduce effort or give up. I pursued strategies to engage them.			
	19. I sustained the belief that our team can positively influence one another's practice.			
Emotional intelligence	20. I noticed when my colleagues exhibited emotions such as distress, anxiety, sadness, boredom, and so on.			
	21. I demonstrated cross-cultural sensitivity and empathy. I brought levity when appropriate.			
	22. I noticed when I felt emotions such as distress, anxiety, sadness, boredom, and so on.			
	23. I was able to self-regulate my emotions in front of others.			
Responsiveness to team hurdles	24. I noticed when my cultural positioning or implicit bias influenced my interpretation and response.			
	25. I anticipated and avoided team hurdles when possible. I responded effectively to hurdles that I could not avoid.			
	26. I explored multiple causes for team hurdles, including the role of school culture and my own leadership.			
	27. I was responsive to the needs of my group.			

FIGURE 32   STL Self-Assessment Tool Examples

The following provides examples for the reflective statements in the STL Self-Assessment Tool (Figure 31).

INTENTION	
1. I optimized learning conditions for collaboration.	Example: I advocated to protect team time when the principal needed to schedule a staff meeting.
2. I established group expectations and responsibilities for collaboration.	Example: I invited my colleagues to rotate co-planning meeting agendas with me.
3. I nurtured a group culture of trust and community.	Example: I showed vulnerability by telling my colleagues a story about my lesson that did not go well.
4. I designed and planned learning experiences for my team meeting.	Example: I activated learning with discussion about a significant quote related to our topic of inquiry.
5. I engaged others in learning and fostered positive interactions with and among my colleagues.	Example: I managed my own level of participation so as not to dominate talk at the table.
6. I led with purpose and direction.	Example: I reframed our teacher-practice goal to name the learning outcomes we wanted for students.
7. I promoted data use to advance learning.	Example: I fostered a healthy team data culture where no one blamed others for lack of student progress.
8. I engaged others in analytical thought, creative problem solving, and clear decision making.	Example: I modeled evidence-based decision making when examining data.
9. I facilitated implementation of new learning.	Example: I led the team in planning a peer observation of a new practice we studied.
10. I assessed the function and impact of our team.	Example: I got feedback from my colleagues about our meeting on a Google Form.
VALUES	
11. I made decisions based on my core values (e.g., about equity) and personal values (e.g., transparency).	Example: I disaggregated data by race so that we could analyze and address inequities.
12. I modeled our school's core values through my words and actions.	Example: Responsibility is a school value. I took personal responsibility for students' confusion on an assessment question that I wrote.
13. I aligned teamwork to research-based, widely accepted guiding principles about teaching and learning.	Example: I led teachers in unpacking the language of a standard.
MINDSET AND EFFICACY ABOUT STUDENTS	
14. I acted on the belief that all students, regardless of cultural or social identity (i.e., race, gender, ability, etc.), can learn and reach high expectations.	Example: I reframed a negative assumption about students who have a history of trauma.
15. I sought to understand why students might reduce effort or give up. I pursued strategies to engage them.	Example: I shared with my colleagues a successful strategy that I used to help a student who would not do homework in any classes.
16. I acted on the belief that our team can positively influence outcomes for all students and families.	Example: I facilitated creative problem solving.

MINDSET AND EFFICACY ABOUT ADULTS	
17. I acted on the belief that all team members can learn and reach high expectations for students.	Example: A veteran teacher was dismissive of trying a new approach where students led the book talk. I helped her craft a class contract with students so that she could successfully implement the new student-centered approach.
18. I sought to understand why colleagues might reduce effort or give up. I pursued strategies to engage them.	Example: My colleague comes to our meetings late and leaves early. Our team is frustrated. I approach my colleague 1:1 to learn what is going on.
19. I sustained the belief that our team can positively influence one another's practice.	Example: I have been teaching this skill the same way for 10 years. I showed a video clip coupled with student work and asked my colleagues to give me feedback.
EMOTIONAL INTELLIGENCE	
20. I noticed when my colleagues exhibited emotions such as distress, anxiety, sadness, boredom, and so on.	Example: I noticed pushback from my colleagues in setting this goal. I recognized that they were feeling overwhelmed.
21. I demonstrated cross-cultural sensitivity and empathy. I brought levity when appropriate.	Example: Someone took offense to the term *struggling learners*, so I changed my language to "when students demonstrate struggle."
22. I noticed when I felt emotions such as distress, anxiety, sadness, boredom, and so on.	Example: I was angry that a school leader did not consult teachers on the decision.
23. I was able to self-regulate my emotions in front of others.	Example: I did not send an angry email to the school leader. Instead, I led a conversation with my team on ways we could implement the decision.
RESPONSIVENESS TO TEAM HURDLES	
24. I noticed when my cultural positioning or implicit bias influenced my interpretation and response.	Example: I was taught that interrupting someone was rude. My colleague views interrupting as a means of showing active participation and engagement. I realize my colleague is not intending to be rude when he interrupts.
25. I proactively avoided team hurdles when possible. I responded effectively to hurdles that I could not avoid.	Example: I had a misunderstanding with a colleague and checked in 1:1 with her after the meeting.
26. I explored multiple causes for team hurdles, including the role of school culture and my own leadership.	Example: Our team did not learn much from looking at student work together. I should have been more thoughtful about the pieces of data we selected to analyze.
27. I was responsive to the needs of my group.	Example: I had planned for everyone to implement the strategy next week, but it became clear that my team did not fully understand it. Instead I will do a dry demo of the strategy with the team next week.

10.8 Set leadership growth goals.

When I do an internet search for "how to approach self-improvement goals," here's some of what comes up: "42 Practical Ways to Start Working on Self-Improvement." "7 Steps to Writing Your Own Simple Self-Improvement Plan." "10 Tips for Personal Self-Development." "80+ Self-Improvement Tips That Will Change Your Life." Are you inspired or overwhelmed? Skillful team leaders (STLs), regardless of their years of experience, set leadership growth goals. Knowing where to start and how to improve can be challenging, and it is not uncommon for teacher leaders, in particular, to question if leading their colleagues is right for them.

How to set leadership growth goals:

Begin with reflection. Use the STL Meeting Reflection Tool (Figure 29) and the STL Self-Assessment Tool (Figure 31, with examples in Figure 32) to focus on the areas where you want to improve. Solicit feedback from those you lead and from those who support you as a leader (e.g., a coach or administrator). If you find multiple areas for growth and aren't quite sure where to start, consider three things:

1. *Relevance.* Which leadership area makes the most sense to work on now given the scope and responsibility of my work as a team leader?

2. *Obstacle.* Which leadership area is most getting in the way of our team functioning well and positively impacting students?

3. *Reward.* Which area, once improved, will make me feel proudest and most eager to continue my leadership work?

Then move through the basic process of goal setting: Envision how you want yourself to grow. Set the intention to get there. Learn what might get in the way of reaching your goal and why. Take what feels right as the first action step and make incremental moves.

In action:

Aaron: When I took the STL self-assessment, I could not point to specific examples where I facilitated implementation of new learning. I am a strong leader in getting people to talk about what worked and didn't when they implemented the strategy we studied, but I have not yet had us observe each other's practice. I'm going to be the first to open my classroom. I'll model a strategy related to our inquiry work for my colleagues to view and give me feedback. It will take courage on my part and a lot of logistical coordination. [*Relevance*] This goal is relevant because everyone is already implementing the new strategy, but not publicly. [*Obstacle*] Without this, we will be missing out on valuable peer feedback. [*Reward*] When I reach this leadership goal, our team will have reached a new level of trust.

10.9 Admit missteps.

If there is one lesson I aimed to convey in my first book (MacDonald, 2013) and can now, almost 10 years later, testify still holds true, it's this: No matter your expertise, no matter your years of experience, you will make missteps when leading your colleagues. Skillful team leaders (STLs) expect to make errors in judgment and expect that they will make moves that don't work. They admit their missteps to their colleagues and to themselves.

How to admit missteps:

Don't grovel. Don't berate yourself. If what you've done requires a formal apology, then offer it. But usually, a simple acknowledgement of your misstep will suffice. Seek to repair any relationships that may have been impaired, and learn from your mistakes.

STL recommendation:

"Give yourself grace." This is the advice my good friend, a former principal, recommends to principals in the Learning Forward article "How School Leaders Manage Stress and Stay Focused": "No principal can address every challenge and meet every goal she sets for herself. Accept imperfection and recognize the many successes you do achieve. This can help you focus on your most important responsibility—upholding your school's vision for academic achievement" (E. Becker, 2019, p. 25). This is also true for team leaders. I am the first to admit that accepting anything less than perfect is extremely hard, particularly when the stakes are high for students. Don't take your eye off student learning, but do expect hiccups. At some point, you will likely design a meeting that flops; make a facilitation move that throws the meeting off; lose your sense of direction and talk aimlessly; feed into negativity instead of steering out of it; escalate tension instead of defusing it; make unfounded assumptions; judge or gossip about others instead of seeking to understand them; be unable to muster the courage to address bias, low standards, or tacit norms that are long overdue for an overhaul; unintentionally violate someone's trust; and unintentionally fail a student or colleague. Such missteps are hard to overcome, and, for the more serious ones like violating someone's trust, you will need to actively make amends, but you can still give yourself grace to learn and grow.

Find the right words:

- *That was definitely a misstep on my part. Might we be able to start afresh?*

- *In hindsight, I shouldn't have . . . and now I know. I'm sorry you had to experience that. What can we do to move forward?*

- *I recognize that I could have handled this better. Let me make it right.*

- *I acknowledge my part in fueling this conflict. I want to take responsibility for moving past it.*

- *Please accept my sincere apology. I had good intentions. I hope you'll give me the opportunity to earn back your trust.*

10.10 Practice mindfulness.

Only 7% of employees ages 18–70 surveyed in one research study believed that stressed leaders could effectively lead their teams (Life Meets Work, 2017). Only 11% of those employees reported that stressed leaders kept them highly engaged at work (Life Meets Work, 2017). Bottom line: If you are a stressed leader, you aren't helping your team (or yourself). Skillful team leaders (STLs) practice mindfulness as one means to manage stress, regulate their emotions, and foster a healthy collaborative climate.

How (one method) to practice mindfulness:

There are many mindfulness moves you can practice. I learned one method to be fully present from an accomplished actress I once worked with: *Breathe. See. Speak.* I have adapted her advice to help leaders manage their own emotions.

- *Breathe.* Notice the emotions harboring in your body and what effect they are having on you physically. Common spots include a clenched jaw, wrinkled brow, raised shoulders, upset belly, tight chest, shaking leg, and shortness of breath. (These sound like side effects in a drug commercial, but they are all real manifestations of the emotional state you are in.) Pick a breathing technique that will allow your body to release the emotion you hold. It might be a basic three slow breaths from your diaphragm. Or it might be a quick release in which you take one big deep breath, hold it, and, before you release, inhale a bit more until you can't anymore, then let it all gush out. Allow your breath to flow deeply through the parts of your body where you feel tension, uneasiness, and the like.

- *See.* Be present. See your physical surroundings. See the circumstances with clarity, unclouded by emotion.

- *Speak.* There is a reason this step is last. Once you have centered your emotions, once you are grounded in the present, then respond to the situation.

STL recommendations:

Visualize. Assign an image to what you feel. For instance, if you feel nervous and scattered with an upset belly, then imagine many tiny rapidly fluttering wings (sort of like the Snitch in the Harry Potter series) running loose manically throughout your body. Then change the image. Picture your hands gently capturing the fluttering wings and holding them quietly and calmly at your center until the fluttering pauses.

Ground your feet. A small adaptation to getting centered is to stand up (or sit in a straight-back chair) and push down into your feet. Press your heels to the soles of your shoes straight through to the ground so that your body leans ever so slightly back, enough to put you off-balance for a moment, but your core should keep you from tipping backward or losing your footing. Then sway slightly forward to a centered, balanced position where your body feels comfortably positioned over your feet. Gently wiggle your toes. Feel your body weight shift to your feet. You are supported and strong.

Practice mindfulness with others. It can be a powerful moment when everyone in a room gets centered and focused together. Some might, at first, be uncomfortable or even unwilling. (That is OK. They can choose to participate in a way that feels right for them.) Even if there is some eye rolling, as soon as people feel a physical difference from the group-centering exercise, they often realize the value in it. Just be sure to monitor your time, keeping it to under five minutes, as this is not intended to be a meditation class.

10.11 Build capacity.

"Here I come to save the daaaaaaaay!" Such were the lyrics to the Mighty Mouse cartoon theme song. (If you want a laugh, search Andy Kaufman singing it.) This mindset is fine for an animated superhero, but unadvisable for a school team leader. Doing everything for your team can cause burnout of a leader, as well as social loafing from team members (see Part II, Chapter 4). It also makes it difficult for teams to sustain progress, particularly when leadership changes. Skillful team leaders (STLs) avoid these superhero(ine) pitfalls by intentionally building capacity.

How to build capacity:

The following section explores ways in which you can build capacity in others and in yourself.

Build capacity in others.

Think about the long-term vision that you and others have for students and educators. While today you may be spearheading this work by facilitating meetings, modeling lessons, or leading subcommittees, seek opportunities to bring other people in. Think macro and micro.

At a big-picture level, work with school leaders to design systems and structures that make space for adults to lead one another. For example, have teachers lead and design in-house courses for their colleagues. Have students present at a teacher workshop.

At the micro level, appreciate the strengths of your colleagues. Notice when someone takes an interest in leading. Create opportunities to lead in your team meetings with Move 2.9. Support your colleagues beyond your meetings by encouraging them to lead a workshop, observe teachers at another school and report back, represent the team at a district meeting, or present at a national conference.

In action:

New teacher orientation in STL Karen Coyle Aylward's school used to be facilitated by one school leader. One summer, Karen and the literacy coach (with approval from the principal) arranged compensation for teachers to lead the training. Karen and the literacy coach supported teachers in the design and facilitation of the training. It was so well received that it became the model for orientation thereafter.

Build capacity in yourself.

Robert Glazer, author of the 2019 book *Elevate*, defines capacity building as "the method by which individuals seek, acquire, and develop the skills and abilities to consistently perform at a higher level in pursuit of their innate potential" (p. 1). In other words, it's what you need to do to become your best self. His model complements the skillful intentional approach I write about in Part I, Chapter 1. His framework consists of four elements through which individuals can build their capacity. They are explained as follows:

Spiritual capacity. Build your spiritual capacity by making decisions guided by your core values and beliefs. Try writing down on paper your life's purpose statement with goals and core values. Refer to this paper when making tough decisions.

Intellectual capacity. Build your intellectual capacity so that you can achieve your goals and reach your life's purpose. Seek out learning and mentorship. Implement small actions that can over time yield big results. For example, try starting every day with a consistent morning routine in which you make it a habit to set your intention, specific goals, and plan for the day.

Emotional capacity. Build your emotional capacity so that you can positively relate to others. No leader wants to be labeled "emotional." Yet, when you are able to emotionally connect with the people you lead, they perceive you as caring and empathetic, both desirable qualities in a leader. Try noticing the effect of your emotions on others. Aim to be responsive, not reactive. See Move 10.10 for a mindfulness technique that can help you manage your emotional response in a challenging moment.

Physical capacity. I remember the first day I taught high school students in a block schedule for which I had first period off and then taught straight through until the end of the day with a mere 22-minute break for lunch. I never sat down. I was "on" the whole time. When I got home, I was so exhausted, physically and mentally, that I was asleep by 8 p.m. I had to build my capacity.

Physical and mental well-being are critical to an STL's endurance. Leading teams can be demanding. And if you lead adults and teach students, like many teacher leaders do, then you are taking on a lot. Managing the workload can be hard. Share leadership by building the capacity of others (see the previous section). Also, try working with school leaders to make educator health and well-being a school-wide priority. For example, I worked with leaders in one school who opened each meeting with a five-minute walk. Focus, too, on self-care, whatever that means for you. And lastly, build your capacity by collaborating with other team leaders. You are each other's support systems.

In closing:

Earlier in the book I make the analogy that team leaders are like bakers on *The Great British Baking Show*. I write, "Two people can follow the same recipe and have the same ingredients, but how things turn out depends on the baker. This book makes the moves visible; you are what makes them work." So, as the hosts of the show say at the start of every challenge,

"On your mark, get set, *bake*!"

Bibliography

25 books that leave a legacy. (2007, April 9). *USA Today*. https://usatoday30.usatoday.com/life/top25-books.htm

Adams, C. B. L. (2021, February 23). How important is diversity in thinking? *Psychology Today*. https://www.psychologytoday.com/us/blog/living-automatic/202102/how-important-is-diversity-in-thinking

Aguilar, E. (2013). *The art of coaching: Effective strategies for school transformation*. Jossey-Bass.

American Institutes for Research. (2016, August). *How to succeed in school turnaround: Practices that characterize successful turnaround schools in Massachusetts*. https://www.air.org/sites/default/files/downloads/report/How-to-Succeed-in-School-Turnaround-Massachusetts-August-2016.pdf

Amplify Education. (2020, June 29). S1-26. The basic science in reading instruction: Daniel Willingham [Audio podcast episode]. In *Science of Reading*. https://www.listennotes.com/podcasts/science-of-reading/s1-26-a-conversation-with-GEv5QoVeKIS/

Anderson, L. (1997). *Argyris & Schön's theory on congruence and learning*. http://www.aral.com.au/resources/argyris.html

Anderson, T. (2020, July 16). *Respond, reimagine, restart* [Webinar]. Association for Supervision and Curriculum Development.

Anstiss, T., Passmore, J., & Gilbert, P. (2020, May). Compassion: The essential orientation. *The Psychologist*, *33*, 38–42. https://thepsychologist.bps.org.uk/volume-33/may-2020/compassion-essential-orientation

Argyris, C. (1993). *Knowledge for action: A guide to overcoming barriers to organizational change*. Jossey-Bass.

Atwell, N. (2017). *Lessons that change writers*. Heinemann.

Bagozzi, R. P. (1992). The self-regulation of attitudes, intentions, and behavior. *Social Psychology Quarterly*, *55*(2), 178–204.

Bagozzi, R., Dholakia, U., & Basuroy, S. (2003). How effortful decisions get enacted: The motivating role of decision processes, desires, and anticipated emotions. *Journal of Behavioral Decision Making*, *16*, 273–295. https://doi.org/10.1002/bdm.446

Bagozzi, R. P., & Edwards, E. A. (2000). Goal-striving and the implementation of goal intentions in the regulation of body weight. *Psychology & Health*, *15*(2), 255–270. https://doi.org/10.1080/08870440008400305

Bailey, K., & Jakicic, C. (2011). *Common formative assessment: A toolkit for professional learning communities at work*. Solution Tree.

Baird, B., Smallwood, J., Mrazek, M. D., Kam, J. W. Y., Franklin, M. S., & Schooler, J. W. (2012). Inspired by distraction: Mind wandering facilitates creative incubation. *Psychological Science*, *23*(10), 1117–1122. https://doi.org/10.1177/0956797612446024

Balcetis, E. (2020). *Clearer. Closer. Better: How successful people see the world*. Ballantine Books.

Baumeister, R. F., & Hutton, D. G. (1987). Self-presentation theory: Self-construction and audience pleasing. In B. Mullen & G. R. Goethals (Eds.), *Theories of group behavior* (pp. 71–87). Springer Verlag.

Becker, E. (2019, October). Keep the focus on instructional leadership. *The Learning Professional*, *40*(5), 25. https://learningforward.org/wp-content/uploads/2019/10/2the-learning-professional-october2019.pdf

Becker, J., & Smith, E. (2019, August 13). Research: For crowdsourcing to work, everyone needs an equal voice. *Harvard Business Review*. https://hbr.org/2019/07/

research-for-crowdsourcing-to-work-everyone -needs-an-equal-voice

Bellack, A. A., Kliebard, H. M., Hyman, R. T., & Smith, F. L., Jr. (1966). *The language of the classroom*. Teachers College Press.

Berckemeyer, J. (2013, November/December). *The battle over student engagement*. AMLE. https://www .amle.org/the-battle-over-student -engagement/

Berry, B. (2019, March 25). Teacher leadership: Prospects and promises. *Phi Delta Kappan, 100*(7), 49–55. https://kappanonline.org/ teacher-leadership-prospects-promises-berry/

Bintlif, A. (2014, July 22). *Talking Circles: For restorative justice and beyond*. Learning for Justice. https://www.learningforjustice.org/magazine/ talking-circles-for-restorative-justice-and-beyond

Bloomberg, P., & Pitchford, B. (2017). *Leading impact teams: Building a culture of efficacy*. Corwin.

Bocala, C., & Boudett, K. P. (2015). Teaching educators habits of mind for using data wisely. *Teachers College Record, 117*, 1–20.

Boudett, K. P., City, E. A., & Murnane, R. J. (2005). *Data Wise: A step-by-step guide to using assessment results to improve teaching and learning*. Harvard Education Press.

Bregman, P. (2016, January 11). The right way to hold people accountable. *Harvard Business Review*. https://hbr.org/2016/01/ the-right-way-to-hold-people-accountable

Brouillette, L., & Graham, N. J. (2016). Using arts integration to make science learning memorable in the upper elementary grades: A quasi-experimental study. *Journal for Learning Through the Arts, 12*(1), https://www .artsedsearch.org/study/using-arts-inte gration-to-make-science-learning-memorable -in-the-upper-elementary-grades-a-quasi-experi mental-study/

Brower, T. (2019, March 3). Boost productivity 20%: The surprising power of play. *Forbes*. https://www .forbes.com/sites/tracybrower/2019/03/03/ boost-productivity-20-the-surprising -power-of-play/?sh=134658257c05

Brown, B. (2020, November 9). Inclusivity at work: The heart of hard conversations with Aiko Bethea [Audio podcast episode]. In *Dare to lead*. Cutler Media LLC. https://brenebrown.com/podcast/ brene-with-aiko-bethea-on-inclusivity-at-work -the-heart-of-hard-conversations/

Brown, B. (2021a, April 5). Armored versus daring leadership, Part 1 of 2 [Audio podcast episode].

In *Dare to lead*. Cutler Media LLC. https://bren ebrown.com/podcast/brene-on-armored-ver sus-daring-leadership-part-1-of-2/

Brown, B. (2021b, April 12). Armored versus daring leadership, Part 2 of 2 [Audio podcast episode]. In *Dare to lead*. Cutler Media LLC. https://bren ebrown.com/podcast/brene-on-armored-ver sus-daring-leadership-part-2-of-2/

Bruhn, A., & McDaniel, S. (2016, October 27). *Tier 2 progress monitoring: Using data for decision making*. Center on Positive Behavioral Interventions & Supports. https://www.pbis .org/resource/tier-ii-progress-monitoring-us ing-data-for-decision-making

Bursztynsky, J., & Feiner, L. (2021, September 14). *Facebook documents show how toxic Instagram is for teens, Wall Street Journal reports*. CNBC. https://www.cnbc.com/2021/09/14/facebook -documents-show-how-toxic-instagram-is-for -teens-wsj.html

Clay, B. (2001, October). *Is this a trick question: A short guide to writing effective test questions*. Kansas Curriculum Center. https://www.k-state .edu/ksde/alp/resources/Handout-Module6.pdf

Conzemius, A. E., & Morganti-Fisher, T. (2012). *More than a SMART goal: Staying focused on student learning*. Solution Tree Press.

CORE Education Digital Media. (2012, September 21). *Professional learning that makes a difference to students* [Video]. Vimeo. https://vimeo.com/ 49954142

Cort, J. (2020, October 26). Creating space for a diversity of thought [Audio podcast episode]. In *Third space with Jen Cort*. https:// www.spreaker.com/user/voicedradio/ creating-space-for-a-diversity-of-though

Covey, S. M. R. (with Merrill, R. R.). (2006). *The speed of trust: The one thing that changes everything*. Simon & Schuster.

Csikszentmihalyi, M. (1990). *Flow: The psychology of optimal experience*. Harper & Row.

Cuomo Prime Time. (2020, April 2). *Story of late ER doctor has Chris Cuomo fighting tears*. CNN. https://www.cnn.com/videos/ health/2020/04/02/cuomo-remembers-er-doc tor-coronavirus-cpt-intv-vpx.cnn

Curriculum Associates. (2022). *About i-Ready assessment*. https://www.curriculumassociates .com/programs/i-ready-assessment

Cushman, K. (1999). The cycle of inquiry and action: Essential learning communities. *Horace, 15*(4). http://essentialschools.org/horace-issues/

the-cycle-of-inquiry-and-action-essential-learning-communities/

The Dalai Lama (with Hougaard, R.). (2019, February 20). The Dalai Lama on why leaders should be mindful, selfless, and compassionate. *Harvard Business Review.* https://hbr.org/2019/02/the-dalai-lama-on-why-leaders-should-be-mindful-selfless-and-compassionate

The Danielson Group. (2021). *The Framework for Teaching.* https://danielsongroup.org/framework

De Bono, E. (1999). *Six thinking hats.* Back Bay Books.

Devine, P. (2018, May 6). Empowering people to break the prejudice habit. *Wisconsin State Journal.* https://madison.com/wsj/discovery/empowering-people-to-break-the-prejudice-habit/article_7afd069e-97a7-5011-844e-56f3f-c25c3d0.html

Dimock, K. V., & McGree, K. (1995). Leading change from the classroom: Teachers as leaders. *Issues About Change, 4*(4). https://sedl.org/pubs/catalog/items/cha14.html

DogTime. (n.d.). *Bringing home your new dog: Preparing and first steps.* https://dogtime.com/dog-health/general/262-adults-bringing-home

Doig, B., & Groves, S. (2011). Japanese lesson study: Teacher professional development through communities of inquiry. *Mathematics Teacher Education and Development, 13*(1), 77–93. https://files.eric.ed.gov/fulltext/EJ960950.pdf

Donohoo, J. (2013). *Collaborative inquiry for educators: A facilitator's guide to school improvement.* Corwin.

Drago-Severson, E. (2009). *Leading adult learning: Supporting adult development in our schools.* Corwin.

Dreikurs, R. (1968). *Psychology in the classroom: A manual for teachers.* Harper & Row.

Duhigg, C. (2016, February 28). What Google learned from its quest to build the perfect team. *The New York Times Magazine.* https://www.nytimes.com/2016/02/28/magazine/what-google-learned-from-its-quest-to-build-the-perfect-team.html

Dweck, C. S. (2008). *Mindset.* Ballantine Books.

Earl, L. M., & Timperley, H. (Eds.). (2009). *Professional learning conversations: Challenges in using evidence for improvement.* Professional Learning and Development in Schools and Higher Education (Vol. 1). Springer, Dordrecht.

Eide, B., & Eide, F. (2011). *The dyslexic advantage: Unlocking the hidden potential of the dyslexic brain.* Hudson Street Press.

Feldman, J. (2018). *Grading for equity: What it is, why it matters, and how it can transform schools and classrooms.* Corwin.

Ferlazzo, L. (2020, March 10). Culturally responsive teaching is not a quick fix. *EdWeek.* https://www.edweek.org/teaching-learning/opinion-culturally-responsive-teaching-is-not-a-quick-fix/2020/03

Fisher, D., Frey, N., Quaglia, R. J., Smith, D., & Lande, L. L. (2018). *Engagement by design: Creating learning environments where students thrive.* Corwin.

Frey, N., Fisher, D., & Smith, D. (2020, October). Trauma-informed design in the classroom. *Educational Leadership, 78*(2). http://www1.ascd.org/publications/educational_leadership/oct20/vol78/num02/Trauma-Informed_Design_in_the_Classroom.aspx

Fullan, M. (2001). *Leading in a culture of change.* Jossey-Bass.

Fullan, M., & Rolheiser, C. (1997). *Breaking through change barriers.* Ontario Institute for Studies in Education of the University of Toronto.

Gallagher, K. (2004). *Deeper reading: Comprehending challenging texts, 4-12.* Stenhouse.

Gallagher, K. (2011). *Write like this: Teaching real-world writing through modeling and mentor texts.* Stenhouse.

Gallagher, L. (2017). *The Airbnb story: How three ordinary guys disrupted an industry, made billions . . . and created plenty of controversy.* Houghton Mifflin Harcourt.

Gallo, A. (2020, March 30). What your co-workers need right now is compassion. *Harvard Business Review.* https://hbr.org/2020/03/what-your-coworkers-need-right-now-is-compassion

Gass, R. (2013). *The Fabulous POP Model.* http://stproject.org/wp-content/uploads/2014/11/the-fabulous-pop-model.pdf

Glazer, R. (2016, October 21). Urgent vs. important (#42). *Friday Forward.* https://www.robertglazer.com/friday-forward/urgent-vs-important-matrix/

Glazer, R. (2019). *Elevate: Push beyond your limits and unlock success in yourself and others.* Simple Truths.

Goleman, D. (2004, January). *What makes a leader?* Harvard Business Review. https://hbr.org/2004/01/what-makes-a-leader

Grant, A. M., & Hofmann, D. A. (2011). It's not all about me: Motivating hospital hand hygiene by focusing on patients. *Psychological Science, 22*, 1494–1499.

Gratton, L., & Erickson, T. (2007). Eight ways to build collaborative teams. *Harvard Business Review, 85*, 100–109, 153. https://hbr.org/2007/11/eight-ways-to-build-collaborative-teams

Guskey, T. R. (2016). Gauge impact with five levels of data. *Journal of Staff Development, 37*(1). https://tguskey.com/wp-content/uploads/Professional-Learning-1-Gauge-Impact-with-Five-Levels-of-Data.pdf

Güver, S., & Motschnig, R. (2017). Effects of diversity in teams and workgroups: A qualitative systematic review. *International Journal of Business, Humanities and Technology, 7*(2), 1–29.

Haigh, M. (n.d.). *Conflict resolution in sport.* Athlete Assessments. https://www.athleteassessments.com/conflict-resolution-in-sport/

Hall, G. E., & Hord, S. M. (1987). *Change in schools: Facilitating the process.* SUNY Series in Educational Leadership. SUNY Press. https://eric.ed.gov/?id=ED332261

Hammond, Z. (2015a). *Culturally responsive teaching and the brain.* Corwin.

Hammond, Z. (2015b, April 9). Four tools for interrupting implicit bias. *Culturally Responsive Teaching and the Brain.* https://crtandthebrain.com/four-tools-for-interrupting-implicit-bias/

Hargreaves, A., & O'Connor, M. T. (2018a). *Collaborative professionalism: When teaching together means learning for all.* Corwin Press.

Hargreaves, A., & O'Connor, M. T. (2018b, April). *Leading collaborative professionalism.* Seminar Series 274. Centre for Strategic Education. http://www.andyhargreaves.com/uploads/5/2/9/2/5292616/seminar_series_274-april2018.pdf

Hattie, J. (2021). *The Visible Learning research: What works best to improve learning?* Corwin. https://us.corwin.com/en-us/nam/the-visible-learning-research

Heinz, K. (2021, November 29). What does diversity, equity and inclusion (DEI) mean in the workplace? *Built In.* https://builtin.com/diversity-inclusion/what-does-dei-mean-in-the-workplace

Hemingway, E. (1952). *The old man and the sea.* Charles Scribner's Sons.

Horn, I. S. (2007). Fast kids, slow kids, lazy kids: Framing the mismatch problem in math teachers' conversations. *Journal of the Learning Sciences, 16*(1), 37–79.

Howard, Y. (n.d.). *Types of unconscious bias: Examples, effects and solutions.* EW Group. https://theewgroup.com/blog/different-types-unconscious-bias/#Perception-bias

Human Dimensions. (2018, January 17). *Conflict Matters Conference: Myrna Lewis, Deep Democracy, South Africa* [Video]. YouTube. https://www.youtube.com/watch?v=ydt_Sxukevw

Hurt, J. (2012, January 31). *10 brain-based learning laws that trump traditional education.* Velvet Chainsaw Consulting. https://velvetchainsaw.com/2012/01/31/10-brainbased-learning-laws-that-trump-traditional-education/

Intervention Central. (n.d.). *How to: Structure classroom data collection for individual students.* https://www.interventioncentral.org/blog/assessment-progress-monitoring/how-structure-classroom-data-collection-individual-students

Iris Center. (2021). *What types of accommodations are commonly used for students with disabilities? Page 4: Selecting an accommodation.* Vanderbilt University. https://iris.peabody.vanderbilt.edu/module/acc/cresource/q2/p04/

Jackson, J. (2020, July 15). Growing up Black in all the wrong places. *Boston Globe Magazine.* https://www.bostonglobe.com/2020/07/15/magazine/growing-up-black-new-hampshire-one-americas-whitest-states/

Jacobson, D. (2010). Coherent instructional improvement and PLCs: Is it possible to do both? *Phi Delta Kappan, 91*(6), 38–45. http://journals.sagepub.com/doi/full/10.1177/003172171009100611

Janis, I. L. (1972). *Victims of groupthink: A psychological study of foreign-policy decisions and fiascoes.* Houghton Mifflin.

Jensen, D. (2021, June 23). Time management won't save you. *Harvard Business Review.* https://hbr.org/2021/06/time-management-wont-save-you

Jensen, K. L., & Minke, K. M. (2017). Engaging families at the secondary level: An underused resource for student success. *The School Community Journal, 27*(2), 167–191.

Jhagroo, J. (2020). Review of L. Grudnoff, F. Ell, M. Haigh, M. Hill, & K. Tocker: Enhancing equity through inquiry. *New Zealand Journal of Educational Studies, 55*, 275–278. https://doi.org/10.1007/s40841-020-00159-z

Johnson, C., Chávez-Linville, D., & Healy, L. (2018, December 13). *How to find culturally appropriate reading materials for English learners.* Renaissance. https://www.renais sance.com/2018/12/13/blog-culturally-appro priate-reading-materials-english-learners/

Kahn, W. A. (1990). Psychological conditions of personal engagement and disengagement at work. *Academy of Management Journal, 33*(4), 692–724.

Karlgaard, R., & Malone, S. (2015). *Team genius: The new science of high-performing organizations.* HarperCollins.

Katzenmeyer, M., & Moller, G. (2001). *Awakening the sleeping giant: Helping teachers develop as leaders.* Corwin.

Kegan, R. (2009). What "form" transforms? A con-structive-developmental approach to transforma-tive learning. In K. Illeris (Ed.), *Contemporary theories of learning: Learning theorists . . . in their own words* (pp. 35–52). Routledge.

Kegan, R., & Lahey, L. (2001, November). The real reason people won't change. *Harvard Business Review.* https://hbr.org/2001/11/ the-real-reason-people-wont-change

Kegan, R., & Lahey, L. L. (2009). *Immunity to change.* Harvard Business Review Press.

Kharbanda, S. (2020, July 30). Neurodiversity in the workplace (No. 24) [Audio podcast epi-sode]. In *Perspectives of change.* https:// podcasts.apple.com/us/podcast/24-neurodi versity-in-workplace-sonsoles-alonso-30-july/ id1038492994?i=1000487091347

Killion, J. (2018). *Assessing impact: Evaluating pro-fessional learning.* Corwin.

Knight, J. (2013). *High-impact instruction: A frame-work for great teaching.* Corwin.

Knowles, M. (1975). *Self-directed learning: A guide for learners and teachers.* Pearson Learning Group.

Kuppler, T. (2015, August 28). Edgar Schein on culture. *Leadership & Change.* https:// www.leadershipandchangemagazine.com/ edgar-schein-on-culture/

Latané, B., Williams, K. D., & Harkins, S. G. (1979). Many hands make light the work: The causes and consequences of social loafing. *Journal of Personality and Social Psychology, 37,* 822–832.

Leading in schools on the edge. (2013, October 1). ASCD. https://www.ascd.org/el/articles/leading -in-schools-on-the-edge

Learning Forward. (2022). *Standards.* https://learning forward.org/standards-for-professional -learning/

Learning Forward. (n.d.). *Develop a culture of continuous improvement in our schools.* https://services.learningforward.org/services/ teacher-learning-teams/

Lencioni, P. (2002). *The five dysfunctions of a team: A leadership fable.* Jossey-Bass.

Lewis, M. (2016, May). *Deep Democracy.* Compassion to Lead. https://www.compassiontolead.net/ wp-content/uploads/2016/05/Compassion_ InspirationCards-03.pdf

Lewis, M., & Woodhull, J. (2018). *Inside the NO: Five steps to decisions that last.* Deep Democracy.

Life Meets Work. (2017, March 27). *Life Meets Work survey finds stressed out leaders harm employees' job performance.* Cision PR Newswire. https:// www.prnewswire.com/news-releases/life-meets -work-survey-finds-stressed-out-leaders-harm -employees-job-performance-300429678.html

Lindsey, R. B., Robins, K. N., & Terrell, R. D. (2009). Foreword. In D. P. Robles (Ed.), *Cultural profi-ciency: A manual for school leaders* (3rd ed.). Corwin.

Little, J. W. (2008, Summer). *Declaration of inter-dependence* (Vol. 29, No. 3). National Staff Development Council.

Little, J. W. (2012). Understanding data use prac-tices among teachers: The contribution of micro-process studies. *American Journal of Education, 118*(2), 143–166.

Little, J. W., Gearhart, M., Curry, M., & Kafka, J. (2003). Looking at student work for teacher learning, teacher community, and school reform. *Phi Delta Kappan, 85,* 184–192.

Love, N. (2008). *Using data to improve learning for all: A collaborative inquiry approach.* Corwin.

Love, N., Smith, N., & Whitacre, R. (2015, December 7). *Coaching teams to use formative assessment for results.* Learning Forward Annual Conference, Washington, DC.

MacDonald, E. (2013). *The skillful team leader: A resource for overcoming hurdles to professional learning for student achievement.* Corwin.

MacDonald, E. (2015, June 1). *A school on the move.* ASCD. https://www.ascd.org/el/articles/ a-school-on-the-move

Margolis, J. (2009, February). How teachers lead teachers. *Educational Leadership, 66*(5). www .ascd.org/publications/eudcational-leader-ship/feb09/vo166/num05/How-Teachers-Lead -Teachers.aspx

Marzano, R. J. (2013, May 1). Art and science of teaching/targets, objectives, standards. How do they fit? *Faces of Poverty, 70*(8), 82–83.

Maslow, A. (1943). A theory of human motivation. *Psychological Review, 50*(4), 370–396.

Massachusetts Institute of Technology. (n.d.). *A short guide to consensus building: An alternative to Robert's Rules of Order for groups, organizations and ad hoc assemblies that want to operate by consensus.* http://web.mit.edu/publicdisputes/practice/cbh_ch1.html

MathsPathway. (2020, June 11). *Exploring the productive struggle: Teacher talk with Dan Finkel* [Video]. YouTube. https://www.youtube.com/watch?v=G5pYziQ6M0A

McKinsey & Company. (2021, September 27). *Women in the workplace 2021.* https://www.mckinsey.com/featured-insights/diversity-and-inclusion/women-in-the-workplace

Meichenbaum, D. (n.d.). *Understanding resilience in children and adults: Implications for prevention and interventions.* http://www.coping.us/images/Understand_Resilience_of_Children_Adults.pdf

Motter, S. (2020, July 15). *TPS sets example for school districts nationwide.* WIBW. https://www.wibw.com/2020/07/15/tps-being-featured-in-national-webinar-over-reopening-of-schools/?fbclid=IwAR3Uvpiw5RYwhXZECEhMypF6PFl7trplgtjpi8ubDdfTcalKyIHNJPtjHwc

Murkoff, H., Eisenberg, A., & Hathaway, S. (1984). *What to expect when you're expecting.* Workman.

National Education Association. (2020, July). *The Teacher Leader Model Standards.* https://www.nea.org/resource-library/teacher-leader-model-standards

National Governors Association Center for Best Practices & Council of Chief State School Officers. (2010). *Common Core State Standards for English language arts and literacy in history/social studies, science, and technical subjects.* http://www.corestandards.org/wp-content/uploads/ELA_Standards1.pdf

National School Reform Faculty. (2017, October). *Suggestions for bringing student work: Developed by Gene Thompson-Grove.* https://www.nsrfharmony.org/wp-content/uploads/2017/10/sugg_bring_stud_work_0.pdf

National Science Teaching Association. (2014). Science and engineering practices. *NGSS@NSTA.* https://ngss.nsta.org/Practices.aspx?id=4

Neeley, T. (2015, October). Global teams that work. *Harvard Business Review.* https://hbr.org/2015/10/global-teams-that-work

Nelson, J. (2006). *Positive discipline: The classic guide to helping children develop self-discipline, responsibility, cooperation, and problem-solving skills* (Revised ed.). Ballantine Books.

O'Connor, M. C., & Michaels, S. (2007). When is dialogue "dialogic"? *Human Development, 50,* 275–285. doi:10.1159/000/106415

OCALI. (n.d.). *Learn about UDL: History of UDL.* https://www.ocali.org/project/learn_about_udl/page/udl_history

Organisation for Economic Co-operation and Development. (2020, March 23). *TALIS 2018 results (Volume II): Teachers and school leaders as valued professionals.* https://doi.org/10.1787/19cf08df-en

Pentland, A. "S." (2012, April). The new science of building great teams. *Harvard Business Review.* https://hbr.org/2012/04/the-new-science-of-building-great-teams?referral=03759&cm_vc=rr_item_page.bottom

Pink, D. H. (2018). *When: The scientific secrets of perfect timing.* Riverhead Books.

The Princeton Review Canada. (2015, August 13). *GMAT resources: 3 tools for spotting assumptions.* QS Leap. https://www.qsleap.com/gmat/resources/3-tools-for-spotting-assumptions

Question Everything. (2013, April 11). *The Asch experiment* [Video]. YouTube. https://www.youtube.com/watch?v=qA-gbpt7Ts8

Quora. (2017, May 15). How food brings cultures together. *HuffPost.* https://www.huffpost.com/entry/how-food-brings-cultures-together_b_5913e153e4b002274b9469c8

Rello, L., & Baeza-Yates, R. (2012, November 19). *Text customization for readability online symposium.* https://www.w3.org/WAI/RD/2012/text-customization/r11

Rennie Center for Education Research and Policy. (2014). *Making space: The value of teacher collaboration.* EdVestors. https://www.edvestors.org/wp-content/uploads/2016/05/EdVestors-Making-Space-The-Value-of-Teacher-Collaboration-2014.pdf

Rock, D., & Grant, H. (2016, November 4). Why diverse teams are smarter. *Harvard Business Review.* https://hbr.org/2016/11/why-diverse-teams-are-smarter

Rogers, P., & Blenko, M. W. (2006, January). Who has the D? How clear decision roles enhance organizational performance. *Harvard Business Review.* https://hbr.org/2006/01/

who-has-the-d-how-clear-decision-roles-enhance-organizational-performance

Rose, C. (2017, February 1). *Ursula Burns* [Video]. https://charlierose.com/videos/29786

Roy, P. (2013). *School-based professional learning for implementing the Common Core*. Unit 4: Standards for Professional Learning. Learning Forward. Three Pages Publishing Services. https://learningforward.org/wp-content/uploads/2017/09/school-based-professional-learning-unit-4-packet.pdf

Sawchuk, S., & Sparks, S. D. (2020, December 2). Kids are behind in math because of COVID-19. Here's what research says could help. *Education Week*. https://www.edweek.org/teaching-learning/kids-are-behind-in-math-because-of-covid-19-heres-what-research-says-could-help/2020/12

Schein, E. H. (2013). *Humble inquiry: The gentle art of asking instead of telling*. Berrett-Koehler.

Schildkamp, K. (2019). Data-based decision-making for school improvement: Research insights and gaps. *Educational Research, 61*(3), 257–273. https://www.tandfonline.com/doi/full/10.1080/00131881.2019.1625716

Scribner, J. P., Sawyer, R. K., Watson, S. T., & Myers, V. L. (2007). Teacher teams and distributed leadership: A study of group discourse and collaboration. *Educational Administration Quarterly, 43*(1), 67–100. https://doi.org/10.1177/0013161X06293631

Senge, P. M. (1990). *The fifth discipline: The art and practice of the learning organization*. Currency Doubleday.

Senge, P. M., Kleiner, A., Roberts, C., Ross, R. B., & Smith, B. J. (1994). *The fifth discipline fieldbook*. Currency Doubleday.

Serravallo, J. (2015). *The reading strategies book*. Heinemann.

Serravallo, J. (2017). *The writing strategies book*. Heinemann.

Shand, R. (2017, December 5). *Promoting productive collaboration through inquiry: The limits of policy mandates*. Albert Shanker Institute. http://www.shankerinstitute.org/blog/promoting-productive-collaboration-through-inquiry-limits-policy-mandates

Singleton, G. E., & Linton, C. (2006). *Courageous conversations about race: A field guide for achieving equity in schools*. Corwin.

Steinke, P., & Fitch, P. (2017, Winter). Minimizing bias when assessing student work. *Research and Practice in Assessment, 12*, 87–95. https://files.eric.ed.gov/fulltext/EJ1168692.pdf

Stone, D., & Heen, S. (2015). *Thanks for the feedback*. Portfolio Penguin.

Stone, D., Patton, B., & Heen, S. (2010). *Difficult conversations: How to discuss what matters most*. Penguin.

Sue, D. W., Capodilupo, C. M., Torino, G. C., Bucceri, J. M., Holder, A. M., Nadal, K. L., & Esquilin, M. (2007). Racial microaggressions in everyday life: Implications for clinical practice. *American Psychologist, 62*(4), 271–286.

Suzuki, S. (1970). *Zen mind, beginner's mind: Informal talks on Zen meditation and practice*. Weatherhill.

SXSWedu. (2017, April 7). *Brené Brown: Daring classrooms* [Video]. YouTube. https://www.youtube.com/watch?v=DVD8YRgA-ck

Taglang, K. (2021, February 19). Broadband solutions to pandemic problems. *Weekly Digest*. Benton Institute for Broadband & Society. https://www.benton.org/blog/broadband-solutions-pandemic-problems

Talks at Google. (2014, March 31). *Thanks for the feedback: Doug Stone and Sheila Heen* [Video]. YouTube. https://www.youtube.com/watch?v=SggjK0Gm3I4&t=2850s

TEDx Talks. (2014, May 4). *Building a psychologically safe workplace: Amy Edmondson: TEDxHGSE* [Video]. YouTube. https://www.youtube.com/watch?v=LhoLuui9gX8

Timperley, H. (2008). Evidence-informed conversations making a difference to student achievement. In L. M. Earl & H. Timperley (Eds.), *Professional learning conversations: Challenges in using evidence for improvement* (pp. 69–79). Professional Learning and Development in Schools and Higher Education (Vol. 1). Springer, Dordrecht. https://doi.org/10.1007/978-1-4020-6917-8_6

Tuckman, B. (1965). Developmental sequence in small groups. *Psychological Bulletin, 63*(6), 384–399.

University of Stavanger. (2011, January 24). Better learning through handwriting. *ScienceDaily*. www.sciencedaily.com/releases/2011/01/110119095458.htm

University of Toronto. (2016, June 23). A better way to predict diabetes. *ScienceDaily*. https://www.sciencedaily.com/releases/2016/06/160623115738.htm

U.S. Department of Justice Community Relations Service. (n.d.). *Understanding bias: A resource guide*. Community Relations Services Toolkit for Policing. https://www.justice.gov/file/1437326/download

Von Frank, V. (2011, February). Teacher leader standards: Consortium seeks to strengthen profession with leadership role. *Teachers Leading Teachers*, *6*(5). https://learningforward.org/the-leading-teacher/february-2011-vol-6-no-5/

Vygotsky, L. S. (1978). *Mind in society: The development of higher psychological processes*. Harvard University Press.

The W. Edwards Deming Institute. (2021). *PDSA cycle*. https://deming.org/explore/pdsa/

Wagner, T., & Kegan, R. (2006). *Change leadership: A practical guide to transforming our schools* (7th ed.). Jossey-Bass.

Wallas, G. (1926). *The art of thought*. New York: Harcourt Brace.

Webb, N. (1997). *Criteria for alignment of expectations and assessments on mathematics and science education* (Research monograph no. 6). Council of Chief State School Officers.

Wenz, J. (2018, March 19). How to write a *Jeopardy* clue. *Popular Mechanics*. https://www.popularmechanics.com/culture/tv/a19435419/how-to-write-a-jeopardy-clue/

WestEd. (2016). Team Tool 4.2: Personal reading history protocol. In R. Shoenbach, C. Greenleaf, & L. Murphy (Eds.), *Leading for literacy: A reading apprenticeship approach* (p. 75). Jossey-Bass. https://readingapprenticeship.org/wp-content/uploads/2021/02/rl-team-tool-4-02-reading-history.pdf

Wheatley, M. J. (2002). *Turning to one another: Simple conversations to restore hope to the future*. Berrett-Koehler.

Wikipedia. (2022, January 18). The Eisenhower Method. In *Time management* (3.3). https://en.wikipedia.org/wiki/Time_management#The_Eisenhower_Method

Williams, J. C., & Mihaylo, S. (2019, November/December). How the best bosses interrupt bias on their teams. *Harvard Business Review*. https://hbr.org/2019/11/how-the-best-bosses-interrupt-bias-on-their-teams

Writing Explained. (n.d.). *What does clear the air mean?* Phrase and Idiom Dictionary. https://writingexplained.org/idiom-dictionary/clear-the-air

Zins, J. E., Weissberg, R. P., Wang, M. C., & Walberg, H. J. (Eds.). (2004). *Building academic success on social and emotional learning: What does the research say?* Teachers College Press.

Index

A SAGE Publishing Company

Helping educators make the greatest impact

CORWIN HAS ONE MISSION: to enhance education through intentional professional learning.

We build long-term relationships with our authors, educators, clients, and associations who partner with us to develop and continuously improve the best evidence-based practices that establish and support lifelong learning.

THE PROFESSIONAL LEARNING ASSOCIATION

Learning Forward is a nonprofit, international membership association of learning educators committed to one vision in K–12 education: Equity and excellence in teaching and learning. To realize that vision, Learning Forward pursues its mission to build the capacity of leaders to establish and sustain highly effective professional learning. Information about membership, services, and products is available from www.learningforward.org.

Lead teams with intention.

Impact learning and achievement.

Shape school culture.

Every team seeking to improve student learning comes up against hurdles. With a skillful, intentional approach, leaders can facilitate high-functioning, high-impact teams— and all schools can leverage their learning communities to advance equity.

ELISA B. MACDONALD
Educator, Author, Consultant

I view team leaders as powerful change agents for teacher and student learning, and as positive influencers within school culture. With three decades of combined experience teaching, leading and consulting in schools, I have trained and developed hundreds of team leaders. I'm ready to support you and your school leaders in skillfully leading the teams you have, and developing into the leaders you want to become. Consulting services are available virtually and in person.

ENVISION AND STRATEGIZE	DEVELOP TEACHER LEADERS	MAXIMIZE TEAM IMPACT
Collaboratively craft a meaningful district or school mission, vision, and action plan with teacher leadership as key drivers for change.	Implement a robust system of support for your teacher leaders, instructional coaches, and the district/ school leaders who support them.	Recharge your leadership and teacher teams so they function at the highest level and positively impact student learning.

Learn more at www.elisamacdonald.com